THE PHILOSOPHY OF BARUCH SPINOZA

**STUDIES IN PHILOSOPHY
AND THE HISTORY OF PHILOSOPHY**

Founding editor: John K. Ryan (1960-1978)
General editor: Jude P. Dougherty

**Studies in Philosophy
and the History of Philosophy**   **Volume 7**

The Philosophy of

BARUCH SPINOZA

edited by Richard Kennington

THE CATHOLIC UNIVERSITY OF AMERICA PRESS
Washington, D.C.

Paperback Edition Copyright © 2018
The Catholic University of America Press
All rights reserved

The paper used in this publication meets the minimum requirements of the American National Standards for Information Science – Permanence of paper for Printed Library Materials, ANSI Z39.48-1984.
∞

ISBN 978-0-8132-3100-6 (pbk)

Library of Congress Cataloging in Publication Data
Main entry under title:
The Philosophy of Baruch Spinoza.

   (Studies in philosophy and the history of philosophy; v. 7)
   Includes index.
   1. Spinoza, Benedictus de, 1632-1677—Addresses, essays, lectures. I. Kennington, Richard, 1921- II. Series.
B21.S78   vol. 7   [B3998]   108s   [199'.492]   79-9556

TABLE OF CONTENTS

Abbreviations vi

SPINOZA'S *ETHICS*

   1 Some Pivotal Issues in Spinoza, Paul Weiss 3

SPINOZA'S METAPHYSICS

   2 The Deductive Character of Spinoza's Metaphysics, Michael Hooker 17
   3 Spinoza's Ontological Proof, Willis Doney 35
   4 Spinozistic Anomalies, Jose Benardete 53
   5 Some Idealistic Themes in the *Ethics*, Robert N. Beck 73
   6 Spinoza's Dualism, Alan Donagan 89
   7 Objects, Ideas, and "Minds": Comments on Spinoza's Theory of Mind, Margaret D. Wilson 103
   8 Parallelism and Complementarity: The Psycho-Physical Problem in the Succession of Niels Bohr, Hans Jonas 121

SPINOZA'S PHILOSOPHY OF POLITICS AND RELIGION

   9 Spinoza's Political Philosophy: The Lessons and Problems of a Conservative Democrat, Lewis S. Feuer 133
  10 Notes on Spinoza's Critique of Religion, Hilail Gildin . 155
  11 Spinoza and History, James C. Morrison 173

SPINOZA AND GERMAN PHILOSOPHY

  12 Kant's Critique of Spinoza, Henry E. Allison 199
  13 Hegel's Assessment of Spinoza, Kenneth L. Schmitz .. 229

ALTERNATIVE APPROACHES TO SPINOZA

  14 Spinoza's Logic of Inquiry: Rationalist or Experientialist?, Isaac Franck 247
  15 *De Natura*, Stewart Umphrey 273
  16 Analytic and Synthetic Methods in Spinoza's *Ethics*, Richard Kennington 293

Index to Propositions of the *Ethics* 319

Index of Names 321

ABBREVIATIONS

I. Spinoza's Writings

- E : *Ethica (Ethics)*
- CM : *Cogitata Metaphysica (Metaphysical Reflections)*
- Ep. : *Epistolae (Letters)*
- KV : *Korte Verhandeling van God, de Mensch, en deszwelfs Welstand (Short Treatise on God, Man, and his Well-being)*
- DPP : *Renati Des Cartes Principiorum Philosophiae (Philosophic Principles of Rene Descartes)*
- TdIE : *Tractatus de Intellectus Emendatione (Treatise on The Correction of the Understanding)*
- TP : *Tractatus Politicus (Political Treatise)*
- TTP : *Tractatus Theologico-Politicus (Theologico-Political Treatise)*

Parts of works "demonstrated in geometric order"

A	: Axiom		L	: Lemma
C	: Corollary		P	: Proposition
Df.	: Definition		S	: Scholium
Dm.	: Demonstration			

II. Editions of Original Texts used

- Gebhardt : *Spinoza Opera*, ed. C. Gebhardt, 4 vols. (Heidelberg: Carl Winters, 1925)
- Land : *Benedicti de Spinoza Opera, Quotquot Reperta Sunt*, ed. J. van Vloten and J. P. N. Land (The Hague: Martinus Nijhoff, 1882)

III. English translations used

- Boyle : *Spinoza's Ethics and De Intellectus Emendatione*, trans. A. Boyle (London: J. M. Dent & Sons, Ltd. 1910)
- Britan : B. Spinoza, *The Principles of Descartes' Philosophy*, trans. H. H. Britan (Chicago: Open Court, 1905)
- Elwes : *The Chief Works of Benedict de Spinoza*, trans. R. H. M. Elwes, 2 vols. (New York: Dover Publications, 1955)
- Wolf (a) : *The Correspondence of Spinoza*, trans. & ed. A. Wolf, (London: Frank Cass, 1966)
- Wolf (b) : *Spinoza's Short Treatise on God, Man, and His Well-being*, trans. & ed. A. Wolf (New York: Russell & Russell, 1963)

SPINOZA'S
ETHICS

1 SOME PIVOTAL ISSUES IN SPINOZA

Paul Weiss

I.

Spinoza's most central and major ideas have been subject to radically divergent interpretations. For the most part, we have been urged to choose between different emphases, all of which find some support in the text. Rarely are we asked or shown how to accommodate all, or most, or even two. Though I have not found it possible to reconcile all of Spinoza's statements, I think that it is possible to reconcile more of them than most writers permit. To do this, it is sometimes necessary to make distinctions that Spinoza himself did not make, but which are not, I think, inconsistent wtih his main claims.

My primary intent is to deal with Spinoza as a major philosopher who is trying to understand man and his place in the universe. I take seriously the idea that he wrote an ethics. I hold that he wanted to show how a man can become blessed and attain peace of mind by identifying himself with what is eternal, that one is virtuous only to the degree that he knows who he is, and that such knowledge requires him to know what is ultimately real. Though a man can never escape a bondage manifested in the form of sufferings, confused ideas, and impotence, he can minimize this side of himself by attending to what is completely intelligible and forever. To make these claims more evident, I will concentrate on seven issues: the geometric method; the attributes of God; the proofs of God's existence; the nature of God; the reality of the modes; man and his knowledge; human bondage and salvation.

II. *Method.*

The geometric method can be understood in three ways. It is a mode of exposition and demonstration; it expresses an attitude; and it offers a warrant for setting aside various topics as unintelligible or irrelevant. The exposition, in imitation of Euclid, sets up a number of definitions, axioms, and postulates, and then attempts to prove various theorems. The attitude assumed, following the lead of Descartes, attempts to deal with the passions dispassionately, as though they were geometrical entities, the objects of a pure reason (E III, Pref.). The pursuit of the method precludes the consideration of final causes (E I, Appendix). Each of these deserves some attention.

The procedure of Euclid is imitated by Spinoza, not duplicated. A duplication would require Spinoza to provide nominal definitions, i.e., those which merely explicate what is meant, without making any claim that what was defined answers to what occurs in fact. But Spinoza wants to talk about what is—we are said, for example, to have an adequate knowledge of God (E II, P47). When we say that God has an infinite number of attributes we are supposedly saying what is certainly true. Spinoza's definitions are real, telling us about the presumed nature of ultimate and derivative realities. And, unlike Euclid's axioms, his can be denied without self-contradiction. There is no contradiction in maintaining, in opposition to E I, A3, that an effect does not necessarily follow from a given determinate cause, unless one means by "necessarily follows," "logically entailed by" in a domain where there is no time and no activity separating and connecting causes and effects. A Euclidean geometry, too, can be formally presented, using the symbols and procedures of symbolic logic; it can even be given an algebraic formulation. But this cannot be done for Spinoza, as Boole showed (*Laws of Thought*, vol. 2, chapter xiii). Spinoza, moreover, departs from the Euclidean method again and again. He adds an appendix at the end of Book 1, introductions to book 3 and 4, an appendix to book 4, and a preface to book 5.

Still, Spinoza does follow the method some of the time. He does succeed, too, in treating the passions with serene objectivity. His method, too, supports his desire to consider only what is necessitated, to put aside a consideration of what is contingent, to reject teleology, and to provide an exposition which was in consonance with his own austere, stoical, detached interpretation of man's problems and their solution. It provides the kind of agency which God might use to recapitulate and order what he clearly knows. And it provides us with a perpetual reminder of the nature of Spinoza's intent, and his understanding of what is more, and what is less, important.

III. *The Attributes.*

It is quite common to hold that the attributes of God are only "subjective," expressing our distinctions, having no reality of their own. Spinoza himself says that an attribute is what the intellect *perceives of* Substance *as if* constituting its essence (E I, Df.4). And God, he insists, is one, undivided and indivisible (E I, P13). But Spinoza also says that God's attributes are immutable (E I, P20, C2), that God has an intellect and, more strikingly, that he is extended (E I, P15, S). Indeed, God is explicitly defined by Spinoza (E 1, Df.1) to be a "substance consisting of infinite attributes."

The two positions can be reconciled by distinguishing God's essence from his *natura naturans*, and this from his *natura naturata*. In himself, God is absolutely one, brooking no divisions or distinctions. As *natura naturans* he is all the attributes, distinguishable but not distinct, conjunctively disjoined, related not as a or b or c, but as a-or-b-or-c. In *natura naturata*, the attributes are distinct from one another, enabling one to speak of any of them independently of a reference to another.

When God is recognized to be fecund, powerful, expansive, active, and expressive, the distinction between what he is in himself and what he is as *natura naturans* and *natura naturata* turns out to be a distinction between God at his center, God as manifestable, and God as manifested. He is a self-distinguishing being whose infinite attributes are so many attenuated, specialized versions of himself. To know any one of these is to know his essence from one angle and at some remove from him, the unity who is able to express himself in infinite ways.

To preserve the unity of God, it must be said that the attributes are subjective. To preserve the distinctness of thought and extension, it must be said that the attributes are also separable from one another. To allow that God has an intellect and is extended, that what happens in one attribute has a counterpart in another, one must grant that the attributes are objective as well.

IV. *The Proof of God's Existence.*

Spinoza provides some of the strongest reasons ever given for holding that God exists. I think he succeeds in showing that God exists—but on condition that what is conceived is true of what is outside the conception. That condition can be fulfilled only if thought re-presents God's own self-causation, or if the idea of God both exists and is continous with God's infinite existence.

In E I, P11, Spinoza offers a number of proofs that God exists. One of them holds that God must exist because nothing could prevent him from existing. Another, beginning with existing men, concludes that, since an infinite being has proportionately more power than men, its existence is necessary. In these two "proofs," the existence of God is taken to be the outcome of the exercise of a power by an infinite being. If we are in fact acquainted with that being, we share in its movement from its essence to its existence—but then we are not engaged in proving anything. If, instead, a proof is offered, we will pass only from an idea of God's essence to the idea of his existence. At the very least, the latter type of movement, occurring in our minds, must be attached to the former, to what is occurring in fact. The proof works, but only if it is sustained by an existing God. The issue is important enough to make it desirable to spend some time with some needed distinctions.

Unlike Descartes, Spinoza does not begin with an idea of God in his mind, but with an unlocated idea of God's essence, or with that essence itself. In opposition to Aquinas and Maimonides, he thinks he knows what God's essence is. He does not, as the critics of the ontological argument suppose, take existence to be a predicate. But Spinoza does not define or satisfactorily explicate what he means by "existence." It is consistent with his claims, however, to understand existence to be a produced domain or part of one in which there are distinctions not present in the essence. Existence is essence diversified in the form of distinguishable attributes in the *natura naturans* and in the form of distinct attributes in the *natura naturata*. It is not identical with the essence—otherwise nothing would be proved and there would be nothing which was the outcome of self-causation. Existence, though, is necessitated by the infinite essence; otherwise there would be no self-causation, and no capturing of this in a proof. Existence adds to the essence the status of being diversified but is thereby also denied the dense unity that is characteristic of the essence.

Spinoza's proof rests on a number of assumptions:

a. It supposes that we have an adequate idea, a true, certain idea of God's essence. Indeed, if we did not have it, he thinks, we would not be able to achieve peace of mind and blessedness. These depend on our having such an idea. Yet if we have an adequate idea of an infinite being, it will be of one who is radically indeterminate, since for Spinoza all determination is negation.

b. The proof supposes that we have an adequate idea, not only of the divine essence but of that essence as existing, that essence as possessed of a power which is necessarily exercised. It is an idea of what is not merely possible—which is what Leibniz demanded—but of what is existent, in the sense of having an infinite, undeniable power to exist. Of course, even granted that we have an idea of an existent essence and of the existence that this might produce, it still does not follow that there is an essence which exists outside the confines of that idea, and that its existence has an infinite reach.

c. An argument passes from premiss to conclusion. That passage requires effort. It can be engaged in only by one who exists, using some of his own power to draw the necessitated conclusion. But one cannot reach existence by taking thought. In any case, the move involves a use of existence, of which the argument makes no mention.

d. Since for Spinoza, causation requires that there be something in common to the cause and effect, there must be something in common to God's essence and existence. What can this be but God's self-causation, his act of making himself exist? Such an act, of course, is possible only to an existent. Spinoza's God moves from an existent essence to the existence of that essence and does so by carrying out an existing causal process. If our proof duplicates this move, we will presuppose existence both in God and in our passage.

e. The argument must recapture the necessity which relates God's essence and existence. But in thought the necessity is purely formal, whereas in God it is dynamic, effective, productive. Despite the fact that the one is available to a finite being, and the other is the privilege only of an infinite being, the one is supposed to yield a strict counterpart of the other. This is not possible. God's infinite self-causation cannot be captured either in an entailment or logical deduction, for it involves an insistent self-expressive, productive act by which the essence exhibits itself in a diversified form.

f. The argument does not deal with the God of any of the main western religions, a God who creates, is accepted on faith, and reveals himself through special messages, miracles, and men. It is just as much about the whole of nature, taken to be all-encompassing, unitary, final, self-causing, uncreating, ahistorical, without novelty or spontaneity. But it is only the former which is the proper object of religion, the practical act with which the *Ethics* ends. However, if we identify the essence of nature with the *natura naturans* and the existence of nature with the *natura naturata*, and then treat both as dependent on God's essence, we can allow for religion and yet keep to the view that nothing is freely and deliberately created, since both the *natura naturans* and the *natura naturata* will remain necessitated outcomes.

g. Spinoza takes all plurality to involve determination, all determination to involve negation, and all negation to mark lack, privation, limitation, impotence. But there are many insistent attributes, ideas, bodies, modes, and men. The two positions can be reconciled by distinguishing a determination which is externally produced and outside an entity's control from a determination which is produced from within, expressing in a diversified manner what the entity is in itself. The former type of determination is privational. The latter, instead, is positive, completive, expressing a man's ability, while self-same, to exhibit himself modally.

The strength of Spinoza's arguments lies in their recognition that what is ultimately real cannot be derived from anything else, that existence is not the only or the primary dimension in terms of which we are to understand what occurs, and that the existence of finite entities presupposes a common domain that must itself be grounded in what is more powerful and unified. This is far from showing that there is one primary, perfect essence, that we have an adequate idea of it, that we can derive an adequate idea of its existence, and that our derivations re-present what is final. But could one have an assurance that what one understood of God was true of him, as he existed apart from that understanding, one could know what, for Spinoza, was needed to make one be virtuous, blessed, and forever.

V. *The Nature of God.*

God, for Spinoza, is an absolutely infinite, self-causing reality (E I, Dfs.1,6), eternal, first in the order of knowledge and reality (E II, P10, S2). His power is his essence (E I, P34), and of this he has an idea (E II, P3, P5). He is the permanent, constitutive cause of whatever exists. To be sure, Spinoza also says (E I, P16, C1) that God is an efficient cause but this, I think, is to be understood to mean that God is an effective, empowering ground. God's essence is identical with his eternity (E V, P30); his intellect, so far as it constitutes his essence, is the cause of the essence and existence of things (E I, P17, S). What follows from him is explained by him; God is the self-explanatory rationale of all else. Since, for Spinoza, to understand anything is to grasp its cause, to understand any finite occurrence it is necessary not only to understand what precedes it, but the God who sustains both the occurrence and its antecedent.

God is free in not being compelled by anything else. He is necessitated in that what he does follows inescapably from his nature. He loves himself and therefore loves men; the love of God toward men and the intellectual love of the mind toward God are the same (E V, P36). God also knows himself. Critics have sometimes maintained that, because of this claim, Spinoza is forced to suppose the attribute of thought has a rank superior to other attributes. But God does not know himself in an attribute. He knows himself through it. Were he to attend to himself through the attribute of extension, he would apprehend himself with the same effectiveness, clarity, and completeness that he shows when he attends to himself through the attribute of thought. Cartesian geometry made evident that the formula for a circle and a graphed circle are alternative versions of the essence of the very same circle. Just as that essence differs in unity and power both from the formula and the spatialized version, and just as it has the ability to diversify itself in these two ways, so God's essence differs from all his attributes in unity and power, and in its ability to be expressed in these infinite ways. God is the ground of all laws, all rationality, all connections, the warrant for the fact that what occurs in any one attribute has a counterpart in another.

Spinoza is not a pantheist, for the double reason that his ultimate reality is identified as nature as well as God, and because he explicitly asserts that finite man, with his passions, images, and confusions and therefore as distinct from God, has an existence of his own. Nor is Spinoza a panentheist, for he does not hold that God, while remaining beyond all things, encompasses them. There are laws governing particular items. Nor, since Spinoza holds that God loves men, can Spinoza be rightly said to be an atheist. He is, instead, a religious deist, one who holds that one should love a self-explanatory, all-powerful, eternal God who provides the grounds for the governing attributes in which particular items occur.

VI. *Modes*.

In E I, Df.5, a mode is said to be an affection of Substance. No mention is there made of any attribute. But for the most part, Spinoza takes a mode to be conceived through some attribute—e.g., E II, P23, E II, Df.1, E II, P6. He does not say whether or not there are modes in all the attributes, though I believe it is safe to infer that, since the attributes are on a footing, if one attribute encompasses modes, the others also do. Nor does Spinoza tell us why there should be any modes, or how there could be a number of them in a given attribute. Solutions to both problems can be obtained if one remembers that things have their own finite essences (E I, P24), and that finite essences can have only finite modal exhibitions. No essence could be exhibited in all the attributes unless it were infinite (E I, Df.6), and none could be exhibited as something finite unless its exhibitions were limited by other finite exhibitions in the same attribute (E I, Df.2). The exhibitions of these finite essences are at once joined and separate (as the attributes are), being conjunctively disjunct when they function as mere units subject to the universal laws of motion and logic, while persistently insistent on themselves as independent units.

We do not know whether or not there are finite essences which exhibit themselves in attributes other than thought and extension, for we have knowledge only of what exhibits itself in these two attributes. But we do know that any such essences will be finite and therefore, unlike God, will be manifested in only some attributes, where their exhibitions will be limited by the exhibitions of other finite essences. Once this is granted, it is possible to make sense of such an assertion as "mind has an essence" (E III, P54), for all essences, finite or infinite, are centers of expressed power. Minds, Spinoza holds, no less than bodies, are active, self-preserving, effective.

Though the mere essence of a thing does not involve the existence of the thing, (E I, P14), it does "posit" the thing (E II, Df.2) in a number of attributes and, since ability to exist is power (E I, P11, S), men, animals, things, and even triangles will exist, for their separate essences not only have proportionate abilities but enable them to fit within and thereby share in the existence of those attributes.

Why are there separate, finite essences? For the same reason that there are distinct attributes—because there is a *natura naturata*. Why is there a *natura naturata*? Because God is infinite, fecund, producing all that can be produced. The attributes and essences serve to articulate him, to express him, to let him be for himself as well as to be in himself.

VII. *Man and His Knowledge.*

Spinoza's definitions deal with Substance, attributes, and modes. A man is none of these. He is not Substance, since he is finite. He is not an attribute, since he is expressed in a number of attributes while they, in turn, are referred back to God's essence. He is not a mode, for he is not identifiable either with his mind or his body. What is he then? A man is an essence, with power enough to exist for a while, and to have modal exhibitions in two attributes. Just as a circle has its essence equally well expressed in a formula and a graph, so a man has his essence equally well expressed in his mind and in his body. And just as a circle can be said to have the power to remain within the domain of mathematics, able to manifest itself in equivalent forms, so a man can be said to have the power to be distinct and to manifest himself bodily and mentally. The power of a man's essence is derived from the source of all power, the infinite essence of God. But because it is finite, man's essence can be expressed only in limited ways and for limited times.

Disagreeing with Descartes' claim that mind and body are substances, and not allowing for the knowledge of anything except via an attribute, Spinoza nevertheless takes man to have a reality of his own, able to be adequately portrayed through the mind and body that this reality empowers. If, with Spinoza, we reserve the term "Substance" for what is eternal, self-caused, infinite in range and power, and expressed in an infinite number of attributes, and if with him we take "mode" to refer to a limited occurrence in an attribute, a man must be said to be nothing more or less than a finite, empowered essence, making itself exist in just two attributes. I hesitantly suggest that the ontological argument has truncated forms allowing us to pass from the idea of an empowered, finite, distinct essence to the idea of an appropriate limited existence.

Sometimes Spinoza speaks as though all men had the same essence, differing from one another only in existence. But each man has his own individual essence, exhibiting this in finite activities within the two known attributes of thought and extension. A man is most completely a man only when he is allied with all the rest in a single harmonious whole (E II, P7, L) which each of them mirrors, and which in turn mirrors the eternal nature of God. The essence of each is a fragment of a fragment of the essence of God. To be at his best, each must unite with the other fragments so as to be in consonance with what is at once perfect, self-explanatory, self-causative, and all-powerful.

Men have ideas (E II, A3). When they love or desire, they have ideas of what they love or desire. Each idea is caused by another idea; all of them have a place in the eternal being of God (E II, P9). What is true of ideas must, of course, be true of bodies, but only so far as the bodies are healthy, expressing the essence of the individual, and not so far as the bodies resonate with the effects produced by external causes (E II, P13).

Spinoza speaks of an individual man in two distinct ways—as an aggregate of small units, and as a part of one mankind. The first half of book IV emphasizes the first; the remainder of the *Ethics* the second. The two are not incompatible. They are supplementary. An individual man is the mediator between the smaller units within his confines and the God who exists apart from him. Every man more or less unifies the one, and more or less epitomizes the other.

An idea of the mind is related—Spinoza misleadingly says "united"—to the mind in the way the mind is related to the body. We can therefore know that we know that we know (E II, P21). Once again it is held by critics that Spinoza gives special standing to thought, allowing ideas to form an infinite set and to apply to everything else. But once again it is right to reply that just as what occurs in any attribute has an idea answering to it in the attribute of thought, so may it have a body answering to it in the attribute of extension. And just as surely as there are ideas of ideas just as surely are there bodies which are inclusive of other bodies.

The human body is complex. Each part of it is matched by a distinctive idea within the larger idea of the individual body (E II, P15). Since every body has a distinct idea which is the counterpart of that body, the idea of a bodily part of the human body must have two forms. The idea must be distinct from all others, appropriate to a distinct bodily part and it must be connected with other ideas within the idea of the complex body.

Because of the mixture of hard and soft parts in his body, a man has only a confused idea of its constitution. He therefore views external bodies in terms of the affections they introduce into his body, leaving him with an idea detached from the idea of its cause, a kind of conclusion without a justifying premiss (E II, P28). In God, though, what is thought and what is extended are in perfect accord (E II, P19). The most that men can do is to use adequate ideas, ideas which allow for neither rejection nor qualification. These have their counterpart in what is common to the whole and to the part—the laws of logic and the laws of motion and rest—and in what is at once rational, infinite, and immediate, making possible a justified move from the idea of the essence of an attribute to the idea of the essence of things (E II, 40, S2), thereby enabling men to know who they are and what they can do. Such adequate ideas, and particularly those which relate to God, contain the secret of man's salvation, enabling him to share in eternity while still finite, ignorant, passionate, and in error.

VIII. *Bondage and Salvation*.

Though Spinoza says in E II, P48 that neither man nor God has a free will, he does hold that both are able to express their essences without being externally compelled. While only man has a transient, horizontally used power enabling him to interplay with other finite entities, he, no less than God, has a constitutive or vertical power by which he freely exhibits what he is in essence. Neither involves willing, desire, intent. When one knows, there is no room for a separate act of the will. Willing is just part of the act of knowing, an affirming or negating, inseparable from the content known (E II, P47, P48). If we are confused we must doubt; if we have adequate ideas, we affirm them and with certainty. Affirmations of what is false and denials of what is true are but misspeakings.

An idea insists on itself to the degree that it is true. It exhibits, in the realm of thought, the nature of an essence. Contrary to Descartes, who takes each entity to perish at every moment, requiring God's creative act to reinstate it in consonance with the requirements of the laws of nature, the essence is seen by Spinoza to seek to preserve itself (E II, P45; E III, P7; E IV Pref.). To see how, on such a view, an item could ever interfere with any other, one must understand the effort at self-preservation to be an effort at preserving oneself by trying to make use of what else there be. *Conatus* must not be identified with a biological form of inertia. It is God's love finitized.

Man can escape bondage if he unites his essence with the essences of other men, and then joins the result to the essence of God—acts which require him to have adequate ideas of which the best of all is the idea of God (E IV, P28). Such knowledge is not possible to animals. They are and forever remain in bondage because they have no knowledge of their bondage and therefore are not able to reduce its power or extent.

The great human error is to treat one's passions as though they expressed one's essence. Man is essentially reason, and if he is truly free, perfected, and virtuous, will live in accord with it, curing his mental failures by logic just as he cures his bodily failures by medicine (E V, Pref.). To the degree that a man knows an affect, the more is it in his control and the less he suffers. Since no man has perfect knowledge, all must be content with following good rules of conduct at the same time that they learn as much as they can about the causes of their sorrows, try to be one with fellow men, understand the common properties of things, and love God (E V, P20, S). The last is best of all (E V, P27, P29). But love of God is the same thing as understanding him—and this, of course, is exactly what Spinoza's philosophic account is to make possible. His *Ethics*, presumably, offers us a clear, distinct, unrejectable idea of God and of man. The beginning of the work is intended to justify and to be justified by its end.

IX.

Spinoza was neglected for a long time, but is now known, at least by name, to many who have heard of no other modern philosopher. He is a rationalist who has been enthusiastically embraced by romantics, a realist who is honored by idealists, an ethicist who is studied for his ontology, a metaphysician whom analysts take seriously, a religious man whom believers disdain, a Cartesian without a mind-body problem, and a formalist who has great attraction for poets and novelists. Despite such strange remarks as: laughter and trembling have no answering idea (E III, P59, S); repentance is a function of education; no one thinks too little of himself; you cannot do what you imagine you cannot do; moderation is a kind of ambition; modesty is dread or fear of shame; remorse shows weakness of mind; humility and repentance are not virtues; and knowledge of evil is sorrow, Spinoza is widely viewed as a splendid guide for both young and old. Why? I think it is in good part because he is so uncompromising, so resolute, so clearly occupied with setting down what is at the root of all there is, that he always awakens respect and, more often than not, admiration and even awe. No one can, I think, be satisfied with his method, accept all his theses, or be persuaded by most of his "proofs." But no one, I also think, can ignore him without loss. At the very least, both by his failures and successes, he makes evident what it means to be honest, rigorous, independent, and courageous, concerned with what is at the root of all knowledge and being—in short, a philosopher.

The Catholic University of America

SPINOZA'S METAPHYSICS

2. THE DEDUCTIVE CHARACTER OF SPINOZA'S METAPHYSICS

Michael Hooker

In the brochure advertising this lecture series there is a quote from Stuart Hampshire that cautions against what I propose to do in this paper. I plan to examine in tedious detail a portion of Spinoza's metaphysics from Book I of the *Ethics*, and in that examination I will treat Spinoza as having provided a purely deductive metaphysics. Hampshire cautions that I will be examining a mask and not the living face, and I am largely in agreement with that judgment. However, there is value to my enterprise, and that value lies in dissecting the mask to reveal the face beneath.

In particular, what I will show is that those philosophers are mistaken who have regarded Book I as merely the expression of the deductive consequences of Spinoza's definitions and axioms. Important philosophical presuppositions are absolutely required to give Spinoza the conclusions he draws from his definitions and axioms, and that fact both belies the claim that Book I is purely deductive and helps to explain why Spinoza's metaphysics has not enjoyed the universal approbation of right thinking philosophers. It has not been widely embraced, because many of Spinoza's arguments are literally invalid. They rest upon unacknowledged and possibly questionable presuppositions. This paper will end with an appraisal of those presuppositions.

Let us begin our examination with the proof of E I, P11, Spinoza's ontological argument for God's existence. The argument is brief, too brief in fact for easy analysis. It goes as follows:

> If this be denied (i.e., that God necessarily exists), conceive, if possible, that God does not exist: then his essence does not involve existence. But this (by Prop. 7) is absurd. Therefore God necessarily exists.

The argument is obviously a *reductio ad absurdum*. We are asked to begin by assuming the conceivability of God's non-existence, and from this a contradictory consequence purports to be drawn. It is concluded that God necessarily exists. How should we reconstruct the argument?

On first try one might be inclined to see Spinoza's intended first premise to be Anselm's, i.e., "God does not exist." However, we know that from the first premise we are supposed to deduce that God's essence does not involve existence, and taking Spinoza purely deductively, we cannot get to that consequence from the assumption of God's non-existence. What will give us the claim we are seeking to establish is E I, A7: If a thing can be conceived as non-existing, its essence does not involve existence. So our first premise should be an instantiation of the antecedent of E I, A7, i.e., the assumption that God can be conceived not to exist.

Now we have that existence is not part of God's essence, so our next step is to derive the claim that that is absurd. Here Spinoza tells us to employ E I, P7 which says that existence belongs to the nature or essence (like Descartes, Spinoza uses these concepts interchangeably in relevant contexts) of substance. Of course we need to know that God is a substance, and E I, Df.6 gives us that. We have then contradictory premises to the effect that existence both is and is not a part of God's essence. We conclude that our generating assumption is false, that is, that God's non-existence is in fact not conceivable. Let us stand back and look at the argument we have produced:

1) God can be conceived not to exist. (Assumption)
2) (x) (if x can be conceived not to exist, existence is not part of the essence of x). (E I, A7)
3) If God can be conceived not to exist, existence is not part of the essence of God. (2)
4) Existence is not part of the essence of God. (1,3)
5) God is a substance. (E I, Df.6)
6) (x) (if x is a substance, existence is part of the essence of x). (E I, P7)
7) If God is a substance, existence is part of the essence of God. (6)
8) Existence is part of the essence of God. (5,7)

---

9) Not-(God can be conceived not to exist). (1,4,8, *reductio*)

There is only one problem with our conclusion, and that is that it is not Spinoza's. His conclusion is that God necessarily exists, not that he can't be conceived not to exist. We need to add to the argument steps to get us from the inconceivability of God's non-existence to the necessary actuality of His non-existence. That is, we need to link the world of thought to the world simpliciter, and for that job there is a familiar principle, affirmed most explicitly by Hume, to the effect that what is not conceivable is not possible. Employing that principle, we can complete the argument as follows:

9) Not-(God can be conceived not to exist).
10) What is not conceivable is not possible.   (suppressed)
11) It is not possible that God does not exist.   (9,10)

12 God necessarily exists.   (11)

We now have a good candidate for the primary ontological argument that Spinoza offered in support of Proposition XI. Since our purpose is to assess the extent to which Spinoza's metaphysics is a purely deductive axiomatic system, we need now to assess the soundness of this argument. We should expect our assessment to terminate ultimately in the discovery of the axioms and definitions on which the proof of XI is founded. If we find premises not capable of support solely by appeal to Spinoza's axioms and definitions (in conjunction with acceptable rules of inference) we will thereby have shown his system to be not deductively self-contained.

There are two loose ends to trace out. One is the Humean principle that we have appropriated—call it the "Principle of the Impossibility of the Inconceivable," or the "Principle of Impossibility" for short—which says that what is not conceivable is not possible. The other loose end is E I, P7, which is the only non-grounded support to which Spinoza appeals. Our concern with the Principle of Impossibility will be to assess whether it is either defensible by appeal to Spinoza's axioms or independently acceptable as a principle of inference. For the moment, let us delay that task in favor of laying bare the argument by searching for the grounding of E I, P7.

Spinoza's proof of E I, P7 goes as follows:

Substance cannot be produced by anything external (E I, P6, C), it must, therefore, be its own cause—that is, its essence necessarily involves existence, or existence belongs to its nature.

We can express the argument in the following premises:

1) (x) (y) (if x and y are distinct substances, x cannot cause the existence of y). E I, P6
2) Only substances can cause substantival existence. (suppressed)
3) Everything that exists has a cause. (suppressed)
4) (x) (if x is a substance, there is some substance not distinct from x that is the cause of x). (1,2,3)
5) Substances cause their own existence. (4)
6) (x) (if x is self-caused, existence is an element of the essence of x). E I, Df.1

7) (x) (if x is a substance, existence is an element of the essence of x).

My appeal to E I, P6 in the first premise deviates from Spinoza's own first premise—he appeals to the corollary regarding the impossibility of external causes—however my appeal directly to E I, P6 seems more to the purpose. In any event, Spinoza's argument and my revised version both rest on the defensibility of E I, P6. Premises (2) and (3) are required to be added, and each is thoroughly Spinozistic. Support for (2), the claim that only substances can cause substantival existence, is suggested in Spinoza's belief that the cause of a substance is that through which the substance is understood, and that a mode, the only other candidate for having causal efficacy, is conceived through something, but nothing is conceived through it. Premise (3), the affirmation that everything existent has a cause, follows from the Spinozistic dogma that the universe is rationally explicable and that to understand anything is to know its cause. If everything that exists can be understood and if to understand something is to know its cause, then everything that exists must have a cause to be known. So E I, P7 is deductively respectable, and we should move to an examination of E I, P6.

Before we do that, however, a parenthetical observation here is in order. E I, P7 tells us that existence is an element of the essence of substance and E I, Df.6 tells us that God is a substance. Shouldn't the conjunction of those two claims, which entails that existence is essential to God, give us all we need in the way of an ontological argument? And if so, why didn't Spinoza argue in that fashion? There are two possible replies. One is that Spinoza is willing to grant the meaningfulness of talk about a thing's essence or nature in the absence of assurance that the thing spoken of actually exists. Another line of reply is that Spinoza would countenance the argument and that his purpose in E I, P11 is to prove not just that God exists, but that he does so necessarily. The second ontological argument of E I, P11, as well as the first, is consonant with both hypotheses, and a selection of one over the other would require additional considerations to be adduced. I will return to this question toward the close of the paper.

Proposition VI, which states that one substance cannot be produced by another, is proved by Spinoza as follows:

> It is impossible that there should be in the universe two substances with an identical attribute, i.e., which have anything common to them both (Prop. 2), and, therefore (Prop. 3), one cannot be the cause of another, neither can one be produced by the other.

Setting out the argument in premise fashion, we get the following:

1) There cannot exist two substances of the same attribute. (E I, P5)
2) (x) (y) (if x and y are distinct substances, x and y have different attributes). (1)
3) Two substances having different attributes have nothing in common with each other. E I, P2
4) If two things have nothing in common, one cannot be cause of the other. (E I, P3)
   ___
5) (x) (y) (if x and y are distinct substances, x and y are causally independent of each other).

All that can be said in critical appraisal of this argument is that it is valid and all of its premises are supplied by prior propositions. We should proceed to those propositions remembering that our purpose still is to search for the ultimate axiomatic grounding of the ontological proof with which this exercise began.

E I, P5, the denial that distinct substances can share attributes, is as difficult to assess as it is important to Spinoza's system. In its defense he says:

> If several distinct substances be granted, they must be distinguished one from the other, either by the difference of their attributes, or by the difference of their modifications (Prop. 4). If

only by the difference of their attributes, it will be granted that there cannot be more than one with an identical attribute. If by the difference of their modifications—as substance is naturally prior to its modifications (Prop. 1)—it follows that setting the modifications aside, and considering substance in itself, that is truly (Def. 3 and Axiom 4), there cannot be conceived one substance different from another—that is (by Prop. 4), there cannot be granted several substances, but one substance only.

The importance of the claim that different substances cannot share attributes is obvious. Spinoza's monism follows immediately when we add the fact that God has infinite attributes. God depletes the store of available attributes and since he is precluded by E I, P5 from sharing his attributes with another substance, there can be no other substances. Also it is on the issue of shared attributes that Spinoza differs so markedly from Descartes. While Descartes apparently thought there was only one thing that had the attribute of extension, he certainly held that many things have the attribute of thought. Thinking is essential to each person, so it is an attribute widely shared. As thinking things, on Descartes' view, you and I differ from our fellows only in virtue of the particular modes of thought that we possess but don't share with others. Spinoza rejects Descartes' view, and the justification for his rejection must be found in his argument for Proposition V.

I find this proof excruciatingly opaque. Its argument is simply not decipherable in any straightforward way; however, a number of hypotheses for interpretation can be offered and tested. At first it appears that Spinoza is saying something like this: *Suppose there are two substances that share an attribute. Then they will have to be distinguished either by virtue of their attributes or by virtue of their modes. But they can't be distinguished by virtue of their attributes, because those are the same for each of the two substances. So they must be distinguished by their modes. But they cannot be distinguished that way, because substances are prior to their modes, so the modes must be conceived through the substance, not vice versa.*

What troubles me most about this interpretation of the proof is the putative justification for denying that substances can be distinguished by a difference of their modes. But there are prior worries, and if they were resolved, possibly this misgiving regarding modes would be resolved as well. Foremost among the prior concerns is the question of what Spinoza means when he says that distinct substances must be distinguished one from the other. It is unclear whether he is speaking of a metaphysical distinction or of an epistemological distinction. If he is making a metaphysical point, then to say that distinct substances must be distinguished is to say that they must have some property not in common. That is so in virtue of the principle explicitly enunciated by Leibniz to the effect that two things cannot be exactly alike and differ *solo numero*. On the other hand, if Spinoza is speaking epistemologically, then to say that distinct substances must be distinguished is to say that if they are distinct we must be able to recognize them as distinct, and since we recognize substances through their properties, we must be able to recognize that the one substance has a property the other lacks.

Another perplexity we confront in interpreting the proof of E I, P5 comes in understanding the proposition itself. When Spinoza says that distinct substances cannot have the same nature or attribute, does he mean that the substances cannot share a single attribute and remain distinct, or does he mean that they cannot share all of their attributes in common and remain distinct? Further, when Spinoza speaks of attributes belonging to a substance, what does he see as the relationship between a single such attribute and the essence of that substance? The notion of essence in Seventeenth Century philosophy is confused at best, and it is no help that Spinoza failed to give us guidelines to his usage of the concepts of essence, nature, and attribute.

It is at first tempting to think that Spinoza intends us to read Proposition V as saying that no two distinct substances can share an essence. That would be consonant with his definition of attribute as that which we perceive as constituting the essence of a substance, and with the notion, which Arnauld held, that the essence of a thing uniquely individuates that thing. Then of course no distinct things could share attributes, i.e., essences, since their having the same essence would guarantee their non-diversity. However, considerations speak strongly against this interpretation of Spinoza's intent. One is that he held that one substance (God) has an infinite number of attributes, so no single attribute could constitute the essence of that substance. Its essence would rather be the totality of its attributes, each of which is essential to it, i.e., each of which is one of its many essential properties.

The other consideration that speaks against interpreting Spinoza as concerned with uniquely individuating essences in E I, P5 is that a different tradition regarding essence was predominant in the period, and Spinoza would seem more in line with it. Descartes, who is most representative of this other view of essence, held roughly that the essence of a created substance is either thought or extension, and what makes those two attributes candidates for essencehood is that they are the most general properties under which all other properties of created things can be subsumed as examples. They are determinables of the highest level of generality, and all other properties of created substances will fall under one or the other as a determinate mode of that attribute. An essential property for Descartes might be loosely thought of as the defining property of an Aristotelian natural kind, though that notion may be so vague as to mislead rather than edify. At any rate, Spinoza seems to have such general properties in mind as examples of attributes, and he seems to have thought of such properties as each essential but none as a *haecceitas* or individual essence. In light of these considerations, then, we should understand E I, P5 as affirming not that two substances cannot share a uniquely individuating essence, but rather that they cannot share essential properties. Whether Spinoza means that distinct substances can't share any essential properties or whether he means rather that they can't share all essential properties is a question yet to be settled. We should look at both possibilities. Descartes, we remember, held that substances can share that single essential property, thought, that constitutes their essence, and we will be interested to see why Spinoza thought that an impossibility.

E I, P4 tells us that distinct things may be distinguished one from the other either by a difference of their attributes or by a difference of their modes. The ambiguity regarding E I, P5 is found here too, but we can see that if Spinoza means that distinct substances must be metaphysically distinguished, then that could happen, E I, P4 seems to say, either by their having different attributes or by their having different modes. And if he means that distinct substances must be conceptually distinguished by cognitive agents, then he seems to be saying that this could be accomplished either by attention to their unshared attributes or to their unshared modes. With this interpretaiton of E I, P4 in mind, let us attend again to E I, P5.

There seem to be four possible allocations of attributes and modes to two substances. They can have in common (1) all attributes and all modes, (2) all attributes and not all modes, (3) some attributes but all modes, and (4) some attributes and not all modes. Without taking cognizance of Spinoza's argument to the contrary, it would seem that in only one of these possible allocations of properties would the two substances be indistinct. In the first case, if they shared all of their attributes and all of their modes, then by the Principle of the Identity of Indiscernibles, they would be identical. There is no more to identity than co-extensiveness of properties. However in the other four cases there is some difference of properties to guarantee that the one substance is absolutely distinguished from the other and to enable a cognitive agent aware of that property difference to so distinguish them. Again for Descartes, you and I share attributes—we are both thinking things—but there is no question of our being indistinct since we do not enjoy the same modes of thought.

Evidence that Spinoza intends E I, P5 in its most radical reading, i.e., as denying any sharing of attributes whatsoever, is provided by his use of the proposition in the proof of God's uniqueness in E I, P14. There, after having already established God's existence and infinitude, Spinoza says that there can be no other substance because such a substance would have to have one of God's attributes, since God has them all, and by E I, P5, that cannot be. So E I, P5 is supposed to rule out any sharing of attributes at all, irrespective of whatever unshared attributes two substances might be thought to possess. We need to examine the argument, then, from this understanding of its radical intent. What is the argument's justification and in what is it grounded?

The argument is in two parts. Having established in E I, P4 that distinct substances must be distinguished either by a difference of attributes or by a difference of modes, Spinoza considers the two possible means of distinction for two substances that purport to share an attribute. First he says that the conclusion will be granted if the substances could be distinguished only by a difference of their attributes. It is not clear why that should be granted. Admittedly, if we were required to conceive putatively separate substances solely by thinking of them through a shared attribute, we could not succeed. And if it were solely in virtue of a shared attribute that putatively separate substances were distinct, they would not be so. However there remains unexamined by Spinoza the possibility of their being distinguished or of our distinguishing them in virtue of attributes that they do not share. What is both distressing and important for our purposes is that Spinoza apparently thinks the justification for his claim is obvious. He does not cite prior propositions, axioms or definitions to support himself. If by "attribute" Spinoza meant "essence," and if he understood an essence as a uniquely individuating property, then he would be as obviously correct as he thinks he is when he says that there cannot be more than one substance with an identical attribute. He would be similarly correct if he were talking about things being distinguished solely by their attributes when they have all of their attributes in common. But neither is the case. Spinoza's claim seems not only not axiomatically grounded, but mistaken as well.

Even if Spinoza were correct regarding indistinguishability by attributes, it is not clear that he would be correct regarding indistinguishability by appeal to modes. To see that, consider Descartes' case where all the attributes of two substances are held in common. Can the substances be distinguished by their modes? Viewing attributes as non-uniquely individuating, it would seem that they could. Looked at from the point of view of the metaphysics of the matter, all that is required for diversity is non-co-extensiveness of property possession.

A difference of modes guarantees that condition. Looked at epistemologically, an agent needs only to conceive distinct substances by appeal to non-shared properties in order to distinguish them. However, Spinoza demurs regarding these possibilities.

In turning to consideration of the possibility of distinguishing two substances by appeal to their modes, Spinoza suggests that this can't be done since substance is prior to its modifications. For that reason, Spinoza says, we must place the modifications aside and consider the substances by themselves, which he says is considering them truly. Now it is not clear what the reason is, but it is clear that Spinoza has either sent us back to the attributes for the distinction between substances, or he has sent us beyond the attributes as a way of conceiving substances and straight to the substances themselves. If it is the former, then we know from the first half of the proof that our task will meet with failure, and if it is to the substances directly that we must turn, then all hope of getting an intellectual grip on substance is lost. As cognitive agents we know substance only through its properties.

We now face a double defect in Spinoza's defense of E I, P5. The first half of his proof is not deductively grounded, and the second half, to the extent that it falls back on the first, will be similarly groundless. What makes matters worse still, the support Spinoza offers for refusing to allow us to distinguish between substances by appeal to their modes is inadequate. He refers to E I, Df.3 and E I, A6, the definition of substance as that which is conceived through itself and the axiomatic claim that true ideas and their objects must correspond. The definition of substance I take to indicate that substances are causally independent of properties and other substances, but that does not show that substances cannot be conceived, i.e., thought about, by attention to their attributes and modes. Support for the injunction against distinguishing substances by their modes is still lacking. One possible but specious line of defense Spinoza might be thought to have had in mind would be the claim that since attributes are prior to the modes they subtend, we cannot conceive modes without conceiving them through their supporting attributes. Such an appeal would be specious as a support for his proof, since it does not show that we can't distinguish substances through their different modes. It shows only that to fully comprehend the modes, we must know the attributes that they fall under.

The upshot of all this is that we have found a proposition—in fact possibly the most essential proposition in Spinoza's metaphysics—that is not deductively derived from prior propositions, axioms, and definitions. We conclude that Spinoza's metaphysics is not an axiomatic system in which all non-basic claims can be expressed as the deductive consequences of self-evident truths. It is not surprising that

Book I of the *Ethics* has not commanded universal allegiance. Those who have read the proofs and have thought that something was amiss were right. However, our excoriation of Spinoza must be tempered by the recognition that while the proof of E I, P5 is not straightforwardly valid, and while no obvious repair is suggested by attention to the axioms, on confronting our criticism Spinoza might well have come up with a response we would find compelling. We should therefore continue our examination of the propositions on which the proof of E I, P6 is based.

In addition to relying upon E I, P5, the argument for E I, P6 depends also upon E I, P2 and P3. E I, P2, which says that substances whose attributes are different have nothing in common, is fairly straightforward if it means that substances with no common attributes have no common modes either. Spinoza is not as clear as Descartes is about the relationship between modes and attributes, but surely he understands much the same relationship to hold as Descartes posited. As indicated above, Descartes divided the properties of things into attributes and modes. Attributes are the most general properties a thing can have—either thought or extension—and modes are specific properties under one or the other genus. For example, hoping, wishing, fearing, believing, and surmising are all ways of thinking. Anything that is characterized by one of those mental activities will also have the attribute of thought. On Spinoza's view, then, to say of substances having no common attributes that they can have no common modes either is to say, for example, that if two substances don't share the attribute of thought, they cannot both bear the mode deciding.

E I, P3 tells us that if two things have nothing in common with one another, one cannot be the cause of the other. In proof of E I, P3 Spinoza says:

> If they have nothing in common, one cannot be understood through the other (Axiom 5), and therefore one cannot be the cause of the other (Axiom 4).

This is the first proposition we have encountered that purports to be deductively derived from a conjunction of axioms functioning as a premise set. We should display the axioms to see what rules of inference warrant the deduction:

1) The knowledge of an effect depends upon and involves the knowledge of its cause.   E I, A4
2) Things which have nothing in common cannot be understood one by means of the other.   E I, A5

3) If two things have nothing in common, one cannot be the cause of the other.

The briefest inspection of this argument shows that it is literally invalid. From the premises all that can be straightforwardly inferred are the following two facts about the limitation of human knowledge:

a) If two things have nothing in common, one cannot be known to be the cause of the other.

and

b) If two things have nothing in common and one causes the other, the effect cannot be known.

These propositions rest on the acceptability of the additional assumption that to know that x causes y is to understand y by means of x. To see how Spinoza derives his conclusion we need to ask what in addition to E I, A4 and A5 is needed. It should be mentioned, if only for purposes of dismissal, that in one sense the conclusion follows immediately, but the sense is too obvious for Spinoza to have intended it. If one thing causes another, then clearly one thing they have in common is a causal relationship with each other, and where no such relationship is present, the one cannot have caused the other. No axioms are required to illuminate that fact. What Spinoza surely rather means is that for two things to stand in a causal relationship they must share an attribute, though we know of course that it will later be shown that since this is impossible, the only substantival causality is self-reflexive.

Returning to the proof of E I, P3, we can see that what is needed to be assumed in addition to the two axioms are the following three claims:

1) Everything can be understood (i.e., the universe is rationally explicable).
2) Everything has a cause.
3) To understand something is to know its cause.

Here we have the fundamental unexpressed tenets of Spinoza's metaphysics. The claim that everything can be understood is needed to guarantee that we cannot have two things causally related but having no properties in common. Our being able to understand the effect guarantees that we must know the cause, given the claim that to understand something is to know its cause. The axiom to the effect that where two things have nothing in common, the one cannot be known through the other, will rule out our being able to understand an effect of a cause with which it has nothing in common. So given that we can know everything, there can be no unknowable effect of a cause with which it has no properties in common.

The claim that everything has a cause is presupposed in the view that to understand something is to know its cause. If there were causally bereft orphans in the universe, and if those orphans were knowable, then not everything would be known through its cause. So everything must have a cause for Spinoza's system of metaphysical explanation to work. That is nothing surprising or new to us, of course, but it is somewhat surprising that none of Spinoza's axioms expresses that fact. E I, A3 tells us that causes necessarily produce their effects and that where no cause exists no effect can follow, but it does not tell us that everything that exists is an effect. This lacuna in Spinoza's axiom set is all the more odd in light of the fact that Descartes so often explicitly affirmed universal causality.

It is tempting to opine that part of the reason Spinoza's system of metaphysics exercised no great influence and failed to gain wide adherence is that so many of his generating principles were left largely unexpressed or undefended. For example, philosophers subsequently influenced by Leibniz, Hume and Kant might find objectionable the confidence Spinoza places in the ubiquity of causality. How, it might be asked, does he know in advance that the universe has a cause. We know that he proves that the universe consists of one substance only, and that substance is defined as being self-caused, which facts guarantee that the universe has a cause. However, the proof of monism requires E I, P3, so it appears unpersuasive if not illicit to use uniqueness to get the causality of the totality, which in turn precludes misgivings that might arise about the universality of causality. This appearance of intellectual impropriety, however, is probably misleading, because Spinoza's concept of causality when fully spelled out, is much broader than other Seventeenth Century notions of causality. As Randall observed, Spinoza's concept of causality is akin to formal causality.[1] It is that in terms of which something is to be understood, so whatever the explanation of a thing, that is its cause. Had Spinoza made this adequately clear in the *Ethics*, he would likely have received a more sympathetic reading.

Looking back from our present perspective we can see that much that is required to yield the propositions of the *Ethics*, is not provided in the axioms. It needs to be supplied by the reader, and it is supplied

---

[1] John H. Randall, Jr., *The Career of Philosophy* (New York: Columbia Univ. Press, 1962), I, 439.

mostly from the reader's knowledge of the bedrock assumptions on which Spinoza based his metaphysics. The fact of the incompleteness of Spinoza's axiomatic system gives support to those scholars who have argued that Spinoza's grand vision of metaphysics came prior to his explicit recognition and formulation of the axioms and definitions in which it is purportedly founded. Those who so interpret Spinoza see the metaphysical system he provided as standing or falling on the strength of the explanatory adequacy of the whole.

As an explanation of how the metaphysics was constructed, this view is appealing. It is very unlikely that Spinoza started with his fundamental notions and worked up to deductively derive their consequences, just as it is unlikely that Descartes proceeded in the stepwise fashion of the *Meditations*. However, just as Descartes thought his metaphysics capable of expression through the deductive structure he gives it in the Appendix of his reply to the second set of objections, so also Spinoza thought his propositions derivable from a set of axioms and definitions that would be found intellectually compelling by anyone who would but attend to them.

Having traced the support for Spinoza's ontological argument back to its axiomatic foundations, we have one remaining loose end to pick up. We saw that the argument requires the Principle of Impossibility, which appears as premise (10) and affirms that what is not conceivable is not possible. This principle and its converse—the claim that what is conceivable is possible—have historically provided the link in philosophy between thought and the world. It is not surprising to find Spinoza using the Principle of Impossibility, and in fact he uses its converse, the Principle of Possibility, as well. Still, as essential to the history of metaphysics as these connective principles are, they have not been without their detractors, and serious questions can be raised regarding their acceptability. We should examine them more closely.

Hume affirms both principles when he says:

> 'Tis an established maxim in metaphysics, *That whatever the mind clearly conceives includes the idea of possible existence,* or in other words, *that nothing we imagine is absolutely impossible.* We can form the idea of a golden mountain, and from thence conclude that such a mountain may actually exist. We can form no idea of a mountain without a valley, and therefore regard it as impossible.[2]

---

[2] David Hume, *A Treatise of Human Nature*, ed. Selby-Bigge (Oxford: Clarendon Press, 1888), 32.

Hume's mention of the golden mountain is an example of his commitment to the Principle of Possibility, and his citing the impossibility of a mountain without a valley displays his commitment to the Principle of Impossibility. Descartes appealed fairly often to the Principle's test for possibility, and he more than once acknowledged his allegiance to it. In *NOTES AGAINST A PROGRAM* he says:

> Here it must be noted that the rule "whatever we can conceive can exist," is mine, and true, so long as the question concerns a clear and distinct concept . . .[3]

One of the most notable uses that Descartes made of the Principle of Possibility was in arguing for the non-identity of himself and his body. In *Meditations* VI he argues that it is conceivable that he and his body are separate, and thence concludes that their separate existence is possible. From that he concludes further that since whatever things can exist separately one from another are actually distinct, therefore he and his body are distinct.

Descartes appeals to God to guarantee the truth of the Principle of Possibility. What God does for Descartes, the appeal of human reason does for Spinoza. E I, A7 expresses an instantiation of the Principle of Possibility. The Axiom affirms that the essence of something that can be conceived as not existing does not involve existence. That is, from the conceivability of the non-existence of something Spinoza infers that its non-existence is possible, which is what is meant by saying that its essence does not involve existence. The generalized version of the Possibility Principle is employed by Spinoza repeatedly in establishing his metaphysics. For example, it occurs in the proof of E I, P14 in which Spinoza establishes the inconceivability of substantival pluralism by showing its impossibility. That is an appeal to the contrapositive of the Principle of Possibility.

Granted that Spinoza and the tradition find the Possibility Principle indispensible, we should still ask whether it is valid and in virtue of what is it capable of carrying the metaphysical weight it has been expected to bear. The Principle was given thorough scrutiny by Thomas Reid who argued vigorously for its falsity, only to end up using the principle in his own arguments.[4] Attention to Reid's misgivings serve

---

[3] *Philosophical Works of Descartes*, trans. Haldane & Ross (Cambridge: Cambridge Univ. Press, 1931), I, 437–438.

[4] Thomas Reid, *Essays on the Intellectual Powers of Man* (Cambridge: M. I. T. Press, 1969), Sec. IV, Ch. III. I have examined Reid's arguments in "A Mistake Concerning Conception," in *Thomas Reid: Critical Interpretations*, ed. S. Barker and T. Beauchamp (Philadelphia: 1976), 85–94.

to remind us of Descartes' caveat: The Principle of Possibility is valid only so long as it is restricted in its application to clear and distinct conceptions. What constitutes a clear and distinct conception was left unspecified by Descartes, and there is little of a general nature that we can supply to fill the void. What ultimately must happen is that disputes regarding use of the Principle are heard and adjudicated in the court of reasoned philosophical reflection, and it is the shared wisdom of the philosophical community that finally certifies as legitimate particular applications of the Principle. Its use in general by Spinoza does not warrant our censure. Its use in particular cases must be appraised separately in each individual use.

With respect to the Principle of Impossibility something more definitive can be said in its support. A commitment to the principle is indispensible to intellectual endeavor. Whatever intuitive appeal we find in the laws of logic rests only on the Impossibility Principle. For example, the pursuasive force of the law of non-contradiction derives from the inconceivability of its denial. We are simply unable to imagine a state of affairs correctly described by the schema "p and not-p." I know of no support that could be offered to the fundamental laws of logic beyond an appeal to the Principle, save possibly a pragmatic appeal to the practical value of operating in accordance with them. But while we are pleased to be served by logic, most of us think that our confidence in it rests on more than past practical benefits it has yielded. That additional support is provided by the Principle of Impossibility. Spinoza's use of the Principle, as long as it is applied with honest conviction and open to public corroboration on the test of inconceivability, is on footing no less firm than the laws of logic that enable his movement from axioms to theorems.

We began the preceding investigation by offering an interpretation of E I, P11, Spinoza's ontological argument for God's existence, and we should return to that argument for discussion of one more of Spinoza's generating presuppositions. It is an important one. We saw that E I, P11 makes reference to E I, P7, which says that existence belongs to the essence of substance, and to Df.6, which says that God is a substance. I earlier suggested that if Spinoza's ontological argument is like Descartes', he has all he needs in those two claims to guarantee God's existence. Why should he have offered the more elaborate proof of E I, P11? My hypothesis is that Spinoza would grant that if existence is part of the essence of something, then that thing exists and that in fact his ontological argument assumes at the outset that God exists. Its real function is to prove the necessity of God's existence from the assumption of its actuality. In premise (6) of our version of the argument, I have expressed E I, P7 in quantificational form. It is a universal generalization to the effect that if anything is a substance, then existence is part of its essence. To get the claim that existence is part of God's essence, we need to affirm premise (5) categorically, that is, we assume God's existence in asserting, under authority of E I, Df.6, that he is a substance. While the definition of "God" may define a concept with no existential commitment implied, in order to get God as a value of the variable in premise (6) we need to assume His existence. In a similar fashion, in order to derive premise (4) in the first half of the proof, it must be assumed that God is the actual object of our conception. That is, for purposes of the *reductio* proof we assume the *de re* conceivability of God's nonexistence. Otherwise, we would be left with the *de dicto* conceivability of the proposition that God does not exist, which would establish only that *if* God exists, the existence is not part of his essence. Clearly the first version of Spinoza's ontological argument assumes God's existence in the process of proving its conclusion, which is that He necessarily exists. I think a close look at his other versions of the argument will reveal a similar use of the assumption.

In our search for the grounding of Spinoza's system, then, we have uncovered another Spinozistic assumption, and that is that God exists. The axioms and definitions do not reveal that assumption, since the only mention of God, E I, Df.6, can be viewed as defining a concept without commitment to whether anything exists conforming to it. The importation of God is not made until E I, P11, though E I, P7 may properly be thought to have a categorical rather than a hypothetical conclusion. If it does, then the existence of substance must be assumed there. What of the propriety of Spinoza's assumption here uncovered? It strikes me as no less warranted than his assumptions that everything has a cause, that nature is wholly accessible to reason, and that to know the cause of a thing is to understand that thing. To appreciate the acceptability of Spinoza's assumption of God's existence, it is necessary only to appreciate the explanatory role of the notion of substance in Seventeenth Century philosophy. It was commonplace to assume the universe explicable and to adopt the notion of substance as the foundation of what exists and as the foundation of the explanation of what exists. That something exists was questioned if at all only heuristically, and that what exists is to be explained by appeal to the character of substance was never questioned at all.[5] Where Spinoza incurred the intellectual mistrust of his metaphysical contemporaries and immediate successors was not in assuming the

---

[5] I would argue that this is ultimately so even for Locke, though he never got around to ultimate explanation.

existence of substance, which is all the ontological argument does, but in calling it "God."

The Johns Hopkins University

3. SPINOZA'S ONTOLOGICAL PROOF
Willis Doney

Spinoza states four arguments following Proposition 11 in Part One of the *Ethics*. E I, P11 is: "God, or substance comprising infinite attributes, each one of which expresses eternal and infinite essence, necessarily exists."[1] Employing the classifications *a priori* and *a posteriori*, he tells us that the third argument is *a posteriori* and implies that the other three are *a priori*. If, for Spinoza's "apriori," we substitute the Kantian "ontological," and if we are prepared to say that these arguments are indeed arguments for the existence of God, we can credit Spinoza—for what it is worth—with three ontological arguments or proofs of God's existence. According to Prof. Gueroult, there are in fact five such arguments in Part One of the *Ethics*.[2] Three are more than enough for one discussion, however; and I shall, in fact, be concerned primarily with the first demonstration following the enunciation of E I, P11. It enjoys pride of place. It is also, I believe, intended to be the principal or official Demonstration of this Proposition. In any event, it seems to me to be the most elusive and perplexing as well as the most interesting of the three.

1.

Before turning to problems of interpretation peculiar to it, I want to make some introductory comments of a more general nature.

---

[1] References are to the standard Gebhardt edition: *Spinoza Opera*, edited by Carl Gebhardt (Heidelberg: Carl Winters, 1925), Vol. II, 52. Hereafter, references to Spinoza's works will be by volume and page in the body of the article, using "G" as abbreviation.

[2] Martial Gueroult, *Spinoza* (Paris: Aubier-Montaigne, 1968), Vol.I, Ch. V, 179. According to Gueroult, there are in total seven proofs of God's existence in the *Ethics*, Part One. In addition to the five "ontological" arguments, one proof is a posteriori, and the other is *une preuve de simple vue*.

These apply to the other a priori arguments as well as this one, and in these comments I shall indicate—without trying to defend—my position on certain controversial issues. Reasons for this position, or rather some of them, will emerge farther on.

(a) I said that, *if* we are prepared to say that these arguments are indeed arguments for the existence of God, we can credit Spinoza with three ontological arguments or proofs of God's existence. I said this because some of Spinoza's readers would not be prepared to say that his statements following E I, P11 do comprise arguments for God's existence. Three reasons for denying this can be distinguished. First, since it seems that what Spinoza means by *Deus* is not what we mean by "God," it also seems that, although these arguments can be said to be arguments for the existence of what he means by "God" they certainly are not (at best) proofs of the existence of what we mean by "God"—or, simply and controversially, proofs of the existence of God. Second, some commentators have rightly pointed out that, according to Spinoza, the existence of substance is self-evident and can be intuited; and it has been concluded from this that the "arguments" here are not really intended to be arguments at all but are rather supposed to be expressions or articulations of an intuition. Finally, it has been suggested that the existence of infinite substance or God is assumed or proved before this in the *Ethics* and that in this Proposition Spinoza is simply explaining the sense, or specifying the kind, of existence that is to be attributed to God—or to "God or nature."

With regard to the first reason, I do not want to insist that Spinoza's arguments are indeed arguments for what we mean by "God," but I want to venture that, by *Deus*, Spinoza thinks that he means what others mean, though he of course, also thinks that his conception of God is quite different and—to understate the point—vastly superior. I believe, therefore, that it is a mistake to say with Wolfson that Spinoza's use of the term "God" is "appeasive."[3] To put this point in another way: if I am right, Spinoza thinks that he has discovered *what* God really is. About the second reason, it is perhaps enough to say that, though Spinoza thinks that the existence of substance can be intuited, he also thinks that the existence of infinite substance can be proved, namely, by the arguments following E I, P11. As will be made apparent farther on, I do not accept the third reason, for (among other things) I interpret the conclusion of Spinoza's first argument, that is, "God necessarily exists", not to be "The kind of existence

---

[3] Harry Austryn Wolfson, *The Philosophy of Spinoza* (Cambridge: Harvard University Press, 1948), 177.

that God possesses is necessary existence," but to be "It is necessarily *true* that God exists."

(b) If we were to attempt to diagnose the cause of the difficulty to be found in the arguments here and particularly in the first rather stark and forbidding demonstration, perhaps the most obvious point to be noted (apart from the brevity of presentation) is that the locution "The essence of X involves existence" is in need of explanation. For, even if we pride ourselves on knowing how the terms "essence" and "existence" and locutions like "essence involving existence" are used in the philosophical tradition, there is no guarantee that Spinoza is using them in any one of the usual ways. Indeed, there is every reason to think that he is not using them in just the way that many of his predecessors used them.[4] Part of what he means is explained in the very first definition of Part One of the *Ethics*. Definition 1 is: "By cause of itself I understand that whose essence involves existence, or that whose nature cannot be conceived unless existing"(G II, 45). In this sentence Spinoza indicates that "The essence of X involves existence" and "X is *causa sui*" or "X is self-caused" can be taken to mean the same thing.

(c) It is perhaps too obvious to note that neither in the first argument nor in any of the other apriori arguments does Spinoza invoke, or appear to rely on, a conception of God as a perfect, or a supremely perfect, being. If we were to attempt to say what conception or idea of God is involved in the three arguments, it would not be incorrect to say that it is the conception of God as an absolutely infinite substance. Turning to the first or official Demonstration in particular, we might say that this argument is based on part of that conception, that is, on the notion of God as substance, and that the argument proceeds, by way of a premise about the self-causation of substance, to the conclusion that God, who or which is a substance, necessarily exists. In conjunction with this point, it is also to be noted that, in none of the arguments, is the proposition "Existence is a perfection" an explicit premise, nor, so far as I can determine, an implicit or suppressed premise. It can be made out that "Existence is a predicate" or "Existence is a property" is presupposed in the claim that the essence of God involves existence, but there is no reference at all to the alleged fact that the predicate or property of existence is a *perfection*. None of the arguments is akin, therefore, apart from their being classified as "*a priori*" or "ontological," to an argument which has been taken to be the prototype of *the* ontological argument and which has been located, among other places, in Descartes' Fifth Meditation;

---

[4] See, for instance, Definition 2, Part Two.

namely, "God, a supremely perfect being, has all perfections; Existence is a perfection; Therefore, God has the perfection of existing."[5]

(d) Regarding another possible misinterpretation, the use of "necessarily" in the conclusion, "Therefore, God necessarily (*necessario*) exists," has not gone unnoticed. This—and the use of "essence" in "The essence of substance involves existence"—can be taken to indicate the presence of a "modal" ontological argument, like the argument which Hartshorne finds in Anselm's *Proslogion*, III.[6] In the case of the first argument, this interpretation is conclusively refuted when we look at the citation of E I, P7 and the Demonstration earlier on of that crucial Proposition.

(e) Finally, to anticipate another point, the term *causa* is used in the second argument, and that argument begins with the assertion of a causal principle: "For the existence or non-existence of everything there must be a reason or cause" (G II, 52-53). Although the term "cause" is not used in the statement of the other arguments, a little investigation shows that, in these arguments as well, the concept of a cause also plays a part. In the first argument, for instance, it is expressed in the demonstration of the principal proposition cited, namely, E I, P7. And it is, I believe, fair to say that, but for Spinoza's insistence that principles of causation be applied strictly and universally—to the existence and non-existence of God as well as other matters,—we should have had none of the apriori arguments following Proposition 11. They might, therefore, be appropriately called "causal" ontological arguments.

2.

So much, then, for general remarks. The statement of the first argument is very short—just three lines in the standard edition. After the enunciation of the Proposition, we find:

> If this be denied, conceive, if it be possible, that God does not exist. Then (by Axiom 7) it follows that His essence does not involve existence. But this (by Proposition 7) is absurd: Therefore, God necessarily exists. *Q.E.D.*

About Spinoza's intentions here, one point at least seems clear: that he intends to state in these few lines a *reductio ad absurdum*. But, as we

---

[5] As in Jonathan Barnes, *The Ontological Argument* (London: Macmillan, 1972), 16.

[6] Charles Hartshorne, *Anselm's Discovery* (Lasalle, Ill: Open Court, 1965).

shall see, even this point needs to be qualified. To begin to unpack his meaning, however, I shall give what I take to be a *prima facie* plausible, if not particularly revealing, dissection of the argument into four steps—four steps which can be distinguished in any argument that is a *reductio*. Amplification and qualification will come later.

(1) There is at first the statement of an assumption—an assumption which is supposed to lead to a consequence that is necessarily false or absurd and which is ostensibly the denial of the conclusion to be proved. The statement of the assumption is accomplished in the first sentence: "If", Spinoza begins, "this be denied, conceive, if it be possible, that God does not exist." "This" in "If this be denied..." refers to the preceding statement of Proposition 11; and, when the reference is supplied, the sentence in which Spinoza states the assumption of his *reductio* is, "If it be denied that God, or substance consisting of infinite attributes, each one of which expresses eternal and infinite essence, necessarily exists, conceive, if it be possible, that God does not exist." The assumption of the *reductio* appears to be "God does not exist"; but, as we shall see, even this seemingly obvious point has been queried.

(2) The second step is the derivation of a certain consequence from the initial assumption. This is done with great economy in the next sentence: "Then (by Axiom 7) it follows that His essence [i.e., the essence of God] does not involve existence." Axiom 7 is: "Whatever can be conceived as not existing is such that its essence does not involve existence" (G II, 47). Accordingly, the second step can be expanded: "From the initial assumption in conjunction with the principle that whatever can be conceived as not existing is such that its essence does not involve existence, it follows that the essence of God does not involve existence." In the next section, a problem will be raised about this attempted derivation of the consequence.

(3) The third step of the *reductio* is the contention that the consequence derived in the second step is necessarily false or absurd. Again, this is done with economy: "But this (by Proposition 7) is absurd...." "This" refers to the consequence derived in the preceding step, namely, "The essence of God does not involve existence"; and Proposition 7 is, "It pertains to the nature of a substance to exist" (G II, 49). In the demonstration of Proposition 7, it is made clear that to say that it pertains to the nature of substance to exist is exactly the same as to say that the essence of substance involves existence. Putting Proposition 7 in these terms and making the reference to the previously stated consequence explicit, we get the following expanded version of the third step: "Since it has been demonstrated in Proposition 7 that the essence of substance involves existence, it follows that the consequence derived from the initial assumption, namely, the

consequence that the essence of God does not involve existence, is necessarily false or absurd." There appears to be a suppressed premise here. Proposition 7 is not about God but about substance unqualified or substance *simpliciter*, and it seems that, for the inference in this step to be valid, Spinoza needs the premise "God is a substance." Difficulties deriving from this seemingly obvious and unexceptionable premise will also be dealt with farther on.

(4) The remaining and final step in the *reductio* is the assertion of the conclusion, which is purportedly the denial or negation of the initial assumption. As was noted before, significance has been attached to the fact that Spinoza states the conclusion of his argument (as well as Proposition 11, or part of Proposition 11) in the following way: "Therefore, God necessarily exists."

3.

On the entirely plausible assumption that the argument is a *reductio*, a problem arises with regard to what I have distinguished as the second step. According to the analysis proposed, Axiom 7 is cited in this step to license an inference from the assumption "God does not exist" to the consequence "The essence of God does not involve existence." When we take a look at Axiom 7, however, we see plainly enough that that principle, or that principle by itself, does not license this inference. Axiom 7 is: "Whatever can be conceived as not existing is such that its essence does not involve existence." Rephrased in a terminology which may be more congenial to some, the principle is: "(x) (if x can be conceived not to exist, the essence of x does not involve existence)." This principle can be used to warrant an inference from "God can be conceived not to exist" to "The essence of God does not involve existence," but it does not get us from "God does not exist" to "The essence of God does not involve existence." If we are not to accuse Spinoza of carelessness or lack of rigor or of an all too obvious blunder, it seems that we must rescue his argument from invalidity in some way or other. There are two possibilities. On the one hand, we can supply a suppressed premise which, in conjunction with Axiom 7, will justify the move from "God does not exist" to "The essence of God does not involve existence." Or, on the other hand, we can deny that the second step of the *reductio* is as it was made out to be in the initial analysis. On the second alternative, there are three sub-possibilities. Either, appearances to the contrary, the assumption of the *reductio* is not "God does not exist." Or, appearances to the contary, the consequence is not "The essence of God does not involve existence." Or last, appearances to the contrary, it is not in reality Axiom 7 which is supposed to get us from "God does not exist" to "The essence of God does not involve existence."

In an interesting paper on this argument. Michael Hooker takes the second alternative.[7] As he interprets the *reductio*, the proposition assumed at the outset is not "God does not exist," but "God can be conceived not to exist." What I have called the first and second steps of the *reductio* are, on his analysis, as follows:

1. God can be conceived not to exist. (assumption)
2. (x) (if x can be conceived not to exist, existence is not part of the essence of x). (Axiom 7)
3. If God can be conceived not to exist, existence is not part of the essence of God. (2)
4. Existence is not part of the essence of God. (1,3)

As Hooker of course realizes, the conclusion of a *reductio* that begins in this way cannot be "God exists" or "God necessarily exists." The conclusion is, on his interpretation, "God cannot be conceived not to exist." To explain how Spinoza reaches the conclusion actually stated in the *Ethics*, namely, "God necessarily exists," he imputes to him the following concluding move:

9. Not - (God can be conceived not to exist). (. . . , reductio)
10. What is not conceivable is not possible. (suppressed)
11. It is not possible that God does not exist. (9,10)
12. God necessarily exists. (11)

Amplifying and reconstructing Spinoza's demonstration in this way, Hooker succeeds in what he set out to do, viz., to attribute to Spinoza a valid deductive argument.

4.

There are, however, three objections to this interpretation, each of which is very strong. (a) When we return to the text and look again at Spinoza's statement of his argument, it is in my opinion undeniable that the proposition he asks us to conceive or assume, or try to conceive or assume, at the outset is not "God can be conceived not to exist" but "God does not exist." The argument, to quote it again, begins: "If this be denied, conceive, if it be possible, *that God does not exist*" (my italics). Granted that we have here the beginning of a *re-*

---

[7] "The Deductive Character of Spinoza's Metaphysics," in this volume.

ductio, can there be any doubt that the assumption of the *reductio* is "God does not exist"?

In the latter part of the argument that Hooker attributes to Spinoza, a suppressed premise is supplied: "What is not conceivable is not possible." My second and third objections are directed to this part of the proposed amplification or supplementation of the argument. (b) The principle ascribed to Spinoza, namely, that what is not conceivable is not possible, seems to me to be by no means an unexceptionable, or trivial or obvious, principle. Interpreted in certain ways, it is a substantive principle which can be taken to have rather far-reaching and disturbing consequences. It would appear, therefore, that, if a principle of this sort were part of, or were required in, Spinoza's demonstration, he would have acknowledged it—either by stating it or citing it. Given the system of Definitions, Axioms, and Propositions in the *Ethics*, however, it should have been impossible for him to cite this principle since it is not an axiom nor a definition nor a proposition which is proved. On the assumption that a principle of this sort is not, and would not have appeared to him to be, uncontentious, it seems more than likely that, if he had intended to wield the principle in this important proof, he would have made it explicit at some point or in some way or other and would have acknowledged it in the course of the demonstration.

(c) An objection can be raised on the ground that, if we accept Hooker's construal of Spinoza's Demonstration, we must credit Spinoza with a second view which it seems unlikely he would have accepted; namely, that God's existence can be proved by arguing that His non-existence is inconceivable. There are two reasons why I think Spinoza would certainly not have held this view. First, he was unquestionably aware of the fact that it is not apparent to everyone that the non-existence of God is inconceivable; and he was also undoubtedly aware of the fact that the very people to whom a proof of God's existence might be appropriately addressed, i.e., atheists and skeptics, would retort to an argument along these lines that nothing is easier than to conceive of God as not existing. If, then, Spinoza had thought that his principal proof of God's existence depended in some way on a premise about the inconceivability of His non-existence, he would surely have been of the opinion that the proposition "God cannot be conceived not to exist" requires some support or proof. In his system, however, there is a problem as to how this proposition could be supported. The only support available seems to be the following line of reasoning: "Since the essence of God involves existence, it follows that the non-existence of God is inconceivable." But the suggested defence gives rise to a dilemma. Either "The essence of God involves existence" entails "God exists," or it does not. If it does, it seems unintelligible that Spinoza would have argued for God's existence on the ground that God's existence is inconceivable since this could have been established directly without recourse to that questionable premise. Why, on this alternative, would he have risked an obvious objection regarding inconceivability when the conclusion could be reached without appeal to that provocative point? If, on the other alternative, he thought that "The essence of God involves existence" does not entail "God exists" but does entail that the non-existence of God cannot in a certain sense—"clearly and distinctly" or "adequately"—be conceived, it would have been apparent to him that he still has a problem on his hands were he to argue for God's existence along these lines. An immediate and obvious objection to this line of argument is that, although it may indeed follow from "The essence of God involves existence" that, in a certain sense, God's non-existence is inconceivable, it is not evident that, granted that it can be established that God's non-existence is inconceivable in this sense, it follows that God exists. That inference would have to be defended, and it is not clear how, within the context of Spinoza's system, a plausible case for the defence could be made.

Second, it seems entirely out of character that Spinoza should have argued for God's existence on the basis of the inconceivability of the alternative view. Such an argument would have seemed to him to rest on a highly objectionable appeal to what might very well be mere habit or engrained prejudice. Against preconceptions based on the inability to conceive something, he inveighs again and again. What a person can or cannot conceive or think is, for him, an exceedingly dangerous point of departure for an argument. For example, the inability of a person to think that what he takes to be a freely chosen action has a cause is no ground whatever for concluding that the action has no cause. Yet the latter part of the argument which Hooker attributes to Spinoza is of a similar sort. Not only does Spinoza not explicitly argue in this way, but, if I read him rightly, it is out of character that he should have argued in this way.

5.

If we are to retain the assumption that Spinoza's demonstration consists in a *reductio*, it would, I believe, be better to take the first alternative mentioned earlier and, if a suppressed premise is to be supplied, to introduce it earlier in the argument. The following reconstruction is not subject to two of the objections that I raised against Hooker's reconstruction:

(1) God does not exist. (assumption)

(2) What does not exist can be conceived not to exist. (suppressed)
(3) God can be conceived not to exist. (1,2)
(4) (x) (if x can be conceived not to exist, the essence of x does not involve existence). (axiom 7)
(5) The essence of God does not involve existence. (3,4)

An inestimable advantage of this reconstruction over Hooker's is that the *reductio* has the right assumption. Also, there are two thing to be said for supplying this suppressed premise rather than Hooker's "What is not conceivable is not possible." "What does not exist can be conceived not to exist" *seems* at any rate to be less substantive and more apparent than Hooker's premise. For this reason, Spinoza might not have thought it necessary to state or acknowledge it in the proof. Furthermore, although "God can be conceived not to exist" is not entailed by "God does not exist," it is entailed by "It can be assumed (or conceived) that God does not exist." Though, that is, "God can be conceived not to exist" does not follow from the proposition assumed, it does follow from the assumption of that proposition. It might therefore be that Spinoza, not concerned about a subtle distinction, did not feel called upon to make his argument a strictly or formally valid argument.

Despite these advantages, however, the third objection that was raised against Hooker's interpretation can also be raised against this interpretation. Though the premise "What does not exist can be conceived not to exist" seems at first blush to be more palatable and less contentious that "What is not conceivable is not possible," nonetheless, if we take this to be a step in Spinoza's argument, we again attribute to him the view that God's existence can be proved by showing that His non-existing is inconceivable; and the objections that were raised against attributing that view to Spinoza apply to this interpretation as well as to Hooker's. That we must attribute that view to him is apparent if we consider the contrapositive of the premise supplied and reformulate Spinoza's alleged argument in such a way that it no longer has the form of a *reductio*. His line of reasoning would then be:

God is a substance.
(A) The essence of God involves existence.
(B) God cannot be conceived not to exist.
(C) God exists.

If Spinoza's reasoning is interpreted in this way, we can again raise the following objection. If someone, say a skeptic, questions (B), Spinoza's answer would presumably be that God's non-existence cannot be really, or clearly and distinctly, conceived; and his support for saying this would be (A). But then either (A) entails (C), or not. If it does, what need is there to introduce (B)? If, on the other hand, it is said that (A) does not entail (C) but does entail a qualified version of (B), namely, that God's non-existence cannot be really, or clearly and distinctly, conceived, it can be objected that it has not at any rate been proved that (C) follows from the reformulated and qualified (B).

6.

It seems, then, that this effort, like Hooker's, is unsuccessful. It fails to provide a valid *reductio* which Spinoza would have been prepared to accept as his principal demonstration of the existence of infinite substance or God. What, then, are we to do? It is, I believe, impossible to deny that Spinoza states—however sketchily—a *reductio* in this passage in the *Ethics*. It also seems undeniable that this passage is supposed to contain his principal proof of the existence of infinite substance or God. The solution to this puzzle that I want to propose is that the passage can be taken to contain two arguments, one of which is undoubtedly a *reductio* and the other not. The basis for my claim is the view that Spinoza proposed about assumptions or "fictitious ideas" in *The Improvement of the Intellect* (G II, 19-25)—a view that can be applied to the assumption in the *reductio* in this passage. According to the doctrine of the earlier work, it follows that someone who has an adequate idea of God cannot conceive or assume that God does not exist. Such a person understands that the essence of God involves existence and hence that God exists. For him, the *reductio* in this passage is not only unnecessary but impossible. For him, it is enough to be reminded of Proposition 7, i.e., "The essence of a substance involves existence," and of Definition 6, according to which God is a substance (G II, 45).

For the person who understands at least to some extent the nature or essence of God, the argument in this passage is simple: "God is a substance; The essence of a substance involves existence; Therefore, God exists." This is admittedly rather slim pickings. But all the meat has already been served up in the demonstration of Proposition 7. That is not to say that, in Proposition 7, God's existence has already been proved. There is no mention of God in Proposition 7 or in the demonstration thereof. What Spinoza has proved there (in part) is that, if something is a substance, then it must exist. In Proposition 11, he reminds the knowledgeable reader of this and of the definition of "God" and in this way proves to him that God exists.

But, rather than simply issue this reminder and draw a connection for those who are quick to understand, Spinoza also provides a *reduc-*

tio for those of lesser intellect who fail to see that God's existence follows merely from a consideration of His nature, viz., his nature as substance. These people can conceive or assume that God does not exist. Moreover, for them, a premise regarding what is or is not conceivable is altogether appropriate. On this interpretation, the *reductio* that is undoubtedly present in the passage is intended as an *ad hominem* argument addressed to those of slow intellect who have failed to grasp what has come before. Strictly and formally, the argument proper here is only a certain part of the *reductio*; namely, the third and fourth steps. The premises are: "God is a substance" and "The essence of a substance involves existence"; while the conclusion is, as stated in the fourth step, "Therefore, God necessarily exists."

As evidence that the *reductio* is not the only argument and not the official argument here, I have three facts to point out. First, the assumption of the *reductio* is stated, "Conceive, *if it be possible* . . . " (my italics). The implication of this qualification is that it is not to be taken for granted that this feat of conception is indeed possible and, if I have interpreted the passage correctly, indeed that for some it is impossible. Second, the Demonstration begins, "If this [Proposition 11] be denied . . . . " If I am right, Spinoza suggests that, although it is unlikely that a competent reader will be at all inclined to deny this, nonetheless an argument with some persuasive power can be given for the benefit of those who are less fortunate. Third, there is evidence that the *reductio* was not carefully thought out and was added in some haste. Axiom 7 is used nowhere else in the *Ethics*, and it can be conjectured that it was added *ad hoc* for its use in the *reductio* here. Moreover, what he says or implies in this Axiom conflicts with what he says or implies in Definition 1. According to Definition 1, to say that something cannot be conceived not to exist is precisely the same as to say that its essence involves existence; and it follows that "X can be conceived not to exist" and "The essence of X does not involve existence" are synonymous. According to Axiom 7, however, it is supposed to be axiomatic, and hence ostensibly not true by definition, that, if X can be conceived not to exist, the essence of X does not involve existence.

7.

Turning now to the third step in the *reductio* and to what, if I am right in what I have just said, is part of the main line of argument in the *Ethics*, we encounter a second hurdle in the course of interpreting Spinoza's demonstration. The third step is taken in the sentence, "But by Proposition 7 this [i.e., "The essence of God does not involve existence"] is absurd." This step can be expanded:

1. God is a substance.
2. The essence of a substance involves existence.
3. The essence of God involves existence.

The support for the second premise is, Spinoza indicates, Proposition 7 and his demonstration thereof. What support is to be given for the first premise—a premise which Spinoza does not state no doubt because, in the context of his system, it seemed to him to be so very obvious? If he had made this premise explicit, there can hardly be any doubt that he would have said it was true by definition, specifically, by Definition 6; and, had he made use of a certain terminology, there can hardly be any doubt that he would have said that this premise is "analytic" or "analytically true." Definition 6 is: "By God I understand being absolutely infinite, that is to say, substance consisting of infinite attributes, each one of which expresses infinite and eternal essence." And it seems to be asserted or implied in this definition that "being a substance" is part of what is (to be) meant by "God." If concern were shown about the ostensible use of a proper name—*Deus* with a capital "D"—in the premise, Spinoza could have reformulated it, "Absolutely infinite substance is a substance." This does not seem to be question-begging, and it also seems to be an explicit identity. With this premise he could have proceeded to the conclusion "Absolutely infinite substance exists," at which point he might have said, in the manner of Aquinas, "And this is what is called 'God'."

It would, however, be a mistake to pass over the premise "God is a substance" on the ground that, within the framework of Spinoza's system, it is a trivial and obvious definitional, or analytic, truth. An important objection can be raised at precisely this point. Though I believe Spinoza can answer the objection, nonetheless we need to know exactly what his answer would be if we are to grasp his line of reasoning at this critical juncture. The objection is that, at this point in the argument, namely, the suppressed premise "God is a substance," the argument is question-begging—not for the reason suggested in the last paragraph, but for a different reason which is less easily disposed of.

The charge of question-begging that I have in mind begins with the claim that, on Spinoza's account of what the term "substance" means, to say that X is a substance is in part to assert or presuppose that X exists. In Definition 3 of Part One, "substance" is defined as "that which is in itself and is conceived through itself...." (G II, 45) and it seems that part of what is meant or presupposed by saying "X is a substance" is that X is, or exists, in a certain way, namely, in itself and not, by implication, in another. It seems, moreover, that part of what is meant or presupposed by saying that X exists in this way is, simply, that X exists. But—to spell out what may be obvious—if part of what is meant or presupposed by saying that X is a substance is that X exists in a certain way and if part of what is meant or presupposed by saying that X exists in this way is that X exists, it clearly follows that, if someone were to say that God is a substance, he would be asserting or presupposing that God exists; and the objection can then be raised that he thereby begs the question at issue in this attempted proof of God's existence. More exactly, he would beg the question at issue in the sense that the conclusion of his proof would be asserted or presupposed in one of the premises.

Not everyone who has drawn this implication from the Definitions at the beginning of Part One has been prompted to use it as the basis of an objection. At the outset of my paper, I mentioned a common view that the arguments following Proposition 11 are not intended to be demonstrations of God's existence at all; and I alluded to certain alternative possible interpretations of this passage. It has been supposed, on the one hand, that these arguments, and particularly the first, are meant to be expressions or articulations of an intuition or self-evident truth; and, on the other hand, the view has been proposed that the question of the existence of infinite substance or God has been settled in advance before Spinoza sets himself to establishing Proposition 11 and that his intent at this stage in the development of his system is to make out the kind of existence that such a substance can be said to have, namely, "necessary" or "self-caused" existence. These interpretations seem to have been generated in part for the reason spelled out in the preceding paragraph. The definition of "substance" as that which is, or exists, in itself has been interpreted to mean or entail that, if X is a substance, X exists or—as a "real definition" with "existential import"—to mean or entail that at least one substance exists. On such an interpretation, any attempt to prove the existence of substance or absolutely infinite substance would seem to be otiose; and so, whatever Spinoza may appear to be trying to do in what follows Proposition 11, it is senseless to suppose that he is trying to prove the existence of absolutely infinite substance or God.

8.

Since the arguments following Proposition 11 certainly appear to be attempts to prove the existence of infinite substance or God, the burden of proof is on those commentators who maintain that they are not really intended to be proofs of this existential proposition. Their case appears to rest in large measure on the supposition that it is perfectly clear that, earlier in the *Ethics*, answers to certain existential questions, e. g., the existence of substance, are assumed or settled. In my estimation, this point is not in fact perfectly clear—indeed, it is not clear at all. For it is possible and, as I shall try to show, plausible to read the initial definitions, and particularly Definition 3, hypothetically and not categorically in such a way that the existential question which, on the categorical interpretation under consideration, are closed are in reality left open. On a hypothetical interpretation of Definition 3, for instance, to say that X is a substance is not to say or imply that X exists in itself and afortiori exists but to say that, if X exists, X exists in itself (and not in another). When Definition 3 is interpreted in this way, the question whether substance exists is left open; and, on the alternative interpretation that I want to sketch, this question remains open until we get to Proposition 11, which is the first categorical existential statement in the *Ethics*. Here, for the first time, we are told not just that, if something is a substance, it exists, but that a substance satisfying a certain description, viz., a substance having infinite attributes, etc., unconditionally or categorically exists. There is here, in other words, a shift from a hypothetical assertion to the effect that, if something is a substance, it has certain properties (including existence) to the categorical assertion that a substance having certain properties also has the property of existing.

To support the view that Definition 3 can be understood hypothetically, two things need to be said. (a) A seemingly powerful objection to that view needs to be countered, and the interpretation can in this way be shown to be viable. The objection is based on the claim that, according to Spinoza, the term "exist" is equivocal. It means one thing when it is used to say that something which is a substance exists. In this case, it means "exists in itself." And it means something else when it is used to say that a mode exists, namely, that it "exists in another." Since, the objection continues, "exists" must mean one or the other of these two things, the suggested hypothetical interpretation of the definition of "substance" would be, on Spinoza's doctrine about existence, either vacuous and non-explanatory or necessarily false or absurd. In neither case could it be what Spinoza intends when he gives his definition of "substance." If, on the hypothetical interpretation proposed, "exists" in the clause "If X exists" means "exists in itself," then the ostensible definition "If X exists, X exists in itself" becomes "If X exists in itself, then X exists in itself," and this can hardly be what is meant by a saying that something is a substance. If, on the other hand, "exists" is taken to mean "exists in another," then the purported explanation of what it means to say that something is a substance becomes "If X exists in another, X exists in itself." But this, on Spinoza's view, is necessarily false or absurd; and it, too, cannot be what he has in mind when he gives his definition of "substance."

An answer to this objection can be given which is short and, I believe, decisive. In Axiom 1, Spinoza asserts, "Everything which is, is either in itself or in another" (G II, 46). If we are to make sense of this assertion, we must attribute to him the view that there is a sense of "is" or "exists" other than the two senses which are distinguished and taken to be exhaustive on the interpretation that "exists" is, for him, radically equivocal. What sense, otherwise, can be made of this ostensible division of what in some sense is supposed to be or exist? Whether Spinoza is decidedly or consistently of the opinion that there is a sense of "is" or "exists" which applies equally to substances and modes is another question. But all that needs to be said in answer to the objection that has been raised is that he is not clearly or consistently of the opinion that the term "exists" is, as some commentators have suggested, radically equivocal.

(b) On the hypothetical interpretation, a plausible account can be given of Spinoza's line of reasoning at the beginning of the *Ethics*, viz., up to and including E I, P11. At the outset, he can be taken to be arguing *inter alia* that, if something is a substance, it must have certain properties—*propria*, in Spinoza's technical vocabulary — and that, if something is a substance, it cannot have certain other properties. In E I, P5, for instance, he can be taken to be arguing that, if something is a substance having a certain nature or attribute, there cannot be another substance having that same nature or attribute—in other words, that there is at most one substance having a certain nature or attribute or that any substance is unique. In E I, P6, his claim can be made out to be that, if something is a substance, it cannot be brought into existence, or caused, by another substance. E I, P7 is also to be interpreted along these lines, though here we have a dual conclusion. The conclusion of Proposition 7 is at once that, if something is a substance, it is cause of its own existence and also that, if something is a substance, it of necessity exists. On this interpretation, it is neither asserted nor implied in E I, P7 that a substance exists. When Spinoza goes on to say in Proposition 8, "Every substance is necessarily infinite," his statement there can also be taken to lack "existential import" and can be read, "Necessarily, nothing is both substantial and finite." Only in Proposition 11 do we get a categorical existential statement to the effect that a substance of a certain sort does indeed exist.

9.

Such an account of Spinoza's procedure at the outset of the *Ethics* seems to me to be at least plausible, as is the hypothetical interpretation given of Definition 3. It is not, therefore, clear that, prior to

Proposition 11, Spinoza assumes or settles the question of the existence of substance or of absolutely infinite substance or God. If I am right, both questions are settled only in the proof of Proposition 11.

Dartmouth College

4 SPINOZISTIC ANOMALIES
Jose Benardete

Although the first and second Parts of Spinoza's *Ethics* have been commonly referred to as *De Deo* and *De Mente* respectively, it is only in the first case that the actual title of the Part is quoted verbatim. Not mind but the nature of mind is featured in the title of the second Part. One might indeed wonder whether any difference can be discerned between an account of mind and an account of the nature of mind. "Nature" seems here purely redundant but in any case the first Part strikes one as being quite as much about the nature of God as the second Part is about the nature of mind. How then is the difference in the two titles to be explained? Spinoza evidently thought that there was an underlying difference important enough to be highlighted in the titles. One conjecture would explain the contrast in the titles as follows. *"Deus"* is a singular term denoting a definite entity whereas *"mens"* as a general term fails to denote anything even while it is true of many things. The conjecture gains support from Spinoza's well-known preoccupation with the distinction between singular and general and his commitment to the one combined with his misgivings if not positive hostility to the other. Although the conjecture is no more than that (a conjecture), it does provide a starting-point for further research into the matter.

Waiving this issue, it must be admitted that the title of the second Part cannot be adequately rendered as an inquiry into the nature of mind. The full title reads: *De Natura et Origine Mentis*. It is then the origin as well as the nature of mind that will be studied in the second Part. What is meant here by "origin"? One's first thought, taking Spinoza's eternalism into account, cannot but be that the term is certainly not being used in its primary, temporal sense. More important still, it is not easy to find anything in the second Part that could justify the temporal reading. In the Great Tradition going back at least to Aristotle "origin" or "ἀρχή" comes to take on various senses, above all that of nature (thus *Metaphysics*, 1013a21). To suggest, however, that "origo" could have that sense here would be again redundant to the point of absurdity. There is indeed an obvious way to take the word; the origin of mind is (to be found in) God. That everything in *some* sense originates in God, Spinoza has demonstrated in Part I but one can hardly suppose that Spinoza will merely recapitulate that doctrine in Part II. *How* precisely mind (or the mind) can be said to originate in God would be, however, a legitimate theme for Part II, and it may be that a coherent reading can be given along that line. Spinoza himself provides an exacting test for determining whether or not we have understood what he means by "the origin of mind". In the scholium to E III, P57 he says that once one has understood the origin of mind he can no longer doubt whether brutes feel. If we could only take "the origin of mind" to be equivalent to "the nature of mind," we would find ourselves on fairly firm ground. Spinoza's mind-body identity thesis being taken to belong to his general account of the nature of mind, it is not hard to see how he might well have felt that the identify thesis rules out any Cartesian doubts over the feelings of brutes. According to that thesis, mental processes cannot exist inaccessibly over and above the physical. Granted that this account satisfactorily explains the remark of E III, P57, we have seen that it cannot be taken to square with the title of Part II where "nature" and "origin" are clearly contrasted. There are thus (at least) two bits of data to be accommodated: "origo" as it figures in the remark of E III, P57 and "origo" in its role in the title of Part II.

That "origo" bears the same meaning (whatever it might be) in the two contexts, I have indeed been tacitly assuming, but one can readily insist that far from being inconclusive our inquiry has succeeded in showing that some sort of shift in meaning must be involved. And that raises the more general question as to how strict or how lax, above all how standardized, Spinoza's terminological practice may be presumed to be, across the board. Can we at least find one clear case in which he uses one of his more or less technical terms now in one way, now in another, depending on context? Merely to have in hand one such case would be of no negligible value as a hermeneutic touchstone available for general application in judging all the rest. *Modus cogitandi* offers perhaps as clear a case of a meaning-shift as one can find, though even here residual doubts may remain undispelled. Primarily, a *modus cogitandi* is simply any state of mind where mind is broadly conceived: in the third axiom of *De Mente* it is said to be any *affectus animi* (is *affectus animi* then to be taken as synonymous with *affectus mentis* in Spinoza's lexicon?). The secondary use or sense of the term surfaces (to mention but one example) in the preface to Part IV where perfection, imperfection, good and bad are pejoratively said to be (mere) *modi cogitandi*. Following Joachim, we are advised to gloss the term here as meaning *entia rationis*. That states of mind are not to be confused with *entia rationis* would seem obvious enough, but if one could succeed in reading Spinoza along the lines of Eliminative Materialism he might well entertain the suggestion that when it is said in the third axiom of Part II that love and desire are *modi cogitandi* what is intended is not merely that they are states of mind but that they are *entia rationis* as well. In any case, whether or not one is prepared to view this radical even deviant interpretation with some sympathy, one may choose to doubt that these finer points of nomenclature can be of more than marginal interest as far as the substantive issues of Spinoza's philosophy are concerned. Is there indeed any reason for supposing that an understanding of "origin," say, in the title of Part II should be of any relevance to the understanding of Spinoza's philosophy proper? Well, of course there is but at the present time this (obvious) reason may well be resisted. Rightly so if it can be assumed that one has already in hand, apart from all points of diction, a roughly adequate command of Spinoza's philosophy. Anyone so fortunate who at the same time remains puzzled by the import of "origo" in the title of Part II is perfectly entitled to believe that his puzzlement can have only textual, certainly not philosophic bearing. My own assumption in the present discussion is very much the reverse, namely that Spinoza remains for us if not quite a closed book then certainly a book only partially opened. Although I shall not undertake to defend that assumption except perhaps in indirect fashion, it must be seen to underpin an inquiry that otherwise might amount to no more than a compiling of antiquarian curiosities. Admittedly only curiosities when taken by themselves in isolation, these Spinozistic anomalies may (so goes the hope) afford a fresh mode of access to Spinoza's philosophy after the more conventional methods of interpretation may be presumed to have carried us pretty nearly as far as they can.

If "nature" and "origin" are contrasted in the title of Part II the contrast is reiterated in the title of Part III as well, though here the import of "origo" is fairly plain. Almost certainly it is the temporal sense of the term that is operative or at any rate something very much akin to it. The bulk of Part III is devoted to giving the origins (i.e., causes) of the specific emotions in a perfectly straightforward, naturalistic fashion. Thus a typical proposition (E III, P40) reads, "If we imagine that we are hated by another without having given him any cause for it, we shall hate him in return." Here then is at least one source or origin of hatred where the origin being the efficient cause has an at least quasi-temporal import. I say "quasi-temporal" because in the present context it may well be doubtful whether there is a temporal gap between cause and effect. The "other" major tradition on causation of which Kant is one notable representative (as in *Critique of Pure Reason*, A 202-203=B 247-248) and Spinoza almost certainly another has always insisted that (efficient) causation not only may dispense with a temporal gap between cause and effect but that all such cases far from being exceptions are actually the conceptually central ones. In any case, we can safely say that "origo" in the title of Part III means "efficient cause" whatever doubts may attach to the issue of temporal priority. Can we now equally say of "origo" in the title of Part II that it also signifies "efficient cause"? One would not readily suppose so, and we have seen that in E III, P57 "origo" lends itself most plausibly to being taken to mean nature. This last reference may be felt to be the less significant owing to the fact that it is deposited in a scholium. *Prima facie* one would not be surprised to learn that Spinoza held himself accountable to a high standard of rigor only in the formal demonstrations of his propositions (not to mention the definitions, axioms and postulates) and that he was prepared to relax those standards in his scholia. As a more informal exposition of his thought, the scholia might be allowed to use even the technical vocabulary with at least a relative freedom from systematic constraints. The hypothesis is well worth looking into but a cursory sampling of various scholia fails to yield any easy confirmation of it. Apart from the scholia, there are the titles of the Parts to be considered and here also a certain informality might be expected to obtain, though any such informality—whether in title or scholium—is presumably only to be justified by the trading off of rigor for at least a rough sort of clarity. To be told that Spinoza has a right to equivocate in his use of "origo" in the titles of Parts II and III (assuming for the moment that such equivocation does take place) on the ground that it is only in his demonstrations that rigor is required, can only make sense if some clarity however rough is the result. Equivocation does not, as such, make for clarity, and we are thus driven to ask whether "origo" might be construed against all odds as meaning "efficient cause" in the title of Part II as well as in that of Part III. It must be admitted indeed that even if "origo" does have the force (if not quite the meaning) of "efficient cause" in the title of Part III but not in the title of Part II our command of the notion of synonymy may well be too unsure today to permit us to convict Spinoza of a precise equivocation. How hard it is to weigh the relevant evidence, may perhaps be suggested by my own much too casual use of *Metaphysics*, 1013a 21 in support of the hypothesis that nature can be shown to be one of the various senses of "ἀρχή."

There is a striking feature in the titles of Parts II and III that I have neglected to mention. Although both titles advertise the contrast between nature and origin there remains a small if perhaps only stylistic difference between them. Where the title of Part II is *De Natura et Origine Mentis*, the title of Part III is seen to be *De Origine et Natura Affectuum*. To the logician at any rate it is all one whether one investigates the nature and origin of something (mind, the emotions or whatever) or alternatively the origin and nature of that thing. In the case of almost anyone else, anyone less imbued with *gravitas* than Spinoza, one would suppose that only some turn toward frivolity not to say perversity could explain a proposal to study, on the one hand, the nature and origin of mind and, on the other, the origin and nature of the emotions. About the only explanation of the reversal in Spinoza would be to show that as the earlier and later propositions of Part II are devoted to the nature and origin of mind respectively, so the earlier and later propositions of Part III are devoted—in reverse fashion—to the origin and nature of the emotions. Again, a cursory review of II and III shows that it will not be easy to make good on that explanation. Despairing of any reasonable way of handling the anomaly as an integral element of the text, one may even resort to the hypothesis that the text may be corrupt in this regard. It is only after one has canvassed a wide variety of unclassified perhaps even unclassifiable anomalies in Spinoza that one is forced to conclude that the hypothesis of a corrupt text can have only the most limited application, and if that application is not to be arbitrary in any particular case one must justify the hypothesis on the basis of more than local considerations that go beyond the mere anomalousness of the crux in question. For there are indeed so many anomalies in the text of the *Ethics* that one cannot but hesitate in the end to call them anomalies at all.

If only as curiosities of antiquarian import, these "anomalies" are bound to elicit a bemused interest in their own, independent right. Less evident will be their relevance to the strictly philosophic study of Spinoza's philosophy. Plato, it may be said, may well require such a deviant hermeneutic owing to the fact that none of his works can be classified as a philosophic treatise of the standard kind: textual minutiae may thus be relevant in Plato's case where literary nuances abound. When it comes, however, to a philosophic treatise of the ruthlessly systematic sort of which the *Ethics*, composed *more geometrico*, is an acknowledged paradigm (it is indeed *the* paradigm *par excellence* of systematic philosophy) these minutiae can never be allowed to play an indispensable role. There are standard ways of studying philosophic texts in the strictly philosophic mode, and it cannot be said that these minutiae of disinterested, free-floating scholarship figure in such studies in more than some collateral, subordinate fashion. However compelling these general considerations may be (and I take them to be at least fairly compelling), I am not prepared to concede that as general they can be taken to override the results (provisional as *they* may be) of our specific confrontation with the Spinozistic text which we are by no means alone in finding peculiarly refractory, not least in its strictly philosophic import.

Of our proposed explanation of why "natura" and "origo" exchange places in the titles of Parts II and III one half is much easier to confirm than the other. As Part III ends with the definition of the passions/emotions/affects it may be said to conclude with an account of their nature, and we have noticed that the earlier propositions of Part III may be readily construed as giving their origin (= efficient cause). There is thus a shift from origin to nature in Part III, and if we could detect a comparable shift but in the opposite direction in Part II our explanation would be vindicated. The difficulty here is that if the origin of mind is presumed to lie in God (as contrasted with the origin of the emotions?) one can only be disappointed to recall that it is in the earlier rather than the later propositions of Part II that God largely figures. If the contrast between origin and nature remains puzzling as regards Part II—widely recognized in any case to be the most difficult Part of the *Ethics*—the contrast in Part III proves to be by no means as unproblematic as one might suppose: witness in particular our later comments on images. Spinoza himself seems bent on chastening us in the very preface to Part IV where it is quite possible that a retrospective note is being struck. The contrast between nature and origin is, to say the least, blurred when we learn that "nothing belongs to the nature of *anything* [my emphasis] except that which follows from the necessity of the nature of the efficient cause." Although this "reduction" of natures to origins can be found to fit the structure of Part III almost perfectly (again it is in connection with images that the "almost" will become clear.), it is hard to see how Spinoza expected it to apply to God. One would like to say that as *causa sui* God may be allowed to instantiate the principle if only in a fairly vacuous fashion as a degenerate case (in the mathematical sense of the expression, of course) were it not for the fact that God could be said only to be the formal, certainly not the efficient, cause of himself, not that Spinoza ever chooses to develop the contrast between formal and efficient causes in the ample way in which he develops the contrast between final and efficient. The context at hand does indeed allow, without however positively compelling, us to restrict the scope of the principle to "all the individuals in nature" where *deus sive natura* (the phrase has just been introduced) presumably lies outside. So cogent is that explanation, taken in isolation, that one might well doubt how, or why, anyone could decline to acquiesce in it, there being indeed some small degree of confirmation of the hypothesis as early as Definition 7 of Part II where Spinoza says that by singular things he understands (*intelligo*) things that are finite and have a determinate existence. Seeing that God is at least one singular thing among others if not *the* singular thing *par excellence*, we seem forced to conclude that we are given here a mere nominal or stipulative definition in connection with which the use of *intelligo* with its evocation of the intellect seems strangely out of place. How indeed one is to distinguish the nominal from the real definitions in Spinoza, proves now to raise a new challenge for our hermeneutics. Previously we would have thought that as *intelligo* by its presence must attest to a real definition, so would it identify a nominal definition by its mere absence (as in the case of Definition 7 of Part I where the nominal or purely verbal force of the definition is underscored by *dicitur*). And what are we to make of the first definition of Part IV where we learn not indeed what Spinoza understands but what he will understand in the remainder of the work? That an ostensibly systematic work designed *more geometrico* should play fast and loose with its foundational definitions cannot but give us pause, and it has not escaped our baffled notice that in a work reputed to be a model of impersonality and objectivity a first personal, almost Cartesian note is persistently struck in almost all of the definitions, real as well as nominal. If we deplore the use of "parenthetical verbs" in a "geometrical" treatise, our dismay is by no means confined to Spinoza: recall the ubiquitous use of the assertion sign in the *Principia Mathematica*.

How seriously must be taken the suggestion that God is indeed the efficient cause of himself, comes to sight, albeit somewhat indirectly, in EI, P25 when God having been thematically pronounced to be the efficient cause of the existence (and essence) of (all?) things it is remarked in the scholium that in the same sense which God is said to be the cause of himself he must be called the cause of all things. Accordingly, I take it that there is a sense x on which God is the cause of himself and a sense y on which God is the cause of the finite modes and that $x = y$ and that $y =$ the sense of "cause" expressed by the phrase "efficient causation." God then is the efficient cause of himself, though this seems scarcely compatible with his status as *causa sui* as that term is defined, and understood, at the very outset of the entire work. Suprisingly, nothing in the demonstration proper of E I, P25 so much as suggests that God is the efficient cause of things; there is indeed nothing therein that suggests that he is the cause in any sense whatever of the existence (as contrasted with the essence) of things. Featured in the proposition to be proved, the expression *causa efficiens* is omitted in the proof itself. God is said merely to be the cause (of the essence) of things. The implication is presumably that in general cause = efficient cause, though we are clearly reminded of the fact that in the philosophic tradition "cause" admits of more than one sense (hence the reference to the sense on which God is said to be *causa sui*). More important than the modest conclusion that Spinoza will countenance only efficient causes (endorsed certainly by many Spinozists) proves to be the hermeneutic guidance afforded us for other, perhaps less tractable, occasions. Spinoza is seen to be prepared to practice a kind of innuendo even in his formal proofs where one would least expect it, certainly not from a rationalist proceeding *more geometrico*. From a systematic (and perhaps even from a purely formal) standpoint it can only be a serious defect to omit from a proof a key term ("efficient cause") that is featured in the theorem. On the assumption that the omission was deliberate we seem forced to conclude that in addition to its systematic character the *Ethics* was composed with dialectical intent and not merely with respect to its more informal components but even as regards its canonical demonstrations. Nor can it be said that the dialectical aspect of the work merely supplements the systematic by way of ornamental or rhetorical accompaniment: in E I, P25 at any rate it is found to undermine it. That is to say, the systematic demands of the work are actually sacrificed to the dialectical.

I take it that the present hypothesis is sufficiently radical to be viewed with the gravest suspicion. There is surely no other work in the history of philosophy that is, on the face of it, so singlemindedly dedicated to the systematic as Spinoza's, and there is always his correspondence to consult if a more personal witness to the impersonal character of his work is desired. Finally, there is the accumulated experience of many able Spinozists who will insist on the basis of their own patient submission to the text that only the most tenuous, and never unambiguous, evidence can be found to support the hypothesis. It is not, however, my present intention to engage in any direct polemics on this issue, but I do want to make it quite plain that I am by no means unaware of the *prima facie* implausibility that attaches to my hermeneutic. If a theory can be judged by its fruits I am content that my approach should be judged by its productivity in generating detachable, independently assessable results. These results are designed to be theory-free in the sense of comprising the kind of primary data that any interpretation of Spinoza will want to accommodate.

One such detachable result we have found in the doctrine, never explicitly stated by Spinoza, that God is the efficient cause of himself. That Spinoza acknowledges in general only efficient causes may be familiar enough but no one has succeeded in explaining how *causa sui* may be assimilated to that model. Granted that there is available more than one doctrine of efficient causation—principally the "constant conjunction" account of the empiricists as opposed to the "transmission" theory of the rationalists for whom there is always some specific content that is transmitted from cause to effect (one recalls Descartes' dictum that there must be at least as much reality in the cause as in the effect)—it must be said that the "transmission" theory is almost as unsuitable as that of "constant conjunction" for explaining the concept of *causa sui* where essence entails existence. One is thus forced to ask whether Spinoza has not stretched the concept of efficient causation beyond all tolerable bounds when he assigns it theological import. How indeed God can be said to be the efficient cause even of finite modes, is scarcely less perplexing. Since the efficient cause of one finite mode, say this stone, is always another, antecedent finite mode, God can presumably be the efficient cause of this stone (the expression "the efficient cause of this stone" is surely a definite description for Spinoza) only if he is identical with some finite mode. Although the suggestion is on the face of it absurd, there is a more strictly logical reason for rejecting it. If God is identical with some finite mode x he is for comparable reasons identical with some finite mode y where $x \neq y$, thereby violating the constraints imposed by the transitivity of identity. In general, for any finite mode m_1 there will always be two candidates that compete for the title "the efficient cause of m_1," namely God and some other finite mode m_2. Might it not, however, be the case that m_2 is the proximate and God the remote efficient cause of m_1, the claims of the two rival candidates being thereby reconciled? Spinoza considers this solution, only to reject it (E I, P28 S). Although there is indeed a sense on which God may be allowed to be the remote rather than the proximate cause of things, that sense proves to be totally irrelevant, in Spinoza's judgment, to the point at issue. Spinoza's own solution may or may not be coherent but its overall intent can be conveyed, doubtless somewhat impressionistically, by a formula to the effect that it is God *qua* m_2 that is the efficient cause of m_1 or alternatively it is m_2 *qua* God that is the efficient cause of m_1. How God as infinite substance is related to the world—more specifically, to this or that finite mode—be it transcendently or immanently, has long been recognized on independent grounds to be the central issue of Part I.

The key to Spinoza's "solution" to the problem of divine immanence/transcendence must be connected with his doctrine that everything, mode as well as attribute, expresses (somehow) the essence of God (i.e., *causa sui*). The doctrine is adumbrated in E I, P25 (the corollary), though with less than full explicitness. It is not until we reach Part II that we are afforded two bits of data that enable us to state the doctrine with complete generality. The first bit of data occurs at the very outset (of the formal presentation) of Part II, in the initial definition, where we learn not that everything but that every body expresses the essence of God. (The second bit of data occurs in E II, P1 where thoughts are brought in.) The definition taken as a whole cannot fail to puzzle us by its textual location if not by its content. Awarded pride of place, it seems indeed anomalous in the context of an inquiry into the nature of mind. Mind presumably is to be understood purely under the attribute of thought, and since thought and extension can be (must be) understood independently of one another any reference to body could only be methodologically otiose. From a purely technical standpoint it must be admitted that reference to body would be appropriate if the entire inquiry into the nature of mind were conducted under the attribute of extension not thought. If for any finite mode x and any attribute y a fully adequate understanding of x can be achieved purely in terms of y, such a proceeding would be admissible. Still, any inquiry into mind that was conducted solely under the attribute of extension would be more suitably described as an inquiry regarding body. In any event, it will not be supposed that Spinoza's inquiry into the nature (and origin) of mind is pursued solely under the attribute of extension, being rather prosecuted in terms of a *mélange* of the two, extension and thought. The puzzle might be felt to be removed once one realizes that mind being identical with body Spinoza wants, and needs, to say just that in Part II, and he can hardly be expected to succeed in the undertaking if he is not allowed to help himself to the concept of body. Granted that the purely textual or hermeneutic question is thereby answered albeit in the narrowest of terms, the substantive issue remains, in sharpened form. How can Spinoza have believed that mind (or indeed anything at all, taking mind as representative) can be understood purely in terms of the attribute of thought? Moreover, and here the textual question surfaces anew, why does Spinoza feel obliged to interrupt the flow of his formal argument by sandwiching between propositions 13 and 14 a fairly extended and certainly detailed excursus on the physics or meta-physics of body? It is surely not accidental that once the flow of the principal narrative is resumed, after the protracted interruption of the physical excursus, the concept of body is featured in virtually all of the next sixteen propositions. There is indeed one exception, II, 15, but even here the demonstration begins, "The idea which constitutes the formal being of the mind is the idea of a body," which certainly suggests that to have an (adequate) idea of a mind is to have an idea of (an idea of) a body and not merely to have the idea of a body in some referentially opaque fashion but to have the idea of a body under that very description (body *qua* body). Whether this materialistic interpretation of II, 15 will stand up under further scrutiny, depends very much on how we come to understand the concept of formal being (its Aristotelian provenance is obvious enough) which can hardly be said to be readily available to us today. In general, I take it that virtually no interpretation of any isolated statement in Spinoza, however plausible in itself, can be regarded as being immune to revision in the light of (our reading, doubtless equally vulnerable, of) every other passage in the *Ethics* (to look no further). At once dialectical and holistic, the whole procedure bids fair to being self-correcting, though the issue of scepticism in regard to such an anti-foundationalist not to say self-certifying hermeneutic can only be deferred not avoided. My approach here is relatively (though only relatively) uncontroversial. More radical is my suggestion that Spinoza himself positively intended and designed his work to be read in this dialectical, holistic fashion in contravention of the ostensibly systematic, above all standardly rationalistic, character that the work bears on its face. Even those who are prepared to allow that a dialectical reading may be required *faute de mieux* (having come to despair of any account at once systematic and comprehensive) may well hesitate to go along with me the full distance, to the point of conceding that the systematic character of the work was precisely designed by Spinoza as a foil against which the dialectical story is to be played out. How then explain (one might well ask) Spinoza's thunderous silence in this matter?

I think that once we collect our results regarding mind and body in Part II I can at least bring out somewhat more clearly the force of "dialectical" in these pages. Although the general drift of my meaning will doubtless be plain enough, the term is so loaded even overloaded with Platonic and Hegelian associations that its current use always runs the risk of some obscurantism being incurred in the process. Let me then affirm at once that when I say that the *Ethics* is dialectical in intent I do not mean merely (merely?) that it has an informal, ramshackle character. What I do mean can be brought out by means of a specific example. We learn from a broadly synoptic view of Part II (now dispensing with all details, for we do not always insist on minutiae) that though mind cannot be understood apart from body (thematic references to body abound in the account of mind) body can indeed be understood apart from mind (the physical excursus is antiseptically austere in this regard). Demonstrated *ad oculos* along a massive front of text, this two-fold thesis is bound to escape the notice of any Spinozist who, in conventional fashion, is so preoccupied with what Spinoza says that he neglects to observe what he, often quite ostentatiously, does. It may well be that the only way in which one can argue effectively that body is intelligible apart from mind is to exhibit in detail what that understanding of body consists in, what it looks like. One can then say, "Look! Mind is nowhere to be found here." In effect Spinoza may be taken to have done just that, and in just the same sort of way the "dependence" of mind on body is exhibited at convincing length. One can now scarcely resist forming the hypothesis that the origin or "ἀρχή" of mind is none other than body itself, and bringing the concept of origin in line with that of efficient causation we may propose that the efficient cause of mind is to be found in that union of bodies which is discussed in the definition (of a composite body?) that is embedded in Axiom 2 of the physical excursus. It does *not* of course follow from these considerations that mind is identical with body and indeed one would suppose from Leibniz's Law that it could not possibly be so. How precisely mind is related to body we learn, once again indirectly, from E II, P21 where in the course of stating explicitly for the first time that mind *is* identical with body an alternative account of the relation is given as follows. Mind is united to body in the same way that the idea of the mind is united to the mind. We have then only to understand how the idea of the mind is united to the mind in order to understand how the mind is united, and *a fortiori* related, to the body. It turns out that the idea of the mind is the *form* of the mind, from which we are invited to conclude that Aristotle was right in defiance of the Cartesian revolution: the mind is the form of the body. That mind so understood should be taken to be identical with the body may not be quite so impossible as it sounds. Thus it is certainly arguable that Aristotle himself accepted the Identity Thesis (*De Anima*, 412b5 - 10). Nor should it be assumed that when Spinoza says, or implies, that it is mind that is the form of the body he differs from Aristotle when *he* says that it is soul and certainly not mind that is the form of the body. Although not widely recognized to play a central role in Spinoza's thinking, the topic-neutral concept of form that was already featured in the physical excursus (see lemmas 4-6) provides an important bridge between mind and body. It is, however, only as a first approximation that to Spinoza can be attributed the doctrine that the mind is the form of the body, for he qualifies it radically in its very formulation. Indeed from the physical excursus one would suppose that the form of any body, as therein characterized, would probably (though perhaps only probably) have to be described as a mode of extension rather than of thought. No wonder, then, that Spinoza declines to regard the mind as the form of the body *simpliciter*; it is rather to be seen as the form of the body in so far as it is considered under the limitation of a certain description, namely as a *modus cogitandi*. The form of any (composite) body is the enduring ratio of motion and rest that obtains among its component parts and which enshrines the persistence conditions of the body. The mind is the idea of the body, and this idea is indeed (also) the form of the body (i.e., a certain ratio) but only subject to a decisive qualification. It is the form of the body only to the extent that that form is considered without relation to its object, namely the body. There is of course a puzzle here. If the essential or real definition of mind is "the idea of the body" any adequate understanding of mind must acknowledge the body. We are told, however, that mind is the form of the body considered in abstraction from the body. Presumably, then, an adequate understanding of mind will not view it under its essential description as the idea *of the body*. Instead, it will view it as a mere idea. To understand the mind for what it really is must then be to misunderstand the mind; which is absurd. Is Spinoza trying to tell us that the concept of mind is incoherent? Or is he oscillating like the contemporary materialist between an identity theory (mind = body) and an eliminative account (there are no minds)? At any rate, one is tempted to say that for Spinoza every reference to mind is a referentially opaque reference to a mode of extension. Mind being a certain x (the form of the body) in so far as it is viewed under a certain description (i.e., as a *modus cogitandi*) and hence under a certain limitation (i.e., by way of a certain abstraction from the body) all references to mind must then be non-extensional, and if scientific contexts are committed to being extensional mind must drop out of any purely objective account of the world. All this will be familiar from recent discussions, and it may not be easy to determine how much of this account may be attributed to Spinoza without lapsing into anachronism. Accordingly, I prefer to notice an implication of Part II that probably has no contemporary counterpart but which on the face of it is philosophically challenging in its own right. No one who has read Part II however cursorily has failed to register, if only on a subliminal level, a striking equivocation in Spinoza's use of the term "idea." Sometimes it seems to be used with its classical, objective force, other times (cheek by jowl) with its specifically modern and subjective. That equivocation (and it may well be that in the precise sense of the term) can now be explained in the light of the following principle. Cartesian mentalism arises when the Aristotelian form of the body (understood now much more physicalistically as a ratio of motion and rest) is mistaken for a thing in itself, by way of a radical separation from the body. An idea in the objective sense of the word, the form of the body comes to sight as an idea in the subjective sense (i.e., an abstraction) at the very moment that it is viewed in abstraction from the body. As a *modus cogitandi* or *ens rationis* (relying on Joachim), the mind simply does not exist at all.

That "dialectical" is true of Spinoza's procedure should now be evident. Granted that the term is a portmanteau word in which are packed more than one meaning, I submit that all (well, virtually all) apply, with doubtless greater or less propriety, starting from the core, the Socratic notion of question and answer. Simplifying our results, we can say that there is a first "moment" in which we are officially informed that the attributes of thought and extension being really distinct from one another are each fully intelligible in its own terms, with the consequence that each mode of thought (extension) can be (perhaps even must be) adequately understood in the light of its own proper attribute. According to the second, unofficial, contrapuntal "moment," though body can indeed be fully understood in terms of a single attribute the same does not apply to mind which as the idea of the body can only be (adequately) understood in terms of a "mixed" account that draws on both attributes. What the third, reconciliatory "moment" might consist in, I shall not presume to say, but it cannot be doubted that we are being asked ("asked" is the right, Socratic word) to reconcile the two accounts.

One clue to a reconciliation might lie in an enigmatic remark that Spinoza makes immediately prior to his physical excursus. He says that everything is *animata*. What can Spinoza have in mind when he proposes, in effect that a stone is "animated"? It certainly ill accords with the physically austere account of body that follows. At the very least Spinoza must be understood as saying that in addition to its material components there is the form of the stone to be reckoned with and that this form is the very soul of the stone to the extent at any rate that the form is considered in abstraction from the material components. If this is all that Spinoza's doctrine of the soul of a stone can be shown to come to, it is scarcely to be distinguished from a *reductio ad absurdum* of the very concept of soul, across the board. That Spinoza's doctrine cannot be taken in such reductionist terms, is forcibly urged upon us by his *conatus* doctrine that certainly seems to take the mentalistic aspect of a stone very seriously indeed. With its insistence that everything endeavors to persevere in its being, the *conatus* doctrine is especially useful in allowing us to give some solid content to what in its absence would probably be no more than an empty shell, namely the doctrine that everything, even a mere stone, is fully intelligible under the attribute of thought. But for the *conatus* I think that one would search in vain for what it would be like to give an account of a stone purely in terms of the attribute of thought. When one turns, however, from the *conatus* doctrine itself to the reasons given in its support—two are given in the space of a few lines in E III, P6, one theological, the other purely metaphysical—it is almost totally obscure how the latter (let them indeed be accepted without demur) are supposed to provide grounds for the former, particularly if the mentalistic aspect of E III, P6 is taken seriously.

A few comments on the metaphysical proof might be welcome here, if only for its own philosophical sake, as I think that I can at least convey the drift of Spinoza's thinking on this matter. Let us then imagine a universe with only one body. Moreover, let us posit that this body is not (ever) in motion—of course, if motion is relative that consequence would follow at once. We are also to suppose that the body is altogether unchanging. Most philosophers have held, and continue to hold, that apart from motion and change there can be no time. Let that also then be granted. These conditions stipulated, is it logically possible for the body (ever) to cease to exist? The question is not one that the contemporary philosopher will find easy to answer. On the one hand, he is inclined to answer in the affirmative when he reminds himself that the body is presumed to be a merely contingent entity. On the other hand, acknowledging that something can cease to exist only at some instant of time he will not be happy with the suggestion that though no instant was (previously?) available it cannot be denied that when (i.e., if) the body does cease to exist an instant of time will certainly be ready at hand. If the contemporary philosopher cannot answer the question with the steady assurance that imbues Spinoza's (negative) reply he will be quite prepared to concede that on this point at least Spinoza might well be right. How the goings-on or rather lack of goings-on in our timeless, Parmenidean universe might bear on the hurly-burly of the actual one, might however require some explanation, and yet the relevance of the one to the other is not hard to find. Let one but take the dominant view on motion and time, namely that motion is relative and that time is parasitic on motion, and it follows at once that every stone is only accidentally a temporal entity. Although it has been widely assumed that the materialists are the friends of time, the present considerations show that the opposite is more nearly correct. Body *qua* body, body as it is when viewed in itself independent of all physical and even geometrical relations to other bodies, proves to be free of any essential entanglement in time. It is this "timelessness" of body, waiving all the particular details of my account, that is surely operative in Spinoza's thinking, and though it has usually been taken to be "metaphysical" in import I think that I have said endough to show that it is no less characteristic of a purely physicalistic world-view.

How these considerations, that may indeed be presumed to underlie E III, P6 in one form or another, may be taken to support the *conatus* doctrine remains perplexing. (The theological reason given is only marginally more relevant thanks to its obscurity). In effect, we are being told that the logical feature of "timelessness" that accrues to body when taken by itself somehow entails a self-affirming will to persevere. Although the mentalistic "overlay" may well seem entirely gratuitous, there is at least one consideration that might be adduced here to bridge the gap. Assuming that it has been independently shown that everything can be understood either under the attribute of thought or extension, it follows (some subordinate and relatively innocuous premises being added) that the topic-neutral feature of "timelessness" must have a mentalistic as well as a physicalistic counterpart. The physicalistic counterpart would presumably go by the name of "inertia" taken to be a principle of "least action." As for the mentalistic counterpart, what else could it be but endeavor? Well, it could of course be sloth which is actually closer in spirit to "inertia." The point is not without ethical import. Endeavor or striving corresponds quite obviously to the practical life, as sloth (inactivity, contentment, serenity) is seen by the Great Tradition—allowing for Aristotle's reservations—to reflect the theoretical. That Spinoza came to identify the theoretical and the practical life where the latter is taken to consist largely of the manipulation of bodies (scientific technology in the service of human needs) is at least arguable; and it may not be an accident that the theme is launched in E II, P14 immediately after the physical excursus.

The question of the primacy of body in Part II we found to bring out in the sharpest terms the tension, indeed the conflict between a dialectical and a systematic reading of the work, and it might readily be thought that we must be committed to at least a relative indifference to the proof-theoretical structure of the system taken as such. Not so. That structure preoccupies us both in the small and in the large. Thus in our very concern with precisely *what* it is that is being proved we are trained to notice even such petty details as that while each body is said to express the essence of God each thought is described rather (in E II, P1) as expressing the nature of God. That "nature" and "essence" are used synonymously at least over a wide range of cases in the informal idiom of the Great Tradition, I am not unaware. But that does not quite prove, though it does a great deal more than merely suggest, that in the regimented jargon of the *Ethics* they count as synonymous as well. In the present, early, crude state of our inquiry we have doubtless no choice but to assume that any difference between the two terms must be merely stylistic, and that means—more generally—that we must not expect from Spinoza's formal diction the kind of stringent uniformity that *more geometrico* encouraged us to anticipate.

If this fixation on some merely possible difference between "essence" and "nature" should seem perhaps overly precious, the formal disparity that infects Spinoza's unequal treatment of body and thought in so far as each is said to express the essence of God, the one doctrine being entrusted to a definition, the other to a demonstration, must surely merit serious attention. However one draws the line between a definition and a demonstration, and there is doubtless some freedom in the matter as to precisely how one is to proceed (at any rate, Euclid's distinction between definition and axiom is simply ignored in modern systems), one's whole sense of formal propriety cannot but be offended by Spinoza's puzzling conduct regarding the matter at hand. One may even query whether Spinoza does recognize a formal difference between definition and demonstration (as a rationalist, he would be expected to regard the former as enshrining a self-evident truth) when one notices that Definition 1 of Part II, far from enjoying autonomous status, leans on the authority of E I, P25 in exactly the same way as does the parallel doctrine of E II, P1. There is indeed one formal difference in the two cases. Although antecedent authority is cited in support of the doctrine that it is *qua* thinking thing that God is expressed by each thought, no such authority is cited in support of the comparable doctrine regarding body, though the authority adduced in the one case quite obviously applies with equal force to the other.

The first definition of Part II is by no means the only one that cannot be taken to express a self-evident truth. There is also the last definition of Part IV, and even more to the point regarding our larger inquiry there are the definitions of the affects with which Part III culminates and which no one could suppose to be self-evident truths, seeing that they comprise the fruits rather than the seeds of the investigation. The title of Part III we found relatively easy to explain: the early sections would deal with the origins or causes of the affects while the latter would deal with their natures. We are indeed quite prepared to find that the two accounts might be virtually indistinguishable, an account of the one coming to pretty much the same thing as the account of the other, and that in consequence the title of Part III (and presumably of Part II as well) might express a formal redundancy. The hypothesis is easy enough to put to the test. We have only to compare the earlier account of some particular "emotion," say hope, with its final definition. It turns out, however, that the testing of the hypothesis encounters a certain difficulty. In the earlier account (E III, P18) hope is said to be an unsteady joy arising from the *image* of a future or past thing about whose issue we are in doubt. The final account (E III, P59, Df.12), is scarcely distinguishable from the earlier except in one particular. Hope is now said to be unsteady joy arising from the *idea* of a future or past thing. The difficulty turns on the relation that obtains between image and idea. If mind and body can be identical, why not image and idea? Spinoza is adamant, however, in E II, P49, that ideas and images are not to be confused with one another, though the reason he gives for their diversity is curiously incongruous with the central trend of his thinking. Ideas and images are contrasted as mentalistic and physicalistic items respectively. In the light of this distinction it is hard to decide whether the two definitions of hope are so much as logically compatible. With hope now coming to sight as an uncertain joy arising from the joint occurrence of an idea and image, the two definitions can be taken to be logically compatible *as definitions* only if a definition in the regimented Spinozistic sense of the term need not be (in a fairly plausible sense) complete. How Spinoza's practice here accords with his theory of definition as part and parcel of his general organon, proves to be but one more researchable topic that is generated by our hermeneutic.

More than even the definitions and demonstrations of the work, the very basic words themselves that serve as its mortar than which none are more basic or more ubiquitous than *ens*, *res* and *aliquid*, must preempt the scrutiny of the student who views the *Ethics* as a dialectical enterprise. How explain the fact that in Spinoza's organon these terms are said in E II, P40 to signify ideas that are in the highest degree confused (*hi termini ideas significent summo gradu confusas*)? One would expect any rationalist and indeed any philosopher of any persuasion whatever who has characterized the transcendentals in such opprobrious terms to shun them like the plague at least in his more formal discussions, and yet Spinoza does not hesitate to define (and here we are back to definitions) God as an *ens*. Unless Spinoza is presumed to be writing in some fit of absence of mind, I fail to see how it can be denied that we are being tacitly challenged by Spinoza to confront his theory with his practice (words and deeds, though the deeds are also words) by way of dialectical opposition.

More specifically, we are being invited to reconcile the destructive burden of E II, P40 with the methodologically constructive import of E II, P38, where it is said that whatever is common to everything (part as well as whole) cannot but be adequately conceived. But surely it is *ens* above all that is common to everything, though the Great Tradition was perhaps never prepared to accept the truism without some reservations (see Aristotle, *Metaphysics*, 998b 21). If the term *ens* signifies an idea that is confused to the highest degree one would not suppose that is could equally signify or denote what can only be adequately and never inadequately conceived. Apparently designed as a gloss upon the thematic proposition, the first sentence of E II, P38 says that whatever is common not indeed to everything but to all bodies cannot fail of being adequately conceived. But that cannot be right. Spinoza does not think that whatever is common to all mountains, say, or all rivers enjoys that epistemic privilege. Why then should bodies be assigned a special status, especially in a Part that is expressly devoted to the subject of mind? We would be the less puzzled if Spinoza had spoken rather of all extended things (i.e., God as well as bodies), for we know that everything can be understood under the attribute of extension. The account of E II, P38, not neglecting the corollary, can scarcely be rendered coherent unless "everything" and "all bodies" are taken to be co-extensive.

As only one of very many thematic instances of *res*, the term is featured in E III, P6 where we are told that every *res* in so far as it is in itself endeavors to persevere in its being. Spinoza then does not say that every *res* endeavors to persevere in its being. He says indeed something very much like it but it is not by any means clear what sort of qualification might be intended and how far-reaching that qualification might be. Inevitably, one must ask to what extent the unqualified statement has been diluted, always bearing in mind that in E I, P15 God alone is said, without qualification, to be an entity that is in itself. As a limiting case, one can even conjecture that the extent to which a mountain is in itself as opposed to being in God (E I, P15) is precisely zero.

Although the word *res* is absent from E II, P38, both the W.H. White and R.H.M. Elwes translations choose to supply the English equivalent "thing." By any ordinary standards of exact scholarship their procedure is unexceptionable: "thing" is certainly welcome to fill out the sense of the passage. One must, however, seriously question whether ordinary standards will suffice in the case of Spinoza.

Syracuse University

5 SOME IDEALISTIC THEMES IN THE *ETHICS*

Robert N. Beck

It is only with amazement, I think, that one observes that Spinoza's metaphysical intuitions still elicit contributions to a lengthy bibliography of studies now three hundred years in the making. Amazement, I say, because the metaphysical system he developed is remarkably simple in its basic assertions and extremely narrow in its scope and adequacy. Of course, a second thought arises immediately, for the simplicity of assertion is enmeshed in the complexities of the mathematical method, and the narrowness of scope is countered by the wide range of negations Spinoza came to make. Perhaps it is this very juxtaposition of philosophic qualities which has helped to maintain interest in Spinoza's position and to produce such a quantity of interpretative as well as expository studies. I should emphasize especially the interpretative, for Spinoza is one of the relatively small group of philosophers who has been carefully studied, not only to determine what he said and meant, but also to present him as the precursor of this movement or that. Professor E. M. Curley finds logical atomism in Spinoza, Professor Lee E. Rice a kind of Strawsonian philosophy of science, Strawson himself a kind of scientific materialism, Marxists a materialism anticipating their own views, and so on—to mention only recent writers. Perhaps such interpretations are well and good, though one of the greatest temptations in doing history of philosophy is not to do it.

These remarks about scope and adequacy, I want to emphasize, apply mainly to Spinoza's metaphysics. They do not apply, at least easily, to his ethics, and we must not forget in the study of Spinoza that his stated motivation in turning to philosophy was the question of how he should live. But the assignment given me for this paper is Spinoza's metaphysics; and while I should emphasize constantly Spinoza's overriding ethical concerns and will touch on them briefly later, I accept the restriction this topic places on me.

One more introductory word: my title may suggest that I am trying to make Spinoza into some kind of idealist. This is not my intent or purpose, and however many idealistic themes may be found in Spinoza, I hope our exposition of him will leave him exactly as he was. But I would add that I have argued elsewhere that there are internal grounds in the *Ethics* for viewing the attribute of thought as primary among the attributes and that therefore in a very restricted sense there is something of, or a kind of, idealism in Spinoza. There is also a bibliography on the idealistic elements in Spinoza now extensive enough to make one wonder whether anything really new can be contributed to it. No, I do not take Spinoza's ideas as a full-fledged idealism, and I would further emphasize that Spinoza was concerned not only with Thought but as well with a new understanding of Extension—an understanding which, I believe, was a marked improvement over Descartes'—with the new concept of infinity developing in the sixteenth and seventeenth centuries. Professor Ivor Leclerc says in his recent study of the concept that a change from negative to positive determinations in the notion of infinity "constitutes the ultimate foundation upon which the entire edifice of modern science and philosophy has been raised."[1] At the same time, however, there are interesting reasons for coupling Spinoza and idealism, even if they be only heuristic ones for the study of Spinoza. A number of idealists have examined Spinoza seriously and written extensively on him; some of them acknowledge insights which they have accepted—"all determination is negation," monism, absolutism, come quickly to mind; and Spinoza wrestled with problems which have been uniquely important to a number of idealists.

The "idealistic themes," then, to which my title refers are those ideas in Spinoza which have attracted idealists and have been viewed by them as the same as, or analogous to, basic tenets of an idealistic metaphysics. To achieve the end of identifying these themes and giving them brief exposition, I have chosen to do two things. First, I shall present the reading and interpretation of Spinoza's metaphysics as given by two idealists. The philosophers I have selected for this purpose are Hegel and Royce, authors who will be representative enough for present purposes. In the last part of my paper I shall try to show somewhat systematically, and despite the frequently negative judgments idealists have made on Spinoza, how and why some of his theses can be taken as idealistic.

---

[1] *The Nature of Physical Existence* (London: George Allen and Unwin, 1972), 36.

I

We turn first, then, to Hegel, and especially to Hegel's treatment of Spinoza's metaphysics in *Lectures on the History of Philosophy*.[2] Needless to say, this is an important section in the *Lectures* because Spinoza, along with Aristotle and Kant, is for Hegel one of the three major philosophers in the entire history of philosophy. Hegel also tells us that he had a share in bringing out Spinoza's works in Jena, and it is also here in the *Lectures* that Hegel made his oft quoted statement that "thought must begin by placing itself at the standpoint of Spinozism; to be a follower of Spinoza is the essential commencement of all Philosophy."[3]

Hegel's initial observations about Spinoza are these. First, he says that Spinoza's philosophy is really simple and easy to comprehend, and that it is the method which creates all the difficulties. This is a modest though insightful observation, and we shall return with Hegel to the question of Spinoza's method. Second, Hegel asserts that Spinoza carried the Cartesian principle to its furthest logical conclusions and that his system is that of Descartes made objective in the form of absolute truth. Here we are getting into some of the tangles of Hegel's own position, but Hegel goes on to explain that "the simple thought of Spinoza's idealism [he does call it "idealism"] is this: The true is simply and solely the one substance, whose attributes are thought and extension or nature: and only this absolute unity is reality, it alone is God."[4] Thirdly, Hegel insists that, although Spinoza's grandeur was that he restricted himself to the One, his metaphysics was an Oriental theory of absolute identity, and not a theory of God as Third. Nor did Spinoza prove unity as did, say, the Eleatics.

Now the texts to which Hegel draws our attention include the definitions, which he says really contain the whole of Spinoza's metaphysics—although it is a weakness that he begins with definitions since this method belongs to mathematics alone—and Props. 5, 8, 14, 15, and 16. Spinoza's first definition, we all know, is of that which is cause of itself. "By that which is *causa sui*, its own cause, I understand that whose essence" (or Notion—Hegel's parenthesis) "involves existence, or which cannot be conceived except as existent." Hegel

---

[2] *Lectures on the History of Philosophy*, tr. E. S. Haldane and Frances H. Simson, 3 vols. (London: Routledge and Kegan Paul, 1894). See especially III, 252-90.
[3] *Ibid.*, 257.
[4] *Ibid.*, 256.

finds this a noteworthy expression, for a cause in which the cause is identical with the effect is an infinite cause. But at the same time he says that Spinoza's substance is rigid and philosophically unworkable because the concept of infinite cause is undeveloped.

The second definition is of the finite: "That thing is said to be finite in its kind which can be limited by another of the same nature." Hegel insightfully glosses this definition as identifying the affirmative side of the notion of limit, for a thing is finite insofar as it comes to an end and is not there. What is there is something else, a something which touches the thing, therefore has a relation to it, and which must be of the same nature as the thing. Such a gloss, of course, finds Spinoza's doctrine of the independence of the attributes implied by the definition.

Definitions 3, 4, and 5 identify substance, attribute, and mode. Of substance Hegel does not remark here, as he does in the *Logic*, that Spinoza failed to pass from substance to subject by way of personality, but Hegel's observations in the *Lectures* point to the same conclusion. He says, first, that Spinoza should have deduced rather than merely defined these three concepts. Not having done this, Spinoza did not, perhaps could not, state how substance passes over into its attributes. Further, absence of a deduction means that Spinoza failed to relate universal, particular, and individual, with the result, Hegel says, that modes are only the foregoing "warped and stunted." The third moment is taken as mode alone, which is a false individual. True individuality can never be a "retreat" from the universal.

Hegel next mentions the definition of the infinite, which is really in explanation of the definition of God. "The infinite in its kind," Spinoza wrote, "is not such in respect of all possible attributes; but the absolutely infinite is that to whose essence all belongs that expresses an essence and contains no negation." That Hegel should isolate this statement about the infinite, even though Spinoza did not make it as a definition, is understandable given his interest in—some would say his unique doctrine of—infinity. And in fact the space Hegel gives this statement is more than to any other definition or proposition. What does he make of Spinoza's view? Spinoza, he says, did grasp something of the Notion and thus has a measure of the true infinite in his system. But Spinoza failed to reach the concept of negation of negation, and the Notion falls for him outside of existence, into the thought of existence.

Finally, Hegel comments on the definition of God (the definitions of freedom and eternity are not referred to here): "God is a being absolutely infinite, *i.e.*, a substance consisting of infinite attributes, each of which expresses an eternal and infinite essence." In this observation, Hegel misunderstands Spinoza, I think, for he says that substance possesses not an infinite number of attributes, but only these two, Thought and Extension. Hegel perhaps wants to read Spinoza this way, for he takes Spinoza's infinite, not as the indeterminate many, but positively, "as a circle is perfect infinity in itself."

From these definitions, Spinoza proceeded in what Hegel describes as a formal and simple chain of reasoning to prove that there is only One Substance, God. Hegel then completes his exposition of Spinoza's metaphysics in a paragraph which mentions a number of qualifications Spinoza ascribes to God: his freedom, power, will, activity, and so on.[5] But Hegel says in conclusion that beyond these universals, no advance is made; for as Spinoza said in the *Ep. 50*, every determination is a negation.

Hegel now turns to critique, and though his observations are couched in his own philosophical language, they point to internal and not merely external difficulties in Spinoza's metaphysics. In fact, I will make bold enough to suggest that Hegel pinpointed the tensions in Spinoza that have continued to concern Spinoza scholars to the present day. The greatest difficulty in Spinoza, Hegel asserts, is the relation of the determinate to God. Spinoza did not demonstrate how Thought and Extension evolve from one substance, or why we know only two attributes. Spinoza attempted in his proofs to descend from the universal of substance through the particular (Thought and Extension) to individual, but without success. The mode, or individual, is not recognized as essential or as having true existence; and we can add to Hegel's point that even the doctrine of *conatus* will not do since the only true *conatus* belongs to God. A major reason for the failure of this descent, Hegel says, is that Spinoza conceived of negation in a one-sided way, and omitted the notion of negation of negation which leads to a third, which leads to the conception of Substance as Subject. Spinoza really took negation as Nothing, and of course out of this abyss (God) comes nothing. Hegel here is commenting on the abiding problem in Spinoza, namely, individuality. And even though, as Hegel writes, Spinoza defined *individuum* in *EII, P13, A2, Df.*, it is understood as a mere synthesis, and individuality must in the end be ascribed only to God.

This criticism of the theory of modes is in a way extended by Hegel to the attributes as well. We have already observed that Hegel took as a defect Spinoza's failure to show how Thought and Extension proceed from substance. He also asks how one is to understand the Spinozistic doctrine of the identity of thought and being. Spinoza would have to hold their absolute indifference to one another, since each of them is a manifestation of the whole essence of God.

---

[5] Hegel's footnote refers to EI, P17, P18, P20, P21, P26, P27, P29, P32, P33, with their additions.

The last of Hegel's comments I shall touch upon is not strictly metaphysical, but it is so basic that I take leave to include it here. It is a comment on *ordine geometrico demonstrata,* Spinoza's mathematical method. Hegel writes that this method is not merely a defect in external form, "but is the fundamental defect of the whole position." Mathematical knowledge and method are merely formal and hence they are unsuited for philosophy. Hegel's exposition of this point is couched in his own philosophy of mathematics, which need not detain us. But he notes that a philosophical procedure which begins with definitions and axioms is bound to be unaware of how it arrives at the individual determinations—cause, finite, substance, mode, etc.—which they specify. The resultant philosophy is therefore also bound to be narrow and one-sided—a one-sidedness, we have seen, on the side of universal determination at the expense of the individual. Hegel viewed both Leibniz and Locke as opponents of the distortions of Spinoza, but this is another, albeit fascinating, philosophical story.

II

Although Royce's treatment of Spinoza in *The Spirit of Modern Philosophy*[6] is less extensive and thorough than Hegel's, it is useful here because it emphasizes a side of Spinoza's thought frequently overlooked. That is, that Spinoza's metaphysics was presented in the context of, and is even seemingly designed to serve, an ethico-religious end. Unless we assume an absolute bifurcation of Spinoza's interests, we are forced to conclude that Spinoza's metaphysics is religious, and that apparent in it is the problem of religious value and truth. Such, at least, is what Royce with his idealistic spectacles read in Spinoza's texts.

Royce begins his section on Spinoza with a number of biographical observations. For our purposes, the chief of these is that Royce finds Spinoza's philosophical motivation to be a combination of interests, namely, to understand and comprehend philosophically the scientific view of the universe as it was emerging in the seventeenth century, and to come to grips with—even to reformulate—an ideal of piety. But the search for a satisfying religious life, Royce says, can take two forms. The first is the form of authority, under which the believer finds religious satisfaction through acceptance of commands and prescriptions from a Source whose guidance will be fulfilling. The second form involves coming into the presence of a Truth or Reality believed perfect in some sense or other. Needless to emphasize, Spinoza's re-

---

[6] *The Spirit of Modern Philosophy* (Boston: Houghton, Mifflin and Co., 1892), 41-67.

ligious interest was of the second kind, for he wrote of his longing for such an object and developed his understanding of piety as peaceful reverence for God's eternal order. Spinoza's philosophic heroism, if such it is, is a heroism of contemplation, not action—Royce believed that Spinoza's isolated life made him a poor critic of social relationships—and the need for a mystical resolution of his religious needs is already apparent.

Royce's exposition of Spinoza's doctrine is brief. It is founded, he says, on Axioms 1 and 2 of Part I which state that everything in the world must either be explained by its own nature or by some higher nature. If a thing cannot be explained by itself—and this is the case for everything except Substance—then that thing must be seen as part of a higher nature, in causality as well as explanation. Spinoza then proceeds to the thought that there must be some one highest nature which explains all reality and as well compels all things to be what they are. This highest nature, as Royce was to remark later in *The World and the Individual*,[7] is partly a realistic entity, partly a mystical Absolute.

Now this brief argument, together with its conclusion, is, Royce says, really self-evident if we take the eternal point of view, if we follow Spinoza's injunction to consider things *sub specie aeternitatis*. Even the proposition that God expresses himself in infinitely numerous ways is evident to the eternal, mystical vision. But at the same time, Royce says, there is a marked limitation in the self-evidence and the vision built upon it. The world of Spinoza has but one sublime feature, one object of reverence and piety, and that is the perfection of divine substance. All else tends to fade away, all individuality, all human and thus limited concerns, pale and sink toward the abyss of Nothing of which Hegel has already spoken. Still, the contemplative and mystical religious soul may find religious meaning even in this, and Royce closes his section on Spinoza with a long quotation about the religious life from the conclusion of the *Ethics*.

III

In the course of this exposition of Hegel's and Royce's treatments of Spinoza's metaphysics, I have singled out six basic observations which they have made. Before I turn to the task of developing systematically the idealistic themes in Spinoza, it may be well to list their comments. Fundamentally, these are criticisms of Spinoza, although

---

[7] *The World and the Individual*, 2 vols. (New York: The Macmillan Co., 1901), I, 71.

at the same time they isolate theses which, if developed or altered in the ways Hegel and Royce suggest, would support idealism. These criticisms have been: 1) the limitation of the concept of substance to an identity expressed in the notion of *causa sui*; 2) the failure to relate substance, attribute, and mode; 3) a limitation in the concept of individuality understood as a mere synthesis; 4) inadequacies in the mathematical method; 5) the failure to reach the concept of negation of negation; and 6) the narrowness of Spinoza's religious-metaphysical interests. Now I do not want to imply that these observations are the exclusive property of idealists, for they—or something like them—can be found in many expositions of Spinoza's metaphysics. Being somewhat common property of different philosophers, it may be understandable that one temptation in interpreting Spinoza is to demote God to Nature, logicize the attribute of Thought, and complete one's interpretation by making Spinoza into a proponent, or at least forerunner, of scientific materialism. Even more, some might say, is the temptation to take the attribute of Extension as basic or primary because of the supposed obviousness of the material world in our experience.

But I have quite intentionally come to these criticisms out of idealistic sources, where, I think rightly, this temptation to minimize or drop idealistic elements in Spinoza will hardly be found. To be sure, I remind myself again that I do not intend to make Spinoza into an idealist, at least in any full sense of the word; and I think there is point in Sir Frederick Pollock's observation that Spinoza tried to keep a clear course between materialism and idealism. Such a course is, I think, not really possible to follow, and the criticisms I have just summarized show this. But the idealistic elements remain in Spinoza and are part of the abiding tensions as well as dissatisfactions with his thought.

But first, there is a matter over which we must pause for a moment, and that is the meaning of "idealistic themes." What shall we mean by "idealism"? Like such terms as metaphysics, or ethics, or even philosophy itself, the meaning of idealism could occupy us for this entire seminar, if not the entire course of lectures. Let me therefore be somewhat dogmatic and, following W. M. Urban,[8] say that a position is an idealism, a metaphysical idealism, if it makes or includes three basic assertions: first, that the sense world is not the real world, second, that ideals are in some sense real, and, third, that reality is intelligible. Taken together, these theses imply that mind, or principles derived from mind or the mindlike, is the ultimate metaphysical

---

[8] In *Beyond Realism and Idealism* (London: George Allen and Unwin, 1949), 38-70.

reality. I trust that these assertions are at least minimally understandable and acceptable, for what I now wish to show in this last part of my paper is that Spinoza, tentatively, partially, inadequately as the critique of idealists has shown, held these three idealistic assertions. method is the product of the understanding rather than intuition—a kind of mystical basis upon which everything in it is constructed.[9]

Consider the first of them, that the sense world is not the real world, or that categories derived from it are not ultimate categories. I think there are a number of grounds which can be offered to support the contention that Spinoza was motivated in philosophy consistent with this assertion and that his system embodies it. In *On the Improvement of the Understanding* Spinoza tells us that "love toward a thing eternal and infinite," rather than toward the perishable, "feeds the mind wholly with joy," and the epistemological *conatus* of the work is to try to lift the mind to the highest level of knowledge which is *intuitiva*. Such knowledge gives us an intuition of the whole, of a reality eternal and infinite, which as substance grounds the entire universe and as modes constitutes the entire universe. I agree with Guttorm Fløistad that *scientia intuitiva* really underlies the whole of the *Ethics* as well, giving that work—however much the mathematical

A second reason for asserting that Spinoza does not take the sensed or experienced world as real is his understanding of finitude, and of finite entities. We have touched on this point earlier, and have need only to remind ourselves that the finite is understood by Spinoza by way of limitation and negation. Reality is not to be found in them, but rather in that of which they are the negation. True enough, Spinoza does seem to accept a doctrine of degrees of reality, but this doctrine, debatable as it may be in some quarters, is itself typically if not always identified as idealistic.

As a third reason, I refer to Spinoza's somewhat difficult doctrine of the individual. The nature and meaning of the individual, as well as of body and similar concepts, are frequently treated in the *Ethics*. We are told that individual things are nothing but modes of the attributes of God (EI, P25, C), that one body is composed of several bodies either in contact or moving at the same rate of speed (EII, P13, L3 A2 Df.), and that there is no true individual except God. We may, he says, "conceive the whole of nature as one individual, whose parts, that is, all bodies, may vary in infinite ways, without any change in the individual as a whole" (EII, P13, L7,5). However much, then, the sense

---

[9] "Spinoza's Theory of Knowledge Applied to the *Ethics*," in S. Paul Kashap (ed.), *Studies in Spinoza* (Berkeley: University of California Press, 1972), 249-75.

world, the world of experienced things and thoughts, appears to consist of particulars and individuals, the appearances are not reality. In Spinoza's view, they vanish in the system, and Joachim, whom I follow here, concludes that "in the timeless activity of the modal system, in the completeness of 'natura naturata,' there is no individual 'essentia' or 'existentia' except that of the whole system."[10]

The second assertion of idealism I noted above was that ideals are in some sense real. This theme, too, can be found in Spinoza, though I do not think in any satisfactory way. I remind you of Royce's observation about the inadequacy of this doctrine in Spinoza. Three quick references must suffice for me to make this point, though in fact the notion of *causa sui* contains the link with both infinity and perfection which I am trying to show. The first reference is to Spinoza's use of a version of the ontological argument in EI, P11, and particularly to his statements that "the perfection of a thing does not annul its existence, but, on the contrary, asserts it," and also that God's "essence excludes all imperfection, and involves absolute perfection." Again, EII, Df.6 reads, "Reality and perfection I use as synonymous terms." Now I am not asserting that the ontological argument is exclusively idealistic, but I do suggest that Spinoza's statement of it does appeal to the idealistic thesis of the reality of the ideal. Perhaps, though, EV, P40 supports my point even more clearly. "In proportion as each thing possesses more of perfection, so it is more active, and less passive; and *vice versa*, in proportion as it is more active, so it is more perfect." If we remember that activity and being are related terms, we must read the proposition as again asserting Spinoza's belief that ideals are real, or that perfection is correlated with reality.

The third assertion of idealism, Urban wrote, is that the real is intelligible. Along with the other assertions, this thesis too has been part of the basis from which idealists have concluded that mind or the mindlike, one or many, is the ultimate finality. Now does Spinoza teach any doctrine which reflects or at least suggests this third thesis? This question points immediately to the nature and status of the attribute of Thought; and I want to propose here, as I have done in another study,[11] that Spinoza, perhaps despite some of his intentions, perhaps even at times inconsistently, does teach a kind of priority for Thought. One could also, of course, raise from epistemological considerations the questions of the intelligibility of the real and the status

---

[10] H. Joachim, *A Study of the Ethics of Spinoza* (Oxford: Clarendon Press, 1901), 70.

[11] "The Attribute of Thought," in James B. Wilbur (ed.), *Spinoza's Metaphysics* (Amsterdam: van Gorcum, 1976), 1-12.

of Thought in Spinoza, though I shall not try to cover these here.[12]

The problem of the status of the attribute of Thought is an old one in Spinozistic studies, and was in fact raised even by one of his correspondents, Tschirnhaus. Pollock in his pioneering study of Spinoza observed that "inasmuch as Attribute is defined by reference to intellect, and Thought is itself an attribute, Thought appears in a manner counted twice over."[13] And similarly A. Wolf has written that "Thought appears to have a privileged position among the Attributes: instead of being parallel with one Attribute (like Extension with Thought), it seems to be co-extensive with all the other attributes."[14] Pollock and Wolf argue their point largely from the point of view of the representative function of thought, but I think the same general conclusions can be reached from metaphysical considerations.

To make this point as briefly and directly as possible, I shall present a number of key Spinozistic assertions almost in outline form, keeping commentary at a minimum. Taken together, they imply that Thought is the metaphysically dominant and primordial attribute and that—since attributes express the essence of substance—God or Reality is primordially Thought. Here are the assertions. (1) God is a being who acts—he is not just the logico-mathematical structure of reality. To conceive God in the latter way is a common, but, I think, mistaken view. Spinoza, to be sure, does not use the term "acts" until EI, P17; still, the very first of Spinoza's definitions expresses not only the unity of all reality but as well the notion of a ground or cause of all that is. (2) Thought and Extension are attributes of this activity, for, as the fourth definition states, "By *attribute*, I mean that which the intellect perceives as constituting the essence of substance." (3) The dynamical view of Extension does not embrace, to be sure, a spiritual activity as in, say, Leibniz; it is the activity of substance, which also has in unity (or expresses itself in unity with) the attribute of Thought. Extension, Spinoza says, "is an attribute of God, or God is an extended thing" (EII, P2), a statement which augurs ill for interpretations which would deny Extension and the plurality of attributes—though also a statement which does not of itself answer the question of the relative status of each of the attributes. (4) But the attribute of Extension is incomplete; for except for God's unity, no formal ordering of the

---

[12] See however, the Bibliographical Essay.
[13] *Spinoza: His Life and Philosophy*, 2nd ed. (London: Duckworth and Co., 1899), 153.
[14] See "Spinoza's Conception of the Attributes of Substance," in Kashap (ed.), *op. cit.*, 25.

universe, so critical to Spinozism, has been given. Along with this, therefore, (5) Some principles, at least, of the activity of Extension must be other than Extension.

A few of the key passages on which these assertions, as well as the immediately succeeding ones, rest must now be stated. In EI, P17,5, Spinoza says that "the intellect of God, insofar as it is conceived to constitute God's essence, is, in reality, the cause of things, both of their essence and of their existence." A moment later he adds that "God's intellect, God's will, and God's power are one and the same." Spinoza also holds that minds are active in so far as they have adequate ideas, passive in so far as they have inadequate ideas (EIII, P1). Always having adequate ideas in act, God's intellect is therefore active. In sum, Thought is a principle or "form" of God's activity which modalizes as intellect, and his power of Thought[15] is one with his power of action.

It can next be asserted, then, that (6) God's intellect is the cause of the essence and existence of things. "Things" is here read literally, not just as "ideas," and Spinoza is referring things to thinking as an order of causality. And, as has been noted, (7) God's power of Thought is one with his power of action. Finally, (8) Thought is therefore best understood as the principle of active, ordering activity, and Extension and the other attributes as principles of passive, ordered activity. The implications of this reading of Spinoza are that causality through Thought accounts for things, that Thought is the attribute or "form" of action, that Thought in this formal sense has a metaphysical preeminence over the other attributes because they are the "matter"—things considered as modes of Extension—made active by the attribute of Thought, and that God's activity actively viewed is Thought, passively viewed is the other attributes.

Such is the reading of Spinoza's teaching which I am suggesting, however briefly. If it, or something like it, is true of Spinoza, the third of Urban's theses about idealism is also exemplified in his metaphysics.

I come, finally, to a brief set of concluding remarks. In his monumental study of Spinoza, Wolfson[16] suggested that the chief mark of Spinoza's philosophy is his *daring*, particularly in respect to the unity of reality. With remorseless rigor, Spinoza attempted to adhere to his principle of unity, treating inherited notions like causality, freedom, thought from the point of view of this principle. Even God and the

---

[15] Rather than intellect, as Spinoza says. There is some ambiguity in Spinoza's use of the terms thought and intellect to which I have briefly alluded in "The Attribute of Thought" (see footnote 11).

human self, traditionally exempted from the unity of nature, or at least treated differently from other beings, are brought by Spinoza under his principle of unity or identity.

Perhaps we can agree with Wolfson in this characterization. But we must add to it, I think, the philosophical judgment that Spinoza insightfully failed. We will all make our judgment about this failure—that identity is too impoverished a principle, that an adequate metaphysical vision requires more than one finality, or that Spinoza's idealistic suggestions will find a coherent home only in the mansions of an explicit idealism. However that may be, perhaps there is this much agreement among us anyway, that—as will be quoted so often during this course of lectures—all good things are as difficult as they are rare.

Clark University

---

[16] *The Philosophy of Spinoza,* 2 vols. (Cambridge: Harvard University Press, 1934).

BIBLIOGRAPHICAL ESSAY
ON THE IDEALIST INTERPRETATION

Bibliographical materials on Spinoza are so complete that little if anything can be added to them. The standard works are Adolph S. Oko, *The Spinoza Bibliography* (Boston: G. K. Hall, 1964), supplemented by John A. Wetlesen, *A Spinoza Bibliography, 1940-1970*, 2nd ed., (Oslo: Universitetsforlaget, 1968). E. M. Curley has compiled a bibliography for the years 1960-1972 in Mandelbaum and Freeman, eds., *Spinoza: Essays in Interpretation* (LaSalle, Ill.: Open Court, 1975), pp. 265-316. Rather than aim at an impossible (and unnecessary) completeness, therefore, this essay will only suggest certain materials relevant to an understanding of idealistic themes in Spinoza.

Most thinkers identified as idealists of some kind have commented at least briefly on Spinoza. Four important book-length studies by idealists include John Caird, *Spinoza*, (Edinburgh: Blackwood, 1888); Harold H. Joachim, *A Study of the Ethics of Spinoza*. (Oxford: 1901); Maurice Blondel, *Dialogues avec les philosophes*, (Paris: Editions Montaigne, 1966); and Errol E. Harris, *Salvation from Despair: A Reappraisal of Spinoza's Philosophy* (The Hague: Nijhoff, 1973). Older articles reflecting idealism include J. Clark Murray, "The Idealism of Spinoza," *The Philosophical Review*, 4 (1896), pp. 473-89; A. E. Taylor, "Some Incoherencies in Spinozism," *Mind*, 46 (1937), 137-58 and 281-301; also his "A Further Word on Spinoza," *Mind*, 55 (1946), 97-112. A treatment of some themes related to the references to Royce above is found in F. C. Copleston's "Pantheism in Spinoza and the German Idealists," *Philosophy*, 20 (1946), 42-56.

Discussions of possible idealistic themes in Spinoza can be divided roughly into two groups, epistemological and metaphysical. The latter kind, of course, is the focus of this paper. But epistemological questions about Spinoza's views have been asked since the appearance of the *Ethics*. One of Spinoza's correspondents, Tschirnhaus, wondered especially about the attributes and the status of Thought, though Sir Frederick Pollock in his *Spinoza: His Life and Philosophy*, 2nd ed. (London: C. K. Paul, 1899) was to provide, in the quotations I used above, the *locus classicus* of the query. Also used above was the similar conclusion reached by A. Wolf in "Spinoza's Conception of the Attributes of Substance," *Proceedings of the Aristotelian Society*, 27 (1927). These references suggest the two basic (and idealistic) issues commentators have faced: whether Thought enters into the definitions of the attributes in a unique and primary way—and this has generated a whole literature on Spinoza's doctrines of attributes which can be consulted; and whether Thought, in its representative function, must be taken as primary because the other attributes are re-presented in it.

Two recent discussions of what may be called metaphysical idealism in Spinoza—and the epistemological-metaphysical distinction I use here is really only heuristic—illustrate work complementary to my own. Errol E. Harris has argued in his article, "The Order and Connexion of Ideas," *Spinoza on Knowing, Being and Freedom* (Assen: van Gorcum, 1974), 103-13, that the Hegelian conclusion that Substance be understood as Subject leaves unresolved the problem of Extension and the physical world. How resolve it? By adopting, Harris says, the conception of a "scale of forms" of reality culminating in the infinite mind of God where the whole scale is expressed as Thought, the only attribute properly ascribable to God and his activity. Secondly, J. G. van der Bend has outlined five theses on which to base an idealistic reading of Spinoza (see his Introduction to the above book and the references he gives). These include the tendency in Spinoza to take reality as residing, not in appearances but in the General; the founding of the attributes in a purely epistemological manner; the importance of the infinite mode of infinite intellect; the coordination among *conatus*, reason, and infinite intellect; and, finally, the mind's powers to possess body. These metaphysical theses and their implications remain, of course, debatable; but at the very least they suggest to the student that an easy reduction of Spinozism to some form of materialism is less than warranted.

6

SPINOZA'S DUALISM

Alan Donagan

The title of this lecture, "Spinoza's Dualism" is, in the rigor of the term, a paradox: it flouts an entrenched common opinion. Was not Spinoza a monist of monists? Did he not protest that substance is one, and that there is nothing but substance and the modes in it, of which it is *causa immanens*? And did he not, in the Preface to Part V of his *Ethics*,* utterly repudiate Descartes' doctrine that each individual human being is a union of two finite substances, each having a distinct finite principal attribute, and insist on the contrary that no individual human being is anything more than a mode of the one infinite substance, inasmuch as that mode is constituted by each one of two really distinct infinite attributes? Did he not, then, deny the very doctrines, both about nature and about man, in virtue of which his great teacher, Descartes, is held to be a dualist?

It is quite impossible to deny, nor do I wish to deny, that Spinoza held all the specific doctrines implicitly attributed to him in these rhetorical questions. He did hold that substance is one, and that an individual human being is a mode of that one substance. However, we should not forget a lesson Quine has taught us, which I prefer to put in a Fregean terminology he rejects, namely, that the totality of what anybody believes is a fabric of logically interconnected items, in which the sense of one is affected by the senses of the others.[1] The very

---

* All quotations and references to Spinoza's writings are to Carl Gebhardt (ed.) *Spinoza Opera* (Heidelberg: Carl Winter, 1925), 4 vols., translations being mine; and all quotations and references to Descartes' writings are to Charles Adam and Paul Tannery (eds.) *Oeuvres de Descartes* (Paris: Leopold Cerf, 1897-1913), 11 vols., abbreviated 'AT', translations also being mine. In the latter case, a reference to E. S. Haldane and G. R. T. Ross (ed. and tr.), *The Philosophical Works of Descartes* (2nd ed. corr. Cambridge: Cambridge University Press, 1931), 2 vols., abbreviated '*HR*', is added for all works translated in that collection.

---

[1] W. V. O. Quine, *From a Logical Point of View* (Cambridge, Mass.: Harvard University Press, 1953), 42-3; cf. Michael Dummett, *Frege: Philosophy of Language* (London: Duckworth, 1973), 592-99.

same sentence, uttered by different persons whose other beliefs are different, may express quite different beliefs.

An illustration from Spinoza's own time is ready to hand. Copernicus in 1543 published a heliocentric theory of the planetary system, according to which, unless it be taken as a mathematically convenient fiction, the earth moves around the sun. In 1588, because the Copernican system, taken at face value, violated every extant system of physical theory, Tycho Brahé amended it, and developed a system in which, according to Aristotelian physics, the earth is unmoved in the center of the universe, with the sun revolving around it, but in which all the other planets revolve about the sun. In his *Principia Philosophiae* of 1644, Descartes pointed out what is now commonplace, that if motion is taken as relative, then the Tychonic and the Copernican systems are largely equivalent: the Copernican system showing the movement of the earth, moon and planets relative to the sun; and the Tychonic system showing the movements of the sun, moon and planets relative to the earth. He even remarked that, from the point of view of a relativist theory of motion, the Tychonic system, to the extent that it is not equivalent to the Copernican, assigns to the earth a greater motion, although "in words," because of his false conception of motion, Tycho denied that it moves at all. And so Descartes advanced his notorious claim: *me accuratius quam Copernicum, et verius quam Tychonem, terrae motum negare.*[2]

Yet despite his explicit denial that the earth moves, historians of astronomy do not set Descartes down as an anti-Copernican or a geocentrist. For, while he did formally disavow the proposition that Galileo and realist Copernicans were condemned by the Holy Office for affirming, he accompanied that denial with affirmations of numerous uncondemned propositions that were equally obnoxious to geocentrists: for example, that "viewed *e caelo,* Earth would appear to be only a planet, smaller than Jupiter or Saturn."[3] At the same time, he reconciled his formal disavowal of Copernicanism with his numerous Copernican affirmations by a radical doctrine of the nature of motion which neither Copernicans nor anti-Copernicans had seriously considered in this connection.

My description of Spinoza as a dualist, despite his repudiation of a plurality of substances and of a union of two substances in man, is

---

[2] Descartes, *Principia Philosophiae*, III, 17-19 (*AT* VIII, 85-86; *HR* I, p. 272—and headings of *'principia'* only). The relation of the Tychonic system to the Copernican is lucidly explained in Thomas S. Kuhn, *The Copernican Revolution* (New York: Vintage Books, n.d.), 202-05.

[3] Descartes, *Principia Philosophiae*, III, 8 (*AT* VIII, pp. 82-83, *HR* I, 271).

parallel to the description of Descartes as a Copernican by historians of astronomy, despite his repudiation of the doctrine that the earth moves. I hope to justify my description by establishing the parallel. For that, I must do two things. First, I must show that, just as Descartes accepted numerous propositions that are distinctively Copernican and heliocentric, so Spinoza accepted numerous propositions that are distinctively dualist. And secondly, I must show that Spinoza himself could only reconcile his acceptance of those dualist propositions with his assertion of the unity of substance and his denial that man is a union of two substances, by embracing an obscure doctrine that is unacceptable alike to Cartesian dualists and to their materialist, mentalist and neutral monist adversaries. If I can show both these things, then even if you remain disinclined to call Spinoza a dualist, I think you will have to concede that his work affords the antidualists of our day as little comfort as Descartes' work afforded the anti-Copernicans of his.

Let us begin with his theory of substance. The antipluralist and hence antidualist proposition that besides God, the infinite substance, no substance can exist (*dari*) or be conceived is a theorem in the *Ethics* (I, P14). But consider some of the propositions in the *Ethics* that precede it, especially EI, Dff, 3, 4 and 6, A5 and P1-P8.

In EI, Dff. 3, 4 Spinoza lays it down that a substance is that which is *in se* and is conceived *per se*, glossing "that is, that the concept of which does not need the concept of another thing, from which it must be formed"; and then he defines an attribute as "that which intellect perceives of a substance, as constituting its essence." Both definitions are Cartesian: that of substance being a version of Descartes' definition of that kind of substance "in which only a unique one is intelligible, namely God," supplemented by a specification of how that substance is conceived; and his definition of an attribute is a version of Descartes' definition of the *attributum praecipuum* of a substance, namely of that one property "which constitutes (that substance's) nature and essence."[4]

The first eight theorems of *Ethics* Part I are also plainly Cartesian: so much so that Martial Gueroult, in the finest commentary ever written on it, has described them as constituting Spinoza's theory of substances of one attribute. The most important of these theorems are 2, 5, 6, and 7, in which it is shown that distinct (*diversa*) substances must

---

[4] Descartes, *Principia Philosophiae*, I, 51, 53 (*AT* VIII, pp. 24-25; *HR* I, 239, 240).

have distinct attributes, and can have nothing in common, and that one substance cannot be produced by another, but that it pertains to the very nature of a substance to exist. Here it must be remembered that we are speaking of Descartes' views of substance in that sense of the word in which he held that only God is a substance: namely that of a substance *quae nulla plane re indigeat*.[5] Taking "substance" in this sense, Descartes had no quarrel even with *Ethics* I, 8, that "every substance is necessarily infinite."

It is only at *Ethics* I, P9-P11 that Spinoza begins to part with Descartes, and the breach is not decisive. In EI, P9 Spinoza lays it down as obvious from his definition of an attribute (EI, Df4), that "the more reality or being (*esse*) each thing has, the more attributes belong to it"[6] but at the same time, in EI, P10, he insists, according to his definitions of attribute and substance (EI, Dff. 4,3) that "each one (of the) attribute(s) of a singular substance must be conceived *per se*." A Cartesian need not have denied these propositions, but he would dismiss them as pointless. For he would have held that an infinite substance had to be simple: that is, that a plurality of really distinct attributes could not belong to it. The various names we assign to God—the sole infinite substance—do not stand for really distinct attributes, but rather for different ways in which finite intellects attempt to represent the infinite divine simplicity. If we take "attribute of God" in Spinoza's sense, as referring to something which the intellect perceives as constituting the divine essence—here of course understanding the word "perceives" as elliptical, and meaning "truly perceives"—then Cartesians, and orthodox Jews and Christians generally, allow only one divine attribute, which they identify with God's incomprehensible essence. If, *per impossibile*, there *were* more than one attribute which could be truly conceived as constituting the divine essence, then indeed a being possessing *some* but *not* all of those attributes would have less reality or being than one possessing *all* of them: but the antecedent of this hypothetical proposition is *necessarily* false. So, at least, a Cartesian would hold.

At the present time, it is easy to overlook how radical was Spinoza's readiness to allow that one and the same substance may have really distinct attributes, because if we use the word "substance" at all, we apply it to ordinary finite individual objects, and if we use the word "attribute" at all, we apply it to the properties of these objects, and

---

[5] Descartes, *Principia Philosophiae*, I, 51 (*AT* VIII, p. 24; *HR* I, 239).

[6] Spinoza's words are "*eo plura ipsi competunt*," the metaphor being that of legal ownership.

there is nothing paradoxical about thinking of a rose, say, as both red and fragrant. But what Spinoza was ready to allow is certainly paradoxical, and on one plausible assumption demonstrably absurd. His substance is an infinite individual, and any attribute it has constitutes an infinite essence. And even if we apply his doctrine to Cartesian created substances—individuals that do not exist *in se*, but need the "concurrence" of God, nothing else, to exist—an attribute of such a substance constitutes its nature or essence, and the scientific study of it is primarily an investigation of the implications of being constituted by the attribute. *If an attribute constitutes an essence,* it is hard to escape concluding that really distinct attributes constitute really distinct essences. In what else could their distinction consist? But if that conclusion is sound, then Spinoza's doctrine that a substance may possess a plurality of really distinct attributes entails that *such a substance must in some sense have a plurality of really distinct essences.* Martial Gueroult, indeed, draws this conclusion. And clearly it is difficult either to draw it, or to reject it.[7]

What must be said at this point is that Spinoza secures the unity of infinite substance within his system only by maintaining that really distinct attributes can be attributes of the same substance: a proposition which his contemporaries found paradoxical because of the above difficulties it involves (see, for example, Simon de Vries' letter of 24 February 1663).[8] I shall return to the question of how Spinoza believed his paradoxical doctrine could be upheld, and its bearing on the question whether or not his system is dualist. But first we must examine Spinoza's views about what attributes can be identified as possessed by infinite substance.

Substance, being infinite, according to EI, P11 has infinite attributes. What did Spinoza mean by that? Anybody who now uttered such a sentence as EI, P11 would be understood to imply that infinite substance has an enormous number of attributes, perhaps as many as the number of natural numbers, or perhaps even more. To interpret Spinoza's theorem as implying anything of the kind would, however, be anachronistic. In terms of his own century, I agree with George Kline that the only plausible sense of "infinite," as stating a quantitative property of the divine attributes in Spinoza's system, is "all

---

[7] Martial Gueroult, *Spinoza* (Paris: Editions Montaigne, 1968), Vol. I, 160-166. For a brief comment on Gueroult's position, see a paper of mine in Marjorie Grene (ed.) *Spinoza: a Collection of Critical Essays* (Garden City, N.J.: Doubleday, 1973), 174-77.

[8] Gebhardt, IV, 41 (Ep.8).

without exception."⁹ In other words, what Spinoza says about the number of the divine attributes in EI, Df.6 and P11 is that, taking all the attributes that constitute the essence of an infinite substance, however many they may be, they *all* belong to the infinite substance, and not merely some finite sub-set of them. Hence, depending on whether the number of attributes that expresss the essence of an infinite substance is one (as Descartes and most orthodox Jews and Christians hold) or, say, three or nineteen, or aleph-null, EI, P11 entails that the number of divine attributes is one, or three, or nineteen, or aleph-null.

How many attributes did Spinoza think infinite substance to have? The only certain answer that can be deduced from the argument of the *Ethics* is "at least two." From his letter to Tschirnhaus of 18 August, 1675, we may conclude that his private opinion was that there are more than two; but nothing in his system appears to entail it.¹⁰

The two attributes Spinoza claims to know to express the essence of infinite substance are not formally introduced until *Ethics,* Part II, in the first two theorems of which it is asserted that *cogitatio* and *extensio* are attributes of God. These theorems are proved from the second and fourth axioms of Part II, that man thinks, and that we feel our bodies to be affected in many ways (*modis*), together with the first and third definitions, in which it is laid down that bodies and ideas (in the having of which thinking consists) are modes of *res extensa* and *res*

---

⁹ George Kline, "On the Infinity of Spinoza's Attributes," in *Speculum Spinozanum*, ed. Siegfried Hessing (London and Boston: Routledge and Kegan Paul, 1977), 342-345.

¹⁰ His numerous references to the infinite attributes of God do not show that he thought there to be more of them than the two he discusses in *Ethics* Parts II-V. But his reply to Tschirnhaus's question, "why the mind which represents a certain Modification (*Modificatio*) . . . expressed not only in extension but in infinite other ways (*modis*) . . . perceives only that Modification expressed through extension?" to wit, that "although each thing is expressed in infinite ways (*modis*) in the infinite understanding of God, yet the infinite ideas by which it is expressed cannot constitute one and the same mind of an individual thing, but an infinity of minds," shows him to have held that other attributes besides *extensio* are represented in the *Dei idea infinita* (Epp. 65, 66, Gebhardt, IV, 279-80). In the passage here translated Tschirnhaus used "*Modificatio*" for "*modus*" in the systematic sense defined in EI, Df.5, and "*modus*" in the unsystematic sense in which it merely means a way; and Spinoza, in his reply, followed Tschirnhaus's usage. By translating "*modus*" here as "mode", Wolf introduces a misleading ambiguity (A. Wolf, *Correspondence of Spinoza* [New York: Russell & Russell, 1966], 309-310).

In the paper cited in note 9, George Kline draws attention to Spinoza's practice of using a number of words in both systematic and nonsystematic senses.

cogitans respectively. Are *extensio* and *res extensa*, *cogitatio* and *res cogitans* the attributes and substances Descartes called by the same names? Up to a point, yes. Spinoza agreed with Descartes that Euclid's geometry gives a true account of *res extensa*, although not a complete one; and that *"cogitatio"* stands for the intentionality or, in seventeenth century terminology, the "objectivity" characteristic of all mental operations and "affections"—all *modi cogitandi*, but he held that Descartes had deformed his own fundamentally correct conceptions of these attributes by denying that they express the essence of an infinite substance.

Once this error is corrected, however, Spinoza expresses no disagreement on fundamentals with Descartes' conceptions of *extensio* and *cogitatio*. Of course there is disagreement on derivative matters: for example, on whether *res extensa* has by its very nature the infinite mode *motus et quies*, which Descartes would have denied.[11] Again, Descartes would have denied that *cogitatio*, which involves representation by ideas (EII, A3) is an attribute through which the knowledge of an infinite substance is to be conceived. But Spinoza plausibly held that all such disagreements derive from Descartes' fundamental mistake that *extensio* and *cogitatio* do not constitute infinite essences. On all other fundamental questions about *extensio* and *cogitatio*, Spinoza followed Descartes, and especially on the one that matters most for the topic of this paper: he held that *extensio* and *cogitatio* are really distinct.

Since he did not follow Descartes in the most important conclusion Descartes drew from this fundamental doctrine, it is necessary to be exact about what it is. In *Principia Philosophiae* I, 60 Descartes laid it down that "a *real [distinction]* is properly between two or more substances"; and Spinoza, in his restatement of the *Principia, more geometrico demonstrata*, captured his meaning in the definition "two sub-

---

[11] ". . . I believe that I have shown clearly enough . . . that matter (*materiam* is by Descartes badly defined in terms of (*per*) extension; whereas it must necessarily be explained in terms of (*per*) an attribute which expresses an eternal and infinite essence" (*Ep.* 83), Gebhardt IV, 334. Wolf's rendering of *"definiri per extensionem"* as "defines as extension" is, in context, a mistranslation, which is connected with his misunderstanding Spinoza as objecting to Descartes' conception of *extensio* as static rather than dynamic (Wolf [a], 63, 365). Taken straightforwardly, what Spinoza meant in this passage of his letter was that Descartes defined matter badly because, although he correctly identified its attribute as *extensio*, he mistakenly denied that *extensio* expresses an infinite essence. It is true that he held that it was because of this mistake that Descartes wrongly concluded that *motus* had to be specially created and conserved.

stances are said to be really distinct when each one of them can exist without the other."[12] However, although in the Cartesian system real distinction is defined for substances, the criterion for recognizing it offered by Descartes is for attributes: "and these [i.e. substances] we perceive to be really distinct each from each (*a se mutuo*) from this alone, that we can clearly and distinctly understand (*intelligere*) one without the other"[13]—an attribute being, for him as for Spinoza, that which constitutes the essence of a substance, and through which it is conceived.[14] Although in Spinoza's system the concept of a real distinction between substances has no application, since there is necessarily only one substance, Descartes' criterion for a real distinction between attributes is retained; "two attributes are really distinct (*realiter distinguuntur*) if each one of them can be conceived without the help of the other" (EI, P10 S).[15] And the bearing of this on the question of how far Spinoza's system is dualist is obvious: by reaffirming Descartes' doctrine that *extensio* and *cogitatio* are really distinct, Spinoza renounces any form of reductive monism. Substance under the attribute *extensio* is not reducible to substance under the attribute *cogitatio*, and *vice versa*. It may be remarked that for some materialists today, such as D. M. Armstrong, the doctrine of a real distinction of attributes is classified as an anti-materialist alternative to substance dualism, incurring most of its liabilities.[16]

Spinoza, however, is no attribute theorist like those of our day, who cheerfully ascribe both physical and mental predicates to living bodies. According to him, *cogitatio* no less than *extensio* is conceived through itself. It cannot be a property of anything physical at all: rather, it constitutes the essence of whatever has what he called *modi cogitandi* (cf. EII, A3). In other words, it is Spinoza's position that nothing can believe, desire, hope, fear, or love except as it is considered under the attribute *cogitatio*. None of these modes can intelligibly be said to be in a *res extensa*. And for the same reasons, none of the modes involving motion and rest—nothing in what Spinoza called the *facies totius universi*, which constantly changes according to the same

---

[12] DPP I, Df. 10 (Gebhardt I, 151); cf. Descartes, *Principia Philosophiae* I, 60 (*AT* VIII, 28-29; *HR* I, 243-44).

[13] Descartes, *Principia Philosophiae* I, 60 (*AT* VIII, 28; *HR* I, 243).

[14] Descartes, *Principia Philosophiae* I, 53 (*AT* VIII, 25; *HR* I, 240).

[15] "... *duo attributa realiter distincta concipiantur, hoc est, unum sine ope alterius* ..." (Gebhardt, II, 52).

[16] D. M. Armstrong, *A Materialist Theory of the Mind* (London: Routledge, 1968), ch. 3, esp. 41-42, 45-48.

unchanging physical laws—can intelligibly be said to be in a *res cogitans* (cf. EI, P10; EII, P6).

This position is difficult; but it is not made easier to grasp by contaminating it with notions resurrected from Aristotelianism or stolen from evolutionary biology. Spinoza's infinite substance is not a sort of infinite Strawsonian person, the nature of which is to be *both* extended *and* thinking: on the contrary, its nature is constituted by each *one* of the attributes *extensio* and *cogitatio by itself*—without either needing any help from the other. And, although Spinoza's infinite substance under the attribute *extensio* is a hierarchy of complex modes, each having more or less *potentia agendi* than others, minds in his theoretical sense do not make their appearance in it as emergent properties of the higher complex modes, namely, the higher animals. The whole of nature is *animata;* not in the sense that things we call inanimate, like grains of sand, are really alive, but in the sense that for every such finite mode under the attribute *extensio*, however lowly, there is a corresponding "idea" in infinite substance under the attribute *cogitatio*.[17] Living things as biology investigates them, that is, living things *considered as bodies,* are not animated at all in Spinoza's theoretical sense. Indeed, the biological differences between living things and non-living ones, according to Spinoza, are to be understood in terms of the fundamentally Cartesian physics he expounded in the lemmata to EII, P13 S. That a body is animated, in Spinoza's theoretical sense, means that the very same thing which, under the attribute *extensio*, constitutes a body, under the attribute *cogitatio* constitutes an idea corresponding to that body. Living things in the biological sense are therefore no more *animatae* in Spinoza's theoretical sense than non-living ones, although the ideas corresponding to them (*"mentes"* in Spinoza's technical sense) are more complex and adequate.

This may perhaps be made a little clearer by examining Spinoza's view of the nature of human minds. His doctrine that each and every

---

[17] This amplifies and corrects a rash assertion of mine that "while acknowledging that all the finite modes of nature are in diverse degrees animated (*animata*), Spinoza did not jump to the conclusion that for every material object (*corpus*) there is a corresponding mind (*mens*) " . . . in M. Grene (ed.) *Spinoza: A Collection of Critical Essays* (Garden City: Anchor Books, 1973), 248. In Spinoza's theoretical sense of *"mens"* there *is* a *mens* corresponding to each *corpus* (EII, P13,5). But there are no minds in the everyday nontheoretical sense except as corresponding to complex bodies of comparatively great *potentia agendi*. I owe this correction to Martha Kneale, in correspondence.

individual human mind, or rather its primary constituent, is the idea of a human body actually existing (EII, P11-P13) is on the face of it absurd. For the phrase "human mind," as Spinoza and everybody else uses it, stands for a human being inasmuch as he engages in mental operations, and "idea" as he and his contemporaries used it, stands not for what engages in mental operations, but for that by which mental operations are conducted. Spinoza, however, was not oblivious of this. His system provided him with a substance to which the ideas primarily constituting a given individual human mind can be ascribed as modes: namely, the infinite substance itself. And so, when he speaks of a human mind as subject of ideas—as *percipiens*—he commonly speaks, not of a *mens humana* simply, but of "*Deus . . . quatenus humanae mentis essentiam constituit*" (EII, P11 C *et passim*).

This is offensive to atheists and theists alike: to atheists because it treats human minds as unintelligible except as modes of an infinite mind; and to theists because it not only treats the contents of the divine mind as of the same nature as those of finite minds—namely, ideas—but also ascribes the whole contents of every human mind, bad and good, directly to God as subject. According to this conception, as Spinoza pointed out to Oldenburg, each and every human mind must be related to the divine mind in a way that corresponds exactly to the way in which the human body that is its object is related to the physical universe as a whole.[18] Just as each human body, like a particle of blood in the bloodstream, "must be considered, as part of the whole universe, to accord with the whole of which it is a part (*cum suo toto convenire*) and to cohere with the other [parts]," so each human mind, having a human body as its object, is the infinite power of thinking in which *Deus sive Natura* also consists; "not as infinite, and perceiving all nature, however, but as finite, namely inasmuch as it perceives only a human body; and for this reason I conclude (*statuo*) that human minds are part of the same infinite intellect."[19]

To the objection, already anticipated, that the infinite physical universe and the infinite divine intellect cannot be the same thing under two really distinct attributes, because the infinite physical universe exists in its own right, whereas the infinite system of ideas corresponding to that universe needs a thinker (*cogitans*) to think it, Spinoza's reply is that it is a delusion that the physical universe, as a system of bodies the processes in which are related by transient causation, does

---

[18] EP. 32 (20 Nov. 1665), Gebhardt IV, 171-74; Wolf (a), 210-212.
[19] EP. 32, Gebhardt IV, 173, 174; Wolf (a), 211, 212.

exist in its own right. The physical universe, so understood, is *natura naturata*—and *natura naturata* is a system of modes that is as it is because it is immanently caused by itself as *natura naturans*.[20] Infinite substance is *causa sui:* that is, it is God or Nature *naturans* eternally and immanently causing itself as *naturata*. This view of things, which was rare even in the seventeenth century, is not so much rejected as forgotten today, when the suggestion that a relation intelligibly describable as causal might be reflexive would generally be dismissed out of hand. But that is one more reason why Spinoza is hard for any twentieth century philosopher to understand, and why so many interpretations of his work in our time systematically disregard some of his plainest statements.

Denying, as he does, that the physical universe as a system of physical processes related by transient causation exists in its own right, Spinoza could assert that a system of ideas corresponded exactly to it in order and connection, and at the same time concede that no system of ideas—or modes of substance under the attribute *cogitatio,* can exist without a thinker (*cogitans*). Both physical and mental processes, as *natura naturata* expressed in two really distinct attributes, require a *natura naturans*, expressed under these same distinct attributes as their immanent cause. Strictly, a human mind is not a complex inadequate idea having as its object an existing human body, but rather, as we have seen, it is God, inasmuch as he constitutes the (actual) essence of such an idea; but in the same way, a human body is not strictly a complex finite mode under the attribute of extension having as its *causa transiens* other finite modes under the same attribute, but rather God or nature, inasmuch as it constitutes the actual essence of such a body.

Curiously, Spinoza did not consider it necessary even to mention what to many in our day is a serious difficulty, much less to try to remove it. That difficulty is as follows. Whereas a complex finite mode under the attribute *extensio* can obviously be a physical whole relatively independent physically of the infinite physical whole of which it is a part, because a physical whole is constituted solely by relations of contiguity between its adjacent parts and of causal interaction between processes in those parts, it appears that a complex finite mode under the attribute *cogitatio* cannot be a mental whole relatively independent mentally of the mental whole of which it is a part, because a mental whole is constituted, not by contiguity and

---

[20] EI, P29 S. Cf. Gueroult I, 345.

causal interaction between the various ideas that constitute it, although those relations exist in it, but by those ideas being ideas of the same subject or *res cognitans*. In Spinoza's terms, the relation of immanent causation between all the finite modes under the attribute *extensio* and *natura naturans* under that attribute is *not* what makes the whole physical modal system a single *cosmos;* but unless one accepts a bundle theory of mind (which Spinoza wisely did not) what makes the whole mental modal system into a single mind is that all those finite modes are modes of God: that is, that they are all immanently caused by the same *natura naturans*. And if that is so, finite complex ideas cannot form finite *mentes;* for they too are modes of the same infinite subject. Mental identity, unlike physical identity, seems to involve identity of subject, that is, of immanent cause. And Spinoza provides only one such subject. Irreverently, what he needs is a theory of divine multiple personality—one in which a comprehensive infinite consciousness can subsist in the same subject simultaneously with an multitude of different finite consciousnesses.

We can now return to the topic of dualism, and conclude. The following catalogue of propositions maintained by Spinoza would suffice to convict almost any philosopher of dualism. He held: (1) that *extensio* and *cogitatio* are attributes of substance, although, contrary to Descartes, each one constitutes an infinite essence; (2) that *extensio* and *cogitatio* are really distinct; (3) that each attribute of a substance by itself, and without the help of anything else, constitutes the essence of that substance; (4) that *extensio* and *cogitatio* are attributes both of *Deus sive Natura* and of individual human beings, who are finite modes of *Deus sive Natura;* and (5) that a full scientific account of *Deus sive Natura* with respect to *extensio* and *cogitatio* must be dual, the accounts under both exhibiting the same order and connection of modes, but neither account being reducible to the other, or to an account in terms of some third attribute.

Whether Spinoza's acceptance of these five propositions suffices to convict him of dualism turns on the character of the further proposition by means of which they are reconciled with the antidualist position that *res extensa* and *res cogitans* are not distinct substances but the same substance. That proposition, as we have seen, is that attributes may be really distinct and yet be attributes of the same substance. Is it of such a character that the antidualist position it enables Spinoza to take is more of words than of substance, like the antiheliocentrism that Descartes' doctrine of the relativity of motion enabled him to profess? Or does it so transform the issue between dualists and antidualists that Spinoza can fairly claim to be a substantive antidualist?

As interpreted by Spinoza's greatest commentator, Martial Gueroult, the cardinal proposition is such that Spinoza's antidualism is as much a form of words as Descartes' antiheliocentrism. Spinoza's *Deus sive Natura*, according to Gueroult, is a "union in one unique substance" of "substances of one attribute."[21] Each attribute, taken in itself, constitutes the infinite essence of a substance of one attribute; but no such substances, taken by themselves can exist; for, since there can be no more than one substance of any given attribute, the necessary existence of a substance having infinite attributes—that is, all the attributes without exception—excludes their existence. However, each of the various attributes in which *Deus sive Natura* consists constitutes a distinct infinite essence; hence the unity of *Deus sive Natura* is a unity of what, if they existed independently, would be substances of one attribute, the modes of which exhibit the same order and connection. It is, I think, unnecessary to insist further that Spinoza's infinite substance, as Gueroult understands it, is a magnification to infinity of Descartes' dual natured man.[22] The fundamental differences between them are three: (1) Spinoza's God is not necessarily confined to two attributes, although it has the two Descartes assigned to man; (2) those attributes are taken to express infinite and not finite essences, and hence their union is not the work of a creator, but follows necessarily from the nature of infinite substance itself; and (3) the real distinction of the attributes is maintained more rigorously by Spinoza than by Descartes, and all interaction is rejected. I think it will be agreed that these points on which Spinoza admittedly disagrees fundamentally with Descartes, do not make him less a dualist. A necessary union of really distinct substances of one attribute is not less dualist than a contingent created one.

If, despite Gueroult's authority, we interpret Spinoza as holding that the really distinct attributes of *Deus sive Natura* all constitute one and the same essence, the issue becomes more obscure.[23] On this interpretation, we are confronted with a radically new and unex-

---

[21] "Si les *Propositions* 9, 10 et son *Scolie* rendent possible la construction du concept de Dieu, ... n'obtiennent-elles pas ce résultat par une sorte de renversement des affirmations premières en niant la substantialité de chaque attribut ... ? ... Cependant ... ce renversement n'est pas aussi total qu'il y paraît d'abord, car l'attribut reste un *être substantial*. Certes, dans la mesure où il est l'essence d' *une* substance, ou *une* essence de substance, il ne se confond pas avec l'essence de *la* substance qui comprend en elle l'*infinité* des essences de substance" (Gueroult, I, 165). The expressions in quotation marks in the text are translated from Gueroult's heading to ch. 4 sect. 1 (I, 598).

[22] Gueroult, I, 229-239.

[23] Cf. A. Donagan in Grene, 179-181.

plored concept of essence: as something that can be wholly "constituted" or (in Spinoza's significant alternative term) "expressed" by really distinct attributes.

Even if it is accepted as intelligible that the same essence should be constituted by a plurality of really distinct attributes, so that Spinoza's *Deus sive Natura* is not a mere union of substances of one attribute, but a genuine substance constituted or expressed by really distinct attributes, the principal implications of the real distinction of attributes would remain. And that is what deprives the antidualists of our day—chiefly materialists—of any comfort in Spinoza.

A final *coda*. The Cartesian system is often objected to, not only as being dualistic, but as, even in the realm of created substances, assigning primacy to *res cogitans*. In two respects, this charge must be granted. Descartes' method ensures epistemological primacy to *res cogitans;* and in his *Passions de l'Âme* he is concerned to show how, despite the interaction of mind and body in human beings, the will can for the most part control the passions that are sustained by movements of the animal spirits. And it is true that Spinoza scornfully dismissed this sort of thing. At the same time, there is not a little evidence that Descartes was a good deal more concerned with improving the quality of physical life through medicine and applied science than Spinoza was. Despite his physical determinism, and his repudiation of all interaction between modes under distinct attributes, Spinoza showed comparatively little practical interest in anything but what he called *intellectus emendatio*. There is a theoretical reason for this in his system, into which I cannot now enter, and which is brought out in the key theorem on which his proof of immortality depends, namely EII, P8. In that theorem, Spinoza maintains that his doctrine that "*ordo et connexio idearum idem est ac ordo et connexio rerum*" (EII, p7), contrary to superficial expectation, entails that modes under the attribute *extensio* that are merely possible must be actually "comprehended" in the mode under the attribute *cogitatio* which he calls *Dei infinita idea*. The consequence is that individual human minds, which are ideas of human bodies actually existing, to a greater or less extent can survive the death of the existing bodies of which they are ideas (EV, P23). In Spinoza's philosophy, the doctrine that part of the human mind remains (*remanet*) after the body has been destroyed is much more important than is that of the immortality of the soul in Descartes's.

The University of Chicago

7 OBJECTS, IDEAS, AND "MINDS": COMMENTS ON SPINOZA'S THEORY OF MIND

Margaret D. Wilson

I

Both specialist commentators and writers of textbooks commonly take Spinoza to have staked out a position on "the mind-body problem" of modern western philosophy. There is, of course, much disagreement on how his position should be characterized. Some are willing to endorse such labels as "a sort of materialism," a "double-aspect theory," or whatever. Others deny that Spinoza's position fits neatly into any of the commonly accepted categories—though they may suggest *limited affinities* with central state materialism, the Strawsonian theory of persons, and so forth. In the recent English-language literature, at least, critics who hold different views about how the position should be described, tend remarkably to agree in regarding it as admirable.[1]

---

[1] Some representative recent articles are the following: Stuart Hampshire, "A Kind of Materialism," Presidential Address in *Proceedings of the Eastern Division of the American Philosophical Association*, 1970; Wallace I. Matson, "Spinoza's Theory of Mind," and Douglas Odegard, "The Body Identical with the Human Mind: A Problem in Spinoza's Philosophy," both in Maurice Mandelbaum and Eugene Freeman, editors, *Spinoza: Essays in Interpretation* (La Salle, Illinois: Open Court, 1975); Errol E. Harris, "Body-Mind Relation in Spinoza's Philosophy," in *Spinoza's Metaphysics: Essays in Critical Appreciation*, ed. J. B. Wilbur (Assen, The Netherlands: Van Gorcum, 1976). Harris' careful essay touches on several of the problems in Spinoza's theory that I will examine below, as does Odegard's to a lesser degree. Both are, in my view, overly conciliatory to Spinoza. A non-conciliatory critic, whose detailed criticisms occasionally parallel those to be developed in this paper, is H. Barker, "Notes on the Second Part of Spinoza's *Ethics*," Parts I, II, and III, *Mind*, vol. XLVII (1938), reprinted in S. Paul Kashap, ed., *Studies in Spinoza: Critical and Interpretive Essays* (Berkeley: University of California Press, 1972). I particularly admire the spirit of the following statement of Barker's (though I don't agree with all the details of the reasoning leading up to it):

While I admire Spinoza's philosophical system very much, I do not think it includes an admirable position on "the mind-body problem." In this paper I am going to argue that what passes for an important theory of the mind-body relation in Spinoza is an obviously implausible candidate for that role when rightly interpreted. (I also hold, though I will not explicitly argue the point, that the theory is not aptly assimilated to any influential present-day positions.) My procedure will be to consider seriously the implications of an absolutely fundamental tenet of Spinoza's system: the identification of *minds* with *God's ideas of* finite things insofar as they are finite—and vice versa. I will try to show that this understanding of what a "mind" is does not yield a plausible or tenable account of the human mind in its relation to the human body, despite Spinoza's attempt to use the notion in this way. Contrary to what some commentators have said, Spinoza is unable to reconcile his theory of "minds" with any intelligible conception of mental representation, or any coherent and credible account of the scope of conscious awareness. Thus my objection will not be the familiar (and still important) one that it is difficult really to comprehend Spinoza's conception of the relation between the corresponding modes of different attributes. My contention is that *however* this relation be conceived, the theory of "minds" has unacceptable consequences when construed as the basis for a theory about human minds[2]—as Spinoza tries to construe it.

To focus attention on the significance of Spinoza's identification of minds with God's ideas, I will begin by sketching a few points of comparison and contrast between the Spinozistic position and Leibniz's theory of complete concepts. As a further preliminary, I will also point out some of the major differences between Spinoza's "minds"

In the opening sentence of the scholium [to E II, P13] Spinoza claims that we can now understand what is meant by the union of mind and body, and the commentators seem inclined to endorse his claim and to think that in his doctrine of body and mind he has made a great advance upon the other Cartesians. I cannot see that he deserves these praises. The statements that the mind is the idea of the body and the body is the one object of mind do not really throw any light upon the relationship— naturally, since they are not true. (Kashap, 148–149)

[2] Although my way of speaking throughout the paper may suggest otherwise, I do not really mean to imply that *only* human beings are subjects of consciousness and the other mental qualities that give rise to "the mind-body problem." My assumption is rather that many, many things that have "minds" in Spinoza's system (all the tennis balls in the world, for instance) are not in any degree self-conscious, sentient, decision-makers like ourselves (though whales, for example, might be).

and Cartesian *res cogitantes*. The purpose of this section will be to clarify the nature of Spinoza's conception, and to insist (particularly) on some of its more unusual features. Subsequent sections will examine in detail some obstacles to construing Spinoza's position as a plausible response to the traditional mind-body problem.

II

In Leibniz's philosophy there are major metaphysical differences between God's ideas, and existing particulars, the ideas of which are in God. In the first place, the ideas *are* in God, whereas existing (finite) particulars are merely God's *creatures* (and not "in" him as their metaphysical subject). In the second place, there is in God the idea of every *possible* entity—and according to Leibniz the realm of possibles is much wider than the realm of actual entities. Hence some of God's ideas have corresponding objects, but others (infinitely many) do not. Third, God's ideas and particular entities belong to different ontological categories: at least some particular finite existing entities are *substances*, whereas (I take it) Leibniz did not think of God's ideas of substances—the "complete concepts"—as themselves substances.

There is, on the other hand, one important sort of intimate relation between complete concepts (on Leibniz's theory) and their existing objects (if any). The complete concept (as its designation suggests) must "in some manner comprise" everything true of its object.[3] In at least one place Leibniz relates this claim to the doctrine of God's omniscience.[4] And of course it also follows from God's omniscience that *every* existent has its complete concept in God.

In Spinoza's system God's ideas are (we may say) metaphysically closer to their objects than in Leibniz's. In the first place, the objects like the ideas are merely modes of God: they too are "in God." Second, Spinoza seems to deny that there are *more* ideas in God than there are objects to correspond to them. (Sometimes he seems to hold that the realms of the possible and the actual are coextensive.[5] At

---

[3] See, e.g., G. W. Leibniz, *Philosophische Schriften*, ed. Gerhardt, 7 vols. (Berlin: 1875–90), vol. IV, 433 (*Discourse on Metaphysics*, §viii). Leibniz explicitly construes the complete concept of an individual as allowing derivation of all past, present, and future states of that individual's world. This important feature of Leibniz's theory, bound up with his theory of truth, provides a fundamental limitation on the comparison I am going to suggest between the complete concept theory and Spinoza's theory of God's ideas of particulars.
[4] Gerhardt, II, 131; cf. *ibid.*, 49, 50.
[5] See Gebhardt II, 60, 76. The references are to E I, P16 and P135.

other times he affirms there are "ideas of non-existent objects," but holds that they too somehow have correspondents ["essences"] in the attributes other than thought.[6]) Further, whereas God's ideas and their objects belong to different ontological categories for Leibniz, for Spinoza both are of course included in the *same* category, as modes of God.

Spinoza's denial of metaphysical distance between God's ideas and their objects (in the first instance, modes of extension) is indeed thorough enough to yield the conclusion that they are in some sense *the same thing*. In the Scholium to the crucial proposition, E II, P7 ("The order and connection of ideas is the same as the order and connection of things"), he writes:

> Here, before we go further, we must recall to memory what we showed above; namely, that whatever can be perceived by the infinite understanding, as constituting the essence of substance, all of that belongs to only one substance, and consequently that substance thinking and substance extended is one and the same substance, which is comprehended now under this attribute, and now under that. So also a mode of extension, and the idea of that mode is one and the same thing, but expressed in two ways [*modis*]; which indeed the Hebrews seem to have seen as if through a cloud, who assert that God, the understanding of God, and the things understood by it are one and the same. For example, a circle existing in nature, and the idea of the existing circle, which is also in God, is one and the same thing, which is explained [*explicatur*] by different attributes. . . . (Gebhardt II, 90)

Admittedly, it is difficult really to grasp the sense of the claim that a circle existing (in God), and God's idea of it "is one and the same thing, *quae per diversa attributa explicatur.*" What is important here is that the assertion of identity between a mode of thought and its object derives from a conception about the relation of God's understanding to the world—a conception which makes this relation much closer and more intimate than in the more traditional Leibnizian system.

This lack of metaphysical space between God's ideas and their objects is, I take it, an important condition behind Spinoza's calling the former the "minds" of the latter (see the Demonstration of E II, P12). The two need to be in some sense *united* for this terminology to

---

[6] E II, P8 (Gebhardt II, 90–91). I confess I find this Proposition one of the most baffling in the *Ethics*, especially when compared with those mentioned in note 5.

make much sense. Still, talking of God's ideas as the "minds" of their objects might in itself constitute no more than a curious terminological move. What makes it more than this is Spinoza's identification of God's idea of the human body with *the human mind* (see, e.g., E II, P12). This identification carries with it a commitment to the relevance of the theory of God's ideas to traditional issues and assumptions about mentality. I am going to argue that the attempted identification has thoroughly unmanageable consequences, and leads Spinoza to confusion and incoherence.

Now we must take note of an important point of similarity between Spinoza's position on God's ideas and that of Leibniz. For Spinoza, as for Leibniz, God's knowledge of particulars is infinite and unlimited. There is no particular object of which God lacks an idea (E II, P3), and God's idea of any particular includes knowledge of whatever happens in its object (E II, P9C). It follows that the human mind will contain a knowledge of *every* occurrence in the human body. It further follows that all bodies whatsoever are "minded" in just the sense that the human body is. Spinoza explicitly draws these conclusions. Thus Proposition 12 of Part II reads:

> Whatever occurs [*contingit*] in the object of the idea constituting the human Mind, that must be perceived by the human Mind, or there necessarily is given an idea of the thing in the Mind: That is, if the object of the idea constituting the human Mind is a body, nothing can occur in this body, which is not perceived by the Mind (Gebhardt II, 95).

The Scholium to the following proposition tells us that

> ... these things we have so far proved are completely common [*admodum communia sunt*], and do not pertain more to men than to other individuals, all of which, though in different degrees, are animated [*animata*]. For of anything at all, there is necessarily given in God an idea, of which God is the cause, in the same way as of the idea of the human Body; and hence, whatever we say of the idea of the human Body, that necessarily is to be said of the idea of anything at all (Gebhardt II, 96).

(Spinoza goes on to explain that one idea is superior to another when the body that is the object of the former "contains more reality" than the body that is the object of the latter. I will return to this passage later.)

Of course these brief remarks do not pretend to exhibit fully the relations and differences between Leibnizian complete concepts and

Spinoza's "minds." To do so would require consideration of such highly complex matters as the differences between the two philosophers' views about the reality of extension, the possibility of interaction between finite particulars, and the distinction between confused and adequate knowledge.[7] (Spinoza, for example, both maintains that whatever occurs in a given body is perceived by its "mind," and *denies* that God has *adequate* knowledge of a given particular insofar as He constitutes its "mind"—since adequate knowledge may require knowledge of external causes as well.) For present purposes, the main points are just the following. First, Spinoza facilitates identifying certain of God's ideas as the "minds" of their objects by not allowing the metaphysical space between those ideas and existent particulars that one finds in Leibniz's system. Second, he holds that human minds are just a sub-class of these "minds." Third, in virtue of being God's ideas, these "minds" have certain things in common with the Leibnizian complete concepts. In particular, no existent fails to "have" one, and everything that occurs in an object is comprised in or (as Spinoza rather puts it) perceived by its "mind."

We may now briefly contrast the features of Spinoza's "minds," as so far presented, with those ascribed to the human mind by Descartes. Everyone knows, of course, that on Descartes's theory the human mind is a substance (*res cogitans*), whereas Spinoza regards human minds as modes. But this is barely the beginning. Descartes's conception of mind rests squarely on the indubitable self-consciousness provided by the *cogito*. Descartes repeatedly claims to have established that "there's nothing in me, that is, in my mind, of which I'm not in some manner conscious."[8] But it can hardly be claimed that I'm conscious of all, or even of most, of what occurs in my body. And I don't think it will do to say cheerfully that, after all, Spinoza thinks of the mind's ideas in pretty much the same way as Descartes, *only he recognizes unconscious ones*. Consider the force of "everything that occurs in my body": this carries right down to changes of the relation of the simplest parts—the smallest molecules, the atoms, the electrons of each of the millions of cells. I don't think one can even make sense of the claim that I have something like Cartesian ideas of these things

---

[7] See also note 3, above. Leibniz himself, incidentally, explicitly criticized Spinoza's identification of minds with God's ideas. He argues, among other things, that mind is unlike an idea in being an active, changing entity (whereas an idea is unchanging and abstract). See Georges Friedmann, *Leibniz et Spinoza* (nouvelle edition) (Paris: Gallimard [Bibliothèque des Idées], 1962), 171 ff.

[8] For a detailed discussion of this point, with references, see my *Descartes* (London: Routledge and Kegan Paul, 1978), Ch. IV, §2.

(without, however, being conscious of them, or explicitly conscious, or whatever).

Similarly, a Cartesian *res cogitans* entertains or has in it ideas of very many different things, existent or otherwise. These are just the things it is aware of thinking about. On the one hand, as just noted, these do not include "everything that happens in the human body." On the other hand, they do include many, many things other than the human body. However, the idea that constitutes the human mind is, for Spinoza, just the idea of the human body; the ideas included in it are all ideas of parts, processes, or aspects of the human body. Also, a Cartesian *res cogitans* can represent its objects (the objects of its thought) accurately or otherwise. But Spinoza's "minds," being just God's conceptions of particulars, cannot be inaccurate (although they can, as already observed, be inadequate).[9]

Finally, a Cartesian *res cogitans* is an entity supposed to explain the capacity of certain other entities (live human bodies) for rational behavior. If an entity does not behave rationally, that is grounds for denying it has a *res cogitans*. But Spinoza's position seems to entail that there is *no* relation between whether or not a thing behaves rationally, and its possession of a "mind." It seems to entail (even) that there is no relation between whether a thing's behavior and constitution suggests *sentience*, and whether it has a "mind." Once again, to say of something that it posseses a "mind" is just to say that the idea of it is in God.

Descartes' position on the mind-body issue is notoriously beset with difficulties. Still, the theory of *res cogitantes* does recognize and take account of certain propositions about the mental that seem either self-evidently true or fundamental to the whole concept. These include most (I do not say all) of the features just mentioned: that the mind (in a straightforward and common sense of the terms) *represents* or *has knowledge of* external bodies; that it *is ignorant of* much that happens in "its" body; that having a mind is associated with thinking and being conscious; that mentality is recognizable from behavior of a certain sort, and the absence of mentality from "behavior" of other sorts. Will not Spinoza's theory of "minds" simply *fail to be a theory of the mental* if it carries the denial of all or most of these propositions? More exactly will it not fail to make sense of the specific phenomena

---

[9] See E II, P32 and P33. It is notorious that Spinoza has serious difficulties in providing a coherent and consistent account of false ideas. See, e.g., Thomas Carson Mark, *Spinoza's Theory of Truth* (New York: Columbia University Press, 1972), and my review of Mark in *The Journal of Philosophy*, vol. 72, no. 1 (January, 1975), 22–25.

of human mentality by attempting to construe the human mind as just a circumscribed piece of God's omniscience?

In the next two sections I will consider two parts of a possible response to this challenge on Spinoza's behalf. In section III I consider an attempted defense of the claim that Spinoza *is* able to develop out of his theory of "minds" an account of knowledge or representation of the external world—one that captures the relatively straightforward Cartesian notion while improving on the Cartesian theory. I will try to show that the defense fails utterly as a defense, though I am not concerned to deny that it may correctly explain Spinoza's *intentions*. In section IV I consider versions of the suggestion that Spinoza does want to draw commonsensical distinctions between human minds and mere "minds"—particularly with respect to consciousness—and that his system provides him with adequate materials for doing so. I will argue in detail that his system provides him with no adequate materials for such a distinction. I believe that these arguments and their conclusions show that Spinoza's theory of "minds" provides little basis for a coherent, plausible position on the traditional, post-Cartesian mind-body problem.

III

It is a classical feature of human minds (one particularly stressed by Descartes) that they are able to represent or exhibit to themselves "external objects," whether near or remote; whether existent, possible, or altogether "unreal." The question of how minds do this has, of course, long been considered significant. And it has long been supposed that the answer—at least for many sorts of representation—will have something to do with the human brain and its causal relations to the sense organs and to objects outside the human body. But the question of how it is that representation occurs (or of what goes on in the body when it does) has traditionally been kept distinct from the question of what it is that is represent*ed*, of what is the "object" of the thought or idea. The answer to the latter question is supposed to be in some sense unproblematic, and more or less independent of theory. The object of my thought is just what I'm thinking of—and surely *I* know what *that* is. Answering the former question is generally supposed to require both theorizing and physiological investigation.

Now suppose one identifies the human mind (as Spinoza does) with an idea in God *of the human body*. Can one still make sense of the claim that the human mind represents to itself objects other than the human body? Well, given that states of the human body are causally dependent on states of external bodies, one can develop a *sort* of account of representation: the one that Spinoza in fact gives.[10] Just as states of a given body may have explanations involving external bodies, so many of the ideas that constitute the corresponding "mind" will have their explanation in other, "external," ideas. We may stipulate that such dependent ideas "represent" the objects of the external ideas.

The question I want to raise is whether "representation" will do as an account of the sort of representation classically attributed to human minds. It seems obvious to me that it will not. According to Spinoza's account, my mind "represents" *every* object or physical state that causally affects my own body. So, five minutes ago my mind was "representing" a number of air molecules, the movement of Earth in space, cosmic radiation, etc. But (I would claim) none of these things were objects of my thought in the ordinary sense—even if some degree of non-conscious representation is allowed in the latter category. Further it follows straightforwardly from Spinoza's theory that *every "mind" "represents"* (if you doubt this, look again at the proof of E II, P16). For a "mind" "represents" something just in case its body is causally affected by that thing. And of course all finite modes are in constant causal interaction with other finite modes. It seems then that "representing" is in no way a sufficient condition of representing.

This point can be made still clearer if we look at the argument offered as a partial defense of Spinoza in a well-known paper by Daisie Radner.[11] Radner suggests that Spinoza's theory of representation was meant to overcome certain difficulties of the Cartesian account, according to which an idea represents an object by resembling it. Among the alleged difficulties is the consideration that since thought and extension have radically different natures, it seems that modes of the two couldn't have enough in common to "resemble" each other.[12] According to Radner, this difficulty is overcome by Spinoza in the following way. The mode of extension which is the object of a given "mind," and the mode of thought which is the "mind," are "related as formal to objective reality" (I do not think she explains these familiar but obscure scholastic terms in any non-tautologous way). Then,

> The key to Spinoza's theory of the nature of representation is his distinction between the object of the idea and that which the

---

[10] E II, P17 S, E III P27, Dm. Radner's article discussed immediately below gives further references.

[11] "Spinoza's Theory of Ideas," *The Philosophical Review*, vol. LXXX (July, 1971), 338–359.

[12] *Ibid.*, 345.

idea represents. The term "the object of the idea" is not synonymous with the term "that which is represented by the idea," although in some cases the two terms have the same reference. The object and the thing represented stand in two different relations to the idea. The relation between the idea and its object is explicated in terms of the distinction between objective and formal reality. The relation between the idea and what it represents is explicated in terms of the resemblance of the thing represented to the object of the idea.[13]

But what, we must ask, is the relevant "relation of resemblance of the thing represented to the object of the idea"? Radner notes that for Spinoza (as for Descartes) what is present in the effect must have existed in the cause. Hence the affections of the human body which have external bodies as their causes, must "have something in common with external bodies."[14] Because they do, ideas of these affections of the human body (ideas in the human mind) may be said to represent the external bodies.

> For example, suppose I have an idea which represents the sun to me. This idea is not a mental picture of the sun. It is the objective reality of an affection of my body, an affection which is produced by the action of the sun upon the parts of my body. Since the sun is cause of this bodily affection, and since there must be something in common between cause and effect (E I, P3), there is something in common between the sun and my bodily affection. My idea represents the sun to me, by virtue of the fact that its object is an affection which has something in common with the sun (op. cit., 350).

This attempt to clarify Spinoza's position seems still to allow us to conclude that my mind represents object O just in case O causally interacts with my body. Further, my mind represents O merely "by virtue of the fact that" O has something in common with the effect it occasions in my body. But Spinoza's theory is then open to charges of being too vague as well as charges of being much too broad. For, obviously, *every* candidate for being a physical cause has "something in common with" every candidate for being a physical effect. Such minimal resemblance does not seem likely to provide any useful clarification of the notion of the effect's *representing* the cause.

---

[13] *Ibid.*, 346.
[14] *Ibid.*, 349.

It should be stressed that the critical point I have just been developing is not the same as either of two other objections that have sometimes been urged against Spinoza (and that are discussed by Radner at the beginning of her article). Thus, some critics have objected that Spinoza uses the term 'idea' ambiguously (and equivocates on it in arguments).[15] On one of these usages 'idea' is tied (definitionally?) to the body of which the idea is the "mind"; an idea can have no other object than this body. On the other usage an idea is a representation or concept, which may be of something external. Now perhaps Spinoza *is* guilty of equivocation on 'idea of' in proofs, but that is not my point. My point is that he is unable to provide within his system a satisfactory conception of the human mind's consciously representing external bodies. This is one major respect in which the theory of "minds" (God's ideas) fails to provide an acceptable model of human mentality. Another objection, also different from mine, lies in the claim that Spinoza confuses "the process by which we come to have ideas with the relation that an idea has with its object."[16] In other words, he fails to notice that a particular brain state might be a necessary condition for our having a particular sort of thought, without the thought having the brain state as its object, in any ordinary sense of "object." In my opinion, this objection underestimates Spinoza's intelligence, and also misses the fundamental point that Spinoza's "minds" are God's ideas of particular physical modes. The problem is not that Spinoza has succumbed to such an elementary sort of "confusion." It is rather that he falsely thinks he can handle the classical (and Cartesian) concept of representation within the peculiar theocentric parameters of his own theory.

IV

I turn now to the question whether Spinoza's theory of "minds" can admit of rational distinctions between conscious and non-conscious entities, or between conscious and non-conscious states of a particular individual. But perhaps we should ask first whether he wants to make such a distinction. (Perhaps he really *intends* to hold that all things are in some degree conscious, and that the mind is in some degree conscious of all that happens in the body?) The textual evidence relating to these latter questions is not plentiful.[17] I will con-

---

[15] *Ibid.*, 338–340.
[16] *Ibid.*, 340.
[17] Although Spinoza speaks of the mind as "perceiving" everything that happens in its body, this need not imply anything about conscious awareness. (Leibniz, of course, uses the term "perception" even for the states of those minds that wholly lack consciousness.)

sider four texts that have been presented as evidence that Spinoza did recognize and make room for the ordinary distinction between conscious and non-conscious states or beings. I will argue that the first two are quite inconclusive on this point. The second two do seem to support the claim that Spinoza wanted to distinguish conscious ideas (or "minds") from non-conscious ones. Unfortunately, neither of these shows how such a distinction can intelligibly and plausibly be drawn within his system. Further the two are inconsistent with each other on the question of what is necessary for consciousness to be present. I conclude that Spinoza's system provides no plausible, clear or reasoned view on this fundamental aspect of the traditional mind-body problem.

All four of the texts I will consider have been pointed out by E. M. Curley, either in writing or in discussion. Curley deserves credit for giving careful, critical attention to the problem of consciousness in Spinoza's philosophy—even though his conclusions are, on my view, overly optimistic.

In *Spinoza's Metaphysics* Curley holds that Letter 58 (Gebhardt IV, 266) "implies quite plainly that such things as stones do not possess consciousness."[18] This seems to me an overreading of the text. In this letter Spinoza asks his correspondent to "conceive if you please that [a] stone, while it continues in motion, thinks. . . ." Curley evidently interprets this as an intended counterfactual supposition—which is reasonable but not, I think, strictly required by the text. Curley further suggests that E II, P19 shows that having an idea of an affection of the body isn't sufficient for being conscious of that affection.[19] I find this suggestion even more dubious. E II, P19 reads: "The human Mind does not know the human Body itself, and does not know it to exist, except through ideas of affections, by which the Body is affected" (G II, 107). Curley takes "this as meaning that it is not simply in having an idea of an affection of the body that the mind knows the body" (Curley is taking "knows" to imply "has consciousness of").[20] I don't see this distinction in the text at all. The point Spinoza is making in this proposition is that Gob does not know *the human body itself* insofar as he constitutes the nature of the human mind. Thus the human mind knows the *affections* of the human body, but not the body itself. There is no implied contrast, so far as I can see, between having an idea of an affection and being conscious of that affection.

---

[18] E. M. Curley, *Spinoza's Metaphysics* (Cambridge: Harvard University Press, 1969), 126. See Wolf (a), 295.
[19] *Op. cit.*, 128.
[20] *Ibid*.

However, two propositions of the *Ethics* do contain remarks that suggest Spinoza does recognize some significant distinction between conscious and non-conscious "minds" or states of "minds." The first is E III, P9, the second, E V, P39 (or, more exactly, the Scholium to the latter). Let us examine these two passages in turn, and consider how they might underpin a distinction with respect to consciousness among and within Spinoza's "minds."

Spinoza first speaks of the mind being "conscious of itself" in E III, P9, which reads:

> The mind both insofar as it has clear and distinct [ideas], and insofar as it has confused ideas, endeavors to persevere in its own being for some indefinite duration, and it is conscious of this endeavor (Gebhardt II, 147).

Spinoza first argues for the existence of this endeavor, and then for the claim that the mind is conscious of it. It is the latter proof that interests us. It goes:

> But since the Mind (by Prop. 23, Pt. 2) through the ideas of the affections of the Body necessarily is conscious of itself [*necessario sui sit conscia*], therefore the Mind is (by Prop. 7 of [Pt. III]) conscious of its endeavor (Gebhardt II, 147).

The second proposition referred to here—7 of Part III—tells us that a thing's "endeavor" is just the actual essence of the thing itself. Spinoza seems to take this as sufficient to establish the hypothetical: If a thing is conscious of itself, it is conscious of its endeavor. And evidently E II, P23 is supposed to establish the antecedent with respect to the mind: i.e., to establish that the mind is conscious of itself "through the ideas of the affections of the Body." Now when we turn to E II, P23 itself, we find that it has to do with *ideae idearum*. It says that the mind "only knows [*cognoscit*] itself, insofar as it perceives the ideas of the affections of the Body." The word "conscious" doesn't appear either in the Proposition or the proof. But, reading backward from Part III, we may interpret Spinoza as implying here that the mind is conscious of itself insofar as it knows itself—and it knows itself insofar as it perceives its ideas, or forms second-order ideas of them. If we add the assumption that "consciousness" occurs only when a mind is conscious *of itself*, we get the result that having an idea of 0 is not the same as being conscious, or as being conscious of 0: one must additionally form an idea of one's idea.

Curley regards the doctrine of *ideae idearum* as providing sufficient basis for a distinction between conscious human minds, and other "minds" that are not conscious. He comments,

> We can equate having an idea of an idea with being conscious....
> It is worth noting in this connection that, while every individual
> thing has a "mind" containing ideas of the affections of its body
> (E II, P135), the existence of ideas of ideas is proven only for
> human minds (E II, P20). I infer from this that, although Spinoza
> is willing to assert that everything is animate (in a very odd sense
> of the term), he is not prepared to say that anything except a
> human being is conscious.[21]

I believe (from his preceding discussion) that Curley also wants to hold that the doctrine of *ideae idearum* provides a basis for distinguishing between ideas in the human mind that involve consciousness, and those in the human mind that do not. I want to deny these suggestions.

It is true that E II, P20 is specifically "about" the human mind, in the sense of referring specifically to it. The proposition reads:

> There is given in God an idea, or knowledge [*cognitio*] of the human Mind, which follows in God in the same way, as the idea or knowledge of the human Body (Gebhardt II, 108).

But the specificity is of doubtful significance, given that Propositions 11 through 13 of Part II also refer specifically to the human mind, yet Spinoza *tells* us (in Proposition 13) that they apply not only to men, but to all individuals whatsoever. *And examination of the proof of E II, P20 fails to reveal, I think, any basis for holding that it applies only to the human mind, and not to "minds" generally.* The proof turns on the claim that there must exist in God "an idea of all of his affections, and consequently (by Prop. 11 [of Part II]) of the human Mind." And Proposition 11 is one of those that Spinoza explicitly holds to apply generally, and not just to the human mind. I conclude that there must be in God ideas of all ideas. Hence the doctrine of *ideae idearum* cannot provide the basis for a satisfactory distinction between minds and "minds," or between conscious thought and non-conscious ideas within the human mind—*whether or not* Spinoza himself supposed that it could.[22]

---

[21] *Ibid.*

[22] Peggy Nicholson has suggested to me that Spinoza might intend the following distinction: the ideas of ideas belonging to the human mind are in God in so far as he constitutes the nature of the human mind, whereas the ideas of ideas of non-human minds are in God but not in so far as he constitutes these minds. This is a natural move to try, but I have so far been unable to find textual warrant for it.

If the doctrine of *ideae idearum* does not provide us with a rationale for ascribing consciousness and hence (as it were) special *mentality* to the idea of the human body, is there any other doctrine of the *Ethics* that does provide such a rationale? The one important passage we have not so far considered appears in the Scholium to E V, P39. There Spinoza comments:

> He who, like an infant or a child, has a body that is fit for very few things [*paucissima aptum*], and is very greatly dependent on external causes, has a mind which considered in itself is for the most part conscious of nothing of itself, of God, or of things; and on the other hand, he who has a Body fit for many things, has a Mind which considered in itself is conscious of much of itself, of God and of things.

He continues:

> In this life therefore we should try before all to change the body of infancy into another (insofar as its nature permits, and conduces to this) which is fit for many things, and which is related to a mind [*ad Mentum referatur*] which is conscious of itself, and of God, and of many things; and thus [*sic*] that all which is related to the memory itself, or imagination, is hardly of any moment in comparison to the understanding.... (Gebhardt II, 305)

This passage partly recalls the Scholium to E II, P13 referred to earlier, where Spinoza explains that what distinguishes one "mind" from another, and in particular the human mind from inferior "minds," is that the object of the one is more excellent (or "real") than the object of the other:

> I say ... in general that insofar as any Body is more fit than others to do or suffer many things at once; and insofar as the actions of one body depend more on itself alone, and the less that other bodies concur with it in acting, the mind of that body is more fit for distinctly understanding [*aptior est ad distincte intelligendum*] (Gebhardt II, 97).

The latter passage tells us that Spinoza recognizes *degrees* of excellence and of distinct understanding among "minds"; the former relates this difference to a difference in degrees of "consciousness."

These passages may seem promising, in that they at least take the plausible step of relating the quality of a given "mind" to the degree of complexity of "its" body. So maybe the theory will come out right after all: aren't beings with nervous systems and sense organs more "complex" than those without them? Without attempting to address this rhetorical question, or to examine all the many puzzling features of the two passages, I will try to show briefly why they do not enable us to attribute to Spinoza a coherent and plausible position on the mind-body issue.

First, it is hard to see how the linking of consciousness with intellect or distinct ideas in these two passages can be reconciled with E III, P9 and its proof, which we have previously cited. In E III, P9 Spinoza says that the mind "necessarily is conscious of itself" through the ideas of the affections of the Body," and specifically links this consciousness to the possession of "confused" as well as "clear and distinct" ideas. This suggests that if Spinoza does regard the human mind as distinguished from other "minds" with respect to consciousness, he has no *consistent* account of this distinction. Second, setting aside the issue of internal consistency, we must observe that Spinoza offers us no way at all of understanding why the adult body's fitness for many things should be linked to *consciousness* in the adult mind. It is not even very clear what "conscious" *means* in E V, P39, nor how it might relate to the phenomenon of sentience and subjectivity that seem to provide the core of the traditional mind-body problem. (What does *consciousness* have to do with the priority of understanding over memory and imagination? Do we really want to say that a child "is for the most part conscious of nothing of itself, of God, or of things"?) Finally, even if one does accept the linkage of consciousness with distinct ideas, it turns out that one *still* has not found a way of identifying a subset of God's ideas ("minds") as peculiarly *mental*. For, contrary to what E V, P39 may seem to suggest, Spinoza's principles in fact commit him to the view that every "mind" whatsoever possesses distinct or adequate ideas. Let us see why this is so.

Propositions 38 and 39 of Part II read as follows:
Prop. 38—Those things which are common to all, and which are equally in the part and in the whole, can only be adequately conceived (Gebhardt II, 118).

Prop. 39—That which is common and proper to the human Body, and to any external bodies, by which the human Body is affected, and which is equally in any of their parts and in the whole, of this also there will be an adequate idea in the mind (*Ibid.*).

The proofs of these Propositions turn on the claim that the ideas of the affections of the human body are adequate in God insofar as he constitutes the nature of the human mind. But this claim is ultimately based on Propositions 12 and 13 of Part II, which (as we've seen) are said to apply to all modes without distinction. That is, God has adequate ideas of what is common to all insofar as he constitutes the "mind" of any mode. *All* "minds," and not just human minds, must contain adequate or clear and distinct ideas (cf. E II, P38 C, Gebhardt II, 119).

This result is largely confirmed by propositions 45 and 46 of Part II. P45 is explicitly universal:

> Any idea of any body or singular thing, actually existing, necessarily involves an idea of the eternal and infinite essence of God.

And so is P46:

> The knowledge [*cognitio*] of the eternal and infinite essence of God, which any idea involves, is adequate, and perfect. (127)

It is true that E II, P47 seems implicitly to restrict *having* adequate cognition (as opposed to "involving" it) to the human mind. The Proposition reads:

> The human mind has an adequate cognition of the eternal and infinite essence of God (Gebhardt II, 128).

But the proof rests, again, on the doctrine of *ideae idearum*. It reads as follows (omitting some references):

> The human mind has ideas by which it perceives itself, and its body, and external bodies, as actually existing; hence (by Props. 45 and 46) it has an adequate knowledge of the eternal and infinite essence of God.

But, as we've seen above, it is an apparent logical consequence of Spinoza's system that *every* "mind" has "ideas by which it perceives itself...." By this reasoning, then, every "mind" must not merely "involve knowledge of" the eternal and infinite essence of God. Rather, by Spinoza's principles, every "mind" of every body must like the human mind be said to *have* adequate, or clear and distinct, knowledge of the eternal and infinite essence of God. To tie consciousness to distinct cognition will therefore *not* restrict it to those entities normally thought of as minded. Apparently this awkward result was not intended by Spinoza; it is, however, dictated by the logic of his system.

V

My fundamental claim in this paper has been that Spinoza's system does not provide a plausible or coherent position about (real) minds and their relations to bodies. The basis of Spinoza's account of the relation of the human mind to the human body is a conception of the relation of God's ideas to their objects. This approach has features that have understandably been found attractive by many commentators—including the rejection of the two-substance human being, and avoidance of the problems of mind-body interaction. I hope to have shown, however, that the drawbacks of identifying the human mind with God's idea of the human body are too fundamental to be outweighed by the advantages. They include the consequences that the human mind has to include knowledge of everything that happens in the human body, and that all bodies turn out to have minds just as the human body does. I regard these results as implausible and even unintelligible on any understanding of "the human mind" that has anything much to do with the traditional "mind-body problem." I have further argued against other critics that Spinoza is not successful in accommodating traditional views of mental representation and of consciousness within his theory—even though there is evidence that he wished to do so. (With respect to consciousness, logical difficulties in developing a satisfactory position within the theory of "minds" may well have been compounded by vacillation on Spinoza's part about what view he *wanted* to hold.) I conclude that Spinoza's interpretation of the human mind as God's idea of the human body does not only fail to provide a satisfactory theory of the mind-body relation (who has *not* failed on this score?). It fails to address with even minimal cogency certain issues that lie at the very base of the mind-body problem as it is commonly understood—issues such as the relation between sentient experience and material existence, and the power of "the mind" to represent remote, non-existent, or impossible things.

Spinoza's attempt to integrate the "mind-body problem" inherited from Descartes into a theory of God's ideas and their objects was brilliant, elegant, creative and resourceful. It avoids the major impasses of Cartesian dualism and suggests (if somewhat obscurely) the move to a sophisticated modern theory that brooks no nonsense about the human mind as an "immaterial substance." These notable assets should not blind us to the facts that it has extremely exotic implications of its own, that it fails to capture ordinary notions of the mental, and that it suffers from internal imprecision and inconsistency. In short, it does not work at all.[23]

---

[23] I am grateful to Alan Donagan and Joel Friedman for valuable critical comments on an earlier version of this paper. The research for the essay was supported in part by a grant from the Guggenheim Foundation.

Princeton University

8 PARALLELISM AND COMPLEMENTARITY: THE PSYCHO-PHYSICAL PROBLEM IN THE SUCCESSION OF NIELS BOHR

Hans Jonas

The psycho-physical problem named in the title of this paper was born together with modern science in the 17th century and is the twin brother of its guiding axiom that things corporeal must be explained by corporeal causes alone, or that the latter are sufficient to explain everything in the physical realm, neither requiring nor even admitting the cooperation of mental causes. Indeed, completeness of intraphysical determination excludes the introjection of any non-physical source of action. So put, the axiom—in a stunning break with pre-modern, "Aristotelian" physics—amounts to the thesis of a causal redundancy of mind in nature. This redundancy found its first expression in the disavowal of "final causes," the concept of which is somehow borrowed from mentality. At the root of the radical turn was a reinterpretation of "nature" itself in purely spatial or geometrical terms. This made measurement of magnitudes the main mode of scientific observation, and quantitative equation of cause and effect, i.e., of antecedents and consequents, the ultimate mode of explanation. This epistemic program of the new science received its metaphysical underpinning in Descartes' doctrine of two heterogeneous kinds of reality ("substances" in his language)—the *res extensa* and the *res cogitans*—each defined by its one essential attribute "extension" and "thought" respectively, and each having nothing in common with the other. The gain of this ontological dualism was the setting free of nature for the unrestricted reign of mathematical physics; the cost was that the relation of mind and body became an intractable riddle. Post-Cartesian continental philosophy is one persistent grappling with this riddle: whatever solutions were proposed, the most persuasive assertion of our untutored experience—*interaction* between body and mind—had to be discounted from the outset. This gave 17th century speculation the anti-commonsensical, intellectually violent flavor which characterizes it. The most familiar appearances had to be contradicted. It appears to be the case that an external object, through the intermediary of our bodily senses, "produces" in our mind a perception of it—a mental presence. But this violates the principle that physical causes can have only physical effects. Likewise, it *appears* to be the case that my will produces the raising of my arm, but this violates the even more vital principle that physical effects can have only physical causes and that, therefore, the actual rising of my arm must be completely determined and accountable for by its physical antecedents. Thus, the *apparent* interaction must be replaced by a different, non-interactionist theoretical model.

The philosophically most remarkable as well as least capricious such model was designed by Spinoza in his doctrine of one substance with different attributes. This model provided for the mind-body problem the solution known as "psycho-physical parallelism." Let us briefly recall the general principle of Spinoza's system. Its basis is the concept of one, absolute and infinite *substance* that transcends those specifications, viz., extension and thought, by which Descartes had distinguished between two different kinds of substances. The infinity of the one substance involves an infinite number of *attributes* that "express" the essence of that substance—each expressing it truly though not completely because each does so under just this form or aspect. They are necessary aspects, not because our subjective cognition happens to be cast in that mold, but objectively inherent in substance itself as articulations of its plenitude. Thus there is no going behind them to a hidden ground: that ground itself exists in no other way than through its attributes, which are coeval with it and coequal with one another. None of them is more genuine than the other, and all of them are concurrently actual in each actuality of substance. The same can also be stated by saying that the attributes all together "constitute" the essence of substance, not, however, additively but as abstract moments that are only abstractly separable (as shape and color are only abstractly separable from a visual object).

Now, of these infinitely many attributes of the one cause, we humans know only two, extension and thought. They are the two universal forms under which alone we can and must conceive all things. But these "things" are not themselves substances; infinite substance leaves no room for a plurality of finite substances. Whatever is finite is not a substance but a modification or affection of infinite substance—a *"mode."* With this term we have, after "substance" and "attributes," the third key term in Spinoza's ontology, "modes." Individual items of reality, even what we are most wont to regard as self-subsistent, like molecules and rocks, are states or occurrences rather than entities, variable local determinations of the self-subsistent One *in terms of* its invariable attributes—this particular body, this particular thought. And if in terms of any one, then in terms of all of them: From the very status of "attributes" as merely different aspects of the same, it follows that each such finite affection of infinite substance as it occurs is exhibited, equally and equivalently, throughout all its attributes at once, and with a sequential necessity of succession *within* each attribute that reflects the eternal necessity of the divine nature. These necessities, then, run *"parallel"* in the diverse attributes, being in reality one and the same necessity. Its simultaneous, coequal manifestation in different essential forms means that it can be apprehended with equal truth under each such form by a finite mind that enjoys cognizance of some of them, and with more truth when this mind apprehends its sameness in several of them. Since, in the human case, this is limited to the two indicated, our world consists in fact of body and mind, and nothing else.

The point for our context is that what to Descartes were two separate and mutually independent substances are to Spinoza merely different aspects of one and the same reality, no more separable from one another than from their common cause. And he stressed that this common cause—infinite substance or God—*is* as truly extension as it is thought, or, as truly corporeal as mental; but there is as little a substance "body" as there is a substance "mind." Now since both these attributes express in each individual instance an identical fact, the whole problem of interaction or of any extraneous interrelation vanishes. Each occurrence (mode) as viewed under the attribute of extension is at the same time, and equivalently, an occurrence viewed under the attribute of thought or consciousness, and vice versa. The two are strictly complementary aspects of one and the same reality which of necessity unfolds itself in all its attributes at once. It would even be too disjunctive to say that each material event has its "counterpart" in a mental event, since what externally may be registered as a paralellism of two different series of events is in truth, that is, in the reality of God or nature, substantially the same. Thus the riddle created by Cartesian dualism—of how an act of will can move a limb, since the limb as part of the extended world can only be moved by another body's imparting its antecendent motion to it—this riddle disappears. The act of will and the movement of the body are one and the same event appearing under different aspects, each of which represents in its own terms a complete expression of the concatenation of things in God, in the one eternal cause.

If we had the time we should now go on to present the ingenious theory of organism with which Spinoza focused the general ontological scheme specifically on the biological sphere, where mentality is ordinarily seen to be conjoined to physical fact, and particularly on the case of man.[1] It must be enough to say that Spinoza makes it beautifully intelligible from his general premises that the quality and power of a mind are proportionate to the complexity of the body to which it corresponds, so that the perfection of the human body as a piece of physical organization is a direct yardstick for the perfection of the human mind which, as it were, conformally (or: isomorphously) duplicates the body's physical performance on the plane of thought. Likewise, a horse's mind is the mind conformal to the horse's body, and so down the line. We need not follow that line in its dubious descent into inorganic matter. What Spinoza is really about, and we with him, is the human mind and the human body, and with these alone in view let us try a critique of this solution to the psycho-physical problem.

Surely, Spinoza's parallelism of attributes expressing differently but equivalently one and the same substance was a feat of genius and far superior to all other treatments of the problem at the time. Without interposing a synchronizing deity, as did others, it overcame Descartes' dualistic rift by a monistic reduction, yet retained the full severity of the disjunctions which that dualism had been designed to ensure. Both sides of the coin are evident in the following propositions from the *Ethics*.[2]

> "The order and connection of ideas is the same as the order and connection of things." (E II, P7.)

> "A body in motion or at rest must be determined to motion or rest by another body, which was also determined to motion or rest by another, and that in its turn by another, and so on *ad infinitum*." (E II, P13, L3)

> "The body cannot determine the mind to thought, neither can the mind determine the body to motion nor rest, nor to anything else if there be anything else." (E III, P2)

In short, the parallels never cross, each continues as determined by itself.

My critique is two-fold: 1. the price for parallelism is a strictly necessitarian view of mind; 2. the alleged equal status of the attributes,

---

[1] See my essay "Spinoza and the Theory of Organism" in H. Jonas, *Philosophical Essays* (1974).

[2] Benedicti de Spinoza, *Ethica ordine geometrico demonstrata*. Here quoted in the translation by William Hale White.

the heart of the doctrine, fails to hold up in the execution of the system—notwithstanding all professions to the contrary, matter gains priority and mind in effect becomes an appendix or epiphenomenon of the body.

1. The necessitarian point is obvious: if conformal parallelism is to hold, then the mental sequences must be as deterministic as the physical. Indeed, Spinoza is emphatic in declaring free will to be an illusion. I leave it to the judgment of the reader whether absolute psychological determinism, the denial of any spontaneity of mind, is not too high a price to pay for the solution of a theoretical problem, and an unwarranted price at that, since unlike physical determinism, intramental determinism is without evidence of its own and is merely postulated for the system's sake.

2. The issue of determinism leads of itself to the second objection, viz., that the attribute of thought is, contrary to the claim of parity, in effect subordinated to that of extension. For where is "determinism" itself a determinate concept and not merely a summary assertion? Surely in the realm of matter, i.e., of spatiality, and precisely by virtue of the attribute of extension, which alone offers the kind of manifold where single items can be distinguished by space-time location, and quantitative values can be assigned to them by measurement of defined magnitudes, and paths can be plotted in relation to coordinates, and their intersection predicted and its outcome as a causal event computed—and where all this can be verified or falsified by new measuring observation. There—in the *res extensa*—determinism is well-defined and testable, and even its limits, its margin of imprecision, can be precisely stated in quantum physics. The stream of consciousness, on the other hand, non-spatial and with only the dimension of time, has nothing to match these conditions for vector analysis and for quantifiability in general. Put plainly: neither Spinoza had, nor do we have, a predictive science of mind as we have a predictive science of body, and Spinoza's own heroic attempt at founding such a science by "geometrizing" mind must be deemed a grandiose failure. Thus when I say that the present state of the mind determines its future state with necessity, and this in strict conformity to the parallel determinism of the states of the body, what I am really saying is that we must look to the causal history of the body, the only we have, to tell us by proxy about the otherwise unknown determinism of the mind. The fact that we cannot reverse the procedure, as the principle of parallelism would stipulate as equally eligible, puts the attribute of mind in the position of unilateral dependence on the other attribute of substance.

Add to this that the human mind, according to Spinoza, is already defined with reference to the body, namely, as having this body for the primary object of its thought, that its thinking is a thinking of the body, whereas the attribute of extension that defines the body has no intrinsic reference to mind, so that indeed we can consider body in its terms alone, as physics does, but mind only in conjunction with the body and as reflecting its condition in thought—and we see that matter is master in the match, and that the very rule of parallelism then reduces mind to one-sided dependence on it. At the end of this road stands the view of mind as a mere impotent epiphenomenon of matter, and matter as the one true substance—not at all what Spinoza had intended.

This critique is tinged with reverence for the might and originality of Spinoza's thought. I also confess to the philosophical hunch that, for all the inadequacies of the parallelistic formula, the monistic effort behind it, the vision of one reality in different manifestations, points in the direction where the truth may lie.

Now, with some trepidation, I pass to the question whether "complementarity" in the technical sense evolved by quantum physics, or rather in analogy to it, offers perhaps a better model for handling the psycho-physical problem. The question is prompted not so much by Niels Bohr's having at one time tentatively suggested it[3] (never to take it up again) as by the tempting currency which the formal concept of complementarity has gained outside its native ground, and by its actual use, or abuse, in different spheres, such as the social sciences.

First a few words about the original, quantum mechanical meaning of "complementarity" as coined by Bohr. It concerned the possibility of defining the "state" of a system in terms of two mutually exclusive, conceptual representations. One may say that complementarity, in the sense of Bohr, means that we can ask one of two mutually exclusive sets of questions about a system, but not both. The answer to one question would describe the system as a particle; the answer to the other would describe it as a wave. But the two models are not just optional alternatives equivalent with one another. They stand for different observables; e.g., the position component x_1 is complementary to the impulse component v_1, thus the particle description answering to the measurement of x_1 is complementary to, but not interchangeable with, the wave description answering to the measurement of v_1. The knowledge of one of them precludes the full determination of the other—the more I know about the one, the less I know about the other—yet both are required for a full account of the phenomenon,

---

[3] See, e.g., Niels Bohr, *Atomic Theory and the Description of Nature* (Cambridge, 1961), 24 and 100 ff.

complementing one another in conveying its truth, i.e., the exhaustive knowledge of what is knowable about it. As quantum physicists are wont to say, the entity "is" a particle when I measure its position, and it "is" a wave when I measure its momentum. Thus, whatever it is "in itself," only a dual account can do justice to the object (or, express the "truth" about it), without therefore bespeaking a dual nature of things.

Now, it has proved tempting to think that something similar might also apply to the two-fold account of human action (and of conscious behavior in general), the "outer" and the "inner," and provide a solution to the ancient problem of necessity and freedom. Descriptions of one and the same train of events in terms of physical necessity, on the one hand, and in terms of mental spontaneity, on the other, are "complementary" in the sense of Bohr's principle: the either-or is one of representation, not of fact, and only both representations together *in* their difference convey the truth of the identical fact. As in the case of the particle and wave descriptions, both are equally genuine—and, we should add, equally symbolic. Somehow, the underlying reality thus doubly expressed is supposed to be one in itself, as was the case with Spinoza's "attributes." But the epistemic situation is quite different.

The suggestion is appealing, but I doubt that it works better than Spinoza's parallelism. First, we ask: is the transfer of the complementarity concept to this case *formally* faithful to the original, so that with all differences of content "complementarity" retains the same logical structure? I think not. To "complementarity" in its quantum physical conception by Bohr himself, it is essential that the two descriptions are clearly separate, each complete in itself and neither intruding into the other; the wave description is not to be contaminated by corpuscular terms, and vice versa. The two models are, in short, strictly alternative. But we cannot begin to describe anything "mental" without referring to the "physical," the world of objects with which mind, sense, will, and action have actively and passively to do. That is to say, any speech about mind *must* also speak of body and matter. And when speaking of ourselves, we not only can and do but always *must* embrace with it our physical and mental being *at once*: precisely that *simultaneous* entertaining of *both* sides which quantum theory rules out for its complementary alternatives. From this original, *joint* givenness, after all, the psycho-physical problem arises in the first place. Here, the *isolation* of the two components is an artifact of abstraction, their interlocking co-presence being the primary datum. Even in abstraction the isolation does not really succeed, as the description of one side intrinsically refers to the other: the lines themselves do not run parallel, but cross. On this *transitive* relatedness alone, by which one description draws into itself elements of the other, the purported analogy with the quantum mechanical situation breaks down.

Even simpler, in this formalistic vein, is the objection that in the quantum mechanical case we begin with data of the same kind (space-time measurements) and end up with a duality of representations of our own devising to account for them, whereas in the psycho-physical case we begin with a duality of cardinally different data, not of our making at all, and try for a theoretical unification of them. If in such a unification they are found to be "complementary" in some sense, then "complementarity" itself becomes the unitary representation for a dual phenomenon. Thus the direction of the logical operation in the two cases is opposite, the one yielding a divergent model, the other (hopefully) a convergent one. These purely formal objections, by the way, especially that of the "crossing lines," fall on *all* extramural uses of the complementarity principle I know of (e.g., in the social sciences): they are all forced to violate the (at least) *semantically exclusionary* character the duality has in the original model and come to grief already on this count alone.

More to the point of our discourse than this formal observation is the blunt reminder that what is substantively at issue in the psycho-physical problem is *interaction* and, more particularly (surely so for Bohr's interest in "freedom"), the question of an *intervention* of mind in the affairs of matter. This, if it takes place at all (which is just in question), is nothing like an invariable concomitant, an innocent complement of physical processes, but is a particular event affecting their course. Does this happen? Is it possible? How? Such a question is obviously meaningless in the case of the complementary wave and particle descriptions; i.e., to ask whether, to what extent, on what occasions the wave aspect of events leaves its mark on their particle aspect. But just those questions (with the appropriately substituted terms) are the most meaningful ones to ask in the psycho-physical setting. Complementarity, "noninterventionist" by its formal nature, does not even allow them to be asked when seriously held to apply.

It is equally meaningful to ask *what* of our behavior, even of the mental state in back of it, is conditioned or circumscribed or prescribed by physical necessity, and what *we* truly initiate; i.e., to *apportion* the relative *shares* of the two sides in a given instance, which again is something wholly inapplicable to complementarity in the genuine sense.

In sum, I believe no faithful analogue of "complementarity" as understood by Niels Bohr really applies to our problem, and philosophers should leave it where it belongs. The philosophical interest of its attempted enlistment lies in what it has in common with Spinoza's "parallelism," viz., the *noninteractional* premise. Of this, it seems to offer a more sophisticated version, but it actually is, for that assigned purpose, inferior to the predecessor in one essential respect: Spinoza expressly acknowledges for the attribute of "thought" an intrinsic reference to the attribute of "extension" (but not vice versa!), inasmuch as he *defines* the human mind from the first as being the "idea" of an "actually existing body": that very body, in all of its changing states, is the proximate "ideatum" (=datum) in all of the individual mind's ideations. This permanent "idea" of its own body, as complex as this body itself, is indeed "the first thing" that *"constitutes* the actual being" of an individual mind and that mediates its ideas of all other things. Thus, far from interdicting physical terms in the description of a mental state (as complementarity must do), Spinoza's parallelism stipulates their very employment as integral to any description of mind: the "crossing" of lines, which the evidence displays and complementarity forbids, is here part of the doctrine itself. This brings the doctrine into closer agreement with the facts, but also into some disagreement with itself. For by the general doctrine, all attributes have equal status and no interrelation other than through their common root, "Substance" itself: no direct relationship of one attribute to another should have a place in their mere juxtaposition according to the system. Yet, "thought" of all attributes does have just such a relationship—ideally to *all* the others (as asserted for God's thought) and actually to the attribute of extension in man's case. The asymmetry which this *uniqueness* of mind imports into the doctrine of attributes is one of the major tensions in Spinoza's system and an old crux for its interpreters. "Thought" in God embraces all the other attributes and thereby excels them: it consists in reflecting them (and itself—there being also "ideas of ideas") and thereby is subject to them. Likewise, "thought" in man excels his one other attribute, "extension," whose self-enclosure is deaf to the coexistence of its companion, and by the same token is subject to it because it must reflect it. Mind alone transcends itself towards all the other attributes, while these are simply and immanently themselves. From this, there results a double disparity of mind with the other attributes, a positive in scope and a negative in autonomy, the former a disparity at the conceptual origin, the latter one at the functional consequence. The necessitarian and ultimately epiphenomenalist consequence of the disparity has been noted before; its initial inconsistency with the terms of the system must now be added. The necessitarian consequence, which troubles us, did not trouble Spinoza, the great denier of free-will. The flaw of internal inconsistency (which would have troubled Spinoza indeed) must be seen by us as a great mind's tribute to the force of truth at the cost of systemic symmetry: by this very irritant Spinoza's parallelism is cognitively superior to a "complementarity" model that *must*, under the uncompromising either-or of its representational scheme, rule out the physical reference from the mental description. That reference being, however, a stubborn datum of the evidence, the schema becomes simply inapplicable. What in Spinoza is a crack in an edifice which can still house many insights, would here annul the very foundation. But whatever the logical merits or demerits, these and all noninteractional models of the mind-body relation equally submerge the real sting of the psycho-physical problem: the question of a *power* of mind to intervene in the course of things. No speculative appeasement can ever disarm this sting.

The result of our critical journey, then, is chastening. The signs are that the psycho-physical problem, the mind-body riddle, is today, 300 years after Spinoza's death, still there to haunt us and still poses the same challenge it did to him. My intimation at the end is that the challenge is better met head-on by boldly trying once again the long tabooed "interaction." And for this, quantum mechanics may indeed offer an opening which classical mechanics denied—not by the principle of complementarity but by that of "indeterminacy." This, to be sure, would no longer be in the vicinity of Spinoza and will be discussed in another paper. Suffice it here to say that in the post-Newtonian age, aim can at least be taken again at a solution whose very concept was outlawed by deterministic natural science. After centuries of almost obligatory noninteractionism, of which Spinoza was the mightiest philosophical symbol, there may yet arise an interactional model of the mind-body relation that vindicates, instead of belying, the irrepressible evidence of our thinking and acting experience.

Graduate Faculty, New School for Social Research

SPINOZA'S PHILOSOPHY OF POLITICS AND RELIGION

9 SPINOZA'S POLITICAL PHILOSOPHY: THE LESSONS AND PROBLEMS OF A CONSERVATIVE DEMOCRAT

Lewis S. Feuer

Spinoza has not been a guiding political philosopher for ideologists and revolutionists. This despite the fact that he wrote the most impassioned defence in his time of freedom for thought and speech. For the favored themes of ideologists are lacking in Spinoza's political philosophy; he is no partisan of a law of progress, he has no dramatic historical outlook, he is no advocate of revolution. Yet precisely for these reasons Spinoza's political philosophy is one which speaks forthrightly to this era in which revolution and the achievement of Utopia have become the orthodox creed of intellectuals.

Spinoza is no Condorcet seeing the stages of an evolution of mankind.[1] He does not believe that history has in the offing some novel social or economic system. As far as political affairs are concerned, he is at one with Ecclesiastes in saying there is nothing new under the sun. As Spinoza states it: "I do not believe that we can by meditation discover in this matter anything not yet tried and ascertained, which shall be consistent with experience or practice... And so it is hardly credible, that we should be able to conceive of anything serviceable to a general society, that occasion or chance has not offered, or that men, intent upon their common affairs, and seeking their own safety, have not seen for themselves."[2]

Unlike Marx, Spinoza does not call upon philosophers to change the world. He does not trust theorists or philosophers in politics: "No

---

[1] "He [Spinoza] did not look foward to any improvement in political institutions or expect to make men philosophers by making them better citizens. On the contrary, he thought, as probably most learned persons in Europe did, that no political experiment of importance could still remain untried." Sir Frederick Pollock, "Spinoza's Political Doctrine with Special Regard to His Relation to English Publicists," *Chronicon Spinozanum*, Vol. I, 1921, 47.

[2] Elwes II, 288.

men are esteemed less fit to direct public affairs than theorists or philosophers." Disenchanted with Utopias, he turns for political wisdom to the statesmen who, he says, "have written about politics far more happily than philosophers," to "the most ingenious Macchiavelli," to Antonio Perez, the former Secretary of State to the King of Spain, and to Pieter de la Court, the economist collaborator of the Grand Pensionary of Holland.[3] Thus, Spinoza has separated himself from the "activist" strain which has pervaded the intellectual class from the French philosophers, Voltaire, Diderot, Rousseau, to Lenin in *What is to be Done?*, to the current varieties of neo-Marxism. Spinoza's "free man" is not a philosopher seeking a political mandate.

Thus, Spinoza's political science begins indeed with what Edmund Whittaker called a "principle of impotence,"—the assertion that no novel political system is possible. Whittaker, a physicist, believed that all physical theory could be encapsulated in such principles of impotence, in statements as to what cannot be done, which set limits to all human intervention in nature; thus, for example, the assertions that energy cannot be created or destroyed, or that heat does not flow from cold bodies to warmer ones. So likewise Spinoza would affirm that the forms of political societies are recurrent; antiquity had its despotisms, even socialistic ones as in Egypt, and it had its democratic states, as in Athens, and its aristocratic republics in Rome and Carthage. Moreover, according to Spinoza, the set of recurrent political forms are founded on "the very condition of human nature" that excludes such things as are "new and unheard of."[4]

Now Spinoza's exclusion of political novelty at the outset seems inconsonant with his metaphysics. For Spinoza affirmed in his *Ethics*: "From the necessity of the divine nature infinite numbers of things in infinite ways (that is to say, all things which can be conceived by the infinite intellect) must follow."[5] According to Spinoza, all those ideas in God's thought of conceivable existence must be actualized. But certainly, one might say, Utopian societies have been conceived from Thomas More to Edward Bellamy and William Morris; why then should a society not be possible, and therefore realizable, in which all alienation is indeed overcome? The fact of the matter for Spinoza, however, is that he does not regard a non-Euclidean social psychology as possible; the behavior of the generality of men will not be characterized by altruistic geodesic lines. "[M]an's natural passions are

---

[3] *Ibid.*, 287–288, 315, 334, 360.
[4] *Ibid.*, 288.
[5] E I, P16.

everywhere the same," writes Spinoza. "[T]he mass of mankind remains always at about the same pitch of misery,. . . [and] is always best pleased by a novelty which has not yet proved illusive," a trait which "has been the cause of many terrible wars and revolutions"; "men are more led by blind desire, than by reason."[6] The laws of social psychology are for Spinoza historically invariant; they have a necessary character. Those forms of society that are possible, relative to these laws, will be actualized in time (in accordance with God's power), but a Utopia is impossible and lies outside God's power because it contravenes the laws of psychology.

To be sure, there is a certain ambiguity here in Spinoza's notion of God's power. For at times he writes of that power as manifesting itself in realizing whatever is possible in the sense of an infinitude of diverse ideas and worlds. From such a standpoint, every variety of non-Euclidean geometry, every conceivable scheme of physical laws, and indeed, every imaginable social structure, would somehow be actualized in God's plenitude. But in practice Spinoza accepts, for instance, Galileo's law of motion as logically necessary, as having no alternative, just as he thus regards the laws of human psychology. Galilean physical laws and Machiavellian sociological laws are like geometrical truths. Indeed, many persons have felt themselves drawn to Spinoza's pantheism because they felt it was a kind of ode to the beauty, order, and simplicity of the laws of nature. Einstein, for instance, said that whenever he approached a problem in the structure of Nature, he asked himself: "How would God have solved it?", for there was an order in nature, beautiful, elegant, that was indeed deiform; hence Einstein regarded himself as a disciple of Spinoza. Yet the fact is that Spinoza in his formal metaphysics explicitly repudiates any doctrine of an "order of nature." For, he writes, such a conception is attributed to God not by reason but by the imagination; "men therefore prefer order to confusion, as if order were something in nature apart from our own imagination," and God "has disposed things in the manner in which they can most easily be imagined."[7] But, says Spinoza, "an infinite number of things are discovered which far surpass our imagination."[8] A contradictory duality between Spinoza's practice and his metaphysics here seems to arise as elsewhere. As a mathematician, physicist, and political scientist, he does seek order and beauty, forgetting his metaphysical doctrine that God's power could show itself in infinite confusion and disorder.

---

[6] Elwes I, 292, 313–5.

[7] E I, Appendix.

[8] *Loc. cit.*

The intellectual love of God in scientific practice is tied to a teleological factor, which Spinoza, however, repudiates.

Spinoza's political and moral intuitions are indeed at times sharply at odds with his naturalistic philosophy. Perhaps no event tried him more than the lynching of the Grand Pensionary of Holland, Jan de Witt, in 1672. Spinoza, who much admired de Witt, wanted to go to the street with a placard bearing the inscription "Ultimi barbarorum" (Lowest of barbarians). Whether the mob would have understood the Latin slogan is questionable; nonetheless they probably would have torn Spinoza to pieces; fortunately, Spinoza's landlord barred the door to keep Spinoza from leaving the house.[9] Yet in terms of his naturalistic philosophy, Spinoza should have said: "The mob has more power, hence, more right, and more of God's power than does the free man, de Witt; hence, it is right that they lynch him if they would." Or again, instead of denouncing the mob for their barbarity, he should have said: "God's power shows itself in infinite ways, and one of these is the lynching by barbarians of a free spirit." As in Spinoza's words: "Because to Him material was not wanting for the creation of everything, from the highest down to the very lowest grade of perfection."[10] Spinoza's own spontaneous response called into question, or at least could not be articulated in the terms of, his metaphysics.

Indeed, Spinoza's eloquent advocacy of freedom of thought likewise fails to jibe with his naturalistic premises. Spinoza argues powerfully that it is the state's greatest misfortune when it punishes its most "enlightened" citizens, and sends to the scaffold its "highest examples of tolerance and virtue."[11] He argues, as John Stuart Mill did later, that "such freedom is absolutely necessary for progress in science and the liberal arts." He urges that it is contrary to the state's own interests for it to drive "upright" men to become conspirators against it. And then, says Spinoza, in any case "it is impossible to deprive men of the liberty of saying what they think."[12] Now the utilitarian, pragmatic argument for freedom of thought is a straightforward sociological one based, as Spinoza indicates, on the evidence of "the city of Amsterdam" itself which "reaps the fruit of this freedom in its own great prosperity and in the admiration of all other people."[13] But the philosophical part of his argument, founded

---

[9] Foucher de Careil, *Réfutation inédite de Spinoza par Leibniz* (Paris: E. Brière, 1954) lxiv. *The Oldest Biography of Spinoza*, ed. A. Wolf (London: 1927), 180.

[10] E I, Appendix.

[11] Elwes I, 263.

[12] *Ibid.*, 261, 262, 264.

[13] *Ibid.*, 264.

on his definition of natural right, leads to a pitfall. For Spinoza concedes that the state "has the right to rule in the most violent manner, and to put citizens to death for very trivial causes. . . ."[14] It has the power, hence the right, and is precluded from suppressing freedom of thought and speech only because, as a matter of fact, it cannot prevent men from forming their own judgments, and telling others about them; men, in this sense, as masters of their thoughts, have a natural right to them. What Spinoza has thus done is to make natural right equivalent to an empirical proposition; but it then follows that where that proposition is false, natural right ceases to exist. The pressures of a secret police, abetted by informers, were in Spinoza's time as in our own, effective in suppressing freedom of speech.[15] On Spinoza's premises, totalitarian states would have the natural right to extirpate freedom of thought and speech, for as such books as those of Alexander Solzhenitsyn and Nadezhda Mandelstam have told, most people do cease to be the masters of their thoughts in such societies; dissent is first consciously repressed, and then lingers on only in the subterranean unconscious; moreover, children are indoctrinated. Spinoza, with his strong libertarian feelings, wishes to deny that the state has the right to suppress freedom of thought, yet his own equation of "right" with "power" constrains him against his own feelings.

A similar difficulty confronts Spinoza's call upon all governments to respect the wishes of the majority. That would be advisable, says Spinoza because otherwise the majority might become indignant, then conspire, and reduce the power and right of the commonwealth. To which one can respond: but suppose a government so concentrates power in its hands that it can deny any avenue of expression to discontented persons, and that conspiracy and faction alike are obliterated. Would such a totalitarian regime have the right to suppress the majority? Again Spinoza's democratic impulses make him want to say "No," but his definition of "right" obliges him to say "Yes."

To rebellious sons both of Ghettos and Gilded Mansions, the unswerving naturalism of Spinoza's social standpoint has an exhilarating, masculine quality. When Spinoza asserts that fishes are "naturally conditioned" that "the greater devour the less," and that they do so by "sovereign natural right," for the natural right of every individual thing extends as far as its power, there is a freedom from self-

---

[14] *Ibid.*, 258.

[15] Under the reign of Gallus Caesar in 355 A.D., the fear of informers made people afraid to admit that they even had dreams. *Ammianus Marcellinus*, tr. John C. Rolfe, Vol. I (Cambridge, Mass: Harvard University Press, 1935), 121.

pity, an identification with the law of power that can be emotionally attractive.[16] To many a primitivist intellectual, reacting against his over-civilization, the law of the jungle has had its appeal. Thus, too Marx and Engels could assert magisterially that ethical rights simply express the relationships of class forces, and that to attach to them any other significance was to engage in mythology. And Marx and Engels were indeed following in the path that Spinoza had opened. This was an intellectual experiment worth making, but it is doubtful that it has succeeded. For in the long run, this naturalist or historicist standpoint can be held only if one is prepared to identify one's self sadistically with triumphant force in history, or alternatively, to identify one's self masochistically with those who submit willingly to superior force. Marx and Engels tried to evade the problem by saying that they were on the side of the future, "more durable" morality which coincided happily with a "higher" proletarian morality. But their grounds for regarding the latter as "higher" were obviously independent of their victory, and in any case only a historical masochist would persist in saying that the "durable" is the good. If a bacterial epidemic were to destroy the human race, a pantheistic ethicist would have to say the bacteria were right, and their triumph was that of God's power. Yet the feeling among humans would be that something qualitatively more god-like had succumbed to chemical agents, that that quality of potential human perfection should have survived even if it had meant the extinction of a predator species. There can be little doubt that Spinoza felt this too, and so did Marx and Engels. But the language-rules of their pantheism and historicism respectively make it impossible for them to admit what they would have to regard as teleological. There is no way of proving or demonstrating this teleological proposition. For in philosophy the most we can finally do by way of criticism is to ask whether a man's philosophy expresses or represses the ideas in science or ethics to which he is spontaneously most drawn, whether a philosophy liberates or constrains a man's thought. With respect to at least one other tenet, Spinoza felt obliged to follow his feelings rather than the formal symmetry of his system. From his metaphysics it seemed to follow that the human mind could be no more immortal or eternal than its corresponding brain tissues. Yet, said Spinoza, "although we do not recollect that we existed before the body, we feel that our mind, insofar as it involves the essence of the form of the body under the form of eternity, is eternal... " "Nevertheless, we feel and know by experience that we are eternal."[17]

---

[16] Elwes I, 200, 291–292.

[17] E V, P23 S.

Given his pessimistic realism about human nature and his freedom from ideology, Spinoza was bound to run into trouble in formulating the foundations for democracy. He is the first democrat in the history of philosophy, and enthusiastically so as he wrote of Amsterdam as a democracy in his *Tractatus Theologico-Politicus* in 1670. But when it came to writing his chapter on democracy in his last years he faced, in my opinion, an insuperable problem. There is a certain genre of literature which we might call the "unwritten book." Thus, Lord Acton is said to have been the author of the greatest history of liberty that was never written.[18] Karl Marx during the decade and a half after 1867 could not write a single major book or article. Both Lord Acton and Marx were confronted by challenges to their basic ideas that they could not resolve. And Spinoza's *Political Treatise*, in my opinion, is their analogue in the seventeenth century; his book stops short at the very beginning of the chapter on democracy. A letter that Spinoza wrote describing his proposed work indicates that he had almost gotten to the chapter on democracy; Professor Wolf dates it as having been written therefore in the latter part of 1676.[19] But the only evidence for this hypothesis is that Spinoza died on February 21, 1677; Professor Wolf assumed that Spinoza was writing the book steadily till his death. Yet the letter might well have been written several years earlier, and Spinoza may have found himself during his remaining lifetime baffled by how to deal with democracy.

For Spinoza's aim with respect to democracy was to do with it what he had done with aristocracy and monarchy. By using such successful examples as the Venetian aristocracy and the earlier Spanish monarchy, he hoped to state what the conditions for stability in such governments would be. But where could he find at hand the model of a successful, stable democracy? The lynching mob of 1672 had set at nought his paean to the Amsterdam democracy; free men might have to live endangered lives even in a democratic society. Furthermore, how was a democracy possible if the masses of men were dominated by their passions? Spinoza might have moved, as Hannah Arendt did two centuries later, in the direction of a distinction between the people and the mob. In dealing with aristocracies and monarchies, Spinoza had argued that the best means for safeguarding freedom would be to entrust the tradesmen and commercialists with power. But how could their hegemony be assured under a democracy? Spinoza had no empirical model on which to found his analysis. The Athenian and Roman democracies no doubt seemed to him sullied with class war-

---

[18] Gertrude Himmelfarb, *Lord Acton: A Study in Conscience and Politics* (Chicago: University of Chicago Press, 1952), 2.

[19] Wolf (a), 481.

fare, assassinations, and foreign military ventures, and he was looking for a constitution that would obviate warfare and discord, both internal and external. Then too he changed his mind on one point; he no longer regarded Amsterdam as a democratic model; rather it had been an aristocratic republic. Spinoza's unwritten chapter was commensurate with the answers that could not yet be given as to the prospects for democracy.

Moreover, although a democrat, Spinoza was what we might call a "conservative democrat," not an ideological one, that is, he in no way endorsed any grounds for revolution. An ideological democrat is one who like Jefferson for instance, finds a natural virtue in the people, and justifies a revolutionary act whenever such is the people's will. John Locke, Spinoza's younger contemporary, was the philosopher of the "Glorious Revolution" of 1688, but Spinoza clearly thought that every revolution was inglorious. Together with Leibniz, he deplored the fanaticism of Cromwell's Calvinist party and their execution of Charles II. He felt indeed that successful revolutions were impossible, and "that peoples have often changed their tyrants, but never removed them or changed the monarchical form of government into any other." Of this truth, the English revolution, said Spinoza, was "a terrible example." "They sought how to depose their monarch under the forms of law, but when he had been removed, they were utterly unable to change the form of government, and after much bloodshed only brought it about, that a new monarch should be hailed under a different name..." Furthermore, the political consequences of the English revolution had been deleterious for the peace of Europe. In order to allay discontent, and to "divert" the people's mind "from brooding over the slaughter of the king," Cromwell's regime had provoked foreign war, and accomplished "nothing for the good of the country."[20] Of all our contemporaries, Spinoza's outlook is best exemplified by Solzhenitsyn, in whose judgment the Bolshevik Revolution replaced one tyranny with a worse one, and instituted a Soviet repression, the massive scale of which has dwarfed that of its Czarist predecessor. And the Communist regime by threatening the rest of the world through its satellite parties with a seizure of power and the formation of similar dictatorships contributed to the collapse of European reason and the emergence of Hitler.

Spinoza's democratic political philosophy is thus curiously Dutch-bound in a manner that recalls those later American republicans such as George Washington, who have been doubtful that American political forms could be transplanted to other peoples without a self-gov-

---

[20] Elwes I, 243–244.

erning tradition. In the Netherlands, fortunately, a commercial class had long ruled the towns without the interposition of a king. Dutch democracy was as fortunate an outcome as the American democracy on the open frontier. But where democracy did not already exist, Spinoza proposed only that the political system be so operated as to ensure to the maximum the welfare of the people, and the preservation of free men.

It is likely too that there was a strong Jewish influence in Spinoza's antipathy to revolution. For the Jewish philosophers have always stood for stability, and dreaded instability. Men like Maimonides had encountered mass people's movements, and knew them as invariably intolerant and portending for the Jews ruination, persecution, expulsion, massacre. Spinoza himself in 1648 as a lad of sixteen had doubtless heard much of the Chmielnicki Massacres that year which had destroyed at least one-third of Poland's Jews; bewildered refugees had reached the Amsterdam synagogue, telling of this people's crusade. Jews became revolutionists in the nineteenth century, especially when the phenomenon arose of an excluded university intellectual class. Yet Disraeli was probably right when he regarded this as an aberration from the historical conservatism of the Jews which indeed characterized Spinoza's political theory.

Though Spinoza, however, rejected the revolutionary path as a blind alley, his naturalistic philosophy, however, led perforce in that direction. For according to Spinoza, there is a natural right to break any compact which seems to be working against one's interest: "Everyone has by nature a right to act deceitfully, and to break his compacts, unless he be restrained by the hope of some greater good, or the fear of some greater evil."[21] Unlike Kant, Spinoza does hold that we have the right to lie to robbers; also, says Spinoza, if I promised someone to starve myself for twenty days, and then realized how foolish my promise had been, "I am bound by natural law and right . . . to break my compact."[22] The same natural right would, however, clearly extend to any class or group, whether minority or majority, which felt itself suppressed, even under a democracy. For every person retains the right to cancel his compact with a democracy which, in his judgment, is violating his interests irreparably. Spinoza does affirm that within a democratic state people are "obliged to fulfil the commands of the sovereign power, however absurd these may be," unless they have made explicit reservations, because under a democracy, people have handed over to the state "all their right."[23]

---

[21] *Ibid.*, 204.

[22] *Ibid.*, 203–204.

[23] *Ibid.*, 205.

Nonetheless, he has also set forth as a cardinal tenet that no one can forego the right which he has over all things, which would indeed suffice for a natural right to revolution. Spinoza too recognizes that seditions do reduce the natural right or power of governments; nonetheless, he refuses to sanction any of them.

One wonders, of course, why Spinoza insists on the natural right to abrogate promises, especially since the free man, in his view, is one who acts honorably, and abides by his promises. It seems to me likely that Spinoza brooded much on this problem when as a youth he was making his break with the Jews and their ways. As an adolescent of thirteen, he had given his Bar Mitzvah promise to the Synagogue that he would fulfill the commandments and the rituals such as those of food, with their fasts and taboos. What then was the status of young Baruch's promises? Clearly, says Spinoza, he has the natural right, now that he realizes that he acted foolishly, immaturely, or under communal pressure, to "act as if my promise had never been uttered."[24] The experience of the excommunicate seems to echo in Spinoza's antipathy to promises.

In the last years of his brief life, Spinoza, a conservative democrat, undertakes then to give concrete suggestions as to how the values of free men can be safeguarded in those countries which live not under democracies but aristocracies and monarchies. Always his basic principle of comparative political science is to try to provide for the hegemony of the commercial class, no matter what the form of government. Thus, if a country has an aristocratic state, it should do well to remember that a landed aristocracy will not tend to preserve freedom, whereas a commercial aristocracy, devoted to trade, will value freedom; the Venetian republic, in Spinoza's eyes, was a great confirmation of this truth.[25] If, on the other hand, a country has a monarchical state, then it must allow no one to own land; instead, everyone must "be obliged for the sake of gain, to practise trade. . . ."[26] The land itself would remain the "common property of the commonwealth," and be rented out to those who need and work it; hence, there would be no landed aristocracy.[27] Moreover, Spinoza advises against allowing any standing army to exist under a monarchy, for

---

[24] *Ibid.*, 204.

[25] *Ibid.*, 356. James Madison, citing Jefferson, called the Venetian republic an "elective despotism" but Spinoza would have felt that its authoritarian ingredient was a condition for its stability and liberty. See *The Federalist*, ed. Edward Mead Earle (Washington: National Home Library Foundation, 1937), 324.

[26] *Ibid.*, 331.

[27] *Ibid.*, 337, 338, 317. Also cf. 350.

that would constitute an independent base for absolutist power. Instead, the army is to be composed exclusively of citizen soldiers. Spinoza draws on the histories of Spain, Turkey, and France, where monarchies had evolved toward absolutism; he notes, for instance, that Aragon was a constitutional monarchy until its liberties were subverted by the cruel and war-minded Philip II.[28] To prevent such an absolutist evolution, Spinoza calls for a constitutionally elected national council, representative of all classes, and with the king denied the right to contravene the council's will; he will always confirm its majority.[29] To make doubly sure that the councillors will be uninterested in wars, Spinoza proposes not only that they should be businessmen but also that they should be at least fifty years of age.[30] An elderly bourgeois elite, in his view, is the best guarantee of peace.

The danger to an aristocratic state, on the contrary, comes primarily, in Spinoza's view, from an uprising of the mob. The experience of the brothers de Witt remained poignantly in his mind. Hence, Spinoza was prepared to allow an army of mercenaries as a stabilizing force in an aristocratic dominion. And to prevent a restless moving about of the population, in hard times, the kind of aimless mobility which makes for mobs, underclasses, and lumpenproletarians, Spinoza proposes that there be a widespread peasant ownership; the lands and farms should be sold to the subjects. To safeguard the patrician rule, furthermore, the Guilds, the corporations of artisans, should be excluded from political participation; Spinoza's aim is for a stable state, with a mitigation of class warfare. He recognizes that the projects of a commercial aristocracy, obviously its navy and army, will require high taxes, but he cites the leading Dutch free trade economist who had written that the Dutch have paid heavy taxes willingly when they have gotten in return "peace and liberty."[31] A commercial aristocracy seeks gain, not glory, and is therefore not war-minded.

Like all the classical political philosophers, Spinoza was concerned with the problem of the decay and dissolution of societies. He was aware that peace and prosperity breed their own weakness: "For men in time of peace lay aside fear, and gradually from being fierce savages become civilized or humane, and from being humane become soft and sluggish," and then, aping "foreign" ways, become slaves.[32]

---

[28] *Ibid.*, 335, 341, 344.
[29] *Ibid.*, 332.
[30] *Ibid.*, 329.
[31] *Ibid.*, I, 360.
[32] *Ibid.*, 381.

To counteract this pattern of decay, Spinoza proposed to enlist the most bourgeois of motives, avarice, or as the Marxists say, the passion for accumulation. The republic would do well to harness on its behalf the energies of men's passions. "And therefore the chief point to be studied," writes Spinoza, "is, that the rich may be, if not thrifty, yet avaricious. For there is no doubt that, if the passion of avarice which is general and lasting, be encouraged by the desire of glory, most people would set their chief affection upon increasing their property, without disgrace, in order to acquire honors, . . ."[33]

According to Spinoza, then, it would follow that bourgeois society would decline if the passion for accumulation were to become discredited. Here indeed Spinoza seems to me original and truthful. The "decay of capitalist civilization" did not take place, as the Webbs and Marx would have it, because of the failure to raise the living standards of the "masses." This, indeed, capitalism has done more than any other system. Rather the decline began when businessmen became ashamed of the desire to accumulate, when the entrepreneurial motive was vilified in a huge literature of drama, fiction, and tracts. As Joseph Schumpeter wrote, it was the spread of the anti-capitalistic mentality among and from the intellectuals that portended the corrosion of capitalism.

Then too Spinoza is mindful that the seditious, the schismatics, the agents of hostility to the existing society are usually the young. Ancient writers from Sallust and Cicero onward have known that every conspiracy, beginning with that of Catiline, has drawn its members chiefly from the malcontented young. Spinoza for all his advocacy of freedom has no respect for the "schismatics," the ideologists as we would say today; "schisms," he asserts, "do not originate in a love of truth, . . . but rather in an inordinate desire for supremacy."[34] He proposes therefore to give ballast to government by weighting it on the gerontocratic side. Where Machiavelli would seek to restore political equilibrium through a periodic terror, Spinoza proposes instead a committee of public safety, made up of older, conservative men, "of an age to prefer actual security to things new and perilous," a practice he seems to have found in the Venetian republic.[35] Life expectancies at this time were so short that a gerontocratic elite would have been constituted from small numbers, something which would have added a factor of instability. But that Spinoza who was only 44 years old when he died should have leaned so much in the gerontocratic direction indicates how much the quest for stability, and the

---

[33] Loc. cit.
[34] Ibid., I, 265.
[35] Ibid., 380.

control of lawless violence, envy, and hatred, seemed to him the primary political aims, rather than any abstract ideal of justice.

Always Spinoza's democratic faith seems to run against the recalcitrant facts adduced by his own observations of human nature. Spinoza the political advocate is never quite at home with Spinoza the social psychologist. Democracy, Spinoza declares in his optimistic *Tractatus Theologico-Politicus*, is "of all forms of government the most natural, and the most consonant with individual liberty." In a democracy, he argues, "it is almost impossible that the majority of a people, especially if it be a large one, should agree in an irrational design."[36] Yet Spinoza believed also that the overwhelming majority of men are led by passions: why then would it be so unlikely that a majority would endorse an irrational design? We in our time have witnessed the "mass base" upon which Hitler founded his totalitarian state, but Spinoza in his time had probably heard, for instance, how the Spanish people had largely approved of the Inquisition against the Jews.

Spinoza wishes to see the elite of free men dominant in the councils of democratic society, to see the men of reason prevail, but as long as a great gulf separates the free men from the multitude, there is an inherent disequilibrating vector in society. Is there any hope for making the multitude into free men? Here Spinoza answers with his pessimistic determinism: "Experience, however, teaches us but too well, that it is no more in our power to have a sound mind, than a sound body."[37] The ignorant simply do not have it in their power to live by the dictates of reason; they will strive as much as they can to realize the sort of human beings they are. If ignorant men declare that they best realize their essences when they murder "intellectuals" such as Jan de Witt, Spinoza may call them "barbarians"; but then suppose they say that their envy of superior intellects, of book-learning, is part of their nature, and that anti-intellectualism enables them to fulfill their perfection of their own kind. The barbarian has his barbarian essence to fulfill, and in Nature's chain of being, he is as necessary to its perfection as Spinoza's free men. If Spinoza calls upon him to improve his character, to act as a free man, has he not forgotten his pantheistic determinism? Has he not in practice responded and acted as a voluntarist, who believes that men, even the ignorant, do have it in their power to make moral choices? According to Spinoza's doctrine, we should have to say that Adolf Hitler, engaged in his mass slaughters, was realizing his Hitlerian essence with its extraordinary

---

[36] *Ibid.*, 206–207.
[37] *Ibid.*, 293.

capacities for destructive aggression; we should have to say that this unusual phenomenon in the history of human aggression showed the power of God and the richness of the phenomena which occurred in accordance with His laws of mind; and the very contemplation of this psychological power, says Spinoza, "in itself affords us delight."[38] Though Hitler would arouse Spinoza's indignation as Nero did with his matricide, still he cannot set him down as a "flaw" in nature, or suggest that even God would wish that such actions did not exist; for then God's nature would not be realizing itself in all the infinite possible ways. Pantheistic determinism thus culminates in the most antinomian relativism.

Furthermore, the laws of political and social science hardly seem the kinds of truths which lend themselves to Spinoza's intellectual love of God. It is noteworthy that it is rather physicists such as Einstein who derive from their contemplation of the laws of physics a pleasure akin to Spinoza's intellectual love of God. There is a kind of awesome splendor one feels in such a generalization of astronomy as Hubble's Law that the distant galaxies are receding from the earth with speeds proportional to their distances from it. But I have never heard of any political scientist or sociologist who experienced a similar emotion as he contemplated the laws of his domain. "Men are in the highest degree liable to the passions" [anger, envy, hatred], writes Spinoza; "therefore men are naturally enemies."[39] Does the sociologist of aggression become filled with "pleasure" as he views these phenomena "aright"? Evidently Freud's studies filled him with a melancholy concerning the human race and all existence. Marx and Engels thought of history as a stern goddess exacting the sacrifice of millions of persons; Pareto felt life was not worth living, a sentiment which the sombre spectacle of his enquiry into human irrationalities did not dissipate; Durkheim feeling himself the meaninglessness of existence without Deity had no real answer to the increases in self-destruction that were otherwise inherent in modern industrial civilization; Weber saw a growing emotional disenchantment inevitable as technological rationality increased. In short, empirically speaking, sociology is no path to the intellectual love of God: moreover, God provides no heuristic concept in sociology as He does in physics. I have heard of no political scientist or sociologist asking himself when dealing with a problem as Einstein did: "How would God have done it?" Rather he might be more apt to ask unconsciously: "How would the

---

[38] E III, Preface.
[39] Elwes I, 296.

Devil have done it?" Yet since the devil "has not the least perfection in him," says Spinoza explicitly, he "cannot possibly exist."[40]

All of these misgivings were indeed raised to Spinoza himself by a grain merchant Willem van Blyenbergh, though in return for his efforts he has been called a "bore," and a "limited" one at that.[41] Spinoza, however, hardly answered him adequately, and became rather impatient in the process. The ungodly man, van Blyenbergh observed, serves God even as the godly does, for each can only perform those deeds that correspond to as much essence as God has given him; though the ungodly have less perfection (in Spinoza's terms) than the pious, they serve God in functioning in their fashion. Does it not then follow from Spinoza's premises, van Blyenbergh queried, that "God Himself causes evil?"[42] Spinoza replies in effect with two arguments. One is cryptoteleological: evil, he says, exists only relatively to ourselves, and not to God, for God endows things with their respective characters, their realities, their perfections in their kind, and to talk of their privations, that which they are not, is only a human way of looking at things. Spinoza assumes that from God's standpoint then evil collapses, which is indeed a teleological fulfillment. What Spinoza seems to overlook is that his whole notion of the intellectual love of God would likewise collapse, for if evil is human-relative, so likewise is the notion of a highest good, of the increase in perfection that is achieved in the intellectual love of God; "grades of perfection" imports a human standard too, for that mode is more perfect in a serial order that has more realities that the other lacks. Spinoza's response verges on anger as he repudiates any suggestion that things insofar as they are "dead, corporeal and imperfect" also depend on God; "who ever dared to speak in so vile a fashion of the most perfect Being?", he challenges.[43] But the logical part of his argument, his second, as distinct from his social-emotive appeal, consists in arguing that God cannot be the cause of Evil because Evil is indeed Nothing, and it makes no sense to speak of a cause which has no effect. Or as Spinoza phrases it: "Evil, Error, or Villainy" do not express essence; though God for instance was the cause of Nero's matricide, as a psychological intention and a physical action, still insofar as negative adjectives are used to characterize that intention and action as "ungrateful, unmerciful, and disobedient," nothing real is described; for these adjectives do not denote an actual psychophysical

---

[40] Wolf (b), 143.
[41] Wolf (a), 54.
[42] *Ibid.*, 153.
[43] *Ibid.*, 178.

occurrence.⁴⁴ Spinoza adds too that the order of perfections is one founded on qualitative differences in essence; presumably the "more" and the "less" could be dispensed with too in ultimate terms, for the pious man and the ungodly "differ from one another not only in degree but also in essence," as a mouse, for instance, differs from an angel.

Once more, however, Spinoza's metaphysics is at odds with his political psychology. For as a political psychologist he proposes to study the "passions, such as love, hatred, envy, ambition, pity, and the other perturbations of the mind" as properties pertinent to human nature "as are heat, cold, storm, thunder, and the like to the nature of the atmosphere, which phenomena, though inconvenient, are yet necessary, and have fixed causes,..."⁴⁵ Anger, envy, ambition, all involve pain, frustration; one can say that frustration is a negative term for it connotes non-satisfaction, but it certainly is not unreal, not nothing, not a definition of a null-class, for its experience is one of pain, of acute need, which drives the person as a vector to action. One might just as plausibly argue that satisfaction, or satiation, is unreal, nothing, because it is accompanied by inaction, a cessation of activity, by vacuity. When Spinoza speaks of men as led by desire rather than by reason, he recognizes the reality of unfulfilled longing; when he studies the aggressions of the ungodly and the devouring fishes, the evils in Nature are taken to be as real as the goods. And in recognizing that God's love for Himself rises with the free men's intellectual love of Him, he acknowledges that if there were more free men in the world than the ungodly, there would indeed be progress, that is, an increase in God's love. Thus, a teleological criterion seems to lie in the background of Spinoza's philosophy. Yet his formal metaphysics obliges him, however, to concede to van Blyenbergh that he cannot exclude an antinomian corollary from being derived: "he who saw clearly that he would in fact enjoy a more perfect or better life or essence by pursuing crimes, would also be a fool if he did not pursue them. For in relation to such a perverted human nature crimes would be virtuous."⁴⁶ Spinoza, however, has no basis in his philosophy for calling such a man "perverted"; to Hitler and Stalin, their crimes too would be virtuous.

Curiously too a whole sociological evaluation or standpoint projected itself into Spinoza's notion of the intellectual love of God. According to Spinoza, the more knowledge or science one has, the more one's mind is indeed conceived through and shares God's essence.

---

⁴⁴ *Ibid.*, 190.
⁴⁵ Elwes I, 288-289.
⁴⁶ Wolf (a), 193.

Now this doctrine was a heritage of Jewish mediaeval philosophy. With the high place accorded to scholars, Jewish philosophy, most notably in the case of Maimonides, expressly made scholars more immortal than the common people on the ground that their scholarly thoughts participated in the Active Intellect of God. Spinoza indeed could not believe that a man of science might harbor evil usages for his knowledge; he repudiated any suggestions that Machiavelli might have been endorsing an evil practice in political means. And he would probably have been shaken by the sight of Nobel Laureates in science who became Nazis: what exactly did their intellectual love of God signify? Again one feels that a teleological ingredient is present though unavowed in Spinoza's philosophy. His intellectual love of God seems to be joined to a conviction that the growth of knowledge and science will finally make for free men, that science and human generosity will ultimately converge; granted that in some short run knowledge may seem to lend itself to diabolical usage, to be a servant, as so many people have felt, of the Devil, yet in the long run, the universe in its travail would realize more of God's perfection, the union of love and knowledge. The intellectual love of God is not then a by-product of the mastery of a textbook of physics; rather it is a standpoint with regard to the laws of nature which sees them as themes that somehow convey, or delineate the outlines of a higher existence. One's delight in science is precisely because of such qualities as the order and beauty of its laws, qualities that Spinoza rejects as tainted with the human imagination. But these imaginative qualities are intrinsic to the experience of the intellectual love of God; the recognition of the convergence of the rational and teleological. In this sense, the intellectual love of God in political science would be founded on the intuition that the divine ingredient will transcend the diabolical.

Lastly, there remains for us to consider all too briefly the basic problem that confronts every determinist who proposes a political philosophy. We might call it the "paradox of determinism," and it is one which we find in the writings not only of Spinoza but of Marx, Herbert Spencer, and Auguste Comte. The determinist argues that the laws of psychology and sociology explain completely the behavior of people; yet as a political philosopher, he proposes a program; thus Spinoza presents his constitutions for an aristocracy and monarchy, and proposes that free rational men shall try to realize these constitutional reforms; Marx similarly hopes that by having set forth the inevitable law of social development, society will get on what he calls "the right track," and thereby will "shorten and lessen the birth pangs."[47] Spencer, at the close of *The Principles of Sociology* remarks

---

[47] Karl Marx, *Capital: A Critique of Political Economy*, tr. Samuel Moore and Edward Aveling (Chicago: C. H. Kerr, 1906), 14–15.

that "the study of sociology" would be useless if its generalizations did not enable us to give "consequent guidance to our acts."[48] Auguste Comte argued that as far as social phenomena were concerned, their laws, unlike those of astronomy, allowed for a "larger modification, due chiefly to our own intervention," a view which he said, "stimulates us to action."[49]

Now in every one of these cases, a choice among alternatives is proposed, the resolution of which lies outside the scheme of sociological laws which the writer believes himself to have demonstrated. Thus, in Marx's case, assuming that he has indeed shown that the advent of a socialist society is historically inevitable, there is still the decision to be made: shall one cooperate with the inevitable or resist it? It may be, as some zoologists say, that species of insects will triumph over man; few of us, however, will decide to cooperate with the inevitable.

There is indeed no classical sociologist who in practice can be regarded as a "total historical determinist." Although Isaiah Berlin assailed such thinkers as Marx, Comte, and Spencer for their principle of "historical inevitability," they were perhaps not, in practice, as total sociological determinists as he thought. All of them indicated the existence of some domain for human intervention; the question then becomes: how large is that domain, or how many degrees of freedom for decision does it pose? And then granted such a domain for intervention, are the latter human interventions themselves determined? And if one believes in such a determinism, is it an article of faith, a postulate, or an operationally determinate hypothesis?

We might state the matter formally: that whenever a system of sociological laws is set forth to describe the workings of society, there always exist some events which lie outside that system, and which in part constitute the responses of people to their recognition of the truths set forth by those sociological laws. Every macro-systematic sociological law thus generates some corresponding event which it itself does not causally explain. Thus, we might say that outside of every sociological theory of order n, there lie events of order n + 1. Spinoza would call them "ideas of ideas." To which we naturally query: are not these events of order n + 1 themselves, however, sociologically determined? We might go on to elaborate a further theory trying to deal, for instance, with how different social and generational groups, under different conditions have responded to different aspects of Marxism. There are two facts, however, to be observed. First, as we

---

[48] Herbert Spencer, *The Principles of Sociology*, Vol. III (New York: Appleton, 1897) 590; Part VIII, Ch. XXIII, 846.

[49] Auguste Comte, *A General View of Positivism*, tr. J. H. Bridges (Paris: N.P., 1848). Reprinted, Stanford, n.d., 59–60.

move from laws of order n to n + 1 and n + 2, . . ., the generalizations become more and more uncertain, with larger margins of error and possible variation. From the statement of the general law of the declining rate of profit to a generalization concerning how the sons of the nobility and bourgeoisie will respond to Marxist ideology takes us from a simple collective economic derivation to a complex of human individual emotional responses. The laws of higher order tend to become more and more indeterministic in form. Secondly, both theoretically and in practice, a totally deterministic theory is renounced as something impossible. The shadowy higher orders such as n + 3 are simply excluded as negligible, and the question of a total determinism regarded as metaphysical.

Since a purely scientific solution of sociological determinism is not forthcoming, we can turn then only to the experienced character of the political choice itself. In his own published statement on the ground for his own personal choice, Marx appealed to "the categorical imperative to overthrow all those conditions in which man is an abased, enslaved, abandoned, contemptible being," "that man is the supreme being for man. . . ."[50] It would seem then that Marx was, in Kantian terminology, making an individual choice, freely willed, with respect to historically inevitable trends; that individual free choice, however, stood outside the scheme of sociological causal law, and was not historically necessitated. Thus, likewise Spinoza, after enunciating a socio-psychological determinism, and asserting that men can no more choose to act rationally than to change their bodies, does present them with a book of arguments for freedom of thought and ensuring majority rule, peace and liberty. He, a free man, evidently assumes that other men can make the effort to understand the causes of their passions, and thus decide as free men. "An affect which is a passion ceases to be a passion as soon as we form a clear and distinct idea of it," writes Spinoza.[51] Which is much like Freud asserting that the aim of psychoanalytical causal understanding is "to give the patient's ego freedom to decide one way or the other."[52] On the other hand, if passions make men irrational, nonetheless when men achieve a rational causal understanding of themselves, presumably they discover not only that their irrationality was determined but likewise their rationality. In our self-understanding of our unconscious motives and our bringing them to consciousness, we would still presum-

---

[50] Karl Marx, "The Critique of Hegel's Philosophy of Right," in *Early Writings*, tr. T. B. Bottomore (London: Watts, 1963), 52.

[51] E V, P3.

[52] Sigmund Freud, *The Ego and the Id*, tr. Joan Riviere (New York: Norton, 1962), 40.

ably perceive that our so-called freedom was a determined one. Now this solution to the "paradox of determinism" disturbs those followers of Spinoza who find his determinism repellent. The social philosopher, Erich Fromm, for instance, has tried to detach Spinoza, Freud, and Marx from determinism. He has said:

> "Spinoza, Freud, and Marx were neither determinists nor indeterminists. Indeed, often Spinoza is quoted as determinist; Freud and Marx have been also. The allegation is to some extent true; but the essential part is often ignored, and that is that all thinkers have said, 'Yes, man is determined.' But the task of life is to overcome this determinism, either of economic forces or of the irrational passions in oneself, and to reach an optimum of freedom...."[53]

Now there can be little doubt that Spinoza, Freud, and Marx were all thoroughgoing determinists as far as their philosophical statements were concerned. Erich Fromm would like to make this only true "to some extent" so that the three thinkers would then be agreeing with him, an understandable weakness. What is true, however, is that in their working assumptions as practical political philosophers all tend to contravene their formal doctrine. Spinoza, Freud, and Marx might, however, respond that this is simply the model of discourse of human beings determined to act to influence others, and has no genuine bearing on the truth or falsehood of determinism. They would agree with Spinoza's view that once all unconscious factors are brought to light, and the unbroken causal sequence involved in human acts is inspected, it would be found to be determinist. To which we reply that this assumes that the intellectual experiment of bringing into awareness the unconscious operative factors always confirms the hypothesis of determinism, and that this is not the case. Rather we find that such intellectual experiments bring to light underlying ingredients of unconscious, repressed free decisions; furthermore, we may find that the endeavor to impose deterministic explanations on all psychological experience may itself have included among its conditions a free choice made to placate certain anxieties. A full awareness of the causes of our actions does not necessarily confirm, as Spinoza and Freud believed, the deterministic standpoint; rather we may perceive that the relevant causal factors were not sufficient conditions for the action in question. And in many cases indeed, after introspectively inspecting the causal-decisional sequence

---

[53] Richard I. Evans, *Dialogue with Erich Fromm* (New York: Harper & Row, 1966), 96–97.

of our acts, we may feel the free ingredient to be irreducible without being able to refute the deterministic believer who holds to the conviction that some determinist account does exist. The question then becomes in Spinoza's terms whether the belief in determinism itself is an inadequate idea, that is, whether it would dissolve if all its antecedents, causal and free, were brought to consciousness. To Spinoza goes the honor of the great achievement of having opened for inquiry this whole domain of the unconscious psychological forces.

Might I close on a note of personal intellectual history in the vein of Spinoza's *Improvement of the Understanding*. I belong to that generation of young Jews in the nineteen-twenties for whom Spinoza was a symbol of both revolt and reason. We were the children of the Talmud Torah on New York's East Side, and knew the orthodoxy of its synagogues. But we were also part of the schoolboy crowd that sought a glimpse of Einstein when he came to America telling of strange new ideas of space and time. We felt too the stronger attraction of a more joyful American culture, of baseball and the Yankees and Giants. We felt the constrictedness of the Ghetto's intellectual bounds. Then we heard of the philosopher who had been excommunicated but who had found the way for a man to be both a scientist and believer in God. An occasional Jewish magazine or newspaper would publish an article about the dramatic excommunication. A teacher at high school told that Spinoza had proved the existence of God mathematically. We got hold of the *Ethics* in a public library, though I was disappointed in the proof. But still Spinoza remained the great liberating figure. A society came into existence, the Spinoza Institute of America, half crackpot, to cultivate the study of Spinoza, and at one of its public lectures, I heard New York's philosopher, Morris R. Cohen, discuss Spinoza's conception of Nature with reverence, and close with Spinoza's dictum that "all things noble are as difficult as they are rare." Spinoza's pantheism and determinism have long ago lost their attraction for me, nor would I place much credence in any purported philosophical demonstration. Yet what remained for those of my generation was the sense of a man of unparallelled honesty, moved by a vision which for all its exaggeration grasped a great segment of reality, and in so doing, was inspired to utterances of such simple philosophical beauty that only one who had shared in God's thoughts could have written them.

University of Virginia

10 NOTES ON SPINOZA'S CRITIQUE OF RELIGION
Hilail Gildin

Aubrey's *Brief Lives* contains two short but revealing reports about what Hobbes thought of the *Theologico-Political Treatise*. When an acquaintance who had lent Hobbes the work asked him what he thought of it, Hobbes said, "Judge not that you may not be judged." After recounting this story, Aubrey adds that Hobbes had told him Spinoza's work had "cut through him a bar's length, for he durst not write so boldly." Both reports suggest that Hobbes thought there were important similarities between his work and Spinoza's. The word "similarity" is too weak, however, to convey the sense of the second remark. In that remark, Hobbes speaks of Spinoza as engaged in a project that is not only like his own but the same as his own, with the difference that in carrying it out Spinoza was even bolder than he himself had been. To say this is not to say that Hobbes thought Spinoza was in agreement with him in every respect or even in every important respect. Two men can be at work on the same project and still disagree heatedly with one another like two officers of the same army who differ sharply about the best way to defeat the enemy. Yet the sameness of a project points to an important area of agreement. In what did that agreement consist, according to Hobbes?

According to a well known analysis, the fear of violent death is the passion on which Hobbes' solution to the political problem is founded.[1] The fact that this passion is more powerful than any other assures Hobbes of the solidity of his solution. Yet, the analysis proceeds, there are passages in which Hobbes acknowledges that other passions are more powerful than the fear of violent death. The fear of spirits, of hell-fire, or of God are said by Hobbes to be more powerful than other fears are. The authority of the sovereign owes its being to men's desire to be liberated from the fear of violent death.

---

[1] Leo Strauss, *Natural Right and History* (Chicago: University of Chicago Press, 1953), 166 ff.

But the still greater fear of God can lead men to regard as still greater the authority of those who they think know how to avert or pacify the wrath of God. This fundamental difficulty, which threatens to nullify Hobbes' entire solution, has been said to be the only major objection to his views whose validity he recognized and which he made strenuous efforts to meet.[2] The content of almost half of the *Leviathan*— the last two parts of that four part work—testifies to the importance he attached to removing that difficulty. The difficulty in question *is* Hobbes' theologico-political problem. Failure to solve this problem would, given his analysis, be tantamount to declaring the political problem itself to be utterly hopeless. His own solution to the theologico-political problem requires that the civil authority as civil authority be granted supreme authority over all religious practice and instruction. Hobbes is aware that many adherents of Biblical religion will find his proposal shocking. To meet the attack he anticipated from them, Hobbes advanced new interpretations of the Bible from which it follows that his views are not in conflict with it and attacked those interpretations of it from which it follows that they are. In presenting his interpretations, Hobbes argues more like a lawyer who is seeking to win a case than like an historian who is dispassionately seeking to determine the truth. Arguing like a lawyer does not, of course, rule out making points with a considerable bite to them, turning to one's account truths that are embarrassing to one's opponents, and in general taking advantage of anything in the law which can be construed to favor one's case, even if nothing of the kind was intended by those who wrote it. When someone argues in this way, however, one usually must look beyond his arguments to understand why he wishes to make them. In Hobbes, the answer to this question is to be found in the strictly political part of his teaching, in his political philosophy in the narrow sense. It is there that we learn why he thinks peace is the end of political society and why it is essential to peace for the sovereign to have the right to prohibit religious doctrines which undermine his authority. In other words, the rational core of Hobbes' critique of religion is to be found in his political philosophy.

When we turn from Hobbes to Spinoza's *Theologico-Political Treatise* we find that Spinoza's work is devoted exclusively to the theologico-political problem as that problem is understood by Hobbes.[3] The *Theologico-Political Treatise* was never meant to be a comprehensive

---

[2] Strauss, 198.

[3] Spinoza, *Opera*, ed. Carl Gebhardt, 4 vols. (Heidelberg: Carl Winter, 1925). All references to Spinoza's *Tractatus Theologico-Politicus* (hereafter cited in the abbreviation *TTP*) will be to volume III of Gebhardt's edition. Numbers in parentheses refer to the lines of this edition.

treatise on politics. Spinoza explicitly distinguishes its subject matter from that of both his *Ethics* and his *Political Treatise*.[4] The relation of the *Theologico-Political Treatise* to the *Political Treatise* can be understood from the fact that it is the purpose of the former work to show how the theologico-political problem can be solved. Only where the danger of divided sovereignty is removed can the sound political orders to which the later work is devoted be established. Spinoza not only understands the theologico-political problem in the same way as Hobbes does, but he also requires, as a condition for solving it, that the sovereign be acknowledged to possess the right to determine what is pious and what is impious. Moreover, he likewise attacks all interpretations of the Bible which would lead one to view conformity with his requirements as irreligious and he advances an interpretation of his own from which it follows that conformity with it is not only permitted but required by piety as the Bible understands it.[5] In both his attacks and his construction, he argues, as Hobbes does, more like a lawyer, than like a scholarly historian, despite his well known role in establishing the science of the Bible. It is especially in his attack—but to a lesser degree, also in his construction—that he displays the daring by which Hobbes was so amazed.

The *Theologico-Political Treatise* opens with a discussion of revelation or prophecy. It defines revelation as certain knowledge revealed by God to man. Spinoza immediately infers from this definition that natural knowledge or natural science deserves to be called revelation too.[6] The assimilation of God to Nature and the knowledge of God to natural science sets in with the very opening of the *Theologico-Political Treatise*. In the first chapter, for example, the belief of some pious men that they understood something by seeing it as an expression of the power of God is ridiculed on the grounds that the power of God *is* the power of nature, and that to understand something as resulting from the power of God means to know its natural cause.[7] God is explicitly declared to have no mind (mens), spirit (animus), or soul (anima).[8] Even if one limits oneself to what is advanced in the first chapter of the *Theologico-Political Treatise* one would have to say that Spinoza's God is certainly not Spirit but that He may well be Nature. The temptation some reader might feel to understand Spinoza's denial of mind, soul and spirit to God in the light of the negative way in theology should be resisted if only because in the *Theologico-Political Treatise* Spinoza affirms that men possess a clear and distinct idea of

---

[4] TTP, 60(24–28), 203 (4–11), 221(31)–222(1).
[5] See the subtitle of the *TTP*.
[6] *TTP*, 15(5)–16(5).
[7] *TTP*, 28(7–16).
[8] *TTP*, 25(25–30), 26(10–13), 171(34)–172(6).

God. He makes the same point in the *Ethics* when he declares that "the human mind has an adequate knowledge of the eternal and infinite essence of God."[9]

These assertions by Spinoza are not used by him to affirm that prophecy or revelation in the usual sense is impossible, but only that it is subject to laws of nature although he declares that he no more knows what the laws in question may be than he knows by what laws of nature some men possess the natural gift of improvising poetry.[10] Rather, he uses these assertions to frame a standard on the basis of which he passes judgements on revelation in the usual sense. So, for example, even though natural knowledge or science also deserves to be called prophecy or revelation Spinoza refuses to infer that natural scientists deserve to be called prophets. The interesting reason he gives is that natural scientists can teach what they know to others whereas prophets can not. This leads to the question of how the auditors of a prophet can know that what the prophet reveals to them is true. That question is examined in Chapter 2. Spinoza again compares prophecy in the unusual sense to natural knowledge or science. The result of this comparison in Chapter 2 is, according to Spinoza, that natural knowledge bears the mark of its truth within itself, while prophecy does not. Unlike natural knowledge, revelation is in need of a sign. The prophet, no less than his auditors, needs it in order to be assured that what is revealed to him is true.[11]

After affirming the need for a sign, however, Spinoza proceeds to make the reader wonder whether the uncertainty that makes a sign necessary can ever be removed by a sign. He cites the Bible to show that according to it, miracles can be performed by false prophets as well as by true prophets. It is true that God never deceives the pious, he adds, but no one can be certain of the piety any more than he can be of his revelation.[12] It would seem, then, that according to Spinoza only natural knowledge or science can, strictly speaking, live up to the definition of revelation with which the *Theologico-Political Treatise* opens. The chapter on prophecy began and ended with a comparison between prophecy in the usual sense and rational knowledge. The conclusion of that chapter was that revelation is the work of the imagination *alone*, unassisted by the intellect.[13] After developing an argument suggesting that the resulting uncertainty of revelation cannot be

---

[9] *TTP*, 59(29)–60(3), *Adnotatio* VI (252 f.), *Ethics* II 47. Cf. the remarks by Appuhn on 13–14 of his introductory remarks to his translation of the *TTP* (Paris: Garnier-Frères, 1965).
[10] *TTP*, *Adnotatio* III (252).
[11] *TTP*, 16(6–9), 30(13–34).
[12] *TTP*, 30(34)–31(12), 31(15–7).
[13] *TTP*, 29(5–8), 30(16–17).

removed by any sign, Spinoza proceeds to confirm that suggestion by undertaking an examination of what the prophets learned about God from revelation. The result of his survey is that the prophets had absurd and mutually contradictory beliefs about God and that the revelations they received about God were likewise absurd and mutually contradictory. This is a rather serious contention, since Spinoza is speaking of prophets like Moses, Jeremiah and Ezekiel. Spinoza qualifies the force of his remark by limiting the scope of his attack to the speculative content of prophecy. The point of revelation, he affirms, is not speculative but moral. We are free to think what we please regarding everything except that point, even if what we think contradicts the content of what was revealed, since that content, as he explains it, resulted from God's adapting the revelation to the erroneous beliefs of the prophets in order to make that revelation and its point seem certain to them. Jesus and the Apostles are to be read in the same way, according to Spinoza, although in the case of Jesus the adaptation of what he had to say to the erroneous beliefs of those to whom he was speaking is said to have been made *by* him rather than *to* him.[14] To repeat, Spinoza exempts from the sweeping repudiation of the authority of revelation only the practical meaning of revelation. What that authoritative practical content is, or rather what it is *not*, and in particular that it is not either the Mosaic or any ceremonial law whatever, is the subject of the three chapters that follows the two opening ones on revelation. Before turning to them, however, it would be useful to examine what arguments Spinoza advances to support the bold and far-reaching assertions we have outlined.

The Bible itself, according to Spinoza, is the witness whose testimony supports the denials he voices. He claims that in the absence of living prophets we have no other witness than the Bible regarding what transcends the limits of our understanding.[15] He therefore requires that whatever is affirmed regarding revelation and those to whom it is granted be based on the Bible alone. In particular, he does not wish what is asserted in the Bible regarding revelation to be made to conform with our beliefs (which may be true) regarding what is rationally plausible. In Chapter 15 of the *Theologico-Political Treatise*, Spinoza agrees with Rabbi Alpakhar's refusal to make conformity with the views of natural reason a criterion for determining whether or not something is a teaching of the Bible. He parts company with Alpahkar over the latter's demand that reason submit to what is determined in this way to be the teaching of the Bible even if that teaching is contrary to reason. In claiming that the testimony of the Bible

---

[14] *TTP*, 37–44
[15] *TTP*, 16(26)–17(8).

(alone) is the basis of his denials, Spinoza appears to be doing no more than practicing what he preaches. Yet it is plain, even apart from an examination of the Biblical passages which are supposed to be the evidence for Spinoza's denials, that something more is at work in his argument than the testimony of the Bible. From the outset, Spinoza begins his discussion of revelation by contrasting it with natural knowledge or science. In developing that contrast he interprets natural knowledge or science as a way in which God reveals His decrees to man. Revelation in the usual sense is measured against revelation in Spinoza's new sense and found inferior to it. The Biblical passages Spinoza cites do not simply speak for themselves. They are judged by the standards of the new theology, some parts of which we have glimpsed, which Spinoza outlines in the *Theologico-Political Treatise*. That theology has at least as much to do with the conclusions to which he comes as do the Biblical passages he cites. In fact, it seems very much as though his negative conclusions are already a part of that theology or at least implied by it. Contrary to what Spinoza affirms, his observations regarding revelation are not based on revelation alone, at least not on revelation in the usual sense. They are based on a theology which is not shown by him to be true, but is merely asserted by him. Before seeing what response Spinoza could make to these criticisms it will be helpful to outline briefly the content of the theology he sets forth in the *Theologico-Political Treatise*.

It was stated above that Spinoza assimilates God to Nature in the *Theologico-Political Treatise*. It would be more accurate to say that he calls Nature "God." Equivalents of the phrase "God or Nature," which occurs once in the *Ethics*, are to be found in a large variety of forms in the present work.[16] The tenets of Spinoza's theology, if one may call it that, derive from its decisive first step, which consists, to exaggerate slightly, in calling nature as some atheists conceive of it—a realm every occurrence in which is completely determined by universal and eternal laws that do not will or think or care and that do not originate in a being that wills or thinks or cares—by the name of God. Accordingly, natural reason and science become a kind of revelation because, according to Spinoza, they furnish us with certain knowledge of God (i.e., Nature) and because they owe their ability to do so to a power that they have received from God (i.e., Nature). Not surprisingly, one acquires natural knowledge of God so understood by studying natural things and coming to know their natural causes. The universal and necessary laws of nature are called the eternal decrees of God. God's direction of the world is explained as the prede-

---

[16] *TTP*, 28(3–20), 45(31)–46(12), 57(23)–58(27), 189(12)–190(2), 199(12–15). See especially Chapter 6.

termined order of nature. If one cannot call this view atheistic this is chiefly because, in conformity with the procedure outlined above, a new meaning is assigned to the word "atheism." Atheism is the denial, as distinguished from the ignorance, of God so understood. So, for example, miracles in the sense in which Spinoza is willing to admit their existence—"unfamiliar works of nature"—do not lead to atheism, whereas miracles of the kind he declares impossible, miracles which interrupt and contradict the order of nature, do lead to atheism according to him.[17] This understanding of miracles and atheism underlies Spinoza's assertions that "everything which the Bible truly recounts as having happened, necessarily happened according to the laws of nature, as all things do, and if something is found regarding which one can irrefutably prove that it contradicts the laws of nature or that it cannot be derived from them, one may straightway assume that it was added to the Sacred Scriptures by sacrilegious men."[18] The men in question would be sacrilegious because what they did fosters a belief in "atheism."

Associated with these theological views is a teaching regarding the supreme good of man. That good is declared to consist in the perfection of the human understanding, a perfection which cannot be achieved without the knowledge of "God" (i.e. Nature). That knowledge in turn is drawn from universal concepts which are certain and self-evident and it is perfected by our understanding of things in nature. Man's blessedness consists in the knowledge of God. Whether the basic knowledge of God that flows from the simplest and most universal notions is sufficient to produce that blessedness, or whether the perfected knowledge must be present as well, is not apparent from the outline that Spinoza gives. The knowledge of God is said by Spinoza to give rise to the love of God. Knowledge of God, love of God, and blessedness are inseparable. This permits Spinoza to say that human blessedness consists in the pure love of God. It also permits him to draw the following negative conclusions which he makes use of in determining what the practical teaching of the Bible is or must be: the true love of God cannot result from what is beyond human understanding but only from what is within its grasp. The true love of God does not result from a decision to obey a command to love Him. That love is the spontaneous outcome of the knowledge of God. Everything irrelevant to this knowledge is irrelevant to this love.

---

[17] *TTP*, 28(12–16), 60(3–11), 85(5)–86(4). For miracles as "unfamiliar works of nature" cf. 98(35)–99(2), 81(23). Cf. A. G. Wernhan's introduction to his edition of Spinoza's political works (Oxford: Clarendon Press, 1958), 6.

[18] *TTP*, 91(21–26).

The belief that some important event once took place is irrelevant to the knowledge of God according to Spinoza, hence to the love of God. Performing religious ceremonies brings one no closer to the love of God because it cannot bring knowledge of God. Spinoza calls by the name "divine law" the way of life prescribed by men with a view to their supreme good, i.e., to their knowledge and love of God. The divine law is its own reward. Failure to act in accordance with it is its own punishment. The divine law does not need rewards and punishments foreign to itself. It is called divine because of its object, not because it is commanded by God. The knowledge of God contained in the divine law makes it clear, according to Spinoza, that no laws can be commanded by God because God cannot be a ruler, legislator or king any more than He can be merciful or just.[19] The divine law, understood in this way, determines Spinoza's interpretation and judgement of the practical teaching of the Bible no less than do the speculative views outlined previously.

Spinoza does not attempt to prove these assertions in the *Theologico-Political Treatise*. On one occasion he refers to a demonstration that he gives in another work of what he affirms in this one.[20] In the absence of any demonstration, his theses are nothing but dogmatic pronouncements. And these pronouncements decisively influence Spinoza's own interpretation of the Bible not only in the judgements Spinoza passes on various Biblical teachings but even more in his efforts to show that his dogmas are the teaching of the Bible itself. Thus one finds him trying to show that according to the Bible the chosenness of the Hebrews had nothing to do with their superior understanding of God, or that ceremonies have nothing to do with the divine law, or even that miracles are impossible. Is not the arbitrariness of the way he makes his arguments enough to rob them of persuasiveness? Nor is this all. One of the chief contentions of Spinoza in the *Theologico-Political Treatise* is that the speculative meaning of many Biblical passages is hopelessly unclear, and that the speculative views of one prophet contradict those of another as well as the truth. These contentions conflict with Spinoza's attempts to show that his own speculative dogmas are the speculative teaching of the Bible. Does Spinoza's argument not stand condemned by itself?

Yet Spinoza's attack cannot be dismissed so readily. Those at whom it was directed did not remain unaffected by it. To what does Spinoza's polemic owe its power in spite of its strange character? The dogmatic theses outlined above are not unfamiliar to the student of

---

[19] *TTP*, 59(29)–65(34). Cf. Harry Austryn Wolfson, *Religious Philosophy* (New York: Atheneum, 1965), 241–243.
[20] *TTP*, 46(1–4).

Spinoza. Many of them are carefully set forth in the *Ethics* where an attempt to demonstrate them is made. In the *Theologico-Political Treatise* Spinoza protests against the practice of interpreting the Bible by reading into it Platonic or Aristotelian speculations with which the Biblical authors were unacquainted.[21] Spinoza does not leave it at denouncing such practices, however. He supplies an example of them and of what makes them arbitrary, in his opinion. He uses all means necessary to read into the Bible not the philosophy of Plato or Aristotle but the philosophy of Spinoza. The reader is thus treated to the strange spectacle of seeing the Bible cited in support of such contentions as that God does not ever tell men how He wishes them to act or that miracles are impossible.[22] One does not have to be a Spinozist in order to be given cause to wonder whether there might not indeed be some arbitrariness in the practices which Spinoza both criticizes and obtrusively illustrates. At the same time that he attempts to arouse doubts about the legitimacy of interpretations of the Bible based on later philosophical speculations, Spinoza develops a second line of argument intended to show that the *true* meaning of the most important passages in the Bible concerning God, as that meaning discloses itself to someone who refrains from reading later speculations into the Bible, points to an understanding of God that is utterly unacceptable not only from the standpoint of Spinoza himself but from that of almost any theologian of Spinoza's time. Spinoza seeks to confront his reader with a dilemma by making him choose between an understanding of God which is Biblical but unacceptable and other understandings which, while they are not unacceptable in the same way, are unsupported by the authority of the Bible. This two-fold argument, taken in conjunction with the difficulties Spinoza raises regarding the authorship and composition of the Biblical books, difficulties tending to arouse doubts about how reliable a witness these books are of the events they relate, constitutes the sober side of Spinoza's polemic. The continuing vitality, among theologians, of the debate over demythologization shows that the difficulties raised by Spinoza, while not sufficient to defeat his antagonist, were far from frivolous.

The intention governing Spinoza's treatment of the speculative content of the Bible can be gathered from that treatment itself. The same cannot be said of the intention governing his treatment of the moral teaching of the Bible. The one treatment is no less arbitrary than the other, but in the case of the moral teaching, the arbitrariness is not the reverse side of a serious argument. The goal at which Spinoza wishes to arrive is clear. He wishes to show that the moral teach-

---

[21] *TTP*, 9(1–5), 19(26–33), 167(30)–168(5).
[22] *TTP*, 65(34)–68(31), 95(15)–96(18).

ing of the Bible is one and the same from beginning to end in both the Jewish and the Christian Bible.[23] One can even see why that goal is a desirable one for him. He wants the adherents of the various Biblical religions to stop thinking that the differences between them are important enough to kill or to die for. What is not clear is why Spinoza thinks that the interpretation of the moral teaching of the Bible which he offers will be persuasive to anyone. Some highly important practical teachings of the Bible simply do not appear to be of the character Spinoza affirms. There obviously are important differences between the Law of Moses and the Sermon on the Mount. Moreover, the ceremonial practices required in the two Bibles are not the same. Spinoza deals with this difficulty by denying that the Law of Moses has anything whatever to do with true piety and affirming that it was merely the Law of the Hebrew state, which is why it had for its end the end of all political laws, i.e. comfort and security. He enlarges upon this assertion by setting forth what according to him truly deserves to be called the divine law in contradistinction to the law of Moses. The true divine law is the teaching regarding the supreme good of man outlined above. Spinoza strives to show that the true divine law is the moral teaching of the Bible. Since the divine law is universal, Spinoza concludes that all practices which are peculiar have nothing to do with it, according to the Bible itself. In this way he disposes, as best he can, of the difficulties created for him by the Law of Moses and various ceremonial practices of Christians and Jews. He disposes of the difficulties created by the new teachings of the Sermon on the Mount, teachings which, as new, are not to be found everywhere in the Bible, in a somewhat different manner. He offers curious interpretations of them which, if accepted, would eliminate any conflict between them and other Biblical precepts. So, for example, the precept to turn the other cheek is explained as advice for times of oppression. A similar explanation is given of the precept to love one's enemies.[24] The way would seem to be open for Spinoza to uniquivocally and consistently equate the moral teaching of the Bible with the divine law.

And yet Spinoza does not do so. He cannot do so without acting in opposition to his overriding intention, which is to persuade religions with different beliefs about God to consider their differences as unimportant. If the equation of the core of true religion with the knowledge of God were Spinoza's last word, he could not very well deny that these differences were of great importance. Spinoza equates the true teaching of the Bible with the divine law, the root of which is

---

[23] *TTP*, 77(23)–78(1), 102(26–35), 165(11–33).
[24] See note 25 below.

knowledge of God, as long as his aim is to dispute the right of the precepts peculiar to the Law of Moses or to the Sermon on the Mount to be considered divine. He does this by explaining the purpose of these peculiar precepts to be, in both cases, no more than the temporal well-being of those to whom they are addressed, rather than anything lofty or divine. He tries to show at length that the ceremonial law of the Hebrews was meant to serve an entirely this-worldly end. He tries to show, though far more briefly, that the same end was served by all the precepts of the Sermon on the Mount which he describes in the *Theologico-Political Treatise*. The precept to turn the other cheek is said, as was mentioned above, to be a counsel for times of oppression. The precept to love one's enemies is said to have never been meant to govern the conduct of the citizens of a country towards that country's enemies. Only because Jesus saw the Jewish nation destroyed and the Jews scattered all over the world is he said to have commanded them to be just and charitable to all men, including their enemies and those who persecuted them.[25] Spinoza uses the equation of the true teaching of the Bible with the divine law to eliminate all important rivals to what he intends to declare the simple general teaching of the Bible regarding conduct to be. As long as those rivals are his chief concern, what the Bible means by true religion is declared to consist of the knowledge and the love of God. Once those rivals have been disposed of, at least in speech, Spinoza declares that what the Bible requires of all men is nothing as impossibly lofty and difficult as the knowledge of God but merely obedience to God, i.e., just and charitable conduct.

Spinoza prepares the way for his later assertion that what the Bible requires of all men is not knowledge but obedience even in the argument that is based on the opposite assumption.[26] Even when he affirms that the divine law is the true teaching of the Bible, Spinoza refrains from saying that the divine law is what the Prophets believed or what Jesus and Paul taught. The Prophets, Spinoza claims, were not only ignorant of the divine law but held beliefs about God which were opposed to it. That is why God, adapting Himself to these erroneous beliefs, revealed himself to them as a just and merciful ruler and lawgiver. Unlike the prophets, Jesus and Paul knew the divine law, as did Solomon too. They knew that God could not be any of the things the Prophets thought He was. But, like the Prophets, Jesus and Paul did not teach the divine law, any more than God did when He revealed Himself to the Prophets. Jesus and Paul adapted what they said to the erroneous beliefs of the multitudes they addressed, just as

---

[25] *TTP*, 103(14)–104(14), 233(15–26).
[26] *TTP*, 63(12)–68(31).

God had done before them. The respect with which Jesus and Paul are treated by Spinoza is based not on what Spinoza asserts they taught but on what Spinoza asserts they "doubtless" knew in spite of what they taught.[27] It should be noted, if only in passing, that there is no hint of disapproval in Spinoza's account of the practice he attributes to Jesus, Paul and God. When Spinoza speaks of the divine law as the true teaching of the Bible, he makes it clear that it is very far from being the prevalent teaching of the Bible.

The assertion that the true religion revealed by the Bible is the knowledge and the love of God contradicts the assertion that the universal revealed religion to be found everywhere in the Bible requires not a sublime understanding of God but only such beliefs about Him as will lead men to obey Him. Spinoza frankly admits that such beliefs are utterly incompatible with the knowledge of God. The universal revealed religion requires us to think of God as just and merciful and as a model of true life. The knowledge of God reveals, Spinoza says, that He cannot be merciful or just or a model of true life.[28] Spinoza does not conceal the conflict between the two positions. He frankly declares them to be incompatible and he claims to be an adherent of both of them. The first is true in virtue of reason, for him the highest tribunal. He says that he accepts the second on the authority of the Bible confirmed by the miracles reported in the Bible. He undoubtedly teaches both opinions in the *Theologico-Political Treatise*.

Spinoza does not resolve this contradiction, but he does help the reader understand his unhesitating willingness to embrace it. In the first place, he asserts that the universal revealed religion does not have to be true. In fact, many of its beliefs are not true, according to him.[29] Truth, for Spinoza, is the province of philosophy, not of faith, which is solely concerned with obedience. Moreover, Spinoza leaves men perfectly free to interpret the articles of the universal faith. For example, one is obliged by the universal faith to hold that a just and merciful God exists who is a model of true life. However, "what God or that model of true life is, whether He is fire, spirit, light, thought etc. does not concern faith, any more than it concerns faith in what way He is the model of true life, whether because He has a just and merciful spirit or because all things are and act through Him and

---

[27] *TTP*, 65(8–9; 17).

[28] *TTP*, 64(10–15), 65(13–34), 171(34)–172(6). Cf. 168(27–33), 175(34)–176(18). Cf. note 8 above. For a comprehensive analysis of how the contradictions of Spinoza in the *TTP* are to be understood, see Leo Strauss' *Persecution and the Art of Writing* (Glencoe, Illinois: Free Press, 1952), 142–201, as well as his introduction to *Spinoza's Critique of Religion* (New York: Schocken Books, 1965).

[29] *TTP*, 176(18–22).

consequently we too understand through Him and through Him see what is truly right and good."³⁰ Everyone is free to think whatever he likes regarding these matters. Such freedom can make contradictions not too difficult to live with. Finally, Spinoza recommends the acceptance of the universal faith because of the benefit society will derive from it and because of the consolation it will bring many people. The success of his efforts to separate religion from knowledge would lead, in his opinion, to an end to violent conflicts between religions. What led him to think that there was any hope of securing acceptance of the universal faith he favors by the religions of his time will have to be discussed in the sequel. It is sufficient at present to draw attention to the fact that, according to Spinoza, solid advantages are to be gained from the universal faith and that most men cannot be expected to achieve the sound understanding of God required by the divine law. These facts alone would lead one to expect Spinoza to accommodate himself in some measure to the beliefs of the universal faith by imitating the practice he ascribes, without disapproval, to Jesus, Paul, and God.

Spinoza claims that the universal faith consists of what the Bible teaches everywhere. It is not difficult to show, on the basis of what Spinoza himself says, that this is not the case. In order to maintain that it is the case he has to deny the fundamental importance, for the practical teaching of the Bible, of both the Law of Moses and the Sermon on the Mount. Yet in other contexts he cannot help recognizing the fundamental importance of these.³¹ Further, the beliefs concerning God of the universal religion are said to be taught everywhere in the Bible. Yet he asserted in the second chapter of the *Theologico-Political Treatise* that many prophets, including the one he calls the greatest of them all, Moses, held opinions about God that were in conflict with these beliefs.³² It is difficult not to conclude that Spinoza says that the universal revealed religion is what it is because that is what he wants it to be. To see why he wants it to be that and why he thinks he can persuade others that it is that one must turn to the political part of his argument. If there is a sober side to Spinoza's treatment of the practical teaching of the Bible, it will have to be found in his political philosophy.

Spinoza's political philosophy thus bears an enormous burden in his argument. When one turns to it, though, one wonders whether it

---

³⁰ *TTP*, 178(13–20).

³¹ See the summary of the Bible from Genesis to the end of Kings, *TTP*, 126(9–24). Consider the omission of law in *TTP*, 98(30)–99(12). Also see 163(7–10) and 152(1–5).

³² Compare *TTP*, pp. 37(19)–41(17) with the passages cited in note 23 and the dogmas of the universal faith (177[20]–178[10]).

can sustain that burden. His argument seems to depend on the doctrine of Hobbes, even when diverging from it. Yet Hobbes felt he had to argue his way to conclusions which Spinoza appears to simply start from. Hobbes' immortal description of what men are like, a description the validity of which he claims men can confirm from their experience of each other and of themselves, is the basis of his political philosophy. No such description is offered by Spinoza, who plunges directly into an analysis of natural right and the state of nature. Does Spinoza's argument, then, not rest on a foundation which is itself in need of a foundation that he fails to supply?

To draw this conclusion would be to underestimate what unites Hobbes and Spinoza. It would be to think of each of them as engaged in constructing his own separate edifice—his "philosophy"—with the difference that in Spinoza's case a proper foundation is lacking for some of the features he took over from what Hobbes had erected. A far better understanding of the relation between the two thinkers is suggested by the following passage from Leo Strauss' *Thoughts on Machiavelli*:

> We have devoted what at first glance seems to be a disproportionately large space to Machiavelli's thought concerning religion. This impression is due to a common misunderstanding of the intention, not only of Machiavelli but also of a whole series of political thinkers who succeeded him. We no longer understand that in spite of great disagreements among those thinkers, they were united by the fact that they all fought one and the same power—the kingdom of darkness, as Hobbes called it; that fight was more important to them than any merely political issue. This will become clearer to us the more we learn again to understand those thinkers as they understood themselves and the more familiar we become with the art of allusive and elusive writing which all of them employ, although to different degrees. The series of those thinker will then come to sight as a line of warriors who occasionally interrupt their fight against their common enemy to engage in a more or less heated but never hostile disputation among themselves.[33]

Spinoza is not engaged in a project different from that of Hobbes, but in the same project.[34] He finds that Hobbes' proposal is radically

---

[33] Leo Strauss, *Thoughts on Machiavelli* (Glencoe, Illinois: The Free Press, 1958), 231.

[34] Cf. Robert J. McShea, *The Political Philosophy of Spinoza* (New York and London: Columbia University Press, 1968), 137-38.

defective in one crucial respect. Men who take their religions seriously will never recognize the sovereign's right to supremacy over the practice of religion, a right both Spinoza and Hobbes agree the sovereign must have. Spinoza believes that he has discovered a new way to overcome this difficulty thereby opening the way for a rational solution to the political problem. The new way does not presuppose anything as illusory as the abolition of false religious beliefs. Such beliefs, together with other errors, have their source in human nature and can never be eliminated in most men. Just as the *Federalist Papers* seeks to safeguard political society against the dangers of ambition not by abolishing ambition but by using ambition to counteract its own ill effects, so Spinoza seeks to safeguard political society against the dangers that threaten it from false religious beliefs by making religion counteract religion. The toleration for which he argues is intended to accomplish this.

Instituting freedom of speech and of religion would, Spinoza thought, depoliticize religion and end religious hatred and wars. Spinoza does not explain why the freedom he favors should have such an outcome. His assertion that it will is supported by the example of Amsterdam rather than by any explanation.[35] That toleration should have such an outcome for Spinoza might even seem surprising to begin with in the light of Spinoza's own description of the savage hatred and indignation which differences regarding religion can arouse according to him. Spinoza refers more than once to the fact that what moves one man to devotion moves another to laughter and derision.[36] If toleration does no more than perpetuate mutual irritation resulting from mutual derision, how can it promote peace between different religions? Two remarks by Spinoza are important for understanding his answer to this question. The first occurs in the *Political Treatise*, where Spinoza declares that it is impossible to make men revere things which arouse ridicule or disgust.[37] The other passage which can shed light on our question is Prop. 31 of Book III of the *Ethics*: "If we imagine that someone loves, desires or hates something which we ourselves love, desire or hate we shall on that account love, desire or hate the thing more steadily. If however we imagine him averse to the thing we love or the reverse, we will then suffer vacillation of mind." The effect of toleration on someone wishing to continue adhering to his religion can be inferred from the foregoing. He will seek whatever will reinforce his convictions and try to avoid whatever would weaken them. He will begin to regard whatever his religious

---

[35] *TTP*, 245(31)–246(25); cf. 7(21–28).
[36] *TTP*, 11(1–8), 176(33)–177(6).
[37] Chapter 4, Paragraph 4.

beliefs have in common with the religious beliefs of his fellow citizens as what is most important about them and his fellow citizens will begin to do the same. The peculiarities of each religion would begin to appear to be of relatively minor importance by contrast. Courtesy rather than mutual ridicule and hatred would be the result. The universal religion which Spinoza teaches in the *Theologico-Political Treatise* would triumph not because men have been swayed by his questionable arguments for it but because of the ingenious working on religious beliefs of the new situation created by toleration. The more the various religions cease to regard what differentiates them from each other as the most important thing about themselves, the less their relations will be characterized by hatred. The less they are characterized by hatred, the less of a threat to the sovereign they will be. Spinoza's solution presupposes the presence of many religions, at least some of which will be saying many of the things that one reads in the *Theologico-Political Treatise*.[38]

According to Spinoza, the sovereign cannot credibly assert a right over the practice of religion. However it cannot abandon that right without exposing itself to challenge from an authority which men are disposed to consider as no inferior to itself. Spinoza's way out of this dilemma is to propose that the sovereign tolerate all religions that do not attack its authority. This it can do without appearing to overstep its bounds. It can also, without appearing to overstep them, compel religions which are not inclined to be tolerant to treat other religions properly whether they wish to do so or not. It can be the impartial tribunal which stands above the various religions and passes judgement on whether they are conducting themselves as they should in their relations to each other. Freedom of religion enforced by the sovereign will give the sovereign all the authority over the practice of religion that it requires, an authority that it will never obtain if it tries to exercise it directly.

Leo Strauss, in the last essay that he published on Hobbes, notes that at one point in the *Leviathan* Hobbes explores the possibility that the sovereign might refrain from establishing any religion whatever and simply leave it at permitting the practice of all religions which are not seditious.[39] If that were to happen, Hobbes observes, it could not be said that the commonwealth "is of any religion at all." But what for Hobbes is, at least at first glance, merely one somewhat marginal possibility, is in Spinoza the only arrangement which results in the

---

[38] See this author's "Spinoza and the Political Problem" in *Spinoza: A Collection of Critical Essays*, ed., Marjorie Grene (New York: Doubleday, 1973).

[39] Leo Strauss, *What is Political Philosophy?* (Glencoe, Illinois: The Free Press, 1959), 186.

attainment of the goals for which men entered political society. Like Hobbes, Spinoza describes these goals as peace, comfort and security. Unlike Hobbes, Spinoza's notion of security includes security from oppression by the sovereign. Accordingly, Spinoza can also speak of freedom as the end of political society. In taking this step, Spinoza prepares the way for the revision of Hobbes' teaching that was later undertaken by Locke and Rousseau.[40]

Queens College, City University of New York

---

[40] According to Spinoza, religion is essential to the stability of bad regimes, i.e., regimes in which security against oppression is absent but it is not essential to the stability of good ones although it can be harmful to good ones, if the proper policy toward it is not adopted. An absolute monarchy—Spinoza's favorite example is that of Ottoman Turkey—needs a powerful established religion, whereas the constitutional monarchy Spinoza describes in the *Tractatus Politicus* has no established religion at all.

11
SPINOZA AND HISTORY
James C. Morrison

> ... Spinoza hat zuerst den Gedanken gefasst, der für die Geschichtswissenschaft des 19. Jahrhunderts in allen ihren Zweigen der massgebende geworden ist, den Gedanken der entwicklungsgeschichtlichen Betrachtung.[1]
>
> —Carl Gebhardt

In his *Theological-Political Treatise*[2] Spinoza gives a critique of religion, theology, and Scripture based on both reason and history. The historical part of Spinoza's critique consists chiefly of a new "method of interpreting Scripture," of which a "history of Scripture" is an essential component. The ultimate result of this critique was the conception of the radical historicity of religion and Scripture. This achievement is now taken for granted by almost all theologians, Biblical scholars, and even laymen. But Spinoza's arguments for the historicity of religion and Scripture have been subsequently extended and applied to philosophy; indeed, to the whole study of man. Spinoza, wholly against his own intentions, has ironically become one of the founders of modern historicism and "the historical consciousness." For historical knowledge, which he employed as a means for liberating human reason from its subservience to the alleged suprarational truth of divine revelation, has been subsequently used by oth-

---

[1] Baruch de Spinoza, *Theologisch-politischer Traktat*, trans. Carl Gebhardt (Leipzig: 1908), xxiii.

[2] When quoting directly from Spinoza we use our own translations. We give page references both to the English version of Elwes, *Works of Spinoza*, Vol. I (New York: Dover Publications, 1951) (hereinafter: TTP) and to Vol. III of the edition of Carl Gebhardt, *Spinoza Opera*, 4 vols. (Heidelberg: Carl Winter, 1924) (hereinafter: Gebhardt)—Acknowledgement is due Mr. Brian Switzer for several helpful comments on an early version of this essay.

ers as a means for binding human reason into a new kind of subservience to the alleged sub-rational fact of the historical process.

In the following study we attempt to clarify some of the basic elements of this transformation of philosophy into historicism by giving an interpretive analysis of Spinoza's understanding and use of history in the *Theological-Political Treatise*. The first part of our study (Section I) deals with the relation of history to religion, theology, and Scripture in general, and Spinoza's historical method of interpreting Scripture in particular. Here is found the ultimate philosophical significance of history for Spinoza. Next (Section II) we discuss the political relevance of history. We then (Section III) turn to a critical examination of Spinoza's attempt to refute the possibility of divine revelation. Finally (Section IV) we indicate an alternative use of history, of which the present study is intended to be an example.

I. The *Theological-Political Treatise* has a philosophical, theological, and political purpose.[3] These are intimately connected. Spinoza says in his Preface that "philosophical readers" will find merely "commonplaces" (TTP 11; Gebhardt 12). This means that the work is written not for actual philosophers but potential ones. The latter are those who could or would become philosophers were they not inhibited by the claims of the Christian and Jewish religions to possess a supra-rational truth which has been revealed by God. The belief in such a revelation inevitably leads to a tension between reason and faith.[4] This tension expresses itself either as scepticism—the subordination of reason to faith and revelation, or dogmatism—the subordination of faith and revelation to reason. The *Theological-Political Treatise*, then, is a philosophical critique of revelation addressed to Christian or Jewish sceptics or dogmatists in order to convert a few of them

---

[3] In a letter to Oldenburg (*Epistola* XXX), probably written in 1665, the year he began to write the *Treatise*, Spinoza states that he has three aims: (1) to expose "the prejudices of theologians" which prevent men, expecially "the more prudent ones," from philosophizing, (2) to defend himself against the popular charge of atheism and (3) to defend "the liberty to philosophize and say what we think" (Gebhardt IV, 1667).

[4] In his discussion of miracles or "that which cannot be explained through natural causes," Spinoza says that he recognizes no distinction between a truth *supra naturam* and *contra naturam* (TTP 87; Gebhardt 86). Since the spheres of nature and reason are coextensive, a truth above reason would be a truth against reason. ". . . For whatever is against nature is against reason, and what is against reason is absurd and so must be rejected" (*TPT* 92; *Op.* 91).

to philosophy and the free use of reason.[5] But the free use of reason is inhibited not only by faith in revelation but also by political and ecclesiastical authority. Spinoza tries to remove this political obstacle to philosophy by arguing that everyone ought to have the freedom to "think what he likes and say what he thinks" (TTP 6, 11, 265; Gebhardt 7, 12, 246-247).[6] He thus addresses himself to present and future rulers in order to persuade them to permit the freedom of conscience and expression.[7] His thesis is that such freedom is necessary and beneficial both for "piety" and "public peace" (TTP 6; Gebhardt 7). In other words, the *Theological-Political Treatise* seeks to free philosophers from persecution by promoting the establishment of a liberal democratic state.[8] But the political and legal freedom to think, speak, and write is ultimately worthless unless reason itself is freed from the limitations imposed by the belief in revelation. The freedom to think without fear of political persecution therefore requires for its full realization complete confidence in the "natural light," i.e., one's capacity to discover and know the truth by one's own reason. For when the philosopher's own capacity to know is doubtful, his will to

---

[5] Cf. Leo Strauss, "How to Study Spinoza's *Theological-Political Treatise*," in *Persecution and the Art of Writing* (Westport, Conn.: 1973), 142, 162-3, 184, 189, 197. (This essay is indispensable to any student of the *Treatise*. Strauss' earlier book, *Spinoza's Critique of Religion* [New York: Schocken, 1965] is also essential and contains a penetrating and masterful discussion of both the historical background and central issues of the major traditional philosophical critiques of religion.)

[6] Cf. the sub-title to the *Treatise*.

[7] Carl Gebhardt, in his Introduction to his German translation of the *Treatise*, maintains that *der wahre grund, dem der Theologischpolitischer Traktat seine Entstehung verdankt, liegt in der Verbindung Spinozas mit* Jan de Witt (*op. cit.*, viii). He calls it *eine politische Tendenzschrift* or a defense of *den wirklichen Glauben der freidenkenden holländischen Regenten*, i.e., of de Witt's party (*ibid.*, xvi-xvii). However, Gebhardt also recognizes Spinoza's more general and permanent concerns of defending himself against the charges of his excommunication and *die Bestreitung des unmittelbargöttlichen Ursprungs der Schrift* as well as his being *der Begrunder der Bibelkritik* (*ibid.*, vii,xxiii). Hermann Cohen substantially agrees with this view. He calls the *Treatise* a *politischen Parteischrift*. Cf. *Judische Schriften*, Vol. III (Berlin: 1924), 294; cf. also 311-2 for Cohen's statement of Spinoza's *drei Aufgaben*. Spinoza himself, in his Preface to the *Treatise*, says that one of the "causes" which led him to write his book was the hypocrisy of Christians, i.e., men who profess to believe in a religion of love but in fact act with hatred and cruelty against their fellows. The conflict between the inner meaning of Christianity and the outer behavior of its adherents shows that its spiritual content has disappeared into "outward forms." The worship of God has been replaced by deference to men and faith has turned into credulity, prejudice, and ritual (TTP 6-7; Gebhardt 7).

[8] Cf. Strauss, "How to Study," *op. cit.*, 163. Cohen calls the *Treatise* a *Grundschrift des politisch-religiösen Liberalismus* (*op. cit.*, 292-3).

know is paralyzed.⁹ The philosophical quest for wisdom would be annulled in advance if one did not have complete confidence in one's ability to become wise. The possibility of revelation or a supra-rational truth leaves open the possibility of a contra-rational truth and hence casts into doubt the certainty of reason's clear and distinct ideas. The "deceiving demon" of revelation must therefore be exorcized by reason and philosophy themselves, which must demonstrate their autonomy and power by demonstrating the limitations and deficiencies of revealed religion. In short, the ultimate aim of the *Theological-Political Treatise* is to refute the revealed religion of Christianity and Judaism and replace it by philosophical wisdom. In order to accomplish this, reason and the philosophical critique of religion form an alliance with history to establish the historical critique of religion.

Historical critique liberates the mind from the external authority of Scripture and faith by providing a *ratio dubitandi* of Scripture and revelation. Spinoza's use of history, like Descartes' use of the method of "doubting all things," frees the mind from the confused ideas or "prejudices" of the past in order to reach a new clear and distinct knowledge of things. While Cartesian doubt leads to the certainty of self-consciousness which will serve as the new "Archimedian point" for constructing the new "edifice" of useful sciences enabling men to become "the masters and possessors of nature," Spinoza's historical critique leads to the liberation of human reason so that man can master himself by means of his own reason and become free of natural necessity. Moreover, by refuting revelation, historical critique removes a major cause of scepticism. For a miracle or interruption of the natural order "would make us doubt all things and lead to atheism" (TTP 87; Gebhardt 87). If miracles and revelations were possible, men could never be certain of anything.¹⁰ A transcendent and

---

⁹ In his Preface Spinoza speaks of the belief that "the human understanding is naturally corrupt" (TTP 7; Gebhardt 8). This belief presumably has a Biblical origin, i.e., the Christian doctrine of the Fall and original sin. If so, then if the Bible can be shown to have no authority, the belief in the insufficiency of the human mind is undermined. That Spinoza himself is free of this debilitating belief is clearly attested by his remark in a letter *(Epistola* XXI) to van Blyenbergh: "I acquiesce wholly without any mistrust in what my intellect shows me . . ." (Gebhardt IV, 126). Cf. also Section III below.

¹⁰ "In the pristine moment, the divine commanding Presence does not communicate a finite content that the human recipient might appraise and appropriate in the light of familiar standards. On the contrary, it calls into question all familiar content, and, indeed, all standards." Emil Fackenheim, *Encounters Between Judaism and Modern Philosophy* (New York: 1973), 45.

revealing God is a "deceiver" Who could confound all human truths and plans.[11] This would mean that philosophical knowledge and wisdom are unattainable. And since certain theoretical knowledge is necessary for certain practical knowledge, and the latter for happiness, human happiness would also be unattainable. Spinoza's ultimate goal of liberating men from superstition or "hope and fear" and thus from their impotent dependence on natural necessity would be undermined. If it is true that universal doubt would lead to atheism, it is no less true that atheism is necessary to avoid universal doubt. Theism or belief in revelation must be replaced by atheism or denial of revelation.[12]

Spinoza claims to demonstrate that "there is no correspondence or affinity between faith, or theology, and philosophy" (TTP 189; cf. 42,194-195, 198; Gebhardt 179; cf. 44, 184-185, 188). The "purpose" of philosophy is "truth," while that of faith or theology is only "obedience and piety" (TTP 189; Gebhardt 179). Spinoza attempts to establish this conclusion by means of both rational argument and historical fact. Knowledge of historical fact is relevant to religion, faith, and theology but not to philosophy. The "foundations" of faith lie in "histories and language" and are to be sought in Scripture and revelation, whereas the "foundations" of philosophy lie in "common notions, and must be sought only from nature"

---

[11] Spinoza refers to God's "tempting" the Hebrews, His "deceiving" the Egyptians, and false prophets confirming their prophecies with signs (TTP 81-88; Gebhardt 87-88).

[12] In effecting this displacement, Spinoza imitates the procedure of Descartes in the *Meditations*. Descartes mentions the "old opinion" of a God "who can do all things" and thus could bring it about that "no extended thing, no figure, no magnitude and no place" exist, and even that the most simple truths of mathematics be false. But immediately after considering this possibility, he says that "perhaps God has not wanted to deceive men because He is said to be supremely good." But this does not solve the problem, for even if Descartes is not "always deceived," he cannot deny that "sometimes I am deceived." Thus Descartes (like Spinoza after him) suggests that "we not oppose" the view of "some who would rather deny the existence of so powerful a God than to believe that all things are uncertain." He then continues the argument of *Meditation* I on the assumption that "all this about God is fictitious" and replaces the "omnipotent" and "best" God with "an evil genius, supremely powerful and cunning, who has done all he can to deceive me," i.e., a finite not infinite power. (The latin version describes the evil genius as *summe potentem & callidum*, whereas the French version describes him as *non moins rusé et trompeur que puissant.*) René Descartes, *Meditationes de Prima Philosophia*, J. Vrin (Paris: 1966), 21-3. Cf. Richard Kennington, "The Finitude of Descartes' Evil Genius," *Journal of the History of Ideas*, Vol. XXXII, No. 3 (1971), 441-6.

(TTP 189; Gebhardt 179). Philosophical knowledge is rational knowledge based on nature; religious knowledge is revealed knowledge based on history and language. Nevertheless, both philosophy and theology use an historical *method*. For philosophical knowledge of nature rests on a "history of nature"[13] and theological knowledge of the meaning of Scripture rests on a "history of Scripture" (TTP 195; Gebhardt 185). The historical method of investigating *nature* "consists chiefly in arranging the history of nature, from which, as from certain data, we infer the definitions of natural things" (TTP 99; Gebhardt 98). Although Spinoza does not tell us explicitly what the "history of nature" or the "certain data" are, the latter presumably refer to the changes that occur among natural things and the former to facts about them. The historical method of interpreting *Scripture* begins by "providing an accurate history of it, and from this, as from certain data and principles, infers by legitimate conclusions the intention of the authors of Scripture . . . " (TTP 99; Gebhardt 98). Here too, as in the case of nature, one begins with a "history" of "certain data" and then infers something else. But what is inferred from the history of Scripture is not a "definition" but the "intention" or "mind" (*mentem*) of the author of the text. Thus, whereas the historical method of interpreting nature yields general definitions of natural things, the historical method of interpreting Scripture yields knowledge of the individual authors of Scripture.

The above account of the historical method is amplified and somewhat modified a few pages later when Spinoza says that in interpreting Scripture one aims at understanding "the intention of the prophets and the Holy Spirit" (not the authors of Scripture) and that in interpreting nature one begins with "the most universal and common things of all nature, namely, motion and rest and their laws and rules, which nature always obeys and by which it continually acts . . . . " According to this, the "certain data" mentioned earlier are universal phenomena found in all natural things. From these "most universal and common things" one proceeds "gradually to other less universal things." Similarly in the case of Scripture, one begins with "what is most universal" and "what is commended by all prophets to all men

---

[13] The term "history of nature" *(historia naturae)* is, of course, a central one in *Bacon*, from whom Spinoza may have taken it. (It is an odd expression for Spinoza to use, and, as far as we know, does not occur in any other of his writings.) For Bacon, however, a history of nature is a collection of observations of particular phenomena from which an "induction" is made to general statements or "laws." Cf. Francis Bacon, *The Advancement of Learning*, ed. Arthur Johnston (Oxford: 1974), Books II, I.2 and VII.3.

as an eternal and most useful doctrine." The latter is "the basis and foundation of all Scripture," from which one can derive other less general and less essential doctrines (cf. TTP 104; Gebhardt 102).

Here we find one of the crucial principles underlying Spinoza's whole interpretation of Scripture: what Scripture really means is identical with its most universal teaching. This principle is derived from the interpretation of nature. For just as the essential nature of natural things consists in the most universal laws covering all natural phenomena, so the essential meaning of Scripture consists in what all of Scripture teaches. And just as nature is intelligible through the knowledge of its most universal laws, so Scripture is intelligible through knowledge of its most universal doctrines. In other words, the true meaning of Scripture is what it says everywhere, or what all writers of Scripture consistently teach. From this principle of interpretation Spinoza derives a correlative principle of *criticism:* whenever one finds in Scripture that "opinions are irreconcilable, one should then suspend judgement about them" (TTP 102; Gebhardt 101). Thus, if one teaching is ever contradicted by another, the reader should assume that Scripture teaches *nothing* about the subject.

Spinoza also asserts that, in addition to its universal meaning, the true meaning of Scripture is its *literal* meaning: the true meaning of Scripture is what Scripture *itself* says and not what has been attributed to it by interpreters or traditional authorities. In order to discover this literal meaning one must view Scripture "carefully" with a "free mind"; one must avoid all "human fictions." Above all, one must not assume in advance that Scripture is "everywhere true and divine" (TTP 8; Gebhardt 9). For the truth and divinity of Scripture is a *conclusion* to be proved after an interpretation of what Scripture means, not an initial premise to be used to interpret what it means. To view Scripture as the true word of God leads only to distortions of Scripture, not to a clear insight into what it is in itself. Spinoza thus replaces the subjective enthusiasm of faith with the objective detachment of reason: one must become neutral, an "agnostic," in order to interpret Scripture accurately. Faith in the divine or revealed character of Scripture is a "prejudice." The only unprejudiced point of view is the one which does not judge in advance that Scripture is divine, but which assumes that it is *not* divine. This is what Spinoza means when he says, "we are trying only to examine the texts of Scripture so that, as from the data of nature, we might draw our own conclusions" (TTP, 25; Gebhardt 28). For just as natural phenomena cannot be understood as the expression of intelligence or will, so to examine the Biblical texts as "natural data" means they cannot be understood as the testimony of a transcendent God revealing Himself to men. A literal interpretation of Scripture implies that it can be understood only as a *human* book.

The history of Scripture consists of three parts. (1) The first is a study of "the nature and properties of the language" in which Scripture was written and which its authors spoke (TTP 101; Gebhardt 99-100). (2) The second is a classification of "the opinions of each book" according to appropriate headings. This will allow one to establish the context of each passage, which in turn will provide the basis for distinguishing clear passages from obscure ones. Here Spinoza emphasizes the necessity of keeping distinct the question of the meaning of a text from that of its truth and the priority of the former to the latter (TTP 101; Gebhardt 100). For we cannot know whether a statement is true unless we know what it means and we cannot determine what a statement means by presupposing that it is true. Above all, one should not interpret the meaning on the basis of what seems reasonable or unreasonable (TTP 102; Gebhardt 100-101).[14] (3) The third element of a history of Scripture involves a number of complex investigations. One deals with the books themselves: the "occasion and time, to whom and in what language" they were written. Another deals with the "fortune of each book": how it was received, into whose hands it fell, the different versions which were made of it, and why it was accepted as sacred and included in the Bible. It is especially important to acquire historical knowledge about the authors, their "life, customs, and studies," for "we are able to explain the words of someone more easily, the better we know his mind and temperament" (TTP 103; Gebhardt 101-102).[15]

Spinoza claims that his method is "the only true one" for discovering the meaning of Scripture. If the meaning of a passage cannot be clarified by his method, the passage must be judged to be obscure, for each part of the method is a necessary condition for understanding a Scriptural text (TTP 108; Gebhardt 106). Spinoza warns, however, that the use of his method is attended by many "difficulties" and "impossibilities." In regard to the application of the first part, he states that no method could ever be found "which teaches how to discover with certainty the true meaning of all the speeches in Scrip-

---

[14] As an example of how to apply this rule, Spinoza mentions two passages, that God is a fire and that God is jealous, which he at first calls "very clear" (although he thinks them most unreasonable) and then, after discussing the possibility of interpreting them metaphorically rather than literally, he decides that they express "one and the same opinion" (TTP 102; Gebhardt 101). The point of this rather ironical and facetious analysis seems to be either that Moses was unable to distinguish between literal and metaphorical speech or that his idea of God was inconsistent (since fires cannot be jealous).

[15] Cf. Section IV and note 44 below for our discussion of the ironical application of this principle to Spinoza himself.

ture" (TTP 108; cf. 110; Gebhardt 107). This is due mainly to the fact that it is now impossible to trace the whole history of the Hebrew language, but also to the fact that past interpreters and editors may have altered the text (TTP 107; Gebhardt 106). Spinoza supports his claim with many examples of the grammatical and linguistic defects of ancient Hebrew (TTP 109-110; Gebhardt 107-108). In regard to the second part, he argues that often a comparison of parallel passages is useless since one cannot always infer what one prophet or apostle meant from another. This could be illustrated, he says, by "many inexplicable speeches" in Scripture (TTP 110-111; Gebhardt 108-109). Finally, in regard to the third part of the method, Spinoza says "another difficulty arises from the fact that it requires the history of all that has happened to the books of Scripture, of which we are for the most part ignorant." For example, of the authors "we are either wholly ignorant or in doubt of them"; "nor do we know" the occasion or time they wrote or what happened later to their books; nor do we know the various versions or how many versions there were (TTP 111; Gebhardt 109). Moreover, some books are not extant in the original language (TTP 112; Gebhardt 110). But in the case of any book which narrates "incredible or imperceptible things" it is absolutely essential to know something about its author and his intentions if we are to understand it (TTP 111; Gebhardt 109). The Bible is, of course, such a book, for it contains accounts of miracles, prophecies, and revelations.[16] Spinoza concludes that he considers all these "difficulties" of using his method "so great, that I do not hestitate to affirm that in very many passages we are either ignorant of the true meaning of Scripture or can only guess without certainty" (TTP 112; Gebhardt 111). Despite the fact that his method requires only the use of "the natural light," which all men possess to some degree, Spinoza "concedes that it does not suffice for explaining with certainty all things which occur in the Biblical texts" (TTP 113; cf. 119; Gebhardt 112; cf. 117).[17]

The arguments of the succeeding chapters (Chapters VIII-X) serve to confirm the above conclusions. For example, Chapter VIII opens with the assertion that the "foundations and principles" of the knowledge of Scripture need a "trustworthy history" of Scripture

---

[16] Spinoza here compares the story of Orlando Furioso driving a winged monster through the air (and a similar story in Ovid about Perseus) with the Biblical account of Elijah ascending to heaven in a fiery chariot (TTP 112; Gebhardt 110).

[17] Nor, Spinoza adds, may traditional authorities be appealed to, for the authority of the "Popes" and "Pharisees" is itself questionable (TTP 118; Gebhardt 116).

itself which, although "especially necessary, the ancients had neglected." For since "what they wrote and handed down has perished by the ravages of time," a "large part of the foundations and principles of this knowledge has been destroyed" (TTP 120; Gebhardt 117-118). Spinoza supports this claim by discussing the many defects of the Biblical texts, the various editions and lost versions, incompetent and even dishonest editing, wrong chronology. etc. (TTP 121 ff.; Gebhardt 118ff.).

Having enumerated in detail all those problems, Spinoza says that "someone" might object that he is trying "to overthrow Scripture completely" by arousing suspicion that it is "everywhere faulty." He protests against this charge by affirming that his purpose is to distinguish between the corrupt and incorrupt parts of Scripture and that just because some are corrupt we cannot infer that all are. Also, no one suspects that a book is "everywhere faulty" "when the speech is lucid and the intention of the author is clearly perceived" (TTP 154-155; Gebhardt 149). To the irrelevance and irony of these replies Spinoza adds the rhetorical device of placing the burden of proof on his critics. He claims that those who would prove the authenticity of Scripture must do so for each passage and book and that this requires in turn the authority of "councils" (TTP 155; Gebhardt 150). Here too Spinoza is being ironical, for he had already given ample evidence that this is impossible in "very many" cases and had rejected all traditional authorities.

According to Spinoza's rules, the true teaching of Scripture consists in its "universal" or "eternal doctrine," i.e., "what is commended by all prophets." In one place he gives as examples the doctrines that "a single and omnipotent God exists," that He alone should be worshipped, that He "loves above all others those who worship Him." Spinoza says that "Scripture teaches these things everywhere so clearly and explicitly that no one was ever in doubt about their meaning" (TTP 104; Gebhardt 102). But he then immediately contradicts this by saying that Scripture "does not expressly teach as eternal doctrine" anything about "what God is" or His providence and that "the prophets had disagreed among themselves about these things" (TTP 104; Gebhardt 102-103). Moreover, he had earlier given instances from Scripture where each of these is contradicted. For he says that the Hebrews recognized the existence of other gods and the right of other peoples to worship them (TTP 36-37; Gebhardt 38-39), that God required natural causes for miracles in addition to His "absolute fiat" (TTP 90-91; Gebhardt 90), that God was "equally propitious to all" (TTP 49; Gebhardt 50), and that "the direction of God" and "providence" mean merely "the fixed and immutable order of nature" (TTP 44, 82; Gebhardt 45, 82).

Spinoza goes on to discuss fundamental inconsistencies concerning the *moral* teaching of the Old and New Testaments. For Christ taught that when injured one should "turn the other cheek," whereas Moses taught that "an eye should be given for an eye."[18] This contradiction is explained, Spinoza says, by the fact that Christ and Moses lived in very different historical situations, for Christ lived in a corrupt and unjust commonwealth (TTP 105; Gebhardt 103-104). Elsewhere Spinoza explains the difference between the Christian and Mosaic teachings by saying that the latter was "not universal" but intended only for the Hebrews (TTP 61; Gebhardt 61), that Christ adapted his teachings to "each man's opinions" (TTP 41; cf. 70-71; Gebhardt 43; cf. 70-71), and that Paul spoke to the Jews as a Jew and the Greeks as a Greek (TTP 89; Gebhardt 88). Furthermore, in every case prophesies varied according to the character, temperament, mind, and circumstances of the prophet (TTP 27; Gebhardt 30). Finally, not only do the prophets of the Old Testament disagree among themselves and with the apostles of the New Testament, but the latter also disagree among themselves. For Paul teaches that "salvation depends only on God's grace," whereas James teaches that "man is justified by works and not only by faith" (TTP 163; Gebhardt 157). All this means that the real meaning and teaching of Scripture remain obscure, for if the most universal things are obscure, then everything else which "derives from them like rivulets" is also obscure.

In one place Spinoza says that the highest precept of Scripture, which "we perceive without any difficulty and ambiguity," is this: "to love God above all things and one's neighbor as oneself" (TTP 172; Gebhardt 165). The whole Bible commends "the teaching of charity" above all else (TTP 173; Gebhardt 166). This is "the foundation of all religion, which, if removed, would cause the whole edifice to collapse" (TTP 172; Gebhardt 165). Having said this, Spinoza then goes on to argue that what is meant by charity in the Old Testament is quite different from what is meant in the New Testament. For although the Hebrews were bidden to love their neighbors as themselves,[19] "neighbor" meant to them other Hebrews or "fellow-citizen," and while they had their own state they hated their enemies (TTP 230, 250; Gebhardt 216, 233). But in the time of Christ, after the Hebrews had lost their commonwealth and were living scattered

---

[18] Cf. Matthew V:43-44, where both teachings are mentioned together and the new teaching is explicitly said by Christ to replace the old one. Spinoza here refers only to Matthew V:43 (TTP 250; Gebhardt 233)

[19] Spinoza refers here to Leviticus XIX:17,18.

throughout the world, Christ "taught that all men without exception should cultivate piety" (TTP 250; Gebhardt 233). Thus Christ, unlike Moses, taught that *all* men were neighbors, and that the Hebrews should love strangers and enemies as well as their fellow-Hebrews. Whereas the Mosaic Hebrews had a "most intense hatred" for other peoples and sought to separate themselves from them as much as possible, the Christians sought to live peacefully among other peoples (TTP 229, 250; Gebhardt 214, 233).[20]

Spinoza asserts that the power of reason "does not extend so far as to be able to determine that men can be blessed by obedience alone without an understanding of things" (TTP 194; cf. 198; Gebhardt 184; cf. 188). If one should ask, then, *why* one should believe that one can be blessed through obedience alone, i.e., why one should believe that the basic teaching of Scripture and theology is true, the answer is that there is *no* reason why one should believe it to be true.[21] Indeed, such a belief is contrary to reason. For reason teaches that knowledge of the nature of things is necessary for knowledge of what will make us blessed. "Natural science" teaches us both about nature and "ethics and true virtue" (TTP 67; Gebhardt 68). Furthermore, reason teaches that the conception of God as a law-giver who lays down precepts and enjoins us to obey them is a demonstrably false conception of God. And to obey a precept which has not been prescribed by any being, divine or human, is also unreasonable (cf. TTP 64-65; Gebhardt 64-65). In short, the basic teaching of Scripture is neither reasonable nor true.

At the beginning of Chapter XII Spinoza says that those who consider the Bible "a letter of God sent from heaven to men" will object that he is maintaining that "the word of God is faulty, truncated, and corrupt." But "if they would consider the matter" they will keep silent, for they will see that "the eternal word and pact of God, and true religion, have been divinely inscribed in the hearts of men, that is, in the human mind."[22] Furthermore, this is the *only* sense in which

---

[20] Spinoza suggests that Christ's teaching is fundamentally antipolitical, for his advice that one should not fear or resist injury removes the major purpose of political life, namely, "security and convenience" (TTP 251, 47; Gebhardt 234, 48). Moses' teaching, however, is necessary for establishing and maintaining a just and stable commonwealth.

[21] This is not to deny, of course, the political "utility and necessity" of Scripture for the "multitude." Cf. TTP 198-199; Gebhardt 188, and Section II below.

[22] Spinoza scoffs at those who mistake the word of God for "paper and ink" (TTP 166; Gebhardt 159).

Scripture has been transmitted to us incorrupt (TTP 165; Gebhardt 158). Spinoza's point here is not difficult to grasp. For insofar as the divine word is inscribed on the human mind, it can be discovered by men's natural faculties, i.e., their reason. And insofar as this is so, it is not revealed or divine but rational and natural. This in turn implies that reason or philosophy can replace Scripture. For the "divine word" is found in any book which contains a rational teaching about true virtue and happiness. The expression "the word of God" is used "metaphorically for the order and fate of nature" and "the true way of living" (TTP 169; Gebhardt 162). For "the reason God should be understood to be the author of the Biblical texts [is] on account of the true religion which is taught in them, not because He wanted to communicate to men a certain number of books" (TTP 170; Gebhardt 163). From this it is easy to infer that, since Spinoza himself claims to teach both the order of nature and the true way of living in his own *Ethica*, the latter may be called the divine law and word. Spinoza thus replaces Biblical religion with the "true religion" of his own philosophy. He replaces the transcendent God, Who created nature and reveals Himself to and cares for men, with a self-caused divine nature, which neither understands nor wills, whose essence is power, which does not act for any end and which is therefore indifferent to men. This blasphemous substitution of the *Ethica* for the Bible is the ultimate implication of Spinoza's general purpose of wholly undermining the authority of Scripture in order to liberate philosophical reason from theological belief. For once liberated from its former master, reason can overthrow and replace it.

II. We have argued above that the ultimate *philosophical* aim of Spinoza's critique of Scripture is the liberation of reason from "theological prejudices." We must now add an important qualification, for this achievement is meant to apply only to "the very few," namely, to potential philosophers. The *political* aim of Spinoza's critique is a very different one, and is meant to apply to "the many." Correspondingly the function of *history* in his critique is different. For a "trust in the histories of the Bible" is necessary for the "vulgar" "whose minds are not strong enough for perceiving things clearly and distinctly."[23] The Biblical histories teach useful opinions to those who are incapable of attaining rational knowledge of how they ought to live. They are necessary for persuading those who are incapable of

---

[23] Spinoza compares the Biblical histories to "pastors," who are needed to explain things in simple terms to people with weak minds. The Old Testament and New Testament narratives are better than "profane" ones only because of the "salutary opinions" they express (TTP 79; Gebhardt 79).

knowing and can only believe and obey (cf. TTP 78; Gebhardt 77-78). Only a few men can acquire "the disposition of virtue by the guidance of reason alone,"[24] but all men can obey or be made to obey. Spinoza therefore insists that "the utility and necessity of Sacred Scripture, or revelation [is] very great." For without it, "we would have to doubt of the salvation of almost everyone" (TTP 198-199; Gebhardt 188). It is in the light of this need for Scripture and simple obedience by the non-philosophical multitude that Spinoza designs his critique of religion and Scripture on two levels.[25] On one level he seeks to *separate* the speculative (or theoretical) content from the moral (or practical) content and to preserve the latter as the only authentic and essential Biblical teaching. On the other level he seeks to *destroy* the whole content and authority of Scripture in order to replace it with philosophical knowledge. While on the first superficial level the teaching of Scripture is reduced to the empty platitude of "justice and charity," on the second deeper level this content is refuted in order to make room for its replacement by a new teaching, namely, the rational plan of living presented in the *Ethica*.[26]

History is also "very useful" to the philosopher in regard to "civil life." For "the customs and conditions of men" are best known from their actions, and the more we know about these, "the more cautiously[27] we shall be able to live among them and the better we shall be able to accomodate our actions to their temperament as reason dictates" (TTP 61; Gebhardt 61-62).[28] Although history cannot teach "the highest good," it can teach ordinary prudence, for it can show the philosopher how to avoid the potential dangers inherent in civil life. By revealing the nature and actions of men, history teaches the philosopher to be constantly aware of the injuries he might suffer from his unreasonable fellows.[29] The philosopher must not be naive.

---

[24] Cf. the last sentence of the *Ethica*: *Sed omnia praeclara tam difficilia, quam rara sunt.*

[25] Cf. the closing paragraph of the Preface (TTP 11; Gebhardt 12).

[26] The fact that Spinoza presents his argument on different levels, constantly shifting back and forth between them, is a major source of the deliberate and initially confusing contradictions that pervade the entire *Treatise*. Only when the reader grasps the ironical dissembling of Spinoza's way of writing will his real intentions become clear and a coherent doctrine emerge. On this whole question, cf. Strauss, "How to Study," *op. cit.*, 169 ff. and Elmer Ellsworth Powell, *Spinoza and Religion* (Boston: Chapman, 1941). 61-5.

[27] *Cautius.* The motto on Spinoza's signet ring was *caute.*

[28] Cf. Spinoza's description of the first of his "rules of living" laid down in the *Tractatus de Intellectus Emendatione* (Gebhardt II, 9).

[29] *Cf. the reference to "brutes" in the Preface* (TTP 7; Gebhardt 8).

He must not assume that other men are well-disposed towards him and his activities; indeed, he must assume that they are not. History shows the necessity to live under cover and under guard. In short, history reveals the ever-present danger of persecution.

A final political use of history lies in its relation to actual political practice. Chapters XVII and XVIII contain a lengthy discussion of the Hebrew theocracy. This is a kind of corollary to one of the central themes of the *Theological-Political Treatise,* namely, the relation between religion (and theology) and politics. Spinoza uses the history of the Hebrew state as an object lesson for present and future statesmen. For by learning what policies and institutions have succeeded or failed in the past, one gains valuable knowledge about what could or should be done in the present or future.[30] Thus, by considering "the histories and successes" of the Hebrews one can discover "what chiefly should be conceded to subjects by the supreme powers for the greater security and increase of their dominion" (TTP 216; Gebhardt 103). In addition, the history of the early Hebrews shows how a state is founded. For after the exodus from Egypt, the Hebrews were in the "state of nature." Since they had no laws or institutions it was necessary to establish a state by compact (TTP 218-219; Gebhardt 205). The kind of state they established was a theocracy. They transferred their natural right to God and recognized Moses as the sole interpreter and executor of God's laws. Thus, the religious and civil authorities were united in one man and all the people were subjects of God (TTP 219; Gebhardt 206). Spinoza suggests that the belief that the ruler and the laws derive their authority from God is a useful way of solving the problem of the "conservation of sovereignty," which requires the "virtue and constancy of mind" of the subjects and that "they prefer public right to private advantages" (TTP 216-217; Gebhardt 203). Spinoza introduces his discussion of Moses' founding of the Hebrew theocracy by several examples of pious frauds by Alexander, Augustus, and Cleon (TTP 217-218; Gebhardt 204-205). He then says of Moses that "he played the part of God." For the Hebrews, in making Moses the sole interpreter of God's revelations, equated obedience to God with obedience to Moses, agreeing to obey "all that God shall tell Moses" (TTP 219-221; Gebhardt 205-207). After Moses' death, however, the religious and political functions

---

[30] Spinoza is here imitating *Machiavelli.* For he uses the Old Testament account of the history of the Hebrew theocracy in much the same way as Machiavelli used Livy's account of the history of the Roman republic. For Spinoza's (extremely favorable) opinions about Machiavelli, cf. the *Tractatus Politicus,* Chap. V, 7. (Gebhardt III, 296-297).

were divided, for one tribe (the Levites) were given the priestly duties and privileges, whereas political authority was given to others (TTP 221-222; Gebhardt 207-208).

Among the initial advantages of this system were the following. The separation of the "priests" who interpreted the laws from the "princes" who administered them removed a major cause of abuse by the princes (TTP 226; Gebhardt 212). By equating piety with patriotism, the Hebrews came to have a very strong love of their country and "hatred" of all other peoples. Property was secure; the people readily endured poverty; civil war was avoided. Everyone obeyed the laws strictly and willingly. For one of the major beneficial results of the belief that the civil laws are divine is that men obey them without external compulsion (TTP 231; Gebhardt 216-217). Further, religious sects and hence religious dissension were absent (TTP 238; Gebhardt 222).

However, the post-Mosaic separation of the religious and civil authority led to many serious problems and ultimately the complete ruin of the Hebrew state. The title of Chapter XVIII mentions "some political doctrines that can be inferred from the republic and histories of the Hebrews." Spinoza begins by saying that, although the Hebrew state could have been "eternal," "no one can imitate it now, nor is this advisable."[31] Nevertheless, "although it is not imitable in everything, it had many very worthy characteristics" (TTP 237; Gebhardt 221). The latter are in fact, however, chiefly negative, since the main political lessons of Hebrew history show what mistakes the Hebrews made and thus what policies should be avoided. For example, the priests (after the Babylonian exile) "usurped political right and obtained absolute sovereignty" (TTP 236; Gebhardt 220-221). Religion sank to superstition. The prophets, by their "liberty to admonish," "incited rather than reformed men" by assuming the authority to judge right and wrong, thereby becoming a constant source of dissension (TTP 239-240; Gebhardt 223-224). But the establishment of a monarchy was the ultimate error, for it led to civil wars which divided and weakened the Hebrews and eventually made them a prey to their enemies (TTP 240; Gebhardt 224). Spinoza concludes that it is "harmful" to both religion and the state to give priests political

---

[31] Spinoza's ironical reason for this is that a "compact of God" is no longer possible because the apostles of the New Testament have taught that such a compact is not written "on stone tablets" but "in the heart." (The real reason is, of course, that there is no God with Whom men can make compacts.) Spinoza also ironically says that a theocracy like that of the Hebrews is "useful" only for people who "live without foreign relations" (TTP 237; Gebhardt 221).

power, it is "dangerous" to establish laws about "speculative things" and about opinions which are always subject to dispute, and it is "fatal" for people unaccustomed to monarchy to establish one (TTP 241-242; Gebhardt 225-226).[32] He suggests that the best way of avoiding these "evils" is "to place piety and religious ritual in deeds alone, that is, solely in the exercise of charity and justice." Also, it is "necessary" for both religion and the state "to concede to the highest [political] powers the right of deciding what is right and what is wrong," i.e., of judging actions (TTP 242; Gebhardt 226).

Although Spinoza views Moses' establishment of a theocracy as a brilliant and effective stratagem for solving some of the fundamental and persisting problems of politics, he believes that in the long term it led to disaster. Moses was indeed initially able to deal with the "stubbornness" of the Hebrews by persuading them to accept and obey his laws because these laws came from God. But Spinoza also says that "if it must be admitted that the Hebrews were stubborn beyond all other mortals, this must be imputed to a defect of their laws or customs" (TTP 232; Gebhardt 217). The ultimate source of the ruin of the Hebrew state was therefore present in the very beginning of Moses' foundations. For the ultimate defects of the Hebrew theocracy are those of theocracy itself. The chief political lesson of the history of the Hebrews is that one should establish a state in which the religious and political authorities are separated, the political power is superior to the religious, and complete freedom of thought and expression is allowed. Only when religious practices lead to direct conflict with the law does the political authority have the right to interfere and regulate religion. In short, the history of the Hebrews as recorded in the Old Testament shows the desirability of a secular liberal state.

III. As we have seen, Spinoza's critique of revelation consists of both historical and rational arguments. In his Preface Spinoza tells the reader that he has "constructed a method of interpreting the Sacred books" in order to inquire into such questions as the nature of prophecy, how God revealed Himself to the prophets, why He chose those He did for His revelations, why the Hebrews were called God's chosen people, the divine law and miracles (TTP 8-9; Gebhardt 9-10). These questions are dealt with primarily in Chapters I-VI, while the method itself is not explained until Chapter VII. But toward the end of Chapter VI ("On Miracles") Spinoza says he has chosen a

---

[32] Spinoza concludes his whole discussion of the Hebrew theocracy by emphasizing the basic (Machiavellian) principle that "the form of each sovereignty must necessarily be retained, and cannot be changed without the danger of its total ruin" (TTP 244; Gebhardt 228).

different method in dealing with miracles than in dealing (in Chapter I) with prophecy. For in the latter case he inferred everything from "the basic writings revealed in the Sacred books," whereas in the former case he has drawn his conclusions "only from principles known by the natural light" (TTP 95; Gebhardt 95). In fact, however, after beginning Chapter I with an orthodox Biblical definition of "prophecy or revelation" as "certain knowledge revealed by God to man" and supporting this with unorthodox comments on the Hebrew word for prophet *(nabi)*, Spinoza gives a quite different definition of prophecy as a kind of "natural knowledge." This latter definition is, of course, quite opposed to the first definition. Spinoza defends this revision of Scripture by a doctrine taken from his own philosophy, namely, that since our mind "participates" in the "nature of God," all our natural knowledge and hence all prophetic knowledge depends on our knowledge of God and His eternal laws. Finally, he says that God "reveals" things to men "which go beyond the limits of natural knowledge and also which do not" (TTP 13-14; Gebhardt 15-16). Thus, Spinoza begins his discussion on a Biblical basis and then abruptly shifts to the terms of his own philosophy, and, within the compass of only two pages, he opposes prophecy and natural knowledge, includes the one in the other, and distinguishes them. This procedure is typical of almost the whole argument of the *Theological-Political Treatise*.[33] For example, in Chapter VI he begins with the common "opinions" about miracles and goes on to criticize these opinions from the point of view of his own philosophical knowledge in order to show that they are unreasonable and absurd.[34] He then claims to "demonstrate" several theses, for example, that "nothing happens against nature" and that "by providence nothing can be understood except the order of nature" (TTP 82; Gebhardt 82). These too are rational philosophemes, not revealed Biblical teachings. Since prophecy "surpasses human understanding"[35] it is a "theological" question (TTP 95; Gebhardt 95). Thus it was necessary for him "to collate the history of prophecy." But since the question of miracles is "purely philosophical, " he needed to appeal only to "the natural light of reason." Although this procedure was

---

[33] Cf. our reference to Spinoza's use of irony in note 26 above.

[34] Chapter VI opens with the statement, "As men have been *accustomed* to call divine the knowledge which goes beyond human understanding, so also they are *accustomed* to call divine, or the work of God, any work of which the cause is not commonly known..." (TTP 81; Gebhardt 81; our italics).

[35] Spinoza later explains this "transcendence" as merely the prophet's faculty of imagination, for "the nature of the mind" is "the primary cause of divine revelation" (TTP 14; Gebhardt 18).

"wiser," Spinoza goes on to say "he also could have easily solved the problem solely from the doctrines and foundations of Scripture." He then proceeds to do this, adducing evidence that Scripture "several" times teaches that nature is "fixed and immutable" (TTP 96; Gebhardt 95).[36]

Spinoza's procedure in his discussions of prophecy and miracles exemplifies his procedure throughout the earlier chapters wherein he repeatedly uses his method of interpreting Scripture before actually explaining it. For example, in his critique of prophecy at the very beginning of Chapter I he appeals to historical facts about revelation recorded in Scripture (TTP 13; Gebhardt 15). And his lengthy analysis in Chapter I of the meanings of the Hebrew word *ruagh* is in fact an application of the first part of his method of Chapter VII (cf. TTP 19ff., 101ff.; Gebhardt 21ff., 99ff.). Indeed, Spinoza implicitly refers to his method by asserting that "whatever can be said about these things [prophecies] must be sought from Scripture alone" (TTP 14; Gebhardt 16). This is followed by the assertion that an examination of Scripture shows that all God's revelations were by means of "words and figures." He then analyzes several passages in the Old Testament dealing with prophecy in order to show when these words and figures were "true" and when "imaginary" (TTP 15; Gebhardt 17). It is obvious, then, that Spinoza employs his method and presupposes its validity at the very beginning and throughout his critique. For as he himself insists, any critique of the *truth* of a Biblical text presupposes a correct understanding of the *meaning* of the text: before one can judge the truth of prophecy or revelation one must know what Scripture says about them.[37] And this is precisely the point of his method. For the aim of his method of interpreting Scripture is to disclose the "literal" meaning of Scripture *before* raising any questions about its truth. In other words, an historical study of Scripture is prior, both logically and methodologically, to a philosophical critique of it.

In fact, however, as we have seen, the actual literary order of Spinoza's chapters is the opposite of this. And when one examines the kinds of arguments and evidence he uses in Chapters I-VI one sees a complex mixture of interpretation and criticism, of appeals to the authority of Scripture and to the authority of reason. In other words, Spinoza does not consistently distinguish between interpreting Scrip-

---

[36] Earlier Spinoza had said that Scripture does *not* try to explain things "by their natural causes nor to teach about merely speculative matters" (TTP 89; Gebhardt 89).

[37] Cf. Strauss, *Spinoza's Critique of Religion, op. cit.,* 258, 262.

ture from itself and interpreting it from another and superior standpoint. His "interpretations" are at once re-interpretations and criticisms: while clarifying Scripture he corrects and replaces it.[38]

A partial explanation of this confusing mixture of interpretation and criticism lies in the fact that Spinoza is trying to refute two quite different opponents, the sceptics and the dogmatists. The only common ground he has with the former is Scripture itself, while the common ground he shares with the latter is reason and science.[39] Thus the critique based on an appeal to the authority of Scripture cannot succeed until a method for interpreting Scripture has been worked out. And the critique based on reason cannot succeed unless confidence in reason is justified. Spinoza must therefore proceed in a zig-zag manner, assuming knowledge of both the real meaning of Scripture and the validity of reason before actually grounding them.

Since Spinoza's historical knowledge of Scripture is independent of, and ultimately irrelevant to, his philosophical knowledge of nature, the historical critique of religion is independent of the truth of Spinoza's philosophy. But since the rational critique of religion ultimately presupposes (at least in part) the truth of Spinoza's philosophy, and since this truth must in turn be established independently of and prior to that critique, the final refutation of revealed religion presupposses that Spinoza's philosophy is true and has been proved to be true.[40] But this is possible only if divine revelation is *not* possible, which is precisely what Spinoza's historical and rational arguments claim to prove. But they *can* prove this only if divine revelation is not possible: reason can have the last word only if faith has no word at all. On the other hand, if Spinoza's philosophy is not true, his claim to possess a final and complete refutation of faith is undermined. A space would then be left open for a truth beyond reason.

When speaking of the interpretive rules of Alpakhar, who subordinates reason to the authority of Scripture, Spinoza says, "I praise him insofar as he wishes to explain Scripture by means of Scripture, but I marvel that a man endowed with reason should desire to destroy it" (TTP 191; Gebhardt 181). For, Spinoza asks, if reason be submitted to Scripture, is this done "with or without reason?" "If the

---

[38] As Strauss puts it, Spinoza's "hermeneutics" really consists "not in understanding the Biblical authors exactly as they understood themselves but in understanding them better than they understood themselves" ("How to Study," *op. cit.*, 146.).

[39] Cf. Strauss' distinction between critique *based* on Scripture and critique *of* Scripture. *Spinoza's Critique of Religion, op. cit.*, 28 and 140 *passim*.

[40] Gebhardt affirms that the *Ethica* was virtually complete when Spinoza wrote the *Treatise* (cf. Gebhardt. trans., *Theologisch-politischer Traktat*, xv).

latter, we are then embracing Scripture only by the command of reason, which therefore, if it be repugnant to it, we should not embrace." For it is reason which assents or denies. Thus, if reason assents to something which it also denies it contradicts itself. Spinoza expresses his astonishment at men who "should want to submit the greatest gift and divine light to dead letters which could have been corrupted by human malice " (TTP 192; Gebhardt 182). For to despise the "divine light" of reason which alone enables us to distinguish the true from the false, to submit willingly to "prejudices," is "to change men from rational beings into brutes" (TTP 7; Gebhardt 8). It is sub-human for human reason to submit itself to anything other than itself.

Spinoza claims that the only point of view from which Scripture can be understood is an historical one: the Bible is a *human* book. But every point of view implies the possibility of another point of view. The other point of view in this case is the religious one: the Bible is a *divine* book. Every point of view predetermines what can be seen from that point of view. For what is viewed appears and can appear only within the limits or perspective from which it is viewed. What *can* be seen depends on what one's point of view *lets* be seen. Thus, the "conclusion" of the human historicity of the Bible is determined in advance by the initial "premise" of its human historicity. From such a point of view, no possible evidence for the divinity of the Bible would be admitted, for all such evidence would be interpreted as specious and reduced to a merely human phenomenon.[41] Conversely, from the opposite point of view of the divinity of the Bible, no possible conclusive evidence for its being merely human would be admitted. In other words, each claims that its point of view is absolute or the only true point of view, that is, not *a* point of view at all but *the* view of the whole as whole.[42] But neither can establish this without presupposing in advance that the other is wrong. Reason can establish its supremacy only by presupposing that faith in revelation is an illusion, and faith in revelation can establish its supremacy only by presupposing that

---

[41] As Emil Fackenheim points out in his critical discussion of empiricist arguments against religious faith and revelation, "the Divine is not among the data of the scientific consciousness, the psychical no more than the physical, for the former include at most the *feelings* of a divine Presence, not the Presence itself" (*op. cit.*, 13; cf. Strauss, *Spinoza's Critique of Religion, op. cit.*, 179, 195, 200, 204.).

[42] For Spinoza, the true view of the whole is presented in his *Ethica*, which *begins* with absolute knowledge of the whole: nature or substance. Spinoza's implicit claim in the *Ethica* to *be* wise is the presupposition of his explicit claim in the *Treatise* to have demonstrated conclusively the impossibility of revelation.

reason is limited. Reason establishes its claim to supremacy by reason, faith by faith, but in doing so each presupposes that the other is subordinate. What each claims to establish as a conclusion is in fact at the same time a premise. Each thus begs the question.[43]

IV. Spinoza presents his historical method as necessary for understanding "obscure" books like the Bible. It is not necessary, or even relevant, for understanding "clear" books. Spinoza's example of a clear book is a mathematical treatise, Euclid's *Elements*. Mathematical books are clear because their doctrines have a rational origin and content. They deal only with "things which are very simple and completely intelligible." Since the language in which Euclid wrote is not corrupt, one needs no history of it. The reader requires at most only an elementary knowledge of the language in order to understand it. He requires no historical knowledge whatsoever about the author, his life, mentality, historical situation, etc. (TTP 113; Gebhardt 111). Spinoza considered his own as well as all genuinely philosophical books to be clear. They are completely intelligible through themselves and presuppose no historical knowledge or "hermeneutics" to be understood.

Spinoza's views on this matter are not shared by most scholars today.[44] For modern scholarship has in effect adopted Spinoza's historical method of interpreting Scripture as the basis for interpreting philosophical books as well. Indeed, his method of interpreting Scripture has become the method of interpreting old books simply. The assumption behind this extended application of Spinoza's method is that philosophical books are not intelligible through themselves but are "obscure." Their obscurity arises from the fact that the authors of these books have been conditioned by the historical situation in which they lived. The conditioning influences of history must be revealed before the thought expressed in their books can be understood. Since past thinkers were not themselves aware of these influ-

---

[43] As Strauss puts it, "... the refutation of religion is possible only if faith and unfaith have some ground in common. Otherwise the critique never reaches the position under criticism" (*Spinoza's Critique of Religion, op. cit.* 165).

[44] A particularly instructive case in point regarding Spinoza himself is J. Freudenthal's *Spinoza: Sein Leben und Seine Lehre*, 2 Vols. (Stuttgart: 1904), the motto of which is: *um so leichter werden wir Jemandes Worte erklären können, je besser wir sein Wesen und seinen Geist verstehen.* This is, of course, taken directly from Spinoza's discussion of "obscure" books and was in no way intended by him to be applied to his own works. (Spinoza left instructions that after his death his name not be appended to the *Ethica* when it was published.) A further irony lies in the fact that Freudenthal's book is dedicated to Dilthey and Diels.

ences, the modern interpreter who *is* aware of them claims implicitly to have a perspective for interpreting the books of the past which is *superior* to that of the authors themselves. Present-day thought which is explicitly aware of history through its "historical consciousness," looks down on the past from the higher perspective of the present. It claims to be able to understand the authors of old books better than they understand themselves even before studying these books and even totally disregarding the rules or wishes which the authors of them may have suggested or explicitly laid down.

Spinoza's use of history to discredit the traditional claim of Scripture to teach men a universally valid truth is now used to discredit the traditional claim of philosophers, and Spinoza himself, to possess universally valid knowledge. Indeed, it is asserted that even the pursuit of such knowledge is absurd, for there are no questions which concern men as men or even are intelligible to all men. All knowledge, pursuits, and questions belong to and are inseparable from the constantly changing historical situations out of which they arose. One may presume that Spinoza himself did not anticipate the ironical result that his own use of history to liberate philosophy from the old servitude of "theological prejudices" would be used by others to bind philosophy to the new servitude of the "historical process." But the initial irony which led to historicism points to a new irony which can lead out of it. Historical knowledge can again become philosophically relevant by calling attention to the fact that philosophy was formerly distinguished from historicism. For if history can cast doubt on the claim of the past to be able to know something valid for all men by showing that not all men have agreed with this claim, it can also cast doubt on historicism by showing that in the past not all men have agreed about the truth of historicism. If the historicist takes history seriously, he will see that history compels him to transcend history. In this way a study of history and of the history of philosophy in particular can provide a *ratio dubitandi* of the present-day historical consciousness and thus a motive for overcoming it. In a post-philosophical age of historicism, history can be used to liberate philosophy from history and return it to itself. Historical studies can thereby provide an opening onto the past which will make possible the recovery and renewal of what philosophy, despite all historical accidents, always essentially is.[45]

University of Toronto

---

[45] For a further discussion of the question of the relation of the *Treatise* to historicism, cf. Strauss, "How to Study," *op. cit.*, 144,149-58 *passim*.

SPINOZA AND GERMAN PHILOSOPHY

12 KANT'S CRITIQUE OF SPINOZA

Henry E. Allison

The sudden emergence of the philosophy of Spinoza as a major force in the spiritual life of Germany in the last fifteen years of the eighteenth century is a fascinating and frequently discussed episode in intellectual history. The catalyst for this emergence was the "*Pantheismusstreit*," inaugurated by Jacobi and Mendelssohn in 1785, and joined in 1787 by Herder as a defender of Spinoza. Whereas formerly Spinoza had been treated, to use Lessing's words, as "a dead dog,"[1] that is, as an atheist hardly worthy of serious philosophical consideration, he was now regarded in many circles as a profound, and at times even genuinely religious thinker, who articulated the true conception of the divinity and of man's relationship thereto.[2]

As is well known, the philosophy of Spinoza, so conceived, exerted a considerable influence on the development of post-Kantian German idealism. To be sure, Fichte first thought of himself as establishing

---

* I should like to express my gratitude to my assistant, Mr. John Hasenjaeger, for his help in collating the numerous references to Spinoza and to Spinozism in the various versions of Kant's lectures.

[1] F.H. Jacobi, *Werke*, Leipzig, 1819, reprinted by Wissenschaftliche Buchgesellschaft, Darmstadt, 1968, Vol. IV, I, 68.

[2] Admittedly this is somewhat of an exaggeration. There was a tradition of Spinozism in Germany throughout the 18th century which included figures such as Dippel and Edelmann. It was, however, only in the 1780's that Spinoza's philosophy became a topic of central concern. For a discussion of the earlier reception of Spinoza in Germany see Moses Krakauer, *Zur Geschichte des Spinozismus in Deutschland wahrend der ersten Halfte des achtzehnten Jahrhunderts*, Breslau, 1881, Leo Bäck, *Spinozas erste Einwirkungen auf Deutschland*, (Berlin: Mayer & Müller, 1895), Max Grunwald, *Spinoza in Deutschland*, (Berlin: S. Calvary, 1897), and Walter Grossmann, *Johann Christian Edelmann, From Orthodoxy to Enlightenment*, (The Hague, Paris: Mouton, 1976).

Kant's philosophy on a new and more solid foundation, free of all of the inconsistencies and obscurities with which Kant himself presented, it, e.g., the doctrine of the thing in itself. Spinoza, for Fichte at this stage of his development, was simply the greatest of the dogmatists. His claim was that dogmatism and criticism constitute the basic philosphical options, and that victory must ultimately be awarded to criticism (as conceived by Fichte), albeit on practical rather than theoretical grounds.[3] In the "objective" or "absolute" idealisms of Schelling and Hegel, the onesidedness of the "subjective idealism" of Kant and Fichte is a constant refrain. Consequently, the philosophy of Spinoza is seen not as a simple antithesis, but as a necessary complement to this subjectivism. The claim is that philosophy must transcend this finitistic, subjectivistic standpoint and, following the path indicated by Spinoza, arrive at the standpoint of the absolute. Thus, despite his frequent and sharp criticisms of Spinoza, it is entirely appropriate for Hegel to claim: "Thought must begin by placing itself at the standpoint of Spinozism; to be a follower of Spinoza is the essential commencement of philosophy."[4]

These considerations, taken in conjunction with the fact that this emergence of interest in Spinoza took place precisely at the time in which Kant was engaged in the completion of the "critical synthesis," lend considerable interest to the question of Kant's own views on Spinoza and Spinozism. At first glance, however, this does not seem to be a particularly promising line of enquiry. Kant's actual references to Spinoza in his published writings are relatively few and far between. The first references from the critical period occur in the essay: "What is Orientation in Thinking?" (1786), which was Kant's own response to the *"Pantheismusstreit"*. There is a brief discussion of "Spinozism" as the logical consequence of the denial of the ideality of space and time in the *Critique of Practical Reason*, but the only thing resembling a systematic critique is to be found in the *Critique of Judgment*. To make matters even worse, the references that we do find hardly suggest any intimate acquaintance with the thought of Spinoza. The situation is reminiscent of Kant's scattered criticisms of the "good Bishop" Berkeley. Certainly, there is nothing like the ongoing concern that Kant exhibited with the thought of Leibniz and Hume.

---

[3] For the question of the development of Fichte's views on Spinoza see Grunwald, op. cit., 153–159.

[4] G.W.F. Hegel, *Lectures on the History of Philosophy*, Eng. trans. by E.S. Haldane and F.H. Simson (London: Routledge and Kegan Paul, 1955) Vol. III, 257.

In fact, if we are to trust Hamann in the matter, Kant himself confessed never to have really studied Spinoza and never to have been able to understand him.[5]

If, however, one turns to the various versions of Kant's lectures on metaphysics and rational theology, his *Reflexionen*, and the latest portions of the *Opus Postumum*, a somewhat different picture emerges. The references to Spinoza and Spinozism found in these places suggest that Kant did have a firm, if not particularly well-informed conception of Spinoza's philosophy. These references cannot be given priority over Kant's published remarks, but they do constitute an invaluable and hitherto neglected supplement to these remarks. It is as such that I propose to use them in the present study. The goal is to show that, when Kant's published criticisms of Spinoza are viewed in the light of some of these unpublished discussions, they not only become considerably more intelligible than they initially appear, but they can even be seen as providing the outlines of a genuine *Auseinandersetzung* with Spinoza. The significance of this *Auseinandersetzung* will be shown to lie in its metaphilosophical nature. In striking anticipation of his idealistic successors and critics, Kant seems to have become aware that the real opposition between his philosophy and that of Spinoza is one of "standpoint." An examination of this conflict of standpoints will not only help us to gain a deeper understanding of the critical philosophy, but also of why the dissatisfaction with this philosophy quite naturally expressed itself in the form of a return to Spinoza.

I

As already noted, "What is Orientation in Thinking?" constitutes Kant's official contribution to the *"Pantheismusstreit"*. His concern was not with the question of Lessing's alleged Spinozism, which initially set off the controversy, and only marginally with the interpretation of Spinoza, which soon became the central issue. Rather, it was with the underlying philosophical issues that really divided Jacobi and Mendelssohn. Jacobi presented Spinoza's thought as atheistic and deterministic on the one hand and as the most consistent expression of human reason on the other. The moral which he drew from this was the necessity of a leap of faith in order to affirm the existence of a

---

[5] cf. Hamann's letters to Jacobi of Sept. 28, 1785 and Nov. 28, 1785, Jacobi's *Werke*, Vol. IV, III, 8f. and 114.

personal, providential God and of freedom of the will. Mendelssohn, for his part, maintained the possibility of a demonstration of the theistic position and of a purely philosophical refutation of Spinoza. For Kant then, the dispute was between the advocacy of an irrational faith and of a dogmatic use of reason, both of which were completely opposed to his own critical standpoint, with its emphasis upon the limitation of reason and its notion of a rational, i.e., moral faith.

Despite this opposition, Kant was ardently wooed by both sides. From Jacobi's side the wooing was undertaken largely by their mutual friend Hamann, who functioned as a middle man between Kant and Jacobi.[6] Mendelssohn approached Kant directly, sending him a copy of *Morgenstunden*, and complaining in rather pathetic fashion about Jacobi's anti-rationalism, as well as about his treatment of "our Lessing" and of himself.[7] Kant left Mendelssohn's appeal unanswered, never even acknowledging the receipt of the book; and in January 1786 Mendelssohn died. In a letter to Kant written shortly thereafter, Marcus Herz complained about the behaviour of Jacobi and his followers and implored Kant to "take the opportunity to say something on behalf of your deceased friend against the contemporary and I suppose future irrational Jacobites."[8] Kant responded by dismissing "*die Jacobische Grille*" as nothing more than the efforts of inspired fanatics to make a name for themselves; but suggesting that he might publish something to expose their fraud.[9]

This something turned out to be the essay: "What is Orientation in Thinking?". Instead, however, of defending the memory of his deceased friend (as Herz had requested), Kant responded to the challenge which both Mendelssohn's dogmatism and Jacobi's fideism posed to the critical philosophy. Thus, Kant praised Mendelssohn for affirming the necessity of orienting oneself with the help of "authentic and pure human reason," but criticized him for granting too much to speculation. His point is the familiar one: "A pure rational

---

[6] The definitive treatment of this whole topic is provided in Alexander Altmann, *Moses Mendelssohn: a Biographical Study* (University, Alabama: The University of Alabama Press, 1973) especially 698–712.

[7] Mendelssohn's letter to Kant, October 16, 1785, *Kants gesammelte Schriften*, ed. by the Königlich Preussischen Akademic der Wissenschaften (Berlin and Leipzig: Walter de Gruyter & Co.), 1901–,Vol. X, 413–414.

[8] Marcus Herz's letter to Kant, February 27, 1786, *Kants gesammelte Schriften*, Vol. X, 431–433.

[9] Kants letter to Marcus Herz, April 7, 1786, *Kants gesammelte Schriften*, Vol. X, 442–443.

belief is the signpost or compass by which the speculative thinker can orient himself in his rational excursions in the field of supersensuous objects".[10] Jacobi, as one might suspect, received harsher treatment. His recognition of the ungrounded nature of the pretensions of dogmatic reason is acknowledged, but he is castigated for substituting for such reason a blind, irrational faith. Significantly, Kant cited as evidence of Jacobi's intent the fact that "He (Jacobi) sees the Spinozist concept of God set up as the only one conformable to the principles of reason, even though it is a worthless concept."[11] To make matters even worse, Jacobi had actually suggested connections or parallels between particular doctrines of Spinoza and certain tenets of the *Critique*.[12] This made it necessary for Kant to publically disassociate himself from the views of Spinoza, and it is within this context that he presents his critique of Spinoza's philosophy. This actual critique occurs in a footnote, which I here quote in full:

> It is hard to conceive how supposed scholars could find support for Spinozism in the *Critique of Pure Reason*. That work clips the wings of dogmatism with respect to knowledge of supersensuous objects, and here Spinozism is so dogmatic that it even competes with the mathematician in rigor of proof. The *Critique* proves that the table of the pure concepts of the understanding contains all the materials of pure thinking; Spinozism speaks of

---

[10] *Kants gesammelte Schriften*, Vol. VIII, p. 142, Eng. trans. by Lewis White Beck in Immanuel Kant, *Critique of Practical Reason and other Writings in Moral Philosophy* (Chicago: University of Chicago Press, 1950) 301 (subsequently referred to as "Beck").

[11] *Kants gesammelte Schriften*, Vol. VIII, 143–144, Beck, 303–304.

[12] Jacobi in fact refers a number of times to Kant in order to illustrate Spinozistic doctrines. Most notably, he appeals to Kant's doctrine of space and time as infinite given magnitudes in which the whole is prior to the parts in order to explicate Spinoza's conception of the relation between substance and the infinite series of finite modes (*Werke*, Vol. IV, I, 176) and to Kant's doctrine of the transcendental unity of apperception in connection with Spinoza's conception of absolute thought (192). Jacobi himself, however, explicitly denied that Kant was a Spinozist. Kant's view of the matter was probably colored by a letter from Christian Gottfried Schütz (*Kants gesammelte Schriften*, Vol. X, 430) informing him that Jacobi describes Kant's ideas on space and time as "entirely in the spirit of Spinoza," and in an anonymous review of Jacobi's book which appeared in the *Jenaer Literaturzeitung*, February 11, 1786, no. 36. For a discussion of this review see H. Scholz, *Die Hauptschriften zum Pantheismusstreit zwischen Jacobi und Mendelssohn*, (Berlin: Reuter Reichard, 1916), LXXVIII.

thoughts which think themselves and thus of an accident that exists for itself as subject—a concept that is not in human understanding and cannot be brought into it. The *Critique* shows that it by no means suffices to the assertion of the possibility of a thing thought through itself to prove that there is nothing contradictory in its concepts (although merely to assume its possibility must then, if necessary, be allowed). Spinozism, however, pretends to understand the impossibility of a being, the idea of which consists merely of pure concepts of the understanding, from which only all conditions of sensibility have been abstracted, in which, therefore, a contradiction can never be found. It is, however, utterly unable to support this unlimited presumption. Precisely for that reason Spinozism leads to fanaticism. On the other hand, there is no sure means of uprooting fanaticism except to determine the limits of the pure faculty of reason.[13]

This passage contains four distinct criticisms. I propose to discuss each in turn, referring, when necessary, to remarks about Spinoza found elsewhere in the Kantian corpus.

1) *Spinozism is dogmatism.* This is an obvious objection for Kant to raise, and, given his critical principles, a perfectly just one. In the *Critique of Pure Reason* Kant had characterized "dogmatism in metaphysics" as the procedure whereby philosophy "confidently sets itself to the task (metaphysics) without any previous examination of the capacity or incapacity of reason for so great an undertaking" (B7). Such a broad brush covers all pre-critical metaphysics, including that of Spinoza. As the passage indicates, however, the charge is levied against Spinoza specifically because of his use of the *more geometrico*. The distinction between the mathematical and the philosophical method was a major concern of Kant's, long before he wrote the *Critique of Pure Reason*.[14] Consequently, any philosophy which attempted to demonstrate its theses in geometrical fashion would immediately be suspect. Moreover, in his lectures, Kant went beyond this general charge and attempted to argue that Spinoza's erroneous conception of substance is the direct consequence of his manner of proceeding geometrically, that is, of beginning with arbitrary defini-

---

[13] *Kants gesammelte Schriften*, Vol. VIII, Beck, 302. I have substantially modified Beck's translation of this passage.

[14] Cf., Kant's *Untersuchung über die Deutlichkeit der Grundsätze der natürlichen Theologie und der Moral* (1764).

tions and deriving propositions from them. Such a procedure, Kant held, is perfectly appropriate for the mathematician, whose object is constructed in pure intuition, but it is totally inappropriate for the philosopher, who must begin with marks (*Merkmale*) and can only then proceed to formulate definitions.[15] In developing this line of objection, Kant was in all probability simply following Wolff, who criticized Spinoza, together with Descartes, for a failure to justify the reality of his definitions.[16]

2) "*Spinozism speaks of thoughts which think themselves and thus of an accident that exists for itself as subject.*" Taken by itself, this remark is unintelligible and hardly recognizable as an expression of Spinoza's views. Nevertheless, when construed in light of Kant's overall critique of Spinoza, it can be seen as a cryptic expression of his basic line of objection to Spinoza's metaphysics. Like the criticism noted above, this line of objection owes a good deal to Wolff. Moreover, it is to be found in various forms and with various degrees of development in Kant's lectures. Rather than going through these texts noting the minor differences, I propose to simply present a composite sketch of the Kantian critique.[17]

The target of Kant's attack is naturally enough Spinoza's conception of substance. According to Kant's Latin rendering of Spinoza's definition: *substantia . . . est cujus existentia non indiget existentia alterius*.[18] Given this definition, which Kant (following Wolff) claims to have been taken over by Spinoza from Descartes, it follows that there is only one substance (independent being or *ens a se*) in the universe. Moreover, since there is only one such being, it also follows that all particular things (Spinoza's finite modes) must be conceived of as accidents inhering in it. The result is thus the "*systema inhaerentia*", wherein the dependence of all things *upon* God is identified with their inherence *in* God. Finally, as Kant notes in one place, it also follows

---

[15] *Philosophische Religionslehre nach Pölitz, Kants gesammelte Schriften* Vol. XXVIII, 2.2, 1041–1042.

[16] Christian Wolff, *Theologia Naturalis*, section 679; H. Scholz, op, cit., pp. XLVII-XLIX.

[17] The main sources for this sketch are *Metaphysik Volckmann, Kants gesammelte Schriften*, Vol. XXVIII, 2.1, 429, 457–458, *Metaphysik Schön*, 510, *Metaphysik L 2*, 563, 600–601, *Philosophische Religionslehre nach Pölitz*, op, cit., 1040–1042.

[18] *Philosophische Religionslehre nach Pölitz*, op, cit., p. 1041. See also *Metaphysik Schön*, op. cit., 510.

from this definition that the world is a phenomenon of God and that we intuit all things in God.[19]

One of Kant's most frequently expressed objections to this conception, which will be further considered in connection with the discussion of Spinoza in the *Critique of Judgment*, is that it involves the conflation of the relation of dependence, which holds between an effect and its ground or cause, with that of inherence, which holds between substance and accident. The pitfalls of Spinozism, according to Kant, can be avoided simply by keeping these two relations distinct. Kant's main tactic, however, at least in his lectures, is to dismiss as arbitrary the definition from which the consequences listed above presumably follow. In its place he substitutes, admittedly without very much further argument, his own, essentially Aristotelian definitions of substance, as that which can exist only as subject, and of accident, as that which can exist only as predicate or determination of a thing. Substance, so construed, is the "something in general," which functions as the subject of predication, and which is only known through the accidents predicated of it. Its characteristic mark is being *per se* or in itself, which is contrasted with the being in another or inherence of accidents, but which must also be sharply distinguished from the being *a se* or ontological independence, which characterizes Spinoza's substance and the God of the theistic tradition. By treating substance in this manner, Kant, in effect, equated it with the concept of a thing.[20] This, Kant argued, removed all the difficulty in talking about a plurality of distinct substances (things), and made it perfectly reasonable to view these substances as causally dependent upon (not inhering in) an extramundane God, who alone is *ens a se*.

In addition, Kant endeavored to construct a *reductio* of the Spinozistic conception itself. To this end he introduced the notion of the ego as a thinking substance. The basic idea is that in order to be conscious of myself as thinking, I must be able to predicate all of my thoughts of an abiding thinking subject (in the *Critique* this "subject" is described as the "logical subject of thought"). In this sense self-conscious thought can be said to presuppose the reality of a substance (*ens per se*) that thinks. Despite appearances, this does not really contradict the argument of the Paralogisms; for Kant does not make any synthetic *a priori* claims about thinking substances. Quite the contrary, the notion of a thinking substance is introduced merely in order to

---

[19] *Metaphysik L 2*, op. cit., 601.
[20] Cf., *Metaphysik Schön*, op. cit., 511.

show that one cannot coherently consider the ego as the predicate of another substance. Given this, Kant thought that the Spinozist, with his conception of a single substance in which everything inheres, is confronted with an unavoidable dilemma, both horns of which lead to absurdity: either the ego must consider itself as God, which contradicts its alleged dependence, or it must view itself as an accident, which contradicts the very concept of an ego as logical subject of thought.[21] At times Kant seems to have attributed the former absurdity to Spinoza, thus characterizing Spinozism as "egoism."[22] At other times he attributed the latter view. This is the case in the passage presently before us wherein Spinoza is accused of speaking of "thoughts which think themselves and thus of an accident that exists for itself as subject." Although virtually unintelligible as it stands in the text, this claim can be seen as the consequence of a consistent line of argument that Kant has sketched in his lectures.

3) "*Spinozism ... pretends to understand the impossibility of a being, the idea of which consists merely of pure concepts of the understanding ... in which, therefore, no contradiction can be found.*" The being that Kant has in mind here is obviously God as traditionally understood, the transcendent *ens realissimum*. Spinoza is thus being viewed with Jacobi (and, of course, with Bayle) as a dogmatic atheist who is offering a rational proof of the non-existence of God, a kind of reverse version of the ontological argument. Kant's objection to this procedure rests upon the supposition that the concept of God is a product of pure reason, composed entirely of pure concepts, and that, as such, it cannot contain a contradiction. Granted this supposition, it follows that there is no way to demonstrate the impossibility of such a being.[23]

4) *Spinozism leads to fanaticism (Schwärmerei)*. Four considerations are necessary in order to understand this claim. The first is Kant's general and familiar charge that the dogmatic use of speculative reason can lead to fanaticism since it involves a venture into the supersensible that is unchecked by any appeal to experience.[24] Secondly, a dogmatic use of speculative reason which leads to atheistic conclusions (presum-

---

[21] *Philosophische Religionslehre nach Pölitz*, op. cit., 1052–1153.

[22] Cf., *Metaphysik L.* op. cit., 207.

[23] In support of this interpretation it should be noted that Kant made essentially the same point in a more explicit manner in his prefatory remarks to Ludwig Heinrich Jakobs' *Prufung der Mendelssohn'schen Morgenstunden*, *Kants gesammelte Schriften*, Vol. VIII, 151.

[24] Kant argues in this manner with specific reference to Spinozism in *Das Ende aller Dinge*, *Kants gesammelte Schriften*, Vol. VIII, 335.

(presumably Kant's reading of Spinoza) can lead indirectly to fanaticism because it seems to leave no alternative except an irrational leap of faith to the defender of traditional religious belief, e.g., Jacobi.[25] Thirdly, both Jacobi and Mendelssohn provide a basis for the linkage of Spinoza's thought to fanaticism, for both connect it to the Cabbala. Thus Jacobi affirms straight out: "The Cabbalistic philosophy is, as philosophy, nothing other than undeveloped, or newly confused Spinozism."[26] Similarly, Mendelssohn maintains that Spinoza's philosophy has its roots in "Cabbalistic fanaticism," and he says of the pantheistic principle: *"one in all and all in one"*, which he equates with Spinozism, that "fanatics and atheists have united in accepting it because it seems to combine their opposed errors."[27]

Finally, and most significantly, Kant had independent reasons for linking Spinoza's thought, as he understood it, with fanaticism. These stem from Kant's conception of the place of this thought in the history of Western philosophy. As is evidenced by certain *Reflexionen*, Kant viewed Platonism, neo-Platonism and Spinozism as three connected stages in the history of "philosophical fanaticism."[28] This history begins with the Platonic doctrine of recollection, which Kant considered to be a philosophically respectable attempt to explain the origin of *a priori* knowledge, especially in mathematics, by means of an appeal to the intuitions of archetypes in the divine mind. In neo-Platonism, with its doctrine of grades of being and theory of emanation, this conception began to lose philosophical respectability. This led finally to Spinozism, which Kant characterizes as "the true culmination (*Schluss*) of dogmatizing metaphysics"[29] and as "a theosophy through intuition."[30] As the context makes clear, Kant locates the fanaticism in the fact that Spinoza's doctrine requires us to conceive of all things, including ourselves, in God, which implies that genuine knowledge requires insight into the divine mind. Such formulations suggest the possibility of a confusion on Kant's part of the views of

---

[25] *Philosophische Religionslehre nach Pölitz*, op. cit., 1052 and *Danziger Rational theologie*, p. 1269.

[26] F.H. Jacobi, *Werke*, Vol. IV, 217–220.

[27] Moses Mendelssohn, *Morgenstunden*, XIII, *Schriften aur Philosophie, Aesthetik und Apologetik*, edited by Moritz Brasch (Hildesheim: Georg Olms Verlagsbuchhandlung, 1968), Vol. I, 393.

[28] *Reflexionen* 6050, 6051, *Kants gesammelte Schriften*, Vol. XVIII, 434–438.

[29] Ibid., 436.

[30] Ibid., 435.

Spinoza with those of Malebranche, which he also characterizes in a similar manner. This seems to be especially true when one considers the numerous references in the *Opus Postumum* to Spinoza as affirming the intuition of all things in God.[31] Nevertheless, it is not necessary to attribute any such confusion to Kant. Rather, as we shall see in more detail later, the formulations reflect Kant's own understanding of the Spinozistic standpoint, with its well known requirement that we conceive things *sub specie aeternitatis*. It is this standpoint which Kant characterizes both as "fanaticism" and as the "culmination of dogmatizing metaphysics" and to which he opposes his own.

II

The period between the outbreak of the *"Pantheismusstreit"* and the publication of the *Critique of Judgment* (1790) was marked by the appearance of Herder's *Gott, einige Gespräche* (1787). In this extremely influential work Herder defended Spinoza against Jacobi's charge of atheism and attempted to argue that Spinoza's philosophy is compatible with the concept of divine providence. As his spokesman poetically puts the matter, "The highest Power must necessarily also be the wisest, that is to say an infinite goodness ordered according to inherent, eternal laws...".[32] Jacobi had responded to this in the Second Edition of his "Letters" (1789) with a refutation of Herder's position. He also sent a copy of this new edition to Kant, who responded:

> For the newest edition of your handsome book on Spinoza's theory my warmest thanks. You have earned distinction, first of all for having clearly presented the difficulties of the teleological road to theology, difficulties which presumably may have led Spinoza to his system.[33]

---

[31] This is maintained by Erich Adickes, (*Kants Opus postumum*) (Berlin: Reuther & Reichard, 1920) 730. Adickes limits this charge of confusion to the references in the *Opus Postumum*, thus using it as evidence of Kant's senility. He totally fails, however, to recognize that Kant already referred to Spinoza's doctrine in just these terms in his lectures and *Reflexionen* stemming from the 1780's.

[32] J.G. Herder, *God: Some Conversations*, Eng. trans. by F.H. Burkhardt (New York: Hafner Publishing Co., 1949), 123.

[33] Kant's letter to Jacobi, August 30, 1789, *Kants gesammelte Schriften*, Vol. XI, 75–76, Eng. trans. by Arnulf Zweig, *Kant, Philosophical Correspondence 1759–99* (Chicago: The University of Chicago Press, 1967), 158. I have substantially modified Zweig's translation of this and the succeeding passage.

After gently chiding Jacobi for juxtaposing his brand of faith to Spinoza's dogmatism, ignoring thereby "the compass of pure reason," Kant continued:

> You have thoroughly refuted the syncretism of Spinozism and of deism in Herder's God. All syncretistic talk is commonly based on insincerity, a property of mind that is especially characteristic of this great artist in delusions (which, like magic lanterns, make marvelous images appear for a moment but which soon vanish forever, though they leave behind in the minds of the uninformed a conviction that something unusual must be behind it all, something, however, that they cannot catch hold of).[34]

The significance of the first passage lies in its anticipation of the concern with teleology which is the focal point of Kant's refutation of Spinoza in the *Critique of Judgment*. Jacobi had sharply criticized Herder's attempt to reconcile Spinoza's doctrine with the acceptance of final causes, or, as Herder puts it, "a wise necessity." In fact, already in the First Edition, before the appearance of Herder's work, Jacobi had denied the possibility of any reconciliation between Spinoza and theism. This is reasserted in the *Beilagen* dealing with Herder in the Second Edition. Theism is here explicitly linked with "the system of final causes." This linkage is based upon the presumed connection between this system and the conception of God as a being possessed of intelligence and will. Spinoza's rejection of final causes is seen, accurately enough, as a consequence of his denial of these attributes to the divinity. For the same reason he is also called an atheist. Given this, Jacobi felt entitled to deny:

> ... that there can be between the system of final causes and the system of merely efficient causes, a mediating system (conceivable to us men). Understanding and will, if they are not the first and highest, if they are not one and all, are only subordinate powers, and belong to created, not creative nature.[35]

In the *Dialectic of Teleological Judgment* Kant presents this conflict between the two "systems" in the form of an antinomy. His solution to this antinomy can be seen as his answer to Jacobi, although it also deals with an issue that is central to Kant's philosophy. It is within

---

[34] Ibid., 76.
[35] Jacobi, *Werke*, Vol. IV, II, 92.

the context of this solution that he develops his critique of Spinoza. Before turning, however, to these matters, it will be necessary to review some of the central conceptions of the *Critique of Judgment*. First and foremost is that of reflective judgment (*reflectierende Urteilskraft*) which Kant contrasts with determinant judgment (*bestimmende Urteilskraft*). The latter is the function which Kant examined at the transcendental level in the *Critique of Pure Reason*. It is concerned with the subsumption of particulars under given concepts (pure concepts of the understanding). The former is concerned with finding empirical concepts and laws under which given particulars can be subsumed and with the systematic unification of these laws into a body of scientific knowledge. Kant recognized that the possibility of realizing these goals, and thus of developing an empirical science of nature, rests upon the conformity of nature in its particularization to our reflective activity. Unless particulars are in fact subsumable under concepts (fall into classes or natural kinds) no empirical knowledge of any kind would be possible. Similarly, unless particulars are likewise subsumable under empirical laws which are themselves systematically interconnected, empirical science would not be possible. But this conformity was not guaranteed by the *Transcendental Analytic*, which merely established the necessary conformity of nature to the transcendental laws imposed upon it by the human understanding. Consequently, Kant argued that this conformity, which he characterized as "logical" or "formal purposiveness" (*Zweckmässigkeit*), must be recognized as an additional *a priori* principle which pertains to judgment in its reflective capacity.[36]

The concept of purposiveness is the trunk from which the two branches of the *Critique of Judgment* spring. Our concern, however, is only with the second of these branches (teleological judgment). The problem is that the principle of "logical" or "formal purposiveness" does not of itself provide a ground for teleological judgments. It requires us to assume as an *a priori* principle of reflection that the manifold of appearances is unifiable under a set of empirical laws and that nature in this sense embodies a systematic unity (a unity constituted by the idea of the whole). But these laws could all very well be mechanical, thereby leaving no scope for any specifically teleological

---

[36] *Kritik der Urteilskraft* (subsequently to be referred to as "K. d. U."), *Einleitung*, IV, *Kants gesammelte Schriften*, Vol. V, 179–181. Passages cited in the text are, with some modifications, taken from the English translation of the *Critique of Judgment* by J.C. Meredith (Oxford: The Clarendon Press, 1928, reprinted 1957).

judgments. These, Kant claimed, require a "real" or "material purposiveness," which can be of two kinds, yielding two classes of teleological judgment. The two kinds of purposiveness are termed "relative" and "intrinsic" or "absolute." The former involves the conception of something functioning as a means for something else, e.g., grass for the sake of cows, cows for the sake of man, etc. The basic problem with this type of judgment is that it rests upon an assumption that can never be justified by the observation of nature; viz., that some natural being (man) is an end or purpose of nature (*Zweck der Natur*), for which everything else is intended to serve only as means. [37] The latter mode of purposiveness concerns the *manner in which* a given entity or class thereof must be thought of as being produced. An entity is deemed to be purposive in this sense, i.e., be a natural purpose, (*Naturzweck*) if the possibility of its production cannot be conceived of according to mechanical laws but requires an appeal to an intelligent cause. This occurs when the form of the entity exhibits systematic unity, that is, when the parts are so interconnected and related to the function of the whole, that this arrangement can only be understood by reference to the idea of the whole.

The central claim of the *Analytic of Teleological Judgment* is that organisms fall into this category, and hence that they must be judged or estimated (*beurteilt*) teleologically. This claim is based upon an analysis of the essential functions of organic beings; viz., the self-regulative, self-preservative and self-generative functions, each of which is held to defy mechanistic explanation. Kant first suggests this by offering a preliminary characterization of an organic being as one that is both cause and effect of itself. This is intended to reflect the ability of such a being to reproduce its own kind and to grow.[38] Then, taking a hint from Hume, he attempts to clarify this by drawing the contrast between an organism and a mechanism such as a watch. The latter is certainly an organized being, each part of which exists for the sake of the whole (fulfills a certain function). An organism shares this feature (organization) with a mechanism. It differs from a mechanism in that it is not merely organized but self-organized. Thus, whereas one part of a watch exists for the sake of another, it can hardly be said to exist by the agency of the other. Similarly, a watch can neither produce other watches nor repair its own causal disorders. But organisms pos-

---

[37] Ibid., 369.

[38] Ibid., 370-372.

sess just these characteristics and fulfill these functions. Consequently, Kant argues, in order to conceive of the possibility of such a product of nature, it is necessary to abandon mechanistic explanation and appeal instead to a causality, which, in Hume's language, "bears a remote analogy" to our own causality according to purposes, that is, to a creative intelligence.[39] The point, of course, is not that we are entitled to assume the reality of such a causality, but merely that we are compelled to appeal to it as a model in our reflections upon these products of nature.

Having thus established a proper territory for teleological judgment, Kant turns in the *Dialectic* to the conflict between this result and the principle, presumably established in the *Transcendental Analytic* of the *Critique of Pure Reason*, that all genuine explanation is mechanical. As already noted, this can be seen as Kant's reformulation of Jacobi's characterization of the conflict between the "systems" of final and efficient causation. The "critical" nature of Kant's reformulation of the conflict consists in the fact that it is seen to hold between competing maxims of reflection rather than between contradictory metaphysical claims. The first maxim or thesis asserts: "All production of material things and their forms must be estimated as possible on mere mechanical laws." The second maxim or antithesis asserts: "Some products of material nature cannot be estimated as possible on mere mechanical laws (that is, for estimating them a quite different law of causality is required, namely, that of final causes)."[40]

The actual structure of Kant's argument is quite complex. The resolution of the antinomy seems to rest both on the assertion of the merely regulative status of the maxims and on an appeal to the supersensible (noumenal) ground of phenomenal nature. The former move, which is frequently equated with Kant's complete solution,[41] occurs in a section (71) which Kant characterizes as a preparation (*Vorbereitung*) to the solution of the antinomy. Kant's point here is simply that by viewing the thesis and antithesis as regulative principles of reflective judgment rather than as constitutive principles of determinant judgment, one avoids the necessity of viewing them as genuine contradictories. Construed regulatively, the principle of mechanism tells us that "I *ought* at all times to reflect upon these things

---

[39] Ibid., 375.
[40] Ibid., 387.
[41] For a discussion of this issue see J.D. McFarland, *Kant's Concept of Theology* (Edinburgh: University of Edinburgh Press, 1970), 120–121.

according to the maxim of the simple mechansim of nature ... because unless I make it the basis of my research there can be no knowledge of nature in the true sense of the term at all."[42] But this, Kant tells us, is perfectly compatible with the possibility that occasions may arise (as happens in the case of organisms) wherein this principle is inapplicable and it becomes necessary to adopt a radically different principle, that of final causes. [43] Since one is then not claiming that the phenomena in question are impossible on mechanistic principles, but merely that their possibility cannot be made intelligible, no contradiction occurs. This is to be contrasted with the constitutive interpretation of these same principles as "objective principles for the determinant judgment" which would yield the contradictory claims: "*Thesis*: All production of material things is possible on mere mechanical laws. *Antithesis*: Some production of such things is not possible on mere mechanical laws."[44]

The function of the second move (the appeal to the supersensible), which seems to constitute the actual solution, is to indicate the possibility of a reconciliation at the noumenal level of these two principles. Such a reconciliation is necessary because within experience these principles are mutually exclusive (the estimation or explanation of a given phenomenon may be *either* mechanistic or teleological but not *both*).[45] Both, however, are required for reflection upon experience, and thus for the development of empirical science. The possibility of such a reconciliation is based upon their possible derivation from a common, to us unknown, ground. This solution obviously shares certain features with the solution of the third antinomy in the First Critique (the conflict between determinism and transcendental freedom). In both cases we find that the appeal to the noumenal is intended to establish the possibility of both thesis and antithesis being true. The basic difference is that in the First Critique the possibility of the compatibility of thesis and antithesis was affirmed by assigning them to separate "worlds." In the present case they are both referred to the phenomenal world (as principles of reflection), while the possibility is left open that the phenomena which are reflected upon by these means may be derived from a common noumenal source.

The critique of Spinoza is largely contained between these two discussions and it helps to form the transition from the one to the other.

---

[42] *K. D. U.*, 387.
[43] Ibid., 387–388.
[44] Ibid., 387.
[45] Ibid., 411–412.

It constitutes the centerpiece of a general argument that no form of dogmatism is able to deal adequately with the concept of purposiveness in nature. Kant's analysis begins with the somewhat strange assertion that "No one has ever yet questioned the correctness of the principle that when judging certain things in nature, namely organisms and their possibility, we must look to the conception of final causes."[46] This seems strange because one would have thought that not only Spinoza but many other thinkers, e.g., Descartes, had denied such a claim. Kant's actual point, however, is that even these thinkers must acknowledge a *prima facie* difference between organisms and other entities and that the difference compels us to think of the former in terms of final causes. The issue concerns the interpretation of this universally acknowledged difference. Some contend that the difference is "objective," i.e., grounded in the very nature of things; so that the existence of organisms provides evidence of a distinct kind of causality (final causes) and perhaps of an intelligent cause (God). Others contend that the difference is merely "subjective," i.e., grounded in the limits of human knowledge; so that organisms are conceived of as extremely complex mechanisms and everything is ultimately explicable in mechanistic terms (for God or perfected science). The former position is entitled the "realism" of final causes, natural purposes or purposiveness (Kant seems to use all of these expressions interchangeably). A defender of this position may be either a theist, who views purposiveness as the product of design, or a hylozoist, who views purposiveness or order as inherent in matter. The latter position is termed the "Idealism" of final causes, etc., on the grounds that it denies objective reality to the ideas of purposiveness and design.

The two versions of idealism are termed respectively the "accidentality" (*Casualität*) and "fatality" (*Fatalität*) of natural purposiveness. The former is represented by Epicurean atomism. Spinoza is described as the "accredited" author of the latter. By this means Kant gives expression to the view, suggested in his lectures, that the philosophy of the historical Spinoza is to be seen as a modern version of an ancient philosophical doctrine. Atomism is dismissed in summary fashion. The basic point is that its appeal to blind chance as the source of purposiveness is not an explanation but rather the abandonment of any attempt to provide one. Spinozism fares somewhat better. Although Kant dismisses its conception of the "original being" as un-

---

[46] Ibid., 389.

intelligible, he does acknowledge that it at least attempts to provide an explanation. The essential feature of this explanation is the derivation of purposiveness from the necessity of the divine nature rather than from the divine intellect. This derivation entails that any purposiveness is undesigned and it is for this reason that the position is characterized as an idealism. By further describing Spinoza's doctrine as "fatalism," Kant is simply following Wolff, who called Spinoza a *"fatalista universalista."*[47]

Kant's critique of Spinoza on this point essentially amounts to the claim that his attempt to derive the phenomenon of purposiveness directly from the necessity of the divine nature is bound to fail because it cannot account for two of the three conditions that must be met by any successful treatment of purposiveness. The condition that Spinoza does meet can be termed the *unity condition*. Kant acknowledges that only if nature is considered as grounded in a single source can we think of it as unified or in any sense ordered. This would be true *a fortiori* of a teleological order. Spinoza's root conception of a single substance of which all things are modes obviously fulfills this condition admirably. Hence Kant writes with reference to the Spinozists:

> Their object is to derive from this substance the unity of source which all purposiveness presupposes. And in fact thanks to their purely ontological conception of a simple substance, they do something to satisfy *one* condition of the problem - namely that of the unity implied in the reference to an end.[48]

The problem, however, is that mere unity of source is not enough; especially when, as the above passage indicates, this unity is conceived of in strictly ontological terms, that is, merely as a simple substance in which accidents inhere. First of all, this conception fails to account for what can be called the *causality condition*. Kant is here merely reaffirming in connection with the problem of purposiveness the general criticism of Spinoza's doctrine of substance which we previously noted. The point, it will be recalled, is that Spinoza's erroneous conception of substance led him to conflate the relations of causal dependence and of logical inherence. Since dependence and inherence are quite distinct notions, the conception of modes as inhering in a substance is

---

[47] Wolff, *Theologia Naturalis*, Part II, section 709.
[48] *K. d. U.*, 421.

not adequate to account for their causal dependence on, or production by, that substance. It is this thought that underlies Kant's claim that Spinoza is able to deny that organic beings (*Zweck der Natur*) are products of design because he denies that they are products at all. As he characterizes Spinoza's position:

> They are, rather, accidents inhering in an original being. This being, he says, is the substrate of natural things, and, as such, he does not ascribe to it causality in respect of them, but simply subsistence.[49]

Secondly, it fails to account for what can be called the *intelligence condition*. Not only must organic beings be conceived of as products of a cause rather than as accidents inhering in a substance, which holds of everything in nature - the organic and the inorganic alike - but this cause must be conceived of as an intelligence acting in accordance with the idea of an end. The necessity for such a cause, as well as that of the other conditions, is clearly expressed in a passage which can be seen as a summary statement of Kant's critique of Spinoza on the question of purposiveness:

> It [purposive or organic unity (*Zweckeinheit*)] does not follow from the nexus of things in one subject, or the beings of the world in an original being. On the contrary, it implies emphatically (*durchaus — bei sich fuhrt*) relation to a cause possessed of intelligence. Even if all the things were to be united in one *simple* subject, yet such unity would never exhibit a final relation unless these things were understood to be, first, inner *effects* of the substance as a *cause*, and, secondly, effects of it as cause by *virtue of its intelligence*. Apart from these formal conditions all unity is mere necessity of nature, and, when it is ascribed nevertheless to things that we represent as outside one another, blind necessity.[50]

The necessity of conceiving of organic beings as products of an intelligent cause is based upon the contingency of such beings with respect to the laws of nature (mechanical laws). By claiming that they are contingent with respect to such laws Kant meant to indicate that they cannot be explained in terms of them. Underlying Kant's argument is the distinction between a whole that is a mere sum of its parts

---

[49] Ibid., 393.
[50] Ibid., 393–394.

(an aggregate) and one that embodies a systematic unity. Mechanical laws are perfectly adequate to explain the generation of a whole or unity in the former sense. This is the point of the last sentence in the above passage, wherein Kant refers to the unity of things "that we represent as outside one another." Such things are, of course, spatial objects or objects of outer sense. Unity or wholeness is here understood essentially in terms of spatial proximity, and this can easily be seen as the result of the mechanism of nature, of "blind necessity." As the *Analytic* has shown, however, organic beings exhibit the latter mode of unity, which is characterized not merely by the spatial proximity but also by the functional interdependence of the parts. Here the unity can only be understood with reference to the idea of the whole. Consequently, Kant argues, we can only render intelligible to ourselves the possibility of the production of such unity by considering it as the effect of an intelligent cause, i.e., one that is determined by the idea of the whole, and therefore can be said to act designedly or in accordance with ends. Since this is just what Spinoza denied with his rejection of contingency and derivation of everything from the necessity of the divine nature, Kant can claim that Spinoza did not succeed in providing an adequate account of purposiveness.

III

As we have just seen, the Spinoza critique of the *Critique of Judgment* has its roots in Kant's earlier criticisms of Spinoza but goes beyond them in its sharp focus on the question of purposiveness in nature. From the standpoint of the *Critique of Judgment* the most significant aspect of this new attack is that it enabled Kant to point to the denial of contingency as the basic flaw in the Spinozistic system. Indeed, it is no exaggeration to say that the concept of contingency is central to the entire Third Critique. The very necessity of positing a reflective function for judgment, and with it an *a priori* principle, is based upon the claim that "/T/he particular by its very nature contains something contingent with respect to the universal."[51] This, in turn entails the already discussed contingency of empirical laws, derived from the observation of particulars, with respect to the transcendental laws, imposed upon nature by the human understanding. Moreover, as Kant proceeds to argue, this latter contingency necessitates the interjection,

---

[51] Ibid., 404.

for the sake of reflective judgment, of the idea of a supersensible or noumenal substrate of nature, which is used to provide additional support for the central critical doctrine of the transcendental ideality of appearances. All of this, and even the analysis of the beautiful in nature, which cannot be dealt with here, was called into question by the Spinozistic denial of contingency. Because of this the refutation of Spinoza is central, not peripheral, to the overall argument of the *Critique of Judgment*. Only if he can refute the claim that "In Nature there is nothing contingent, but all things are determined from the necessity of the divine nature to exist and act in a certain manner." (*Ethics* I, 29), can Kant succeed in establishing a critical function and an *a priori* principle for the faculty of judgment. And this, after all, is the basic goal of the Third Critique.

Although Kant's target is a metaphysical doctrine, his approach is thoroughly and predictably epistemological or "critical." The strategy is to argue that contingency (and with it purposiveness) cannot be excised from nature, considered as the object of human or, more generally, finite cognition. The defining characteristic of such cognition is its discursiveness. As the *Critique of Pure Reason* showed, this is a consequence of the separation of the functions of sensibility, through which objects are given insofar as they affect the mind, and understanding, through which given objects (sensible particulars) are thought. According to Kant, knowledge of the discursive type (the only type possible for man) essentially involves the subsumption of particulars (provided by sensibility) under universals (produced by the understanding). To know a given particular is to recognize it as an instance of a general kind. But the very fact that the particulars are not derived from the universal is enough to render their accord or subsumability, which is a necessary condition for the possibility of such knowledge, a contingent matter.[52]

The essential point here is the genuinely transcendental character of Kant's claim. This means that it can be construed neither in empirical (psychological) nor transcendent metaphysical terms. Its non-empirical character is reflected in the insistence that contingency is a necessary ingredient in the conceptual scheme of *any* finite intelligence. From this Kant concludes that the distinction between a mechanism and a technic of nature, and with it the appeal to final causes, cannot be construed as a function of the state of science, such that future advances will make possible the reduction of teleological to

---

[52] Ibid., 406–407.

mechanistic explanation. On the contrary, Kant boldly proclaims: "It is utterly impossible for human reason, or for any finite reason qualitatively resembling ours, however much it may surpass it in degree, to hope to understand the generation even of a blade of grass from mechanical causes."[53] Correlatively, its non-metaphysical character is reflected in its limitation to a "finite reason qualitatively resembling ours." This serves to leave open the possibility that contingency (and with it purposiveness in nature) would have no place for a qualitatively different, infinite intellect, which would be acquainted with things as they are in themselves. Consequently, the concept of contingency cannot be applied to things as they are in themselves. We have already seen that this move plays a crucial role in Kant's resolution of the antinomy of teleological judgment.

As Kant himself acknowledges, the cogency of this approach, which involves the reference to certain peculiarities of "our" understanding, rests upon the coherence of this conception of an intuitive intellect with which the discursive manner of cognition is contrasted.[54] Only by reference to "an underlying idea of a possible understanding different from the human" can Kant drive the necessary critical wedge between transcendental claims about peculiarities or subjective conditions of human knowledge and metaphysical claims about things as they are in themselves, i.e., things as they would be for an understanding that is exempt from these (and all) subjective conditions. Of course, such an intellect is completely unknown to us and we are in no position even to establish its possibility. Nevertheless, Kant maintains that the mere fact that the concept of such an intellect does not contain any contradiction allows us to give it a problematic status. Such status is sufficient to justify a purely methodological use of this conception in order to provide a contrast to our "peculiarly human" way of knowing.

Kant had already made use of this mode of analysis in the *Critique of Pure Reason*, especially in the chapter: "The Ground of the Distinction of all Objects in General into Phenomena and Noumena." There the concern was to provide a "critical" interpretation of the distinction between phenomena and noumena, which would make it possible to attribute a role, as a limiting concept, to the noumenon in the face of the (presumably) demonstrated unknowability of noumena or things as they are in themselves. Consistent with the method

---

[53] Ibid., 409–410.
[54] Ibid., 405.

of transcendental reflection, the notion of "object" is construed in epistemological terms as the correlate of a certain manner of cognition. This means that qualitatively different manners of cognition or "intellects" have as their correlates qualitatively distinct "objects." Within this context, the problematic concept of an intellect possessed of non-sensible and hence intellectual intuition is introduced in order to provide the notion of an intellect capable of having noumena as its object. The actuality of noumena (in this positive sense) depends upon the actuality of such an intellect, and this can never be established. Nevertheless, the concept of a noumenon, so construed, is able to fulfill its "critical" function by limiting the "pretensions of sensibility." It does this by underscoring the claim that space and time are merely forms of human sensibility, not properties or conditions of things as they are in themselves.[55]

In the *Critique of Judgment* this line of thought undergoes a significant development. The non-sensible intellect of the *Critique of Pure Reason*, the knower of non-sensible objects or noumena, is now characterized more definitely (although still problematically) as an intuitive intellect. In contrast to "our" (discursive) intellect which moves from the *"analytic universal"* to the particular, that is, from concepts to empirical intuitions (whence the contingency of the fit between the two), the hypothetical intuitive intellect "moves from the *synthetic universal*, or intuition of a whole as a whole, to the particular—that is to say, from the whole to the parts." The claim is that such an intellect, which Kant contends qualifies as an "understanding" (*Verstand*) in the widest sense of the term, would not encounter the contingency of the fit between universal and particular which is a decisive mark of all discursive knowing. For that very reason it would have no use for the idea of purpose and no need to recognize the distinction between mechanism and teleology.[56]

This sketch of the Kantian defense of contingency and purposiveness in nature puts us in a better position to understand both the specific criticisms which Kant levied against Spinoza and why the conflict between them can be characterized as one of "standpoint." The essential feature of Kant's critical standpoint is its emphasis upon the conditions of human knowledge. The central teaching of the *Aesthetic*

---

[55] The account offered here is admittedly extremely sketchy. For a detailed treatment of these issues the reader is referred to my "Things-in-themselves, Noumena and the Transcendental Object," *Dialectica*, Vol. 32, No. 1, 1978, 41–76.

[56] *K. d. U.*, 406–407.

and *Analytic* of the *Critique of Pure Reason* is that human knowledge is subject to certain *a priori* conditions (both sensible and intellectual) which determine the form of the objects of human experience (as enduring spatio-temporal entities standing in causal relations with one another etc.), but which are only applicable to things *qua* objects of human experience. The "moral" of the First Critique is that the neglect of these conditions, or the failure to recognize that they are *only* conditions of objects of human experience (epistemic conditions), not conditions of things as they are in themselves (ontological conditions), is the direct source of skepticism, antinomy, or, more generally, transcendental illusion. The *Critique of Judgment* develops this line of thought by introducing conditions, not of experience, but of reflection upon experience, which likewise have an *a priori* function and hence transcendental status.

I have argued elsewhere that transcendental idealism consists in the claim that the objects of human experience, and only these objects, must be viewed as "in us" in the transcendental sense. This, in turn, amounts to the demand that these objects be considered as subject to the sensible and intellectual conditions noted above.[57] Correlatively, the label "transcendental realism" can be applied to all philosophies which either neglect or misinterpret these conditions. This would hold not only of Spinoza but of all "pre-critical" philosophies; for as Kant himself says: *"Alle Philosophien sind im Wesentlichen nicht unterschieden bis auf die Kritische."*[58] But transcendental realism, as Kant construed it, involves more than simply the failure to achieve the critical standpoint. It also involves a model of knowledge or standpoint of its own. This standpoint can be broadly construed as theocentric. The defining feature of this theocentric standpoint, construed in the broad sense wherein it is applicable to thinkers for whom it is merely implicit, is the assumption that human knowledge must be analyzed and evaluated in terms of its conformity (or lack thereof) to some pregiven ideal or standard. This conception is obviously the heritage of Platonism, but it was shared by rationalism and empiricism alike. The conflict between philosophical schools, even between what Kant calls the dogmatists and the skeptics, is not over this ideal or standard of

---

[57] "Kant's Refutation of Realism," *Dialectica*, Vol. 30, No. 2, 1976, 224–253. I there develop a methodological interpretation of Kant's idealism.

[58] *Kants gesammelte Schriften*, Vol. XXX, 335.

knowledge, but over the extent to which the human mind is judged capable of conforming to it.[59]

Now no modern philosopher, with the exception of Malebranche, maintained the theocentric standard in as explicit a form as Spinoza. Not only did Spinoza affirm this standard, but he also affirmed the possibility of its attainment by the human mind. This is presumably attained in the second and third kinds of knowledge, whereby the human mind is said to view things *sub specie aeternitatis*. Indeed, the second part of the *Ethics* can be viewed as an extended argument, the goal of which is to demonstrate that the human mind can transcend the "common order of nature" (the finitistic perspective, governed by inadequate ideas) and conceive things according to the "order of the intellect," which is equivalent to conceiving them *sub specie aeternitatis*. This argument culminates in the most un-Kantian claim that "The human mind has an adequate knowledge of the eternal and infinite essence of God" (E II, P47). Similarly, the fifth part of the *Ethics* is devoted to the demonstration that the conception of things *sub specie aeternitatis* leads to the *amor intellectualis Dei*, which is not merely the means for the overcoming of the passions, but also the source of human blessedness.[60]

Thus, when seen from a Kantian perspective, Spinoza, who denies the transcendence of God, is none the less a philosopher of transcendence in a radical sense. The realization of this fact enables us to put the previously discussed criticisms of Spinoza in their proper perspective and to more fully grasp both their continuity and their philosophical significance. First of all, it enables us to see more concretely why Kant repeatedly dismissed Spinoza's doctrine as *Schwärmerei*, characterized it as Platonism carried to its logical extreme, and described it

---

[59] This conception has been called by Gottfried Martin the "theological foundation of truth" and he sees Kant as having undermined it in the antinomies: *Kant's Metaphysics and Theory of Science*, Eng. trans. by P.G. Lucas, (Manchester: Manchester University Press, 1955), 60–61. The interpretation offered here differs from that of Martin and others who write in a similar vein largely in the fact that it sees a theocentric standard as operative implicitly in thinkers who would not acknowledge a "theological foundation." For example, Hume's skepticism concerning knowledge of matters of fact can be seen as an expression of this conception because it is based upon an assumption of what genuine knowledge would be like if it were attainable by the human mind. The conception must, therefore, be seen as a methodological assumption, often tacitly adhered to, rather than as a metaphysical doctrine.

[60] I develop this interpretation of Spinoza in my *Benedict de Spinoza* (Boston: Twayne, 1975) esp. 99–114, 147–161.

in terms highly reminiscent of Malebranche. Secondly, it helps to explain why, under the impetus of Jacobi, Kant found it necessary to define his position on purposiveness in nature *vis a vis* that of Spinoza, and to develop his critique in the manner in which he did in the *Critique of Judgment*. Finally, it can perhaps even enable us to understand one of the more enigmatic of the many references to Spinoza found in the *Opus Postumum*:

> We cannot know any objects, neither in us nor as found outside of us, except in so far as we place in ourselves the act of knowing according to certain laws. The mind (*Geist*) of man is Spinoza's God (which concerns the formal element of all sensible objects). And transcendental idealism is realism in the absolute sense.[61]

Apart from its overall obscurity, the most notable feature of this passage is its equation of the human mind with Spinoza's God. One can never be very certain in dealing with passages such as this from the latest portion of the *Opus Postumum*, which are frequently dismissed as manifestations of advanced senility. Nevertheless, the overall context, the reference to the "act of knowing according to certain laws" (presumably the pure concepts of the understanding) and the formal element of sensible objects (space and time), suggest that Kant's point is that in his philosophy the human mind plays the same role that God, or, more properly, the infinite intellect does in Spinoza's. Just as for Spinoza objects are only "adequately" or "clearly and distinctly conceived" by being referred to God or the "order of the intellect," so for Kant objects are only determined or known in so far as they are considered in relation to the conditions of human knowing. The necessity of considering objects in this manner would also explain why transcendental idealism (which does so consider them) is "realism in the absolute sense." Despite the terminological differences, this can easily be seen as a restatement of the familiar critical doctrine that only transcendental idealism is consonant with an empirical realism. Since Spinoza does not recognize the necessity of considering objects in this way, but instead appeals to their intuition in God, it would follow that he cannot be considered a realist in the absolute, i.e., empirical sense. Consequently, it comes as no surprise to find the label "*Schwärmerei*" still applied to Spinoza's thought in the *Opus Postumum*.[62]

---

[61] *Kants gesammelte Schriften*, Vol. XXI, 99; Cf. 51.
[62] Ibid., 19, 48.

Moreover, this puts us in a position to understand Kant's characterization of Spinoza as an idealist. This not only occurs in the *Critique of Judgment*, wherein Spinozism is described as an idealism of purposiveness or of final causes, but also in the *Opus Postumum*, wherein it is given a much more general sense. Indeed, in the latter work Kant speaks in several places of the transcendental idealism of Spinoza.[63] As Adickes suggests, this could be due partly to the influence of Lichtenberg, who both advocated a version of transcendental idealism and spoke glowingly of Spinoza, and partly to Kant's occasional tendency to reconstruct the views of his predecessors and opponents in such a way as to bring them into accord with his own position.[64] Nevertheless, it should be noted that even here Kant does assert that, taken literally, Spinoza's transcendental idealism is transcendent,[65] and that Spinoza's conception of substance can be construed as a regulative but not as a constitutive principle.[66] In light of these remarks, as well as the discussion in the *Critique of Judgment*, it seems reasonable to assume that Kant viewed Spinoza's "idealism" as analogous to the "empirical" or "dogmatic idealism" which he claimed to have refuted in the *Critique of Pure Reason*.

As the name indicates, the defining characteristic of empirical idealism is its construal of ideality in an empirical or psychological rather than a transcendental sense. This sense is incompatible with the objective reality of that which is held to be ideal. In its full blown form, wherein it actually denies all objective, i.e., extra-mental reality, and reduces objects to mere representations in the mind of individuals, this idealism becomes dogmatic. This is precisely how Kant saw Berkeley. In the more moderate form, in which it is found in Descartes, it merely raises doubts concerning the possibility of demonstrating the reality of the "external world." Ideality in the transcendental sense, however, is not only seen by Kant as compatible with the objective, i.e., empirical reality of that which is deemed ideal, but also as necessary for the affirmation of its objective reality. Hence the claim in the passage cited above that transcendental idealism is "realism in the absolute sense."

---

[63] Ibid., 13, 15, 22, 50, 56, 64, 87.

[64] For a discussion of the influence of Lichtenberg on Kant and especially on his views about Spinoza see Adickes, *Kants Opus postumum*, 763 ff. and 840.

[65] *Kants gesammelte Schriften*, Vol. XXI, 22.

[66] Ibid., 89.

The contrast between these two senses of ideality is nicely illustrated by the account in the *Critique of Judgment*. Both Kant and Spinoza reject what Kant calls the "realism of purposiveness" or of "final causes." Nevertheless, they do so for quite different reasons and this gives completely different flavors to their respective versions of idealism. Spinoza's position, at least as Kant construes it, is straightforwardly reductionistic. Final causes are "ideal" (an expression which Spinoza never uses) in the sense that the belief therein is a product of the human imagination, having no basis in *rerum natura*. Given Spinoza's theocentrically oriented epistemology, this means that the ideas of such causes and of a God that acts with an end in view are totally inadequate and cannot fulfill any positive epistemic function. Using the terminology of the First Critique, this would be a clear instance of a "dogmatic idealism of purposiveness." Now Kant, as we have already seen, likewise rejects any dogmatic claim to the effect that God actually acts with an end in view or that organic beings are in fact products of design. On the other hand, he does insist that the concept of purposiveness fulfills a positive epistemic function as a heuristic principle or maxim of reflective judgment. It is, therefore, "ideal" in the sense that it is imposed upon phenomena by the human mind; but it is transcendentally ideal in virtue of its epistemic function.

Kant's critique of Spinoza on this point closely parallels his better known critique of the Leibnizian theory of space and time. In both cases the critique is directed against what Kant takes to be a mistaken, non-transcendental sense of ideality. Leibniz repeatedly termed space and time "ideal," meaning thereby merely that they are "confused representations," due to the limits of human cognition. Such a position is clearly reductionistic. It holds that the spatio-temporal relations between phenomena, and with them the whole sensible content of human knowledge, are reducible (for God) to the purely conceptual determinations pertaining to the monadological realm (noumena). Against this Kant maintained that space and time are *a priori* conditions of human experience which, as such, positively determine the form of this experience. This is why Kant claimed that Leibniz and his followers "falsified" the concept of sensibility and of appearance (A43/B60), that they "*intellectualized* appearances" (A271/B327), and even that they mistook appearances for things in themselves (A264/B320). All of these formulations reflect Kant's fundamental quarrel with the theocentric, transcendentally realistic orientation of the Leibnizian philosophy, with its failure to recognize that human knowledge has its own *a priori* conditions which cannot be explained away by means of an appeal to a transcendent standard of adequacy.[67]

In the last analysis, then, the Kantian critique of both Leibniz and Spinoza comes to much the same point. As he saw the matter, the basic fallacy of both "dogmatists" lies in their failure to recognize that human knowledge, whether it be with regard to sensibility as in Leibniz or judgment as in Spinoza, has its own *a priori* conditions. This can also be expressed, although Kant never quite puts it in this way, by claiming that they failed to recognize the autonomy of human knowledge. On the contrary, their reductionistic program, with its requirement or ideal of the replacement of the inadequate, sensibly conditioned features of human knowledge by the clear and distinct conceptions appropriate to an infinite intellect, can be seen as a species of heteronomy. As such, it shares, for Kant at least, the endemic fate of heteronomy in all of its forms; viz., it explains away precisely that which is presupposed as the fundamental datum to be explained. In the *Critique of Judgment* Kant makes this quite clear with respect to Spinoza's treatment of purposiveness. As I have tried to show, however, this must be seen as merely a reflection of a more fundamental philosophical opposition of which Kant was very much aware.

University of California, San Diego

---

[67] I discuss Kant's critique of Leibniz in more detail in my *The Kant-Eberhard Controversy* (Baltimore: The Johns Hopkins University Press, 1973) and in "Kant's Refutation of Realism," op. cit.

13. HEGEL'S ASSESSMENT OF SPINOZA
Kenneth L. Schmitz

More than any other philosopher before him, Hegel shaped his own thought by means of a continuing meditation upon his predecessors.[1] There is no doubt that for Hegel Aristotle was prince among them. Kant may well be said to occupy a position of importance for Hegel's thought second only to Aristotle. Nevertheless, Hegel's relation to each differs. Kant is a thinker whom he has to confront and overcome, whereas Aristotle is an endlessly suggestive thinker for Hegel's speculative enterprise. After these two philosophers I would put Spinoza in a position of pivotal importance, and in a relation to Hegel's own philosophy that resembles Aristotle's role more than Kant's. There is no confrontation here, though there is criticism and transformation. In his *Lectures on the History of Philosophy* Hegel tells us that Spinoza is the first to take up philosophy where Aristotle had left it, and he insists that in order to philosophize one must be a Spinozist.[2] One thing is essential for the beginning of philosophy, he tells his auditors: thought must place itself at the standpoint of Spinozism.

---

[1] Cf. Quentin Lauer, S.J., "Hegel as Historian of Philosophy," *Hegel and the History of Philosophy*, Proceedings of the Hegel Society of America, 1972, ed. J. O'Malley, K. Algozin, F. Weiss (The Hague: Nijhoff, 1974), 20–46.

[2] *Sämtliche Werke: Jubiläumsausgabe in 20 Bänden*, ed. H. Glockner (Stuttgart: Frommann, 1927–30) vol. 19 (reprint 1959), Bd.III, 376; also, 374: "Entweder Spinozismus oder keine Philosophie." Abraham Wolfson makes these texts prominent in his *Spinoza, A Life of Reason* (New York: Philosophical Library, 1969), 249, 297, 313, although he is critical of Hegel on equally general grounds (155). Cf. *Hegel's Lectures on the History of Philosophy*, 3 vols., tr. E.S. Haldane and F.H. Simson (London: Routledge and Kegan Paul, 1892–96), vol.III, 252–290, especially 257: "Thought must begin by placing itself at the standpoint of Spinozism; to be a follower of Spinoza is the essential commencement of all philosophy."

The reason is, however, that Spinoza has brought philosophy back to its starting-point, the being of the Eleatics.

Indeed, Spinoza's philosophy is so important that Hegel interrupts the march of the categories in the *Science of Logic* in order to delineate the true method to be followed in the interpretation and refutation of another philosopher; and it is Spinoza who serves as the theme of this outline.[3] There is no doubt that Hegel found an affinity with Spinozism that made the task of distinguishing his own thought from it a subtle and challenging affair.[4] Hegel tells us that

---

[3] See *Wissenschaft der Logik*, ed. G. Lasson (Hamburg: F. Meiner, 1934), vol. II, 216–218 (hereafter *WL*). For a recent English version, see *Hegel's Science of Logic*, tr. A.V. Miller (New York: Humanities, 1969), 580–581 (hereafter *SL*). I have quoted this translation unless otherwise noted. An older translation by W.H. Johnston and L.G. Sruthers, under the same title (London: George Allen and Unwin, 1929), has the passage at vol. II, 214–215 (hereafter *JS*). At the beginning of the passage Hegel refers to an earlier discussion of Spinoza in *WL*, II, 164–167 (*SL*, 536–539; *JS*, II, 167–171).

[4] Moreover, Spinozism was in the intellectual air that the young Hegel breathed. See H.S. Harris, *Hegel's Development: Toward the Sunlight, 1770–1801* (Oxford: Clarendon, 1972), *passim*. On the relation between the young Hegel and his contemporaries regarding Spinoza, see also Walther Christoph Zimmerli, *Die Frage nach der Philosophie, Hegel-Studien* (Bonn: Bouvier, 1974), Beiheft 15, 137–155, especially 151–155. Along with others, E. Shmueli, in "Hegel's Interpretation of Spinoza's Concept of Substance," *International Journal for Philosophy of Religion*, vol. I, no. 3, (Fall 1971), 176–191, remarks that Hegel pressed the same argument against Spinoza as he did against Schelling and the Romantics, but it is unlikely that it was a simple misunderstanding (179–180). Already in his first publications he shows a detailed, subtle, complex and critical appreciation of Spinoza's writings. See, for example, his critique of Jacobi's criticism of Spinoza in *Glauben und Wissen*, ed. G. Lasson (1928) (Hamburg: F. Meiner, 1962), 47–57 (*Faith and Knowledge*, tr. W. Cerf and H.S. Harris [Albany: S.U.N.Y., 1977] 104–115), and his discriminating interpretation of Spinoza's absolute principle in *Differenz des Fichte'schen und Schelling'schen Systems der Philosophie*, ed. G. Lasson (1928) (Hamburg: F. Meiner, 1962), 27 ff. (*The Difference Between Fichte's and Schelling's System of Philosophy*, tr. H.S. Harris and W. Cerf [Albany: S.U.N.Y., 1977], 105 ff.) In *Hegel's Development* (211) H.S. Harris remarks that "the contrast between the Absolute as Substance and the Absolute as Subject is not yet [i.e., in 1795] clear in Hegel's mind, because he has surrendered the idea of a *personal* God without as yet finding anything very definite to put in its place." His conception of subjectivity will fill this role, but it reaches its first stable expression in the Jena period just before the *Phänomenologie des Geistes* (1807). For a recent study, see Klaus Düsing, *Das Problem der Subjektivität in Hegels Logik, Hegel-Studien*, Beiheft 15; specifically on Spinoza, 228–233.

the philosophy which adopts the standpoint of *substance* and stops there is the system of Spinoza.[5]

Those familiar with the Preface to Hegel's *Phenomenology of Spirit* will recognize the implied criticism, since in Hegel's view philosophy must not stop at substance, but must go on instead to develop substance into *subject*.[6] Failure to do so is the chief defect of Spinozism.

Nevertheless, Hegel continues,[7] noticing a defect is not the same as refuting it. Refutation is not so easy. In order to clarify his own position with respect to Spinoza, Hegel lays down certain requirements for a philosophical refutation. First of all, of any two philosophical systems, the one taken to be true must not be considered to have only one relationship to the system taken to be false, viz., the relation of opposition. Hegel is not making a general appeal to generosity and broad-mindedness here. He is making a quite precise point: the system taken to be false, if it is indeed a philosophical position, is the development of a fundamental and comprehensive idea (such as the idea of being), and such a system is "a necessary standpoint assumed by the absolute." Such a system is no mere *Weltanschauung*, no mere individual opinion or social point of view, subjectively interesting but objectively groundless. It is a stage along the way by which speculative thought discovers itself. In what, then, does its falsity consist? To the extent that the system expresses a necessary standpoint it is true; "but it is not the highest standpoint." And it is in this alone that its falsity consists. Hegel writes:

> This does not mean that the system can be regarded as false [simply because it is not highest or complete] . . . the only thing about it to be considered false is its claim to be the highest standpoint.

It follows, then, that the true system cannot exclude the other system as false, because it would then exclude some truth; it must rather include it within its own higher standpoint.

---

[5] *WL*, II, 216 (*SL*, 580; *JS*, II, 214).

[6] *Phänomenologie des Geistes*, ed. J. Hoffmeister (Hamburg: F. Meiner, 1952), 19 (*The Phenomenology of Mind*, tr. J.B. Baillie [London: George Allen and Unwin, rev. ed.1949] 80). A new translation by A.V. Miller has recently appeared: *Hegel's Phenomenology of Spirit* (Oxford: Clarendon, 1977), para. 17, 10.

N. Rotenstreich examines this theme in *From Substance to Subject: Studies in Hegel* (The Hague: Nijhoff, 1974).

[7] See fn. 3 above.

The second requirement for a philosophical refutation follows from the first. Hegel writes:

> Further, the refutation must not come from outside, that is, it must not proceed from assumptions lying outside the system in question and inconsistent with it.

For if, from an alien set of assumptions, we point out an alleged defect in the system under attack, that system can simply refuse to countenance the alien set of assumptions, and both critic and criticized will remain in splendid isolation. Unwittingly anticipating Kierkegaard's attack upon his own system, Hegel denies the efficacy of attacking Spinoza's system in the name of the independence and freedom of the individual. In his own way, we are told, Spinoza accommodates subjective consciousness and individuality in his system. Rather, a genuine refutation

> must penetrate the opponent's stronghold and meet him on his own ground; no advantage is gained by attacking him somewhere else and defeating him where he is not.

A true philosophical refutation, then, must recognize the essential and necessary truth of the other position and raise it to the higher and truer standpoint in the name of that system's *own* principles, direction and aspirations. Now, it is just this that Hegel tries to do, and this is to be at once the completion and the refutation of Spinozism. It is carried out at its most profound level in Hegel's *Science of Logic* in the doctrine of Essence, the section on Actuality, the first and third chapters (on the Absolute, and on the Absolute Relation).[8] In the first chapter he takes up the conceptions of Absolute, Attribute,

---

[8] *WL*, II, 157ff. and 184ff., respectively (*SL*, 530ff. and 554ff.; *JS*, II, 161ff. and 187ff.). Eugène Fleischmann insists, in "Die Wirklichkeit in Hegels Logik: Ideengeschichtliche Beziehungen zu Spinoza," *Zeitschrift für philosophische Forschung*, Bd. XVIII, 1964; 3–29, that Hegel had Spinoza chiefly in mind throughout the whole section on actuality. And against G.R.G. Mure and J.N. Findlay he wants to try to show with respect to the chapter on actuality "dass man das *ganze* Kapitel als eine kritische Auslegung Spinozas zu verstehen hat, so wie Hegel eigentlich meinte, und dass ihm vielleicht auch die einheitliche Grundidee nicht fehlt" (3). It is interesting that he considers the texts of the two *Logics* to be sufficient for systematic (wissenschaftliche) purposes (p.4). I think that the nub of the problem is set out in *WL*, and that the Lesser Logic adds nothing essential.

Mode; and in the third, the conceptions of substantiality, accidentality and causality. I will attend especially to the first chapter where the issue is settled.

Hegel begins by identifying the central Spinozistic conception as the absolute, presumably on the basis of the definitions of *causa sui* (definition I) and of God (definition VI).[9] What interests him is the instability of the conception. On the one hand,

> the absolute itself appears only as the negation of all predicates and as the void . . .[10]

Yet, on the other hand,

> it must be pronounced equally to be the position of all predicates.

It must be absolutely indeterminate, so that all determinations may be dissolved in its unity; and yet it must be fully determinate, since it must contain all determinations in some way. Our present task is to understand just how this formal contradiction is to be understood and resolved. According to Hegel, this will refute Spinozism by completing it from within. To add something from without and thereby to change the meaning of the absolute will prove nothing. What is needed is an exposition of the absolute which is *the absolute's own self-exposition*.[11] We will simply try to conform to that exposition as Hegel understands it, and to follow its contours and stages.

---

[9] Gebhardt II, 45: "I. Per causam sui intelligo id, cujus essentia involvit existentiam, sive id, cujus natura non potest concipi, nisi existens... VI. Per Deum intelligo ens absolute infinitum, hoc est, substantiam constantem infinitis attributis, quorum unumquodque aeternam, et infinitam essentiam exprimit." Hegel used the Paulus edition of Spinoza's works. It is interesting to notice that, whereas older Hegel interpreters emphasized the comprehensive universality of Spinoza's definition of substance, more recent commentators are more likely to stress the mutual involvement of existence and essence in the definition.

[10] *WL*, II, 157 (*SL*, 530; *JS* II, 161).

[11] The German reads, "die *eigene* Auslegung des Absoluten," its *own* exposition; the reflexivity is understood but is not verbally explicit. See *WL*, 157 (*SL*, 530; *JS*, II, 161). The full reflexivity is gathered up only in the phrases that recapitulate the movement from the absolute to the modes and back again: "Das Absolute als diese sich selbst tragende Bewegung der Auslegung . . . ist nur als absolutes sich für sich selbst Manifestieren; es ist so *Wirklichkeit*." (*WL*, II, 164)

The absolute displays itself in the modes, and therein lays out what it is. Now this display has both a negative and a positive side to it. It is a negative exposition of the absolute insofar as the absolute shows the modes as its own, and thereby dissolves them; they perish [*untergehen*] in its unity. But there is a positive side to the exposition, too. For the determinations or modes, in passing over into the absolute, pass over into their ground. In going to ground [*zu Grunde gehen*, perishing] they claim that ground for themselves. The determinations, then, have the absolute both for their abyss [*Abgrund*], because they are *only* modes, and for their ground [*Grund*], because they *are* modes *of* the absolute. The negative and positive exposition, however, has told us more about the determinations than it has about the absolute. The absolute remains in formal contradiction: it is both *Abgrund* and *Grund*.[12]

To consider this again, the absolute is absolutely self-identical. It is the unity of all the determinations of being and essence. The determinations are pure negations with respect to it. To that extent they are swallowed up in it [*aufgelöst, versenkt*]. Each determination is indistinguishable from the whole, and is really nothing but the whole. We have seen, however, that just because this self-identical being is absolute, there can be no determinations that fall outside of it, and so it must contain every distinction and every multiplicity. "A variety of content must emerge in it."[13]

Hegel attempts to advance beyond the dilemma by introducing his own category of *show* [*Schein*]. Insofar as the category succeeds in resolving the dilemma, it will be a category that is intrinsic to the self-development of the absolute itself and not merely a subjective category introduced by Hegel from without.

Let me try to make this difficult and obscure conception a bit clearer without recapitulating Hegel's entire doctrine of show and of

---

[12] *WL*, II, 159 (*SL*, 532; *JS*, II, 163).

[13] *JS*, II, 162, renders the technical Hegelian term, *Verschiedenheit*, better here as "variety" than *SL*, 531, whose "difference" more correctly translates the Hegelian term, *Unterschied*. The point is that at this stage of the self-exposition, determinate content is mere variety, indiscriminate determinations. For the German, see *WL*, II, 158.

appearance [*Erscheinung*].¹⁴. The category of show is, perhaps, the most Platonic element in Hegel's thought, for there is not just appearance *and* reality according to Hegel, but appearance *in* reality. The modes are appearances in the reality of substance. Now, show is not mere fiction or illusion (though it is the source of illusion) but is rather an ontological (or precisely a meontological) principle. It differs from quality, although both are determinations. But quality is a positive determinateness that bears a positive relation to a substantial being as to its foundation. Show, on the other hand, has *nothing* for its foundation. That is, its foundation is the *negative* relation which the determination has to its ground; here, to the absolute. Since the absolute is the ground of all determinateness, however, this negative relation (viz., that the determinations are *not* the absolute) is the absolute's *own* self-negation. The determinations (the modes) are, then, the self-show of the absolute. They have no *real* being of their own, no being appropriate to things (*res*), as do qualities; and yet they are not simply nothing: they are appearances, that is, *apparencies*. They are determinations founded on the negative relation and are grounded in the absolute. The puzzling distinction between foundation and ground may be understood in this way: the apparencies, after all, have some self-identity; this self-identity, their character, rests upon their difference from the absolute (and, of course, from each other). Now this determinateness is the character resting upon the negative relation to the absolute, founded upon the diversity between modes and the absolute. The "reality" of show in itself is nothing, however, and the character and the negative relation comprise a determinateness grounded only in the absolute as alone real, as alone *res*.

For all that, the apparency is unstable. The apparency of show is

> the transparency of the finite, which only lets the absolute be glimpsed through it.¹⁵

---

¹⁴ A complete account would call for a consideration of Hegel's doctrine of reflection (*WL*, II, 13-23; *SL*, 399-408; *JS*, II, 25-34). Hegel's own doctrine of reflection is the basis for his charge that Spinoza's exposition of the absolute is developed out of external reflection, and is therefore not intrinsically justified (*WL*, II, 164; *SL*, 536; *JS*, II, 167-168). He also lays the fault at Spinoza's defective understanding of negation (*ibid.*). Cf. S. Rosen, "Hegel, Descartes and Spinoza, "in *Spinoza's Metaphysics: Essays in Critical Appreciation*, ed. Jas. B. Wilbur (Assen: Van Gorcum, 1976), 127. An examination of reflection and negation, however, lies beyond the scope of this paper, and I have confined my present consideration to the concept of "show" [*Schein*]. See *WL* II, 7-13 (*SL*, 394-399; JS, *II*, 20-25).

¹⁵ *WL*, II, 159-160 (*SL*, 532; *JS*, II, 163 [translation faulty]).

Nevertheless, this glimpse of the absolute overwhelms the apparency, since

> there is nothing in the finite which could preserve for it a distinction against the absolute.

Show is a transparent medium which is absorbed by that which shows [Scheint] through it.[16] It is as though show is finite determinateness in the process of vanishing into its ground, and as though it stops for a logical moment to express itself before it vanishes into the absolute. And the determinateness must vanish, since the only non-negative in the process is the absolute itself. Whatever is real in the content is reclaimed by and in the absolute itself. The absolute alone, so to speak, has title, and so all reality is claimed by the absolute and in its own name.

Still, the question remains: where did the content come from in the first place with its determinateness? To which Hegel claims to have an answer: all the determinations which have been developed up to this point in the *Science of Logic* are to be understood as a negative (i.e., a determinate) exposition of the absolute. The job is not yet done, however, even for Hegel, for the absolute still withdraws from its determinations into a simple identity that lies beyond them. But the determinations have been developed out of the unity of being and of essence already, so that (Hegel is certain) they can and will be recovered and integrated subsequently into the absolute in the remainder of the *Science of Logic*. Spinoza, according to Hegel, is in no such position. His conception of the absolute is too immediate, too raw, too unrefined and undeveloped. That, too, is why he proceeds by a mathematical method, laying down definitions of the absolute and proceeding from them.[17] He is driven, therefore, according to Hegel, to introduce differentiation (in the form of the modes) "empirically," i.e., from without, and so by an appeal to sensible experience and to external reflection. As the modes vanish into the absolute they do not meet an already developed implicit content, but meet instead only the abstract claim that all content (i.e., all modes) comes from and returns to the absolute. Hegel thinks that in his own *Science of Logic* the self-

---

[16] *JS*, II, 163. (*SL*, 532, translates *scheint* as "is reflected.")

[17] *WL*, II, 165 (*SL*, 537; *JS*, II, 168) Cf. *Encyclopaedia of the Philosophical Sciences* (1830), para. 151 *Zusatz* (in the English, *Hegel's Logic* [being vol. I of 3 vols.], tr. Wm. Wallace (1873) (Oxford: Clarendon, 1975), 214. The point is controverted, of course, in Spinoza scholarship.

developing absolute recovers the determinate content (i.e., the modes) in a series of evolving contexts that it recognizes as its own.

Nevertheless, Spinoza does carry us beyond the mere dilemma of determinate modes and indeterminate substance. The "absolute absolute" is the pure self-identity into which all of the formal determinations disappear. In the conception of the *attribute*, however, thought relativizes the absolute. We may recall the definition of attribute:

> Per attributum intelligo id, quod intellectus de substantia percipit, tanquam ejusdem essentiam constituens.[18]

The attribute *is* the essence of substance, and so it is the whole, but it is *a determinate totality*, i.e., thought or extension or perhaps an infinite number of others. Now, the determinateness seems at first to be introduced from outside, but if we take the conception of the attribute seriously, then we must conceive the absolute as somehow determining itself, since the attributes *are* the absolute and the absolute *is* these determinate totalities. If they were imposed upon the absolute from outside it, they would not express its essential character and it would remain essentially untouched by them. This means, then, that we must somehow change our way of conceiving the absolute. This is the challenge set forth by this interesting conception of the attribute. The attribute is determinate content in the form of the absolute. Determinateness has undergone a twofold change: (i) it has lost the partiality it has in the modes, and (ii) it has lost even the appearance of subsistence which the modes gave forth. In other words, the determinateness in the form of the attribute has lost finitude, and has become infinite determinateness or determinate infinitude.

Nevertheless, the distinct determinateness of thought and extension seems ungrounded in Spinoza's philosophy. Alas, there is more. For when we ask: What happens to this absolute determinateness? we must (according to Hegel) reply: in the end it is rendered inessential within Spinoza's exposition. For the essential reality and truth of the attribute lies,—not in its thoughtfulness or in its corporeality, but—in its character as totality. Moreover, the warrant that justifies the reality of the attribute comes to it from its absoluteness, and not from its determinacy. Once again, if several attributes do emerge in the ex-

---

[18] Gebhardt II, 45. Hegel distinguishes the "absolute absolute" from both the "absolute attribute" and the "relative absolute" at *WL*, II, 160–162 (*SL*, 532–534; *JS*, II, 164–165).

position (i. e. thought, extension and perhaps an infinity of others), still they reduce in the end to a single attribute: determinate totality. The plurality of attributes in Spinoza's philosophy may seem to be a demand of thought. In truth, however, according to Hegel, it is an empty abstract demand, to be compared perhaps with the Stoic contraction of all the determinations of life into the one bond of servitude and dependence.[19] Since the absolute must by its very nature contain and ground all determinateness, and yet since it cannot in its Spinozistic form, we may conclude that we have not yet reached the "veritable absolute" in Spinoza's philosophy. This should not surprise those familiar with Hegel's thought, however, since the absolute is not a definition with which we begin but a *result* reached only by the labour of thought.

The attribute attempts to build a conceptual bridge in Spinoza's philosophy between the absolute absolute and the determinate modes (which are finite after their own kind).[20] The attribute declares that the absolute is in its very essence determinate. Moreover, in providing the determinate totalities within which a mode receives its own determinate character, the attributes appropriate the modes as belonging in some way to substance.

Of course, the root problem which the conception of the attribute was meant to solve was not the relation between the substance and the modes. It was, rather, a problem within the absolute itself, viz., the problem of identity and difference within absolute identity. The attribute is the first emergence of determinateness within the Spinozistic absolute, and of it. For that reason the attribute differs from a property, which is a determination of a relatively indeterminate substrate. The attribute has a dual character. It is simple self-identity, since it is the very essence of the absolute, the essence of substance; and as such it is positive. But it is also the formal determinateness of the absolute; and as such it is negative.

Now, the mode develops out of the attribute as a reinforcement of its negativity.[21] The mode is the self-externality of the absolute in which

---

[19] *Phän.*, 153 (*Phen*, tr. Baillie, 244; *Phen.*, tr. Miller, para. 199, 121).

[20] Cf. Gebhardt II, 46, the *Explicatio*, for the phrase, "absolute infinitum, non autem in suo genere," from which this is derived.

[21] *WL*, II, 162–164 (*SL*, 534–536; *JS*, II, 166–167). Cf. the passage on show [*Schein*] in fn. 14 above.

the absolute loses itself in the instability and contingency of being.[22]

Again, the mode is

> externality *posited* as externality, a mere way and manner, and hence show as show.

In recognizing show as mere show, as a mere modification of substance, the mode manifests non-show, i.e., it manifests the absolute. This is the movement of reflection by which the absolute reflects back upon what it already is. The mode as show, then, is not just a quality. It is the *affectio*,[23] the modification by which the absolute returns to itself. If the absolute did not pass into and through the determinations, something would escape it and it would not be absolute. The true meaning of mode, then, is: that modification of substance which is not a transition into another; and so it is an immanent, intransitive movement on the part of reality. It is a "going out" into determinations and a "returning" to itself as so determined. It is, then, not merely determinateness or determination, but a self-determining. Now, this is just the principle of subjectivity that Hegel thinks essential to the nature of absolute substance. Subjectivity is the name given to thought insofar as it takes its determinations as its own, through its own activity, and insofar as it determines itself by these determinations without passing over into another, i.e., into non-thought. There is still work to be done to make clear the Hegelian nature of substance as *causa sui*; but when it is done, the absolute will emerge as substance-become-subjectivity through its own self-determination. When it does it will manifest the process of the concept itself [*Begriff*]; and the absolute, attribute and mode will have realized themselves as universal, particular and individual respectively.[24] As sides of the concept they will give to the absolute the form of subjectivity.

The defect of Spinoza's philosophy, then,—and according to Hegel, it is a necessary defect,—lies in the primacy it gives to *substance* and the relative neglect it shows to *subjectivity*. At the beginning of this paper I mentioned the banner of the Hegelian philosophy that Hegel

---

[22] *JS*, II, 166 (*SL*, 535. *WL*, II, 162: "Veränderlichkeit und Zufälligkeit").

[23] Gebhardt II, 45: "Per modum intelligi, substantiae affectiones, sive id, quod in alio est, per quod etiam concipitur."

[24] *WL* II, 204-205 and 238ff. (*SL*, 571 and 600ff.; *JS*, II, 205 and 234ff.)

held aloft in the Preface to the *Phenomenology of Spirit* and elsewhere: Forward! From substance to subject! In short, Spinoza's defect is that he was not a Hegelian! Hegel reminds us that Spinoza neither wholly ignored nor excluded subjectivity, for he included thought within his system as an attribute and minds as an order of modes. The defect of Spinoza's philosophy, then, is not that of a simple absence of subjectivity, as though it is a one-sided objectivism. It is the problem of the way in which subjectivity enters into Spinoza's substance and receives expression there. It is a question of the shape of the Spinozistic absolute.[25]

We have already seen, at the beginning of this paper, how Hegel's own thought stands in relation to Spinoza's. Spinoza's conception of the absolute is correct, and it becomes false only when it insists that substance is the highest standpoint. It is the failure to incorporate the subjective principle adequately and appropriately into his system.

---

[25] *WL*, II, 217-218 (*SL*, 581; *JS*, II, 215). In the article already cited in fn. 14, S. Rosen in *Spinoza's Metaphysics*, 115-132, traces the sense in which Descartes laid down the modern idea of subjectivity that Hegel recognizes as implicit in Spinoza. It remains only to insist equally upon the continuity that binds Hegel to Spinoza in contrast to the discontinuity that exists between Descartes and Hegel. J.B. McMinn, in "A Critique of Hegel's Criticism of Spinoza's God," *Kant-Studien*, vol. 51, 1959-60, 294-314, is correct to speak of "an implicit substantial affinity" between the two systems [of Spinoza and Hegel], but he understates the difficulty when he declares without qualification that both have "the same metaphysical object, viz., the God of Substance and Spirit." Interpretations that work with categories such as "monism" and "rationalism" also underrate the difficulty. Interpretations that rest upon some type of monism miss the great difference between 17th century rationalism and 19th century idealism. Cf. H.A. Meyers, *The Spinoza-Hegel Paradox*, New York: B. Franklin, (1944) 1974; L. Foss, "Hegel, Spinoza, and a Theory of Closed Experience," *The Thomist*, vol. 35 (1971), 435-446; and E. Shmueli, "Some Similarities between Spinoza and Hegel on Substance," *The Thomist*, vol. 36 (1972), 645-657.

Interpretations that work with a category of idealism seem to fare better, although it can be argued that Hegel is an idealist, if at all, then in such a special, even unique sense, that the term doesn't throw light on his philosophy. Still, two recent volumes are interesting in this regard. In *Spinoza on Knowing, Being and Freedom*, ed. J.G. van der Bend, Assen: Van Gorcum, 1974, the editor indicates "some idealistic tendencies" in Spinoza, and the volume ends with a discussion of the relation between Hegel and Spinoza that marshalls a range of opinions (184-186). In *Spinoza's Metaphysics* (see fn. 14 above), Robert N. Beck writes: "In making out this interpretation I have tried not to hurry to some modern position or classification like idealism or scientific materialism, though I do think that Hegelianism of a sort is the proper philosophical heir of Spinozism." (10).

Now, this incorporation of the subjective is, according to Hegel, a demand inherent in the development of philosophical thought itself. In modern times, he writes in the beginning of the *Science of Logic*

> the *subjective* act has also been grasped as an *essential* movement of objective truth.[26]

This is, indeed, the key to Hegel's own philosophical program. Nevertheless, in order to achieve it. Hegel finds it necessary to transform the accepted meanings of subjectivity and objectivity, so that the absolute can assume a determinate shape which incorporates them both, even as it passes beyond the shape they have when opposed to one another. Now, it is just the promise of this transformation that makes Spinoza's philosophy at once a half-way house and a place where we must not rest. For Spinoza himself has pointed out the way that needs to be travelled, and he has done it with his remarkable conceptions of the *causa sui* and the attribute.

The task is nothing short of a reconciliation of thought and being, a task that requires a recovery of the ancient harmony so vital to philosophy: the justification of the intelligibility of being. But this cannot be done without a redefinition of subjectivity and objectivity. In his own solution Hegel assimilates the previous forms of the subjective principle. There is the ancient theological form of the principle. Indeed, philosophy had to become theology in the Middle Ages in order to appropriate this form. There is the modern psychological form of the principle, although Hegel did not foresee the even more radical anthropological turn initiated by Feuerbach, Marx and others. The importance of Spinoza is that he redirected the search for the appropriate form of the subjective principle back to its Eleatic beginnings; and he posed the problem of the appropriate form of the absolute in terms of being (*ens a se*), of substance, of nature (*physis*). It is from this recovered standpoint that Hegel moves out to reach what he takes to be the final shape of the absolute,—not the shape of *theos*, nor of *psyche*, nor of *anthropos*, nor even of *physis* or *natura*,—but the shape of spirit, *Geist, pneuma*.

It remains only to ask whether Hegel has succeeded in his refuta-

---

[26] *WL*, I, 52 (*SL*, 67; *JS*, I, 79).

tion of Spinoza.[27] It is patent that he has taken Spinoza's substance to be filled with the aspirations of the Hegelian absolute. In assuming this, he assumes an identity of philosophical purpose between himself and Spinoza. Indeed, Hegel approaches all of his predecessors as though they are fore-runners in the same speculative enterprise. If this is not in some sense true, then the unity of philosophy is more apparent than real. But that too is subject to debate. Even among metaphysicians of a speculative cast radical differences make communication, comparison and criticism more difficult than Hegel

---

[27] See Errol Harris, *Salvation from Despair: A Reappraisal of Spinoza's Philosophy*, The Hague: Nijhoff, 1973, especially c.2, 15-30. He writes: "Spinoza [is accused] of failure to provide a principle of differentiation intrinsic to God, so that interpretation must oscillate between blank unity and inexhaustibly concrete diversity without finding a satisfactory principle of reconciliation. I believe this criticism to be misjudgment (it is shared by many besides those I have quoted [Caird, and sometimes Joachim], Hegel not the least)" (50). Professor Harris identifies the problem acutely, but he does not, it seems to me, develop the needed reconciliation directly as a refutation of Hegel's interpretation. Moreover, his objections to Caird and Joachim do not meet the genuinely speculative level of the difficulty as Hegel addresses it. (58-60)

Harris' own solution (64-69) simply restates the problem: "What is infinite has, by that very fact, infinite attributes. The more reality a thing has the more attributes it must possess" (*Ethics*, I, p10, S; Harris, 64). The correlation between the infinite and its attributes comes on the scene too late to meet Hegel's problem. He might even agree, but would attach a *proviso*: providing the absolute as infinite has any right to determinate attributes at all. Harris writes again (*ibid.*): "The principle of differentiation, therefore, of God's 'unity' is his very infinity, his necessary all-inclusiveness. There can be no *whole* which is not diversified" [Italics added.] But Spinoza does not justify the conception of substance as a *whole*, whereas Hegel (or so he would claim) has already taken up the conception in his treatment of the Essential Relation (*WL*, II, 138-142; *SL*, 513-517; *JS*, II, 143-147), moving from the Whole and its Parts to the dynamic unity of Force and the distinction of Inner and Outer (*WL*, II, 144-155; *SL*, 518-528; *JS*, II, 149-159). But this categorial development led directly to the level of enquiry at which the question of the Absolute can be *put* (*WL*, II, 156ff; *SL*, 530ff.; *JS*, II, 160ff.); it did not *answer* the question. Now Spinoza never even raised it. Only because Hegel's absolute already contains what he takes to be a *warranted* plurality of categories, can the problem of indeterminacy and determinacy be faced at the level of the absolute. The problem is not resolved even here, however, since only the further march of the categories into realized subjectivity can justify the reconciliation of absolute indeterminacy and absolute determination in absolute self-determination. As N. Rotenstreich, *op. cit.*, writes (20): "The shift from substance to subject places totality at the end of the dialectical movement and not at its beginning."

imagines. His treatment of Spinoza is always serious and often brilliant; but his failure to appreciate the possibility of a radically different philosophical objective means that he has failed to meet his own rigorous criteria for a philosophical refutation, and *a fortiori* that he fails to engage Spinoza at the intimate core of his thought. And so he leaves a lacuna, a negative of a sort that permits Spinoza's God to escape and to play another role than that of Hegel's absolute. Nevertheless, although he has not vanquished Spinoza, he has entered the lists and encroached upon his field. For they do share a common conviction that knowledge—whatever its nature—will not be fulfilled until it rests in contemplative union with the deepest core of reality—however differently they each may understand that to be. Hegel mistakes Spinoza's substance for his own realized embodiment of *Wissenschaft* and finds it to be *dieu manqué*. He places Spinoza's ethics at the periphery of the latter's thought. Nevertheless, he does expose a genuine problem in Spinoza's metaphysics that challenges us to rethink—not only our understanding of Spinoza's philosophy, but—our understanding of the nature of philosophy itself. Hegel thought that he had taken the essential truth of Spinoza's philosophy up into his own, so that it could become a moment of the Hegelian thought-totality. If Spinoza has escaped in some measure, still Hegel has approached Spinoza's thought close enough to continue a conversation with him, even if he has not come close enough to stop it.

Trinity College, University of Toronto

ALTERNATIVE APPROACHES TO SPINOZA

14 SPINOZA'S LOGIC OF INQUIRY: RATIONALIST OR EXPERIENTIALIST?
Isaac Franck

Readers whose approach to Spinoza's philosophy reflects widely held, traditional assumptions concerning Spinoza and Rationalism, frequently espouse two fashionable stereotypes. The first is that, in the title of this paper, the "or" between "Rationalist" and "Experientialist" is necessarily an exclusive "or," and that there can be no intermingling between these two modes of philosophical inquiry. The second stereotype is that Spinoza was a rigid, uncompromising *Rationalist* who " . . . completely separated . . . rational thought and . . . empirical observation [with] no way of getting from one to the other."[1] In this paper I propose to discuss these two still fashionable assumptions.

I

Many years ago, in a lecture on Spinoza, the late Professor Frederick J. E. Woodbridge of Columbia University said that Spinoza's *Ethics* "does not represent the way he arrived at his conclusions, but the way he expressed them."[2] This distinction between the "Geometric Order" in which the *Ethics* is presented, with its formidable deductive apparatus, and on the other hand the putatively different way in which the doctrines of the *Ethics* were arrived at, or could be arrived at, is reinforced by a passage in a powerful but sadly neglected book, published at about the same time as Woodbridge's lecture. I refer to H. F. Hallett's *Aeternitas: A Spinozistic Study*. On page 4 Hallett pointed out that

---

[1] W. T. Jones, *A History of Western Philosophy*, 2d ed. (New York: Harcourt, Brace & World, 1969), Vol. III, 217–218.
[2] Frederick J. E. Woodbridge, *Spinoza*, lecture delivered at Columbia University, January 26, 1933, published as a separate brochure (New York: Columbia University Press [no date]), 9.

"It is because it has not always been remembered that the order of discovery often reverses the logical order, i.e., the real order of nature, that Spinoza's doctrine has commonly been misinterpreted ... And the position is not rendered more safe for the unwary by Spinoza's attempt to identify the order of nature and the order of exposition by the use of the ... geometric form in his chief metaphysical work, the *Ethics*."[3]

The exposition or presentation in the *Ethics* is *ordine geometrico*. From Definitions and Axioms it proceeds deductively to generate theorems, called Propositions by Spinoza, each of which ostensibly claims the right to be part of the deductive system by virtue of a demonstration that shows it to follow logically from: (a) these initial Axioms and Definitions; or from (b) additional Axioms, Definitions, and also a number of Postulates, that are later introduced at various points in the *Ethics;* or from (c) other theorems or Propositions the logical dependence of which upon prior Axioms, Definitions, Postulates, or theorems has already been demonstrated; or from combinations of these. What has occasioned voluminous comment is the fact that these Axioms, Postulates, and Definitions are, like those in Euclid's *Elements*, themselves undemonstrated. This fact, in turn, has inevitably led to the question, whence, for Spinoza, do these Axioms, Postulates, as well as the Definitions derive their truth?

From among the several interpretations to be found in the extensive Spinoza literature, I focus on what appear to me to be three prototypical biases with respect to this question. I shall call them a) The Euclidean Bias; b) The Rationalist Bias; c) The Historicist Bias.

a) *The Euclidean Bias.* Because of its geometric form, and consequently the inevtiable comparison that is drawn between Spinoza's *Ethics* and Euclid's *Elements*, the attempt has often been made to approach this question by way of the traditional interpretation of Euclid, according to which his Axioms have been accepted as self-evident, and his Definitions either as necessarily true, or as nominal explanations of the use of terms and thus neither false nor true. The theorems deduced from these axioms, definitions, and postulates are therefore said to gain their truth from the self-evident certainty of the presuppositions. For a long time Spinoza's *Ethics* was interpreted as having tried to do the same thing, or something similar to it. From allegedly self-evident axioms and definitions he was said to have de-

---

[3] H. F. Hallett, *Aeternitas, A Spinozistic Study* (Oxford: Clarendon Press, 1930), 4.

duced, or drawn out, his entire system; and on the *self-evident* truth of these presuppositions his system supposedly rests.

This interpretation has persisted at least since the year 1661 when Spinoza's contemporary, Henry Oldenburg, criticized his early experiments with the geometric order. Oldenburg wrote to Spinoza as follows:

> "The third question is, whether you hold those axioms, which you communicated to me, as indemonstrable principles, recognized by the light of nature, and standing in no need of proof? It may be that the first axiom is of such a kind; but I don't see how the remaining three can be included in the number of such principles . . . . Since, then, these axioms do not seem to me to be placed beyond all risk of doubt, you will easily conjecture that your propositions which are based on them cannot but be shaky. And the more I consider them, the more I am overwhelmed with doubts about them."[4]

It is interesting to note that, while Spinoza obviously held that his axioms were true, there is no evidence that he placed them at the beginning of the Ethics with any illusions that they would be accepted as self-evident. As a matter of fact, in his reply to Oldenburg's letter Spinoza made no attempt to persuade him that the axioms are self-evident. His reply amounts almost to an acquiescence in Oldenburg's contention. These are Spinoza's words:

> "You proceed . . . . . . to object to my assertions, [and state] that [my] axioms are not to be reckoned among Common Notions. Over this, however, I will not dispute."[5]

It is important also to note that, if self-evidence had been Spinoza's criterion for placing any proposition among the axioms, and if his system were purely a deduction from these self-evident axioms, the beginning portions of the first part of the *Ethics* should hardly have undergone the drastic changes they did undergo from earlier versions[6] to their final form. It would have been inconceivable for propositions, that were originally classed as (self-evident) Axioms, to have migrated later, as they in fact did, into the bulk of *demonstrated* theorems in the text of the *Ethics*. As a result of such migration, we find

---

[4] Wolf (a), Ep. 3, 79.
[5] Wolf (a), Ep. 4, 82.
[6] Wolf (b), Appendix I, 153–156; cf. Wolf (a), 371–373.

the system endeavoring to *prove* some of the propositions that presumably had been, at least at one time, considered by Spinoza to be among its putatively self-evident axioms or presuppositions. Such behavior is hardly what one expects from a respectable deductive system whose starting point is a group of self-evident Axioms.

But Spinoza had no illusions about self-evidence. In his work we find a keen awareness of the fact that what may be self-evident to one person is only too frequently quite obscure to another. We sometimes find him doing what a logically competent person, who is constructing a strict *a priori*, deductive system logically drawn out of self-evident axioms, would be expected never to do, namely, yielding to human frailty, and quite consciously placing, among the theorems to be proved, a proposition which he considered axiomatic. Such is proposition 7 of Part I of the *Ethics:* "It pertains to the nature of substance to exist." In the Scholium to the very next Proposition Spinoza remarks that

" . . . if men would attend to the nature of substance, they would not entertain a single doubt of the truth of proposition 7; indeed this Proposition would be considered by all to be axiomatic, and reckoned among the common notions."[7]

b) *The Rationalist Bias.* Spinoza has been almost universally denominated a Rationalist. In the recent *Encyclopedia of Philosophy* Alasdair MacIntyre refers to him as "rationalist metaphysician," and identifies him, in accord with the traditional, received classification in most histories and textbooks of philosophy, as one of the three "Continental Rationalists."[8] As to the meaning of Rationalism, Bernard Williams, writing in the same *Encyclopedia of Philosophy*, singles out among the "several different outlooks and movements of ideas" included under the label "rationalism," as "by far the most important . . . the philosophical outlook or program which stresses the power of *a priori* reason to grasp truths about the world."[9]

Spinoza's *Ethics* is generally taken to be an example *par excellence* of Rationalist thought, a product of such *a priori* reasoning, which proceeds deductively from certain "innate ideas," or "clear and distinct ideas," perceived by man's *lumen naturale*, or "natural light" of reasons. Such ideas include God, Thought, Extension. They are verbal-

---

[7] E I, P 8 S.

[8] Alasdair MacIntyre, "Spinoza," in *The Encyclopedia of Philosophy* (New York: MacMillan, 1967), Vol. 7, 530–541.

[9] Bernard Williams, "Rationalism," Ibid., Vol. 7, 69.

ized in and represented by the Axioms and Definitions in the *Ethics*. The Geometric Order is deemed the most congenial to this kind of methodology, and indeed, the "Geometric *Method*" (a locution repeatedly used by many commentators as if it were Spinoza's own, though in fact this locution was never used by Spinoza himself) is deemed *the* philosophical method for the discovery of new ideas and facts about the universe. The Axioms and Definitions are thus versions of our autonomous, self-validating innate ideas, uncontaminated by experience, and grasped *a priori* by the *natural light,* through the exercise of *scientia intuitiva*. From these ideas, employing the rational technique of logical deduction, Spinoza spun the logically coherent, rational diagram of the rationally structured universe, bringing forth in the *Ethics* what to W. T. Jones "seems a dream philosophy—a magnificent, even inspiring edifice, but still a dream."[10]

In the face of this prevalent bias it was, for many years, considered ill-mannered and intellectually disreputable to suggest that Spinoza did not resemble quite perfectly the stereotypical portrait of the rigid Rationalist, or that his alleged disparagement of and contempt for experience as a source of knowledge was not as thoroughly immaculate or consistent as believed or claimed. Those who, beginning two or three decades ago, thought they discovered significant empirical or experientialist elements in Spinoza's philosophical methodology, and flirted with the idea that some of the Axioms and Definitions of the *Ethics* may be based on *experience,* and may have been seen as so based by Spinoza himself, therefore constituted a kind of unorganized underground in Spinoza scholarship that began to surface only in the past two decades. Such books as H. G. Hubbeling's *Spinoza's Methodology*[11] and C. De Deugd's *The Significance of Spinoza's First Kind of Knowledge*[12] are examples, as well as more recent individual essays by G. H. Parkinson and E. M. Curley, to which reference will be made later.

c) *The Historicist Bias.* Under this rubric are included those who approach the *Ethics* almost exclusively from an historical point of view, and are engaged largely in tracing its intellectual antecedents to the writings of his predecessors. The most distinguished of these Spinoza scholars was, of course, the late Professor H. A. Wolfson of Harvard. His great and irreplaceable work, *The Philosophy of Spinoza,* throws a powerful new light on Spinoza's work in general and on the *Ethics* in

---

[10] W. T. Jones, Op. cit., Vol. III, 217.

[11] H. G. Hubbeling, *Spinoza's Methodology* (Assen: Van Gorcum, 1964).

[12] de Deugd, Cornelius, *The Significance of Spinoza's First Kind of Knowledge* (Assen: Van Gorcum, 1964).

particular. However, so overwhelming is the cumulative massing of the historical evidence, that questions about the logical, methodological, and epistemological status and sources of the Axioms and Definitions and other central ideas in the *Ethics* are almost lost sight of. It would seem almost as if Spinoza's philosophical ideas propounded in the *Ethics* were not at all based on any processes of philosophical or logical analysis or speculation. It would seem rather as if they were woven altogether out of the ideas of his predecessors and his critical responses to them—from Plato through Aristotle, the Neo-Platonists, the Stoics, the Arabic Philosophers, the Scholastics and Descartes, as well as the thinkers in the mainstream of Jewish philosophy: the Rabbis of the Talmudic period, Philo, Isaac Israeli, Saadia, Solomon Ibn Gabirol, Bahya Ibn Pakuda, Yehudah Halevi, Abraham Ibn Ezra, Moses Maimonides, Gersonides, Hasdai Crescas, Joseph Albo, etc.

II

However, such interpretations are far removed from the spirit, the intentions, and the convictions incorporated in the *Ethics*. Spinoza's chief concern in this work is exactly what the title of his book is, namely, *ethics*. It is a concern with striving for a way of life that will attain the highest good that man is capable of, namely the life of freedom; freedom, in the words of Prof. Woodbridge, "from our unruly wills and emotions that are the causes of our misery",[13] freedom from *perturbationes mentis*. "Everything in the sciences that does not promote this endeavor must be rejected as useless,"[14] says Spinoza. The only way this goal can be attained, according to Spinoza, is through "the knowledge of the union which the mind has with the whole of nature,"[15] and this entails the study of nature. Spinoza wrote the *Ethics* in order to exhibit this very union. He wanted to exhibit the structure of things, and to show man's place in this structure. He did not write the *Ethics* as an exercise in logic, or in *a priori* reasoning, or in the synthesizing or criticizing of the ideas of his predecessors.

The procedure of the *Ethics* is accurately described in its subtitle as *Ordine Geometrico Demonstrata*. The Ethics is a *demonstration*, an ἀπόδειξις, but it is a demonstration in *geometrical* order. Every demonstration proceeds deductively from certain premises, first principles, or, ἀρχαί; in the case of Spinoza's *Ethics*, these premises are

---

[13] Frederick, J. E. Woodbridge, Op. cit., 3.
[14] TdIE, Para. 16.
[15] TdIE, Para. 13.

are furnished by the definitions, axioms, and postulates. Therefore, the question of the truth of the definitions and axioms of the Ethics is not only relevant but of crucial importance. However, in the *Ethics*, as in any demonstration, the truth of the premises is taken for granted or assumed *in the course of the demonstration,* and may be inquired into and discovered only *outside* of the framework or procedure of the particular demonstration itself. To put it succinctly: the order or logic of demonstration is distinct from any order or logic of inquiry or discovery, and questions of the *order* or *logic of inquiry and discovery* are improper to the process of the demonstration itself. The axioms and definitions of the *Ethics* perform the function of putatively true premisses in a demonstration, and these may be discovered, and their truth grasped, *not as a consequence* of the demonstrations of the *Ethics*, but outside of their framework and their procedure.[16]

The *Ethics* is not an *Inquiry;* it is not a *Critique;* it is not a *Discourse;* it is not a set of *Meditations;* it is not a *Summa;* it is not a *Tractatus.* The *Ethics* is a *Demonstration,* or a series of demonstrations, of an elaborate group of doctrines concerning Nature, Man, Man's body and mind, his emotions, his Slavery to his emotions, and his Liberation from this Slavery. This Demonstration, or group of demonstrations, is in the nature of an attempt to show that these doctrines propounded by Spinoza are related as conclusions to the premises (in this case the definitions, axioms, and postulates) that stand at the head of the various parts of the demonstration; and the discovery of which occurs outside and apart from its order. This approach to the *Ethics* as a Demonstration has, as I shall attempt to show, important consequences in its interpretation.

If we ask whether or not the premises of an *apodeixis* or Demonstration are themselves true, we are told that, while the question is legitimate and even imperative, nevertheless the answer to it cannot be given in terms of, or within the framework of, the apodeixis itself. The answer to this question must be sought in an inquiry outside the confines of the demonstration proper. The truth of the premises has its foundation in knowledge that is prior to the deductive procedure and the conclusions of the demonstration. This, of course, is the Aristotelian analysis, according to which "all instruction given or received by way of argument proceeds from pre-existent knowledge,"

---

[16] This and what follows immediately below of course reflect Aristotle's analysis of "demonstrative knowledge" in the *Posterior Analytics* I, 1–4, 71a1–73a23; and II, 18–19, 99b15–100b17.

and demonstrative or apodeictic reasoning is such that by its very nature it assumes an audience that accepts its premises.[17]

If we now proceed to inquire, outside of the framework of the demonstration, in what manner this previous knowledge, or what is the same thing, the putatively true premises, were obtained, it may be answered, of course, that they themselves are in turn conclusions of demonstrations; but this tracing back cannot continue, because, either it will involve an infinite regress, which amounts to a denial of the possibility of demonstrative knowledge; or, if no infinite regress is allowed, it will amount to an admission that all knowledge is circular.[18] But since demonstrative knowledge *is* in fact possible, we must assume the existence of another kind of knowledge, which is "independent of demonstration,"[19] and by means of which it is possible to obtain the "basic truths," the premises, the first principles, on which demonstrated knowledge is based.

The concluding pages of Aristotle's analysis in the *Posterior Analytics* contain the account of how by ἐπαγογή (*epagoge*, generally translated "induction"), by a leading on, knowledge is built up from sense perception, into memory, thence into experience, and thence into scientific knowledge; how νοῦς (*nous*, translated "intuition" in the Oxford Press translation) grasps the universal, and how the universal is then given as premiss for demonstrative knowledge.[20] It can be shown, and has been shown quite clearly by H. A. Wolfson,[21] that Spinoza's explication of the *origin* of knowledge is not as different from that of Artistotle as it has frequently been assumed to be.

Clearly also Spinoza followed Aristotle in his conception of what constitutes scientific knowledge. The premises from which a scientific conclusion is demonstrated are the logical causes, the principles, the *archai*, on which the conclusion depends and through which it is known. Spinoza's principle that "true science proceeds from cause to effect"[22] is only a paraphrase of Aristotle's statement that "we have scientific knowledge ... when we think we know the cause on which the thing depends."[23] Indeed, Spinoza makes it axiomatic that "the knowledge of an effect depends upon and involves the knowledge of

---

[17] Ibid., I, 1, 71a 1–7.
[18] Ibid., I, 3 72b 5–17.
[19] Ibid., I, 3, 72b 18–20.
[20] Ibid., II, 19, 99b18–100b17.
[21] H. A. Wolfson, *The Philosophy of Spinoza*, 2 vols. (Cambridge: Harvard University Press, 1934), II, 151–154.
[22] TdIE, Para. 85.
[23] Aristotle, *Posterior Analytics*, I, 2, 71b20–22.

the cause."[24] Ernst Cassirer, in his classic (and still untranslated) history of the problem of knowledge in the philosophy and science of the modern era, summed up neatly Spinoza's relationship to Aristotle on this issue, in the following sentence:

"So bleibt hier die Aristotelische Definition der Wissenschaft, dass sie die Erkenntnis der Wirkungen aus den Ursachen sei, im Kraft."[25] ("Thus the Aristotelian definition of science as the knowledge of effects through their causes, remains in force here.")

To sum up then, the truth of the premisses is not demonstrable within the particular demonstration itself. Their truth is assumed in the demonstration, and questions of their origin and ground are irrelevant and improper to the course of the demonstration. How the premisses were arrived at, or may be arrived at, is a subject for a separate inquiry. And it is to be noted that the order and logic of inquiry into and discovery of such basic truths, or premisses, or axioms that are employed in the structure of any given apodeictic system, is different and distinct from the order and logic of demonstration of that system.

III

There is an abundance of evidence that Spinoza was keenly aware of this distinction between the proper order and logic of inquiry and the order of demonstration. His decision to write a special treatise, the *Tractatus de Intellectus Emendatione,* for the purpose of showing how the intellect "may be directed towards a true knowledge of things,"[26] testifies cogently that he did not consider the enterprise of this treatise, namely, the enterprise of "directing the intellect," to be part of the task of the *Ethics.* Neither did his correspondents. In one of his letters to Spinoza, Tschirnhaus inquires, "when are we to have your method of controlling reason rightly in acquiring knowledge of unknown truths?"[27] Tschirnhaus was obviously not referring to the *Ethics,* since most of *Ethics* I was already in his hands. The TdIE was never completed, and therefore there are serious lacunae in Spi-

---

[24] E I, A4.
[25] Ernst Cassirer, *Das Erkenntnisproblem in der Philosophie und Wissenschaft der neueren Zeit,* II, 16.
[26] From the subtitle of the TdIE.
[27] Wolf (a), Ep. 59, 298.

noza's theory of the correct order and logic of inquiry. The fact remains, however, that this treatise was begun for the purpose of explaining just what such an order should be, and of thus leading up to some of the premises and first principles on which the demonstration, or group of demonstrations, that the *Ethics* is, logically rests.

It will be instructive to digress here in order to note how this approach to the *Ethics*, as a demonstration the premises of which are discovered outside of the demonstration itself, eliminates some alleged difficulties that seemingly present themselves on other interpretations. The nineteenth century Spinoza scholar, James Martineau, interpreted the TdIE correctly as "laying down the principles of knowledge and the order of discovery," but in the very next breath he proceeded to claim that to this order of discovery "the order of the (*Ethics*) should conform".[28] He thus conceived it to be part of the task of the *Ethics* to *discover* the "substantive truth." Consequently, it seemed paradoxical to him that in the TdIE we find Spinoza's "exposition of the rules of knowing already bespeaking the things known; so that if he had completed his theory of method, he would have told, in the process, the substantive truth which was professedly waiting to take shape from it."[29] This alleged paradox is only a result, first, of erroneously assigning to the *Ethics* the task of *discovering* "the substantive truth"; and, second of being blinded, by virtue of having reserved this assignment for the *Ethics*, to the possibility of achieving this discovery in the course of the inquiry of the TdIE.

It would have been logically impossible, and methodologically inconceivable, to discover this "substantive truth" (meaning of course *God*) in the course of the argument of the *Ethics*, since this truth is itself one of the ἀρχαί, or more properly, the one major fundamental principle that is presupposed by the subject matter of the *Ethics*, and from which this work logically proceeds. The discovery of this substantive truth in the TdIE is not at all paradoxical. In Spinoza's view, the mere exposition of the correct order of inquiry and discovery inevitably leads to some of what this correct order is designed to discover, namely, some of the premises, of the basic truths, from which the demonstration of scientific knowledge must proceed. It would have been strange, in the context of Spinoza's thought, if the TdIE, even in its unfinished state, did not lead us to the two major ἀρχαί, God and the human understanding, the first of which is the major principle involved in the demonstrations of Part I of the *Ethics*, and the second in the demonstrations of Part II.

---

[28] James Martineau, *A Study of Spinoza* (London: Macmillan, 1895), 48.
[29] Ibid, 48–49.

There is also evidence within the *Ethics* itself that Spinoza did *not* consider it among the tasks of that work to inquire into the sources of its axioms or to expound the proper order or logic of such an inquiry. In Part II of the *Ethics*, after having demonstrated that the *notiones communes* are to be included among adequate ideas (Prop. 37–39), Spinoza appends a Scholium to the next proposition, in which he says that it would also be advantageous to discuss further other *causes of other axioms and notions;* such a discussion would enable us to distinguish *useful notions* from *useless* or *partially useful ones,* and to distinguish further those which are *common* and those which are clear and distinct, and those which are ill-founded. Moreover, he says, such an inquiry would tell us "whence those notions called secondary, and consequently whence *the axioms which are founded on them,* derive their origin." But, Spinoza continues, "I have set apart this subject for *another treatise.*"[30] The reference here to the TdIE is unmistakable.[31] First of all, there is evidence that Spinoza worked on the TdIE at the time of the composition of the *Ethics.* Secondly, the description of the subject matter of such a treatise fits fairly accurately the discussions in the TdIE.

This internal evidence, taken from the *Ethics,* is of utmost importance. It points conclusively to the TdIE as the treatise in which matters proper to a method and logic of inquiry are properly discussed. It does away, once and for all, with the assumption that axioms were, for Spinoza, self-evident propositions, concerning the genesis and the truth of which no questions need be asked. Indeed, Spinoza states unequivocally that he has just explained, first *"the causes of those notions which are called common,"* second, that *"of some axioms or notions other causes exist"* (*"cause,"* of course, in the sense of ἀρχή, principle of explanation), and, third, he points to *the problem of whence certain* "axioms .... derive their origin" as a problem that will be treated in the TdIE. Now, a phrase in the passage just quoted from the first Scholium to Proposition 40 of Part II of the *Ethics,* will require some attention. It will show that the prejudice concerning the self-evidence of Spinoza's axioms has even resulted in unnecessary and unwarranted tampering with the Latin text of the *Ethics.* The full passage reads as follows in the Latin:

"Praeterea constaret, unde notiones illae, quas *Secundas* vocant, et consequenter axiomata, quae in iisdem fundantur suam duxerunt originem . . . "

---

[30] E II, P40, S1.
[31] Cf. Charles Appuhn's translation of Spinoza's *Ethics* (Paris: Librarie Garnier, n..d.), I, 422, note b to E II, P40 S1.

258   PHILOSOPHY OF BARUCH SPINOZA

The ordinary and correct translation of the passage should read:

> "Moreover, it should be manifest whence these notions which are called *Second*, and consequently *the axioms founded upon them*, have taken their origin . . ."

This is the translation given by W. H. White, and that of Fullerton is substantially the same. The French translation by Charles Appuhn follows the same reading.

However, two widely used English translations, that of Elwes and that of Boyle (Everyman's Library), find it necessary to alter the passage and render it thus:

> " . . . Whence these notions which are called secondary, and consequently whence *the axioms on which they are founded*, derive their origin . . ."[32]

The difference between the two translations is that one says that *the axioms are founded on the second notions* (which is clearly what the Latin says), and the other says that *the second notions are founded on the axioms* (which requires that the Latin text be read *"inquibus eaedem fundantur"* instead of the universally accepted *"quae in iisdem fundantur"*[33]).

That this is not merely another quibble about an unimportant textual difference becomes obvious when we consider that no scholar has suggested any reason for questioning the authenticity of the text, and when we observe carefully the nature of the difference between the two interpretations. The assumption behind the Elwes and Boyle translations seems to be that the reading ". . . these notions . . . and consequently *the axioms founded upon them* . . ." must be wrong because, they would maintain, axioms cannot be founded upon any other notions, since again, as in Euclid, axioms are self-evident. The translator, in changing the text, seems to be saying that if there is any relation of dependence between *axioms* and *second notions*, the second notions must be founded on the axioms, and not *vice versa*, and any text which asserts the contrary is *ipso facto* corrupt.

Professor H. A. Wolfson follows Elwes and Boyle in their interpretation of this disputed passage.[34] A reading of his book suggests that

---

[32] Spinoza's *Ethics*, Everyman ed., trans. Boyle, 67; also Elwes II, 111.
[33] This textual problem is extensively discussed in Wolfson, Op. cit., II, 122–123.
[34] Ibid.

Wolfson shares the preconception concerning axioms which seems to lurk behind Boyles' and Elwes' translation of the passage. Wolfson treats the doctrine of the *Ethics* as if it were a logically and metaphysically autonomous, self-dependent, self-complete system, based not on an examination of reality, but stitched together out of an examination of the doctrines of previous thinkers. The Axioms, therefore, are for Wolfson not statements concerning the world and experience, but rather summaries or critiques of ideas encountered in Spinoza's reading. Accordingly, in Wolfson's interpretation, the Axioms of the *Ethics* are not derived from other logical foundations or sources or evidence, since they must have been modelled on Euclid, and are identical with the *common notions*.[35] Furthermore, Wolfson finds that Maimonides used the term *second notions* as identical with the theorems in Euclid,[36] and suggests that therefore Spinoza must have meant by *second notions* "the conclusions in demonstrative syllogisms."[37] This, of course, would make it impossible for axioms (if they were *common notions*) to be founded upon *second notions*, since these latter are themselves derived from the common notions.

However, there is no reason to believe that Spinoza equated axioms, i.e., his axioms in the *Ethics*, with the *notiones communes;* nor is there reason to believe that Spinoza could not think that some axioms were founded upon, or had their origin in, what he called *second notions*. What Spinoza meant by common notions we know quite clearly. These common notions are the ideas of those things "in which all bodies agree,"[38] and the things in which all bodies agree are first, that they involve the same attribute, i.e., extension, and second, that "they are capable of motion and rest, and of motion at one time quicker and at one time slower."[39] It is these common notions that are "the foundations of our reasoning."[40] Certainly these notions are not the axioms at the beginning of each of the five parts of the *Ethics*. They are among the first elements in the different steps which the mind, in the pursuit of the logic of inquiry and discovery, follows in building up knowledge. On the other hand Wolfson[41] is correct when he relates these notions to Aristotle's description of the procedure by which the mind builds up knowledge from sense perception, in the closing pages of the *Posterior Analytics*.

---

[35] Ibid., II, 120–121.
[36] Ibid.
[37] Ibid., II, 122.
[38] E II, P38 S.
[39] Ibid., L2, Dm.
[40] E II, P40 S1.
[41] Wolfson, Op. cit., II, 151–154 (cf. supra, note 21).

Whatever Spinoza may have meant by *second notions*, and this appears to be a matter of dispute among philologists and historians of philosophy,[42] it seems obvious that the tampering with the text of the *scholium* under discussion is motivated only by the wrong assumption that Spinoza's axioms are self-evident propositions in the structure of an *a priori* deductive system. However, if we look upon the *Ethics* as a demonstration, or a *systematic exposition* of doctrine, the starting points of which are arrived at as a result of a process of philosophical inquiry, the text in which axioms are spoken of as "founded" on other notions is not only above suspicion, but is fully consistent with the philosophical enterprise as it is exemplified in Spinoza's *Ethics*.

There is an additional body of evidence, out of the history of 16th and 17th century thought, that supports the distinction between the order or logic of inquiry and the order or logic of demonstration, and its application to Spinoza's *Ethics* as shown above, namely, the distinction between the method of *Analysis* and the method of *Synthesis*. It was well-recognized logical doctrine in the 17th century; it is summed up by Descartes in his reply to the Second Objections to his *Meditations;* and is explained by Ludwig Meyer in his Preface to Spinoza's earliest work, *Principia Philosophiae Cartesianae*, significantly characterized in its subtitle as *"Demonstratio More Geometrico."* Descartes (in a text that seems somewhat confusing), differentiates between the methods of *Synthesis*

> "(which) does indeed clearly demonstrate its conclusions, and ... employs a long series of definitions, postulates, axioms, theorems ... (but) does not show the way in which the matter taught was discovered," (and, on the other hand,) *Analysis*, (the method he used in the *Meditations*, that) "shows the way in which a thing was methodically discovered."[43]

Ludwig Meyer's Preface to Spinoza's *Principles of Descartes' Philosophy* paraphrases Descartes. Meyer says he had long hoped that someone would take what Descartes

> " ... had put in Analytic form [and] remold it in Synthetic order and demonstrate it in the more familiar forms of Geometry." Analysis, says Meyer, "is the method by which ... truth is discov-

---

[42] Cf. Wolfson II, Op. Cit., II, 120–123.
[43] *The Philosophical Works of Descartes*, trans. Haldane & Ross (Cambridge: Cambridge University Press, 1934), II. 48–49.

ered," whereas Synthesis is "the method by which it is set in order."[44]

IV

Spinoza's *Ethics* begins with a definition of that which is *causa sui*, that whose "essence involves existence,"[45] namely, God. His *Tractatus de Intellectus Emendatione* opens its discussion of method with an analysis of the different modes of perception.[46] The subject matter which in the order of demonstration, i.e., in the procedure followed by the *Ethics*, occurs in the latter pages of Part II, comes first in the treatise the task of which is to give an account of the nature, instruments, and order of philosophical inquiry. This is as it should be. *In the order of Nature* God is prior to modes; therefore things, and the human mind with its ideas of things, come fairly late in the course of the exposition that reflects this order. *In the order of inquiry* we begin with the ideas we have of ourselves and of things, and, following the interconnections among these ideas, we proceed to the discovery of *the order of nature*, and of that which is first in this order, namely, God.

Spinoza's first steps in the order of inquiry are far removed from the rationalistic method that is usually attributed to him. His procedure is surprisingly experientialist, or empirical. He begins with the data of experience and out of these proceeds to build systematic knowledge. After enumerating the different modes of perception and posing the question as to which of *these modes is the best*, he tells us that the means necessary for making this choice are the following:

"I. To have an exact knowledge of our nature which we desire to perfect, and *to know as much of the nature of things as is necessary*.
II. To gather from these the differences, agreements and oppositions of things.
III. To learn thus exactly how far they can or cannot be modified.
IV. To compare this result with the nature and power of man."[47]

This hardly sounds like deducing a world of things out of a *priori* innate ideas, or like spinning existence out of logic. To examine the

---

[44] DPP, Ludwig Meyer's Preface, 3.
[45] E I, Df. 1.
[46] TdIE, Paras. 18–24.
[47] TdIE, Para. 25.

different modes of perception, we go to experience, and "recapitulate all the modes of perception which I have hitherto employed for affirming or denying anything with certainty".[48] To discover the best of the different modes of perception, we again go to experience and compare what we have been able to learn of the nature and power of man with what we can learn concerning things as a result of gathering their "differences, agreements, and oppositions".[49] Things here are not deduced from something which is antecedent to things and which is accepted as the first datum. A world of things, and man as one among such things, are taken as givens, as data, and the enterprise of philosophical inquiry is the enterprise of pursuing the implications of the fact of our experience that there are things, and that there are observable differences and agreements among them.

His crucial reliance on the brute facts of experience in connection with some of the most important elements in Spinoza's doctrine is consistently overlooked by interpreters with a doctrinaire Rationalist bias about Spinoza's thought.[50] For example, they fail to take note of the fact that the existence of "finite modes," i.e., of the finite, contingent objects of everyday experience, is never *deduced* in the *Ethics*. Indeed, Spinoza says explicitly in his letter to Simon De Vries that "experience" is needed for our knowledge of the finite Modes since, unlike the attributes of God, they "cannot be deduced from the definition of a thing."[51] With the exception of God, whose essence involves existence and who therefore necessarily exists, the existence of no individual object can be positively deduced from the idea of the object—no matter how comprehensible the idea—because, as Leon Roth pointed out more than half a century ago, of "our ignorance of the complete detail of the structure of things. The *naturae ordo*," Roth continues, in a footnote, "is therefore a problem to be worked out and the way is left open to the purest empiricism."[52] "For knowledge of particular things," says Spinoza, "experiments will need to

---

[48] TdIE, Para. 18.

[49] TdIE, Para. 25 (cf. No. II of the four "means" listed above).

[50] Cf. E. M. Curley: "The view that Spinoza was a rationalist . . . is not only mildly inaccurate, it is wildly inaccurate. Experience has a much greater role to play in Spinoza's theory of knowledge than this view allows for ("Experience in Spinoza's Theory of Knowledge," in *Spinoza: A Collection of Critical Essays*, ed. M. Grene [New York: Anchor Books, 1973], 26). Cf. also de Deugd: "Spinoza now and then speaks unhesitatingly of experience as valuable knowledge, and as dependable knowledge at that" (Op. cit., 150).

[51] Wolf (a), Ep. 10, 109.

[52] Leon Roth, *Spinoza, Descartes and Maimonides* (New York: Russell and Russell, 1963), 57 and note 3.

be made,"[53] and H. G. Hubbeling comments here: "Spinoza does not deny the great value of experience for the finding of facts . . ."[54]

Moreover, it is significant that Spinoza found it necessary to include, among his proofs for the existence of God, one a *posteriori* proof, that takes as its first datum an observable experiential fact, namely, the existence of each of us as a finite human being.[55] *Premiss:* We, finite, contingent human beings, exist. Conclusion: (omitting the steps in the proof) *Therefore,* there is *something that necessarily exists;* that necessary existent is God. The procedure here is "Analytic," in that it begins with sense perception and experience of the existence of things generally, and goes on to discover the truth that *something* must necessarily exist. This is the way knowledge is often built up. In the Scholium Spinoza displays a full understanding of this when he explains that he "wished to prove the existence of God *a posteriori,* in order that the demonstration be more clearly understood."[56]

Thus, we go to experience for our data. But, we must not rest there. Analysis of the data of experience and their implications must in turn lead to the order, the system of reality, that will comprehend the very data we begin with, assign them to their proper place in the system, and thus render them fully intelligible; for the truest knowledge is knowledge within the structure of such a system. If the system we arrive at, as a result of analyzing our data, is to be a system of the Real, the reality of the data we start with must be guaranteed. The data must be known to be not illusory, not mere products of the human imagination. Things must be shown to be part of the productivity of nature, part of the whole which nature is. "*Nature* must in the end be both *dator* and *datum.*"[57] Philosophical *inquiry* begins with the data of experience, analyzes them, and proceeds to the discovery of the system that will provide the epistemological and metaphysical intelligibility that these and all other data, or parts of the whole, fit into. *Demonstration,* or systematic exposition, or *deduction,* from the appropriate premisses, is the critical ordering of the system so that it may best exhibit this intelligibility.

Philosophical *inquiry* begins with the data of experience, and proceeds to discover axioms and postulates, i.e., the materials out of which a system may be deductively constructed. *A geometric system*

---

[53] TdIE, Para. 103.
[54] Hubbeling, Op. cit., 10.
[55] E I, P11 Dm. (3d proof) and S.
[56] E I, P 11, S.
[57] Hallett, Op. cit., 150.

starts with such definitions, axioms, and postulates, to which the first data in the *order of inquiry,* and other data, are in turn shown to be related as consequents to ground, or as conclusions to premises. *Philosophical inquiry* begins with experienced things, traces the relations of these things to the ultimately Real, and discovers their place in the scheme of the ultimately Real. On the other hand, *geometric systematization,* in Spinoza's sense, begins with the ultimately Real, and exhibits its structure, and the place of things in this structure.

This is the nexus between Spinoza's experientialist or empirical logic of inquiry and his Rationalism. Neither is complete without the other. A sound Naturalism, such as Spinoza's appears to be, embraces both as two complementary and equally indispensable approaches to the problem of securing knowledge and systematizing it. The geometrical logic of demonstration is *Synthetic,* and the logic of inquiry is *Analytic.* The *Ethics* follows the logic of Synthesis. Spinoza's *Tractatus de Intellectus Emendatione* follows the logic of Analysis. This treatise is, in Sir Frederick Pollock's words, "the analytical preface to Spinoza's latest work."[58] Method, the principal subject matter of the TdIE, is the unfolding of the order or logic of the search for knowledge that will lead us to the postulates of the system. Or, since for Spinoza true knowledge of anything is knowledge of its cause, method is the order that will direct us to the causes of things, and ultimately to the cause of all things. This cause of all things will, in turn, serve as the starting point for the systematic exposition of nature, *in accordance with nature's true order.*

But a search for knowledge implies a search somewhere, among some entities. A method must have a starting point. As Spinoza puts it: "If we wish to investigate the first thing of all, there must necessarily be some *basis* which must direct our thoughts toward it".[59] This sentence seems to contain Spinoza's own refutation of those who view the *Ethics* as an autonomous, *a priori,* intuitively revealed system, which starts with an intuitive apprehension of God, and proceeds to deduce the rest of the universe from the idea of God. Philosophical inquiry must begin somewhere, and its most natural beginning is our immediate, experienced world of extended and thinking beings. We have ideas, of our bodies, of other bodies, of our own ideas, and the *basis* from which our exposition of a method of inquiry begins is discovered through an examination of our ideas, and through research among them.

---

[58] Frederick Pollock, *Spinoza: His Life and Philosophy,* 2d. ed. (New York: American Scholar, 1966), 115.

[59] TdIE, Para. 105.

One of the things that Spinoza tells us repeatedly about method is that method is *"cognitio reflexive"*, or *"idea ideae"*[60]; "it is the way in which truth itself, or the objective essences, or ideas of things (which are all the same) must be sought in their proper order".[61] Method starts with thinking about thinking, thinking about the fact of thought. Superficially, this methodological starting point might seem not to be far removed from the putative epistemology of pure rationalism. However, Spinoza's methodology is wedded to metaphysical convictions which, as we shall see below, transform this seeming rationalism into a concern with things and facts as we discover them in experience. It is our everyday ideas, the facts of accumulated knowledge, that are the first data from which our inquiry must proceed. For Spinoza, a mind without ideas cannot even be assumed: it would be a contradiction in terms. For the mind *is* itself the idea of the body, and the human body is such that its idea, which is "the first part that constitutes the actual being of the human mind,"[62] is capable of having ideas of itself, of the body, and of other bodies as they affect its own body.

But true ideas are ideas of things. When they are true, the ideas are the counterparts in thought of what exist also as extended, as bodies. This metaphysical confidence is basic to all of Spinoza's thinking. A true idea is, axiomatically, an idea which "must agree with its ideatum,"[63] and the proposition that "the order and connection of ideas is the same as the order and connections of things"[64] is central in the *Ethics*. Ideas are not abstract universals, in some detached, Platonic realm. Spinoza's rejection of such "ideas" is complete: his nominalism here is uncompromising. It is not such ideas that serve as the starting point for his method of inquiry. Each idea, for Spinoza, is a judgment concerning some part of the world of things: "An idea, in so far as it is an idea, involves affirmation or negation."[65] In this sense, a true idea is not a *disembodied* existence; on the contrary, it is *literally* "embodied," for it is the counterpart in the realm of thought, of what also exists in the realm of extension, and it is an affirmation of that existence. In the case of man, his mind is the idea of his body. By virtue of its being that idea, the mind is also an affirmation of the

---

[60] TdIE, Para. 38.
[61] TdIE, Para. 36.
[62] E II, P11.
[63] E I, A6.
[64] E II, P7.
[65] E II, P49 S.

existence of its own body.⁶⁶ "From the fact that I know the essence of the mind, I know it to be united to a body."⁶⁷ The very meaning of mind is that it is the objective essence of a body.

This relation between man's body and his mind is also the relation between all other things and their ideas. Spinoza states this quite clearly. Although "like objects, ideas differ from one another," nevertheless, "whatever we say concerning the idea of the human body must necessarily be said concerning the idea of any other thing."⁶⁸ All extended things have the ideas of them in the attribute of thought. Individual material objects are "all, though in various degrees, *animate*,"⁶⁹ i.e., there are in God, under the attribute of thought, *ideas* of all extended things. The ideas of such extended things are affirmations of the existence of the things. Ideas, in this sense, must be distinguished from the mere "*images* of things which we imagine."⁷⁰

Research among ideas, which is the starting point of Spinoza's method of inquiry, involves and implicates the world of extended things. Research among *true* ideas will be in every sense equivalent to research among extended things. A methodology which starts on such terms is, to repeat, far from a procedure that can be accused of eliciting things out of abstract ideas, or existence out of logic. It is firmly anchored in a concern with things, and the fact that the existence of man's mind entails the existence of his body is the most striking illustration of the foundations of such a methodology.

V

This unity of mind and body is the fundamental beginning in an account of the nature, logic, and instruments of philosophical inquiry. But the human mind's first knowledge of its body and of its relation to its own body is confused and inadequate. All we know at first, *as a matter of experience,* is that we think ("*Homo cogitat*," *Ethics* II, Axiom 2),⁷¹ that "we are aware (*sentimus*) that a certain body is affected in many ways,"⁷² and that somehow this fact of thinking and this body

---

⁶⁶ E II, P11–P13, espec. E II, P13 ("The object of the idea constituting the human mind is the body . . .")

⁶⁷ TdIE, Para. 22

⁶⁸ EII, P13 S.

⁶⁹ Ibid.

⁷⁰ E II, P49 S.

⁷¹ E II, A2.

⁷² E II, A4. "We are aware" as translation of "*sentimus*" seems to me preferable to both Boyle's "we feel" and White's and Elwes' "we perceive".

are united, "but what is this feeling and union we cannot absolutely understand."[73] However, our mind cannot remain restricted to this confused and tentative knowledge:

" . . . this Idea (which the mind has of its body) can by no means find rest in the knowledge of the body without passing to the knowledge of that without which the body and Idea could neither be nor be understood . . . "[74]

Our body is obviously not an isolated fact. Our experience, our ideas of the modifications of our body, tell us that we are in continuous intercourse with other bodies. If our body had no relations or commerce with other things (*commercium habere cum allis rebus*), then our mind, which is the *essentia objectiva* of the body, would "also have no relation or dealings with other ideas, that is, we could conclude nothing concerning it."[75] But our body does have relations or commerce with other things. Therefore, the *objective essence* of our body (i.e., our mind), since it must agree in all respects with its *formal essence*"[76] (i.e., its body), and, on the other hand, the ideas it has of the things with which our body is in commerce, "will have the same relations" or commerce with each other as our body has with other bodies.[77] Such relations can be traced and studied, and by means of such study "the instruments of our investigation are increased."[78]

The commerce that our body has with other bodies is of a variety of descriptions. We observe in our experience that our body produces other bodies, and is produced by them.[79] Furthermore, our experience tells us that

"the human body needs for its preservation many other bodies from which it is, so to speak, continuously regenerated,"[80] since " . . . the human body is composed of many parts of different nature which need continuous and varied nourishment so that the whole body may be equally fit to discharge all the duties which can flow from its nature . . . "[81]

---

[73] TdIE, Para. 21.
[74] Wolf (b) II, ch. 22, 134.
[75] TdIE, Para. 41.
[76] Ibid.
[77] Ibid.
[78] Ibid.
[79] TdIE, Para. 41, Note.
[80] E II, Postulate IV following the Lemmas.
[81] E IV, Appendix, 27.

The mind, in experiencing and perceiving the many modifications that take place in its body as a result of its contact with other bodies, must necessarily be able to "perceive the nature of many bodies at the same time as the nature of its own body,"[82] for,

> "the idea of every mode in which the human body is affected by external bodies must involve the nature of the human body and at the same time the nature of the external body."[83]

It is in this manner that the mind, as a result of its determination to study the agreements and differences among things, is able to discover through experience that its body has many things in common with all the other things with which it has commerce. If it had nothing in common with these external bodies it could in no way have commerce with them. The mind then discovers what those things are which its body *has in common with all other bodies,* namely, the observed facts that they are capable of motion and rest, that they may move more quickly or more slowly, and most of the other information that Spinoza gives us in the Lemmas that follow Proposition 13 in Part II of the *Ethics,* as coming from experience.

This is the origin of the *notiones communes* which are "the foundations (*fundamenta*) of our reasoning,"[84] They arise from experience, from the mind's originally confused knowledge of its body, and from the ideas, again at first confused and inadequate, which the mind has of other bodies as they affect ours. They are traceable back to our perceptions of "individual things, represented by the senses to us in a mutilated and confused manner, and without order."[85] Their origin is therefore in our knowledge of *the first kind,* "knowledge from vague experience (*cognitio ab experientia vaga*)."[86] Nevertheless, though they arise from experience, these *common notions* "must be adequately, or clearly and distinctly, perceived by all."[87] The genesis and ground of their adequacy is in the circumstance that they are notions, or ideas, of invariant, common properties of all bodies, and that they are discovered by the mind in its empirical search for the "agreements among things," a search that by its very nature transcends the limited and therefore mutilated individuality of perceived individual

---

[82] E II, P16 C2.
[83] E II, P16.
[84] E II, P40 S1.
[85] E II, P40 S2; cf. Wolfson, Op. cit., II. 125–27.
[86] E II, P40 S2.
[87] E II, P38 C.

things. "Things which we clearly and distinctly understand are either *common properties* of things or what we deduce from them."[88] It is by experience that we come to know them to be *common,* indeed, by a kind of *Induction.*

The same position is outlined in Letter 37, where it is made clear by Spinoza once and for all that he was not committed to what has been interpreted stereotypically as a purely Rationalist procedure, and that his comprehensive method of philosophical inquiry was such that the Baconian inductive procedure found a necessary place in it. Here Spinoza states that

> " . . . as far as the method requires, there is no need to know the nature of the mind through its first cause; it is sufficient to put together a short history of the mind, or of perception, in the manner taught by Verulam."[89]

At this point it begins to be clear that *Ratio,* Spinoza's *second* kind of knowledge, cannot function without the materials given by *Imaginatio* or *Experientia Vaga,* i.e., the *first* kind of knowledge in his classification; and, as will be briefly maintained below, that *Scientia Intuitiva,* the highest kind, must have for its functioning the materials given by *Ratio* if it is to give us significant knowledge.

That Reason cannot operate without the materials given by the senses is quite evident. The common notions have their origin in the confused perceptions of the imagination, and all knowledge of the kind given by common notions is the result of the mind's search for the differences and agreements among those things which it first perceives in a confused manner through the senses. But the Understanding, Spinoza tells us repeatedly, forms clear and distinct conceptions which "depend solely on our nature . . . on our absolute power; . . . . nor do they acknowledge any cause external to us . . . "[90] This has led commentators to assume that Spinoza believed that the Understanding (or *Scientia Intuitiva*) forms its true ideas in *vacuo,* in an *a priori* manner, in total independence of experience.

---

[88] E V, P12 Dm.

[89] Wolf (a), Ep. 37, 228. We find the same methodological procedure described by Spinoza in the *Tractatus Theologico-Politicus:* "As in the examination of natural phenomena we try first to investigate what is most universal and common to all nature—such, for instance, as motion and rest, and their laws and rules, which nature always observes, and through which she continually works . . ." (Elwes I, 104). I am grateful to Richard Kennington for directing my attention to this passage.

[90] Wolf (a), Ep. 37, 227.

Spinoza meant nothing of the sort. Rather, he insisted that while *imagination*, or vague experience, the perceptions of which came from the senses, was *passive*, and had little control over what impinged on its attention, clear and distinct ideas were the result of a conscious, deliberate, critical effort of the mind. It is in this sense that the perceptions of the Understanding "depend solely on our nature," "on the power of the mind,"[91] and not on "fortuitous and unconnected sensations" which arise "from external causes."[92] But this critical activity of the mind can result in the clear and certain perceptions of the Understanding only because it is a critical activity among ideas which the mind had previously formed in the course of its empirical inquiries, and which arose first from *imaginatio*, and only subsequently from *ratio*.

Of course, Spinoza continually endeavors to keep clear and sharp the distinction between *Imaginatio* and *Intellectus* (or *scientia intuitiva*, i.e., the third kind of knowledge). He says, for example, that "the effort or desire to know things by the third kind of knowledge cannot arise from the first kind . . . "[93] Nevertheless, this very same Proposition, in Spinoza's own words, makes it abundantly clear that there is a link between *Ratio*, the second kind of knowledge that depends on experience, and on the other hand *scientia intuitiva:* "The effort or desire to know things by the third kind of knowledge . . . may arise from the second kind of knowledge."[94] Indeed, the connection between Reason and Intuition is affirmed in Spinoza's thought in the early *Short Treatise*. Here of course the terminology is not the same as that of the *Ethics*, but the meaning is unmistakable. "True belief," says Spinoza, and by *true belief* he means the same as is meant by *Reason* in the *Ethics*,[95] "is good only because it is the way to "true knowledge" [meaning knowledge of the highest kind—*Intuition*], and awakens us to things which are truly lovable."[96]

In some of the very recent Spinoza literature there is a reversal of the traditional, stereotypical assessment of the respective roles and importance of experience and intuition, the first kind of knowledge and the third kind of knowledge, in Spinoza's epistemology. Note is

---

[91] TdIE, Para. 84.
[92] Ibid.
[93] E V, P28.
[94] Ibid.
[95] In fact, Spinoza equates the two terms "true belief" and "reason" even in the early *Short Treatise* (Ch. 14 of Part II): "True belief or reason . . . leads us to the knowledge of good and evil . . . " (Wolf [*b*], 99).
[96] Wolf (b), II, ch. 4, 76.

taken of Spinoza's puzzling candor when he said in the TdIE that "The things which I have been able to know by this kind of knowledge [i.e., *Scientia Intuitiva*] so far have been very few."[97] In fact, *what* it is precisely Spinoza claimed we knew through the third kind of knowledge, is still an unresolved and controversial question. On the other hand we are also reminded that two paragraphs earlier in the TdIE Spinoza stated that by experience, or the first kind of knowledge, "I know nearly all things that are useful in life."[98]

De Deugd is an example of this recent reexamination of Spinoza's theory of knowledge, and he has gone further than others. A major conclusion of his is that " . . . untraditional though it may be (and to many even paradoxical) it seems that in Spinoza's system imagination [i.e., the first kind of knowledge] is of more actual value than intuitive science."[99] Among his reasons for this conclusion are: a) his view that the second kind of knowledge, i.e., *Ratio*, would be impossible without the first kind, i.e., experience; "without sense data, it seems there can be no knowledge of the second kind"[100]; b) his view that for Spinoza the distinctions between the three kinds of knowledge "are of a relative rather than absolute character"[101]; and c) the abundance of evidence he finds in Spinoza's texts that "Spinoza does not hold empirical reality in low esteem and that in his system the first kind of knowledge is, in the ultimate sense at least, not considered inferior."[102] Similarly, G. H. Parkinson, in a recent essay, quotes numerous passages in which Spinoza appeals to experience in support of various doctrines or conclusions or postulates.[103] For example, when postulates which are not self-evident can be seen to agree with experience, Spinoza considers this fact as confirmation of their truth; he deems the testimony of experience acceptable when it is not contradicted by deductive reason; and he notes pointedly that men can understand and be more easily persuaded by a doctrine when it is proven by experience even when it has previously been proven deductively. These are among Parkinson's examples of Spinoza's reliance on and appeals to experience in the *Ethics*. There are others in the TdIE as well.

---

[97] TdIE, Para. 22. Cf. E. M. Curley's interesting comment, Op. cit., 54–55.
[98] TdIE, Para. 20.
[99] de Deugd, Op. cit., 185, repeated on 188 and 262.
[100] de Deugd, 153.
[101] de Deugd, 188.
[102] de Deugd, 253.
[103] G. H. R. Parkinson, "Language and Knowledge in Spinoza" in *Spinoza: A Collection of Critical Essays*, Op. cit., 96–97.

These recent reassessments appear to throw additional light on the logic of philosophical inquiry that I have tried to distill here out of what is explicitly present and is implicit in Spinoza's *oeuvre*. The received rigid Rationalist paradigm in the traditional interpretations of Spinoza must be discarded, or, at the very least, radically modified. The paradigm of philosophical inquiry that emerges out of our analysis in the preceeding pages may be crudely restated as follows.

Inquiry begins from knowledge based on *Experience* (inadequate knowledge of the first kind) which is critically examined and refined. It proceeds to the formation of the second kind of knowledge, scientific knowledge, through the exercise of Reason, for which the Common Notions derived from sense observation are fundamental materials. From the disclosures of Reason, *Scientia Intuitiva*, the third and highest kind of knowledge may arise, knowledge that will be completely adequate, and will glimpse something of the total, systematic character and structure of reality, or *Natura*, and understand the interrelationships of things in their true order of nature *(ordo naturae)*. While some of the Axioms, Definitions, and Postulates in the *Ethics* are in the nature of generalizations from empirical observation (e.g., Axioms II and IV of Part II, and Axioms 1 and 2 and Lemmas I and II following Proposition 13 in Part II), most of them are the end product of the progression from Experience to Reason, and some (especially those that stand at the beginning of Part I) are products of the progression from Reason to *Scientia Intuitiva*, and are grasped intuitively as a result of this progression. These, for Spinoza, are known to be true, and known with certainty, not because they are self-evident, nor as products of the apodeictic demonstrations in the *Ethics*, but as products of the mind's search for the implications of the human experiences and their disclosures, with which the mind begins its systematic search for knowledge.

The Kennedy Institute of Ethics, Georgetown University

15 *DE NATURA*

Stewart Umphrey

I.

Spinoza (1632–1677) has not been a major influence in the history of ideas. His moral philosophy, unlike Kant's, falls outside the mainstream of modern thought; his natural philosophy, unlike Newton's, now appears so aberrant as to be in no way worthy of the name "science." Yet Spinoza remains an object of wonder, for at least three reasons. By nearly all reports his was an exemplary life; among philosophers only Socrates, perhaps, has been so venerated. The admirability of his *ratio vivendi* is connected, we imagine, with his thoughts about nature and man's place in it. These thoughts are true according to Spinoza himself (*Ep* 76). In the opinion of many, however, his doctrine is false, even abhorrent, His virtue seems therefore to be the effect of his ignorance, if not identical with it. This is a second reason for our wonder. A third is the uncommon manner in which he presented his teaching in one of his two major books, the *Ethics*. Therein, according to its subtitle, ethical things are demonstrated *ordine geometrico*. In the First Part, for example, the existence, immanence, and omnipotence of God or nature are seemingly deduced. My curiosity about this mode of this account of nature is the starting point of the inquiry recounted herein.

Demonstrations are by definition sound. Hence their conclusions are true. If one knows by demonstration that a proposition is true, then one also knows that the premisses of that demonstration are true. An absolutely primary premiss is indemonstrable. Hence it cannot be known by demonstration. It is knowable *per se*, if at all; it is, let us say, self-evidently true. Hence demonstrations cannot be the sole eyes of the mind, if in truth they are like such an organ in any illuminating respect. The primary instruments of reason must be ungrounded or self-grounding definitions, or axioms, found to be true by intuition.

That an indemonstrable premiss is self-evidently true need not be evident to us. The basic statements of geometry may be non-controversial, but those of metaphysics certainly are not.[1] It is helpful, indeed necessary, to understand such statements in the light of the consequences: their meaning is in a sense their use. But this way of discovery proves insufficient when one tries to understand Spinoza's Ethics I, *de Deo*. Even Leibniz found its starting point to be obscure.[2] The reader needs, in addition to the deduction from first principles there declared, an introduction to those principles. But if Spinoza is right, such a preface would of necessity be not merely extrinsic to the system but moreover informal, unscientific, inadequate (cf. EII, P40 S2 with P10 S2). Here, at least, the criteria of cogency and informativeness are incompatible in their application. The logographic necessity of Spinoza's teaching *de Deo* seems to be logical necessity. This durational likeness of God's eternal activity is therefore opaque to those who might otherwise learn from it. Why, then, did Spinoza write the *Ethics* and endeavor to have it published? But this question seems no more relevant than the question why a mathematician tries to disseminate his findings, or why he happened to become a mathematician. An apodictic account appears autonomous. It invites comprehension without reference to the particular conditions of its coming to be.

On closer inspection, however, *"de Deo"* is found to be less than pure. Unlike Euclid and most other mathematicians, Spinoza admitted into his written account a conspicuous quantity of patter. Most of it is relegated to the thirteen scholia and appendix; but these together constitute well over half the account. Because such interludes predominate, and because they seem relatively easy to understand, it follows that many readers are induced to attend rather to the informal than to the apodictic portions, and to believe that the former are better than the latter. Spinoza should have predicted this, for his psychology in large part explains it. He failed, it seems, to combine first philosophy with rhetoric.

But *"de Deo"* seems impure even apart from this distracting admixture. Some examples: (1) If the definition of substance is to be a real definition, it is misleading to write *"Per substantiam intelligo . . . ."* Perhaps Spinoza wanted the reader to take *"intelligo"* strictly, as referring to understanding. But then why did he write *"dicitur"* in

---

[1] Cf. Descartes, *Meditationes, Sec. Resp., Oeuvres*, ed. Adam-Tannery, 12 vols. (Paris: 1897–1913), VII, 156 ff.; also TTP, ch. 7 (Gebhardt III, 111).

[2] Cf. Gebhardt I, 139 ff.

the second and penultimate definitions, of finitude and freedom respectively? (2) To demand definitions of all terms would betray lack of education. But Spinoza's account does not always satisfy the reasonable and pertinent condition that non-primitive terms be defined before they are used. In one case (P9 Dm) this lapse seems to have resulted in an egregiously bad argument. (3) Nowhere in *"de Deo"* does Spinoza establish that extension and thought are attributes. P14 C2 states that they are either attributes or affections thereof. In P15 S he claims to have concluded that extended substance is an attribute, and in P21 Dm he finally assumes that thought is another (see also P17 S). The former has not been concluded by a demonstration, however, and it cannot be since any attribute is conceived *per se*. (4) Spinoza might have proceeded in this way: It pertains to the nature of a substance to exist (P7); therefore God necessarily exists (by P7 with Df 6); therefore besides God no substance can be given or be conceived (P14, by the foregoing with Df 6 and P5). Spinoza's proof is much less elegant. Furthermore, he gives in passing, it seems, another proof of the proposition that only one substance can exist (P8 S2); and this proof is independent of Df 6. A reader is thereby induced to ask whether that definition is merely nominal, whether Spinoza could as well or better have written *"Per naturam intelligo ...."* (5) One need not read beyond *"de Deo"* in order to conclude that, for Spinoza, the starting point of knowledge is adequate cognition of God, or of any attribute of God. But *"de Deo"* itself is not apparently an argument from an adequate declaration of that starting point. Furthermore, it harbors a concession that attributes are not the only *per se nota* (e.g., P30 Dm, P31 Dm.), and even the assertion that nothing is more clearly perceived by us than intellection itself (P31 S). It thus causes the reader to doubt that the order of knowing need be the same as the order of being.

We conclude that, as an apodictic system, *"de Deo"* is patently ill formed; more precisely, it is not an apodictic system. The fact that the manner of exposition seems so to caricature its subject matter might be thought to warrant the further conclusion that Spinoza was a confused thinker as well as an ineffectual writer. This thought would lack certitude, however. We judge a blind man, but not a stone, to be deprived of sight. One may judge the first Part of the *Ethics* to be defective when one believes that it is supposed to be apodictic throughout. Spinoza did provide reason to believe that such was his intention. But he also provided reason to believe that such was not his sole or chief intention in writing the *Ethics*. The very fact that some of the alleged fallacies and muddles are so obvious warrants the suspicion that he was endeavoring to do something else. This suspicion is confirmed when, on a more thoughtful inspection, *"de Deo"* is found to be rather dialectical than demonstrative. The definitions and axioms were, for the most part, quite traditional. From that agreeable starting point readers were led by Spinoza out of all traditional theology; if they followed his digressive, mixed argument, they arrived finally at the border of "first physics," so to speak, that is, at an incipient understanding of nature as infinite power or absolute necessity, the sole cause, two of whose attributes are extension and thought. The argument is, on the one hand, a declaration of the double foundation of all possible knowledge for us. It is, on the other hand, a critique both of many commonly held opinions about our Maker and of the commonly held opinions about humans on which they are founded. If one agrees that God is absolutely infinite or most perfect—and who would not?—then it is irrational to maintain that God is also an immaterial substance apart from nature, or that he is good or is guided by an end while producing and sustaining the world, or that he is free to act otherwise than he does, or that he cares about us, rules over us as a king over his subjects, and is therefore a fitting subject of entreaty. Mosaic theology is anthropomorphic; more precisely, it depends on a false anthropology (E I, Appendix). Removal of ignorance about oneself is therefore an excellent propaedeutic to knowledge of nature. On the other hand, self-knowledge is impossible apart from first physics, since nothing is for us conceivable apart from extension or thought. *"De Deo"* is like Descartes' *Meditationes de prima philosophia* an introduction to first physics. The instruments by which this introduction is effected include, prominently, deductions from more or less lexical definitions.[3]

According to Spinoza's account, no account can be autonomous. The reasoning expressed by *"de Deo"* cannot be understood apart from its proximate cause. Its meaning now appears to depend, in particular, on what it was Spinoza was trying thereby to accomplish. Hope that subsequent Parts of the *Ethics* will make plain his intention is one reason for reading them. Another springs from the arresting thought that, if Spinozistic physics is true, no satisfactory moral science is possible. For if nature is both omnipotent and fully actual, then we must be impotent, fated to exist and act when and as we do. If it cannot be grasped by appeal to artefactual and political ana-

---

[3] That the definitions are for the most part traditional is a fact elaborately established by H. A. Wolfson, *The Philosophy of Spinoza* (New York: World Publ. Co., 1958), I, 21 ff., 58, 63, *et passim*. Notice that most terms proper to Spinoza's basic teaching are not even used at the outset; but *"substantia,"* for example, is rarely used beyond the First Part.

logues, if it is not illuminatingly like a city or a machine, for example, then nature will seem forever alien to properly human understanding; there will be no passage from what is first for us to what is first in itself. If nature is neither beautiful nor good, it will hardly be deemed lovable. Spinoza's teaching *de rerum natura* may be true, but the truth may not be good for us. If apprehension of the truth causes despair, it must appear odious. He to whom Spinoza's hypothesis indeed seems hideous will quite naturally try to reject or ignore it.

II.

All things are "in" nature. The nature of nature is power. Hence nothing whatsoever can be absolutely impotent: to be is to be efficacious. Every given singular thing is a more or less powerful particular expressing the essence of nature in a certain, determinate way.[4] The power of acting, the *conatus* or appetite whereby each existing thing endeavors to persevere in its own being, is the actual essence of that thing, without which it can neither be nor be conceived.[5] The efficacy of any particular thing cannot be infinite, for each is of necessity a part of nature. In no case, then, is a given finite thing, or its essence, the sole cause of all its modifications; not everything about it follows from the laws of its own appetite alone. To the extent that the nature of each is a partial and not adequate cause of its operations, to that extent the given thing is said to be passive rather than active.[6]

A given human being is an actually existing singular thing "in" extension and thought. Its essence is the corporeal and mental desire whereby it seeks to persevere in its own being. Its being involves its essence. Every given human being desires to persevere in its own desire, or virtue, to be as active in thought and deed as it can.[7] What assists or augments one's power of acting is good, *i.e.*, useful to oneself; what impedes or diminishes one's own efficacy is bad. The highest good is virtue, since by means of it above all is one able to persevere in one's being. Hence the true foundation of virtue, the end of virtue, and the means to virtue is virtue or power itself.[8]

---

[4] E I, P15, P34; P36; E I P24 C with E IV, P4 Dm., E II, P6 Dm.
[5] E III, P7 and Dm; E II, Df2; E III, P9 S.
[6] E IV, A1, E III, Df2; E III, P9.
[7] E III, P9 S, Affectus, Df1, Aff. GnDf, E IV, P19 Dm., P59 Dm.; E IV Df. 8, P52 Dm., P67 Dm.
[8] E IV, Dff. 1–2 and E III, P7, E IV, P18 S, P20 Dm.–P26 Dm., P35 S2, P52 Dm., ApCp32, E V, Praef., P9 Dm., P20S, P25, P41 Dm.; E IV, P28, ApCp4, E V, P28 Dm.; E IV, Df. 7, P18S, E V, P42.

A human mind is a relatively powerful will to power.[9] It is virtuous to the extent that it consists of adequate rather than inadequate ideas, to the extent that its emotions are active rather than passive. Adequate ideas are true cognitions, or understandings; they constitute one's reason or intellect. Mental virtue is knowledge. Active emotions are those whereby, from the dictates of reason alone, one endeavors to persevere in one's own being; they are referred to the mind insofar as it understands. Mental virtue is strength (*fortitudo*).[10]

It is not inappropriate to divide strength of mind into *animositas* and *generositas*. The former is the active desire whereby one endeavors to persevere in one's own being, and whose actions aim at the good of the agent alone. The latter virtue is the active desire whereby one endeavors to assist other human beings, and to join them to oneself in friendship; its actions aim at the good of others.[11] Human beings are those singular things whose natures agree with the generous one's *ingenium*.[12] But experience teaches us that few human beings will become autonomous reasoners; that is to say, few will ever enter into society with philosophers or scientists as such. Even under optimal political conditions the many would be led rather by hopes and fears than by reason. The generous man, as much as he can, helps them to be polite. For example, he hesitates to diminish their humility, modesty, allegedly womanish pity, and other such passions. He manfully shrinks from doing and saying anything that would unleash their ambitions, lusts, hatreds, *etc*. Brutes, and all other things whose natures or desires are contrary to our own, we are to exploit as much as we can in ways conducive to our powers of thinking and doing. The free man understands this and proceeds accordingly.[13] Indeed, to the extent that he is virtuous, to that extent a human being lives by the laws of his own nature alone. *Homo sapiens,* properly speaking, strives actively to be as divine as he can. He is generous, therefore, since among those circumstances conducive to his own felicity are some conducive also to the felicity or relative well being of

---

[9] E III, P9 S, E II, P13 S.
[10] E II, P49 S, E IV, P26, etc.; E III, P29 S, E IV, P73 S.
[11] E III, P59 S; cf. E II, P49 S, E III, P34 Dm.
[12] E III, P31 S, E IV, P29–P35, ApCp7, with E IV, P18 S, E II, P40 S1.
[13] E III, Aff. Df. 48 Expl., E IV, P 35 S, P37 S1-S2, P47 S, ApCpp4, 14, 25, 32, E V, P4 S, P41 S. Cf. Descartes, *Discours de la méthode* VI (Adam-Tannery VI) 62.

some others. He cannot be solely or primarily altruistic, however, nor does he try to be, for reason postulates nothing contrary to nature.[14]

If one considers the content of the *Ethics* together with its form, one concludes that the argument presented in this work is largely an effect of its author's generosity so defined, and not so disinterested as it first appears to be. The highest good for every prospective reader is (not God but) knowledge of God, which is to say, knowledge of nature, of extension and thought. Every one of us has such knowledge. But some have much more of it than others. And many are guided much of the time by inadequate notions both of the first cause and of themselves.[15] The passions consequent on such idiosyncratic or intersubjective conceptions impede their seeking what is truly good. Under the guidance of those passions they may, for example, try to constrain rather than assist the virtue of the philosopher, than whom no singular thing is a higher good, so far as "we" know.[16] Clearly the first Part of the *Ethics* was designed by Spinoza to remove those misidentifications of the first cause which prevailed in his time and place, even among philosophers: it is not transcendent; it is matter, but not at all passive; it is thought, but not at all purposive. The second and third Parts were to assist the reader in achieving rational cognition of the human mind on the basis of common notions awakened, as it were, by *"de Deo."* The fourth and fifth Parts were to assist the reader in his desire to form, on the basis of such knowledge, a rational exemplar of human nature, conformity with which he would endeavor to achieve so far as he could.[17]

But if the *Ethics* is an expression of generosity, or *pietas*,[18] then it must be the case not only that such was Spinoza's intention but also that the composition proceeded under the guidance of reason. It surely seems to be the work of a partisan of rationality; Spinoza has succeeded in being regarded as the exemplary Rationalist. But we found that *"de Deo"* is not strictly apodictic. The first impression it makes on the reader is therefore not quite adequate for understanding it. But if the *Ethics* were truly demonstrative throughout, would it

---

[14] E IV, P18 S with E IV, P27, P31 Dm., ApCp5; E II, P43 S, P49 S, E IV, P45 S, E V, P20 S.

[15] E II, P47 & S with P45 Dm.; E II, P13 S, E IV, P20, P35 C2, P37 Dm., P 56 Dm., P71 S, Apcp4, E V, Praef., P27 S, P24, P27 Dm.

[16] E IV, P35 Cl & S, P38, ApCp9.

[17] Cf. E V, P36 S; E IV, Praef.

[18] E IV, P18 S, P37 S1, Apcp25, E V, P4S.

not then be false to say that it is an expression of reason? For if someone already lives from the dictates of reason, and is therefore free, reading the *Ethics* will not be pedagogically useful to him. But if someone is under the influence of *imaginatio,* and so dreams with his eyes open, reading demonstrations alone would not be pedagogically good; for while they might compel him somewhat, they would hardly be persuasive; they would not effect a turning about of his soul from the private and conventional to the common and to himself as he is in reality. Such souls must be led by the hand, as it were, more than by the eyes; and the hand which rightly leads them needs must be felt rather than seen, inasmuch as they are benefitted by its guidance. Spinoza's *Ethics* may be construed as an exposition of the power or *libertas*[19] of a human being, whereby he naturally and rightly seeks what is to his own advantage. This freedom stands revealed only when and where traditional religion is deprived of its authority. Spinoza endeavored to remove this veil in *"de Deo,"* wherein he answered *more scholastico* the question *quid sit Deus.*[20] He was remarkably ingenuous, if not bold. To refute customary notions of the divine, however, is to weaken the foundation of piety or humility; and experience teaches us that when such obedience or servitude is removed its place is usually taken not by philosophy but by ambition or pride.[21] From the ingenuity of his reason Spinoza sought to preclude this likely consequence by writing *"de Deo"* in a way such that his candid answer to the primary question would in no way encourage those passions rightly condemned by decent men everywhere and always. If the learned reader of *"de Deo"* is educated to believe that determinism is true, it is likely that he will feel less and not more powerful; for it is likely that his conception of self as agent will still involve the idea of free will, of undetermined *conatus.* *"De Deo"* may be construed as an argument for the proposition that *homo liber* is an impossibility.

The endeavor expressed by the *Ethics* appears partially revealed by the foregoing account. Before one tries to complete that account, however, one should ask whether the external cause in question can be known. And, supposing that it can be known, would knowing it be good? Surely it cannot be the highest good according to Spinoza. In-

---

[19] E IV, P66 S, P68 Dm.; cf. E IV, P 70 Dm., P73 Dm., E V, P42 S.

[20] Cf. L. Strauss, *Spinoza's Critique of Religion,* tr. Sinclair (New York: Schocken Books, 1965), 194; and *The City and Man* (Chicago: Rand McNally, 1964), 241.

[21] E IV, ApCp22, E IV, P57 S, E III, Aff. Df. 29 Expl. and E V, P41 S. Cf. Hobbes, *Leviathan,* I, 11.

deed, our endeavoring to follow his or any other account is, by his account, proof of our servitude. Our curiosity has led us astray, it seems. One should rather be trying to amend one's intellect, to augment one's knowledge of extended and cogitative things. One should rather be contemplating one's own power of acting, and loving nature with that love whereby nature, insofar as it is explained through one's own mind, loves itself.[22] But is it the case that the highest good is science of nature and, simultaneously, *acquiescentia animi?* Surely it is, according to Spinoza, not supremely good to believe that it is supremely good according to Spinoza, nor supremely good to opine it simply. Through his *Ethics* Spinoza continues even now to rouse in some readers a desire to remove the veil of philosophic lore and to find out for themselves, through liberal inquiry, whether virtue does consist in knowledge of the nature of things, and whether first physics (as I have called it) is merely difficult and rare or impossible.

III.

Let it be granted that mathematics is knowledge. It cannot be knowledge of the beautiful or good as such; it cannot be about ends. Hence a mathematician, as such, is forever blind to the distinction between elegance and inelegance of proof. He never judges some arguments to be good, others to be unsound. He never holds an internally consistent system to be superior to one containing a contradiction. Questions respecting the propriety of his own discipline do not occur to him. While mathematics is thoroughly non-teleological, however, it appears that an adequate account of mathematics itself must be teleological.[23] For this reason, at least, it is apparently unable to give an account of itself. It cannot be comprehensive knowledge. And this must be no less true of physics insofar as it is mathematical. If physics makes no reference to final causes, however, then it is doubtful whether it can be comprehensive knowledge even of nature. For it appears that knowledge about mathematics must be teleological because it appears that knowledge about mathematicians themselves and all their practices must be teleological. But mathematicians and physicists are presumably natural things. Is physics, then, science either of the nature of some natural things only or of all natural things in some respect only?

---

[22] E V, P36 & Dm.; also E IV, P4 Dm., P18 S, P52 & Ś, ApCp 4.
[23] Cf. J. Benardete, *Infinity* (Oxford: Oxford U. P., 1964), 210–233.

Spinoza affirmed that physics is comprehensive and denied that it is teleological.[24] He rejected the Socratic turn: man is not somehow a kingdom within a kingdom. As a scientist he could not have recourse, with Descartes, to the non-scientific "teaching of nature," in whose abiding twilight the superiority of Galilean to Aristotelian physics became manifest.[25] Nor would he follow Kant in making man a denizen of two worlds, or Ryle in holding that a man is subject to two true descriptions, one of which mentions purposes. Explanation is not supplemented by the ghost of teleological misunderstanding. That the *Ethics* is full of normative discourse appears incongruous, therefore, as well as fitting. In this work Spinoza implies that, given his actual essence and awareness of his partiality, a human being must think in the teleological mode; he must be idealistic.[26] Let this necessity, laughable or not, be granted. It is not then obviously contradictory to say both that human beings must regard themselves as end-directed and that the physiology of human bodies and minds is not all teleological. According to Spinoza, a scientist can describe the difference between *hilaritas* and *titillatio*, for example, and declare that a human being constituted in a certain way prefers the former to the latter. As a scientist, however, he cannot state categorically that the former is to be preferred. He can explain the fact that he himself desires to form a certain exemplar of human nature and to become it so far as he can; but he cannot say that his project, the *scopus* to which he looks, is superior to those formed by weaker, less rational minds. For Spinoza, apparently, it was both necessary and impossible to make a virtue of necessity. It was necessary for his *conatus* considered in its entirety, and impossible for his intellect considered in itself alone. The author of the *Ethics* admitted in this very artefact that its ethical teaching is not entirely scientific owing to the cooperation of "our" creative will, which uses knowledge of itself for the sake of itself. Presumably he was aware of the fact that his stated reason for retaining normative terms is teleological, not explanatory. Clearly he believed that such terms can be translated into, or otherwise reduced to, scientific terms: "end" means "appetite"; "virtue" means "power"; *etc.*[27]

---

[24] E I, Appendix. For us, of course, physics must be of nature expressed as extension and thought, and not otherwise.

[25] Cf. R. Kennington, "The 'Teaching of Nature' in Descartes' Soul Doctrine," *Rev. Metaph.* 26 (1972), 86–117.

[26] E IV, P68 & S; cf. E III, P9 S, E IV, P18 S. This would explain the need for medicine and logic (E V, Praef.) and for ethics (E II, Praef.).

[27] E IV, Praef. and Dff.; cf. E V, P42 S, and E. Harris, *Salvation from Despair*, (The Hague: M. Nijhoff, 1973), 8–9, 15.

The perplexity to which the foregoing account gives rise should not be allowed to eclipse our first question: Is it contradictory to affirm that physics is comprehensive and deny that it is teleological? Spinoza would deny that it is contradictory. But would that statement be true? Its truth value is no more obvious than the truth value of the statement that ethical naturalism is necessarily fallacious.

Let it be granted, for the sake of the argument, that comprehensive knowledge of the nature of things is possible without reference to final causes. It does not follow that physics refers to efficient causes alone. The mathematical model to which Spinoza appeals in his account of the nature of things is at odds with his thesis that this sort of cause alone exists. For mathematics is not knowledge of agents or powers any more than it is of ends and means. In other words, it is not of those sorts of causes whose exemplary cases are supplied by the human things humanly conceived. If physics is mathematical, or like mathematics in this respect, then it must be of formal or material causes alone, if indeed it can properly be said to be aitiological at all.[28]

According to Spinoza, however, nature as cause of an actually existing finite mode is not absolutely identical with nature as cause of an infinite, eternal mode; and the model to which he appeals in his account of the former sort of cause is less the eternal nature of a triangle than the dynamic nature of an enduring individual.[29] Powers of acting, or forces, are exemplary cases of the sort of cause in question. But their operations are in accordance with inviolable laws, according to Spinoza; and such laws, while supposedly causal, are evidently not identical to those forces themselves. Spinoza accepted with reservations the replacement of substantial forms as conceived by Artistotle with nomic universals as conceived by Galileo. But he was no more successful than Aristotle in showing that the immanent formality (law-likeness) of things is identical to their immanent efficacy. The nature of nature is or involves necessity. But *necessitas* is said in more than one way in Spinoza's account: dynamic necessity and nomic necessity cannot be one simply.[30] It does not follow that the power of nature and the regularities of nature are really distinct: "equivocal" is equivocal. But it does follow that the cause of all things is somehow

---

[28] Cf. Artistotle, *Physics* 194b26–31, 195a18–19, 198a16–20, b7–8."
[29] E I, P28, E II, P9 and E III, P7.
[30] Consider the argument from E I, P15 S through P17; also E I, P34, E III, Praef., P25, E IV, P39 Dm. & S. Things are said by Spinoza to occur *secundum* laws as well as to ocucr or be or follow *ex* laws. He seems to use *"ex"* equivocally, to indicate manner as well as source.

complex, and moreover that it is false to say of the sole cause that it is solely efficient.

That Spinoza cannot maintain the simplicity of natural necessity may be shown in another way. A Euclidean geometer often speaks of the objects about which he reasons as if they were active. His doing so may be a necessity. Surely it is laughable, since mathematical objects are in truth immobile. For this reason, at least, the mathematician is necessarily beyond his own purview. The mind or soul must be the object of a different science, if indeed it can be known at all. More generally, while the order and connection of powerful particulars may be held accountable in mathematical terms alone, those particulars *qua* powerful cannot. One may believe that Spinoza's turn from essential to causal definition[31] provides a way of avoiding the otherwise ineluctable distinction between form and agency. But a rule of construction is no more self-actualizing than a formula of the construct itself. The assertion that nature as generator and nature as rule of generation are indiscernible would be reminiscent of the Academic attempt to unify mathematics and psychology (or cosmology) by asserting that soul is self-moving number. The former assertion may seem more plausible to us, but it is no more intelligible. Spinoza did identify agency with activity: the power of acting is the acting itself, paradigmatically so in the case of God. But this identification does not enable one to obliterate the distinction between power and regularity. The assertion moreover involves an utterly confusing metaphorical stretch reminiscent of the Artistotelian endeavor to establish the priority of being-at-work (*energeia*) to potentiality by asserting that the paradigmatic being, god, is simply a being-at-work.

The foregoing aitiological query is merely preparatory to our seeking to understand nature as cause. But let us now attend briefly to a relevant dialectical problem.

Suppose that the intellect perceives, as constituting the essence of substance, the attribute of extension (or matter) and the attribute of thought. To say that extension, or thought, constitutes the essence of substance is to imply that it, too, is *in se* and conceived *per se;* it too is infinite and indivisible; it too necessarily exists. Extension and thought are themselves substantial; substance itself is essentially extended and essentially cogitative, though not extended or cogitative simply. Each attribute is definitive of substance, though not definitionally identical

---

[31] Cf. TdIE, Gebhardt II, 34 ff., and E. Cassirer, *Das Erkenntnisproblem* (Berlin: B. Cassirer, 1922–1923), II, 49 ff., 86 ff., 127 ff.

to it. Hence the constituting relation which obtains between an attribute and substance is far more intimate than that which seems to obtain between any spatiotemporal position of a body relative to ours and that body itself. It is more intimate even than the relation which necessarily obtains between either of two species (determinants) and the genus (deteminable) whereof they are species. For while either species "involves" the genus and so can neither be nor be conceived without it, the genus does not involve this or that species but at most some species. Attribute and substance, on the other hand, are essentially interrelated; neither can be or be conceived without the other.[32] Their relation, I shall say, is one of equivalence.

Spinoza also maintained that extension and thought are expressions of substance really distinct from one another. To say that they are really distinct is to imply that each can be and be conceived without the other. Extension is not essentially cogitative, thought is not essentially extended (or material). Hence the relation which obtains between any two such expressions of substance cannot be one of equivalence. It is rather like the much less intimate relation which may seem to obtain between two spatiotemporal positions of a body relative to us. Just as one can be acquainted with Venus as the Morning Star without being acquainted with it as the Evening Star, so too can one cognize substance as primary matter without cognizing it as primary thought.[33] Substance is *ens perfectissimum,* or so Spinoza wanted to allege, but it cannot be *ens simplicissimum.* Spinozistic Monism implies that not even one monad can exist.

But this doctrine of essential attributes is unintelligible The relation of equivalence, like the relation of likeness, is symmetrical. Unlike the relation of likeness, it is transitive as well. Hence, if x is equivalent to s, and y is equivalent to s, then x is equivalent to y. But if x is equivalent to y, then x and y cannot be really distinct. It is impossible, therefore, both that extension and thought constitute the essence of substance and that they are really distinct expressions of substance.

If one retains the proposition that extension and thought are really distinct expressions, then one must grant that each constitutes a really distinct essence, and hence that extended substance and cogitative substance are really distinct. But then one must give up considerable

---

[32] E I, Dff. 3–5, P5, P10, P15 S, P19–P20, E II, P7 S, P40 S 2 and E II, Df2 with A. Donagan, "Essence and the Distinction of Attributes in Spinoza's Metaphysics," in M. Grene (ed), *Spinoza* (New York: Anchor Books, 1973), 180f. Also Epp 2, 4, 9, 63–66.

[33] Especially E I, P10 S, E II, P7 S.

portions of Spinoza's account. What is more, one must give up the agreeable supposition that there can be two or more *per se* attributes or constituents of one thing. If, on the other hand, one retains the proposition that each attribute constitutes the essence of substance, then one is obliged to ascertain in what way extension and thought are distinct. Spinoza correctly maintained that the distinction cannot be one of reason alone. Nor can it be a *distinctio modalis*. But then, according to Spinoza, extension and thought cannot be distinct at all, since there is no sort of distinctness beyond these three.[34]

One may try to preserve one's thinking from this absurdity by invoking the Peripatetic teaching of that reputed dunce, Duns Scotus, according to whom there is also *distinctio formalis a parte rei*.[35] But if extension and thought are formally distinct attributes of substance, they are essentially related to each other. One must then deny that each is *in se* and conceivable *per se*. And while one can still accept Spinoza's rejection of all Causal Theories of perception and behavior, one cannot accept his thesis that psychology and physiology (narrowly construed) are independent sciences; it will be impossible, not merely difficult, to know the *idea* constituting a mind without having knowledge of its *ideatum*, and vice versa.[36] One need not then accept a materialistic or idealistic Identity Theory, however, for equivalence is indeed a relation, though not an exemplary case of relatedness; the relata are indeed distinct, though not really distinct. One can still accept, for example, the Aristotelian conception of the soul-body relation.

Spinoza would object. He does find, he might say, that mind is conceivable apart from body, body apart from mind. Hence, while each is determinate *in suo genere*, neither is in or under (*sub*) the genus in or under which the other is. These genera or attributes, too, must be conceivable apart from one another.[37] In the first place, however, it is not obviously the case that all mental things are conceivable apart from all corporeal or extended or moving and resting things. Secondly, if Spinoza is going to maintain that attributes are really distinct, I declare again my failure to see how he can then remain invulnerable to the charge of polytheism. Finally, Spinoza's qualified identification of attributes with genera appears mistaken. Extension and thought

---

[34] CM II.5.
[35] Ibid., and Duns Scotus, especially *Opus Oxoniense* II.16. *quaestio unica*, no. 17; IV. i, no. 38.
[36] E II, P5, P7 S, E III, P2, E V, Praef.
[37] E I, P32 Em., E II, P7 S, and DPP I, P8 Dm.

are not even like class conditions in a way that permits their functioning as such for the intellect. Furthermore, while these attributes are superordinate with respect to our natures, they cannot be greatest genera beyond nature itself but must be on a par with it. Spinoza's account of nature as infinite power and as infinite attributes appears to be one of several problematic attempts to combine a precise with a comprehensive account of being.[38]

A second objection is this: If the *per se* attributes of a substance are formally distinct, then one cannot have a clear and distinct idea either of each attribute or of the essence so constituted. It will be erroneous to speak of any one of these attributes, since 'each' is so related to the rest that none is one. It will be misleading even to speak of these attributes, since this locution suggests that they constitute a plurality of elements, whereas in truth one cannot conceive or select or abstract 'any one' of 'them' without conceiving all 'collectively.' It would be laughably oxymoronic to say, for example, that extension-and-thought, or a human being, is an indeterminate dyad or a two-in-one. Countability and accountability require separability in thought at least, and separability even in thought requires *distinctio realis*. Therefore, if the attributes of any thing are countable, they do not constitute its essence, hence they scarcely are what the thing really is; and if 'they' do constitute its essence, 'they' do not fall within the scope of the intellect, hence 'they' scarcely reveal what the thing really is. Hence the nature of nature is unknowable; so too is the nature of any natural thing. Physics is impossible. And this conclusion follows whether reason and discourse identify the putative constituents in question with extension and thought, matter and form, order and power, or whatever.

The conclusion that physics is impossible follows also from consideration of the relation between the essence and existence of nature, or of any attribute of nature. They are not one simply but one and the same. They must therefore be discernible but not really distinct. *Natura naturata* is "in" *natura naturans; natura naturans* is "immanent" in *natura naturata*.[39] Hence each is *in alio* as well as *in se;* and as

---

[38] E I, P16 Dm., P29 S with Df.2 and P5, E II, P7 S, E III, P2 Dm. & S; cf. TdIE (Gebhardt II, 37), Ep 9, IV I. 7, and H. H. Joachim, *A Study of the Ethics of Spinoza* (New York: Russell & Russell, 1964), 22, 26f. Plato, *Sophist* 246a2 and context.

[39] E I, P20; E I, P15, P18, P29 S. Spinoza granted that the infinite, eternal modal system is the same as *natura naturans,* but not that the former is therefore cause of the latter. Hence he could not consistently have believed that x causes y if and only if x is the sufficient and necessary condition of y, since y would then be the necessary and sufficient condition of x.

in alio each is *in se* as well, since the other is in each case the same as that other than which it is; and so on *ad infinitum*. But this explication is no less misleading than the statement that nature as self-causing and nature as self-caused constitute a duality-in-unity. Reason should, in the interest of truth, try to abstain from treating this ontological difference as if it were a real distinction, the essentially related "subsistents" as if they were externally related elements. The relation "between" essence "and" existence is no more like the spatial relation of containment, to which Spinoza's account so often alludes, than an animal that barks is like the eponymous heavenly constellation. One should admit that of such "relata," or "their" unity, no clear and distinct idea can be formed.

The conclusion that physics is impossible follows, thirdly, from consideration of singular natural things. Knowledge based on common notions alone cannot be knowledge of particulars as such. Hence *ratio* is eternally blind to the very essence of any finite thing. It is blind even to the fact that such things exist, since the negativity which defines finitude is necessarily beyond its purview.[40] But rational science is not the only kind of knowledge according to Spinoza. *Scientia intuitiva* necessarily involves knowledge of a finite individual. It is knowledge of its formal and not actual essence, however; it is of the thing as it is contained in "eternal" nature and not as it exists in relation to a certain time and place; it is of the thing as everlastingly necessary and not as "durational."[41] Hence the knower, as such, necessarily overlooks transitory things as such. He must be unaware of the actual essence of any given thing, that without which it can neither be nor be conceived. But cognition of the *conatus* is the proximate basis of physics as well as ethics and politics. What we call science of nature, then, is either epistemically pure and not of given natural things or else of given natural things and not epistemically pure. One may reply that the second-order actuality of a particular is but a figment of the imagination, just as the obdurate *communis ordo naturae* is but a fragmented and confused presentation of the eternal *ordo totius naturae*. Spinoza correctly shrank from making this reduction. There are, he said, two orders of actuality; the *conatus* is not the formal essence simply. He could therefore hardly maintain that all things are in *natura naturans* or *naturata*. On the other hand, he could hardly explain the

---

[40] E II, P37–P38, P40 S2, P44 C2 Dm., and E I, P21, P8 S1. Cf. E. Curley, *Spinoza's Metaphysics* (Cambridge: Harvard U. P., 1969), 62–74.

[41] E V, P36 S with E II, P40 S2, E V, P29 S; also E II, P45 S, E V, P23 S, P37 S, and Wolfson, II, 292.

existence or essence of second-order actuality itself. Trying to understand *duratio* solely within the horizon of *aeternitas,* the being of actually existing natural things solely by reference to the being of necessary truths, is an endeavor that must fail. *Imaginatio* is by definition inadequate cognition. It appears, however, that not everything sensed need be an *ens imaginationis* alone, and moreover, that *imaginatio* is indispensable for any conception whatsoever of given natural things as they actually are. One seems compelled by the phenomena, or by a desire to preserve the phenomena, to admit that being does not entail being understandable.

One may object that the admission of two orders of actuality precludes any successful attempt at understanding the unity of a given natural thing. Dualism rejected reappears in a new guise. But Spinoza's position seems to have been this: of the parts of a human mind, for example, one is its formal essence; the other has come into being, presently lives, and will presumably cease to be. The former part can be and be conceived without the latter, perhaps, but the latter certainly cannot be or be conceived without the former. The actual existence of a mind, and therefore its actual essence, are logically dependent on its formal essence; but its formal essence is separable from its actual existence, perhaps, though not from its first-order actuality.[42]

One may nevertheless argue that Spinoza failed to account for the unity of any given natural thing. A human body, for example, is a compound of bodies. It is called one owing to the perduring presence therein of a certain proportion of motion and rest. But what is the ontic status of this *ratio* or *forma*, or of the fact that it obtains? Of this Spinoza gives no adequate account. Again, he says of a mind both that it is a composite of ideas and that it has ideas; but the way in which an idea has its elements is not made plain. A given individual is essentially the *conatus* whereby it endeavors to persevere in its own being. But every analyzable part of that individual is another individual whose essence is the *conatus* whereby it endeavors to persevere in its own being.[43] What explains the fact that a multitude of *conatus* is one *conatus*? Is it the prevailing one, so far and so long as it prevails? Is a slave, then, part of the body and mind of his owner, to the extent that

---

[42] E V, P20-P40, E III, P11 S. Consider the claim in E IV, P57 S that laws of nature respect the common order of nature.

[3] E II, Df. after A2 before L4, A3 before L4, L4 & Dm., Postl., E IV, P39 Dm., ApCp 27., E II, P15 and, e.g., E III, P19 Dm.; E IV, P7 Dm. (cf. E I, P36).

he is subject to the appetite thereof, or to the prevailing appetite therein? Or must the principle of unity be other than any of the elements of a compound, just as that which makes the syllable ART one cannot be any or all of its letters, or as that which unifies the *Ethics* cannot be any or all of its Parts? But again, natural forms as conceived by Aristotle are rejected as specious by Spinoza.

There is another objection. Spinoza seems to have held, first, that singular things are so interdependent that they constitute not an aggregate but one systematic individual. Any singular thing must be a part of eternal if not also durational nature, and indeed a partial part thereof, since it can neither be nor be conceived apart from the rest. Consequently, any finite power-center is modally but not really distinct both from other such power-centers and from the power-field in its entirety. Still speaking with necessary imprecision, we may say that nature as a whole is the same as the multitude of mutually determining particulars. Self-knowledge involves knowledge of all other individuals. Spinoza surely held, secondly, that each actually existing singular thing is discrete with respect to its essence or laws thereof. Each is an adequate as well as inadequate cause; some of its operations can be understood by reference to its own nature alone. Self-knowledge does not involve knowledge of every other individual.[44] The two theses are plainly inconsistent. They agree in implying that nothing is solely *in alio;* nothing can be only its relations to other things. According to the first thesis, however, no particular can ever be an adequate cause. Furthermore, the way in which it is partially *in se* cannot be distinguished strictly from the way in which it is partially *in alio,* since 'its own' nature is inconceivable apart from the others. No other cause is solely external. Necessity and compulsion are for "each" inextricably mixed. Thus a natural particular is like a point in space or extension. That point necessarily exists. It is unique. Yet it is essentially related both to extension itself, as a unity, and to uncountably many other points. Its position therefore "pertains" to its essence. But its essence is not simply its position. But what more pertains to it is not really distinct from that position. Spinoza's first thesis seems to be a result of reflection on nature in its entirety, on its general laws

---

[44] E I, P15 S, Ep 32, and Harris, 233, 237; also E II, P7 S with E I, A3, E II, P45, E III, P3 S, E IV, P57 Dm., E V, P40 S. On the other hand, E II, L7 S, P11 C, P46–P47, E III, P1, P4, E IV, P60 Dm. (which refers to E III, P6); and notice how frequently *"in se solo"* and similar locutions are used in the Fourth Part.

the generally accepted fact that disparate and indeed refractory agents exist, oneself for example. At any rate, just as he failed to declare adequately the relation between actual existence and eternity, so too Spinoza failed to integrate his account of nature as one's own with his account of nature as the common. One hardly knows how to interpret the implicit proposition that a given free man is essentially a kingdom within a kingdom, a particular God whose partiality is a necessary and therefore pleasant accident. Spinoza's Essentialism is no less questionable than Aristotle's.

The foregoing dialectical query is merely preparatory to our seeking to understand nature, or any natural thing, as a concrete unity or whole. One may claim that it is not even preparatory because physics has nothing to do with substance, mode, essence, or other *entia rationis*. But we can suppose that all such terms are merely appeasive and nonetheless maintain that the problem brought to light by our ratiocination remains to be thought through. Or one may claim that our query is irrelevant because all natural differences are real distinctions. Some are, as even Spinoza wanted to maintain. But some are not, as even the youthful Wittgenstein granted when he said that the world divides not into simple things but into complex atomic facts. And if all distinctions were real, then again the possibility of any sort of physics would be dubitable: its impossibility follows no less from Humean Atomism than from Spinozistic Holism. Furthermore, it would then be obvious that our natural desire to achieve one comprehensive theory is in vain. If, on the other hand, our dialectical query does provide reason to believe that the nature of things is not composite but irresolvably complex, it thereby provides reason also to doubt that knowledge thereof is wholly impossible. Nature very likely does not love to hide; but it has been, presently is, and perhaps will continue to be found perplexing. It is conceivably an eternal problem. For those who very much desire to know the nature of things, who are persuaded as well as compelled by the truth, being so perplexed rejuvenates as well as impedes their inquiry. The appetite so expressed by these philosophers is not obviously love of one's own. The true foundation, the means, and even the end of such endeavor is apparently rather inquisitive wonder in the attractive face of what is problematic *qua* problematic.

Graduate Faculty, New School for Social Research

16 ANALYTIC AND SYNTHETIC METHODS IN SPINOZA'S *ETHICS*

Richard Kennington

I.

The over-arching thesis of Spinoza's philosophy can be simply stated. Final knowledge of the whole ("God or Nature") in its necessitated, non-teleological, character is the necessary condition for human happiness or freedom. This thesis of itself does not evidently demand a) the *order* of exposition of the *Ethics* descending from the one Whole or God in Part I to the parts, modes or finite beings in *Ethics* II - V. It does not demand, to express the point differently, that metaphysics be absolutely prior to physics in the order of knowledge. Moreover, it does not evidently demand b) the *form* of exposition of the *Ethics* as demonstration "in geometric order." If we consider Spinoza's two major writings, the statements of the *Tractatus Theologico-Politicus* (henceforth "*Treatise*"), which describe philosophic order and method, are in striking discrepancy with the procedure of the *Ethics*. In the *Treatise* an empirical "history of nature" (*historia naturae*) is "the foundation of philosophy"; history of nature is prior to "definitions of natural things"; the "examination of natural things" begins not with a metaphysics of substance, as in the *Ethics*, but with what is "universal and common to the whole of nature - as motion and rest ... "[1] The *Treatise* statements about the nature of philoso-

---

[1] *A Theologico-Political Treatise*, In *The Chief Works of Benedict de Spinoza*, tr. R. H. M. Elwes (New York: Dover, 1951), 195, 99, 104, 113; Gebhardt, *Opera*, III, 185, 98, 102, 112. Modifications are sometimes made in this translation of the *Tractatus*, henceforth referred to as "Elwes"; and also in the White-Stirling translation of the *Ethica* and the Elwes translation of the *Tractatus de Intellectus Emendatione*, published together in the edition of J. Gutmann (New York: Hafner, 1955), henceforth referred to as "Gutmann."

phy do not require or even mention geometric order or method.

In the discrepancy between the *Treatise* and the *Ethics* lies the initial basis for the great dispute over the interpretation of Spinoza. The traditional interpretation, which included Hume and Mendelssohn as well as Bayle, understood Spinozism as an atheistic naturalism; it discounted the order of the *Ethics* from God or infinite substance to finite beings; in certain cases it even regarded the geometric order of demonstration as a "pretense."[2] The *Treatise* and the *Ethics* must be understood together; the *Treatise* is not to be dismissed as merely a negative critique of religious prejudice. Precisely as a " pre-philosophic" critique of prejudice it would be an indispensable beginning of Spinozist philosophy. In the pantheist interpretation of Spinoza, which began primarily with Herder in the 1780's and remains dominant today, the *Treatise* has lost its importance. The *Treatise* need not be discussed because its conclusions, as distinct from some of its arguments, are largely accepted. Insofar as philosophy still regards it as necessary to discuss the conflicting claims of philosophy and biblical revelation, it does so on the basis of a tradition of Biblical interpretation which has been decisively altered by the *Treatise*. The doctrine of the *Ethics* remains moot; the success of the *Treatise* is so considerable that it has receded from the philosophic stage. In recent decades study of Spinoza's philosophy is almost exclusively study of the *Ethics*. The absence of the *Treatise* is not felt precisely because the *Ethics* is understood as a self-sufficient writing which descends by geometric demonstrations from the infinite divine whole to the finite beings. This means not only that the question has been begged regarding the interpretation of the *Ethics*, but also that the arbitrariness and limitation of its "geometric order"—so often acknowledged—are deprived of a solution.

The only form in which these issues are found in recent discussion (e.g., Wolfson, Gueroult) is in the question about the appropriateness

---

[2] "He (Spinoza) was accustom'd to this way of pretending to demonstrate things in a Geometrical Method, tho he knew 'em to be false, since thus he had before demonstrated Cartesius's Principles," John Toland, Letter IV, *Letters to Serena* (1704) (reprinted, New York and London: Garland, 1976), 153. ". . Spinoza à donné a ses imaginations une apparence de grands principes de métaphysique, et il a affecté la méthode des géometres, pour donner à son ouvrage un tour d'exactitude et de demonstration," F. de Salignac de La Mothe-Fenelon, *Correspondance de Fenelon*, ed. J. Orcibal (Paris, 1976), 95. "Quoi qu'il ait disposé en ordre Mathematique ce qu'il dit, pour surprendre les Lecteurs; on voit partout de faux raisonnements et un Galimathias perpetuel," J. Le Clerc, Vol. 22 (1724), quoted in F. Mauthner, *Der Atheismus und seine Geschichte im Abendlande* (Hildesheim: 1961), II, 349-350.

or necessity of "geometric" demonstration for the doctrine of the *Ethics*. But even as regards its *form* of demonstration as distinct from its *order* of exposition, this discussion has lacked clarity about the alternative. The alternative to the geometric method is the analytic method. Few today examine, and most merely allude to, the one writing in which Spinoza explains these alternatives. Only in the Preface to his *Principles of Descartes' Philosophy* (henceforth" *"Descartes"*), and nowhere else in his writings, does Spinoza discuss "geometric" demonstration: this is the *locus classicus* for the procedure of the *Ethics*. "Analytic" procedures are there distinguished from "synthetic" ones, and both are geometric or mathematical as well as philosophic procedures. Nevertheless, the synthetic is called "geometric," even in philosophy, because of the authoritative precedent of Euclid.[3] Of course these statements belong to the treasury of information well-known to all Spinoza students. The import of the Preface has been discounted because its ostensible author is not Spinoza but his disciple, Ludwig Meyer. Yet Spinoza asked Meyer to make alterations in the text of the Preface; in the only book he ever published in his own name, he did not ask that the statements on method be modified.[4] Again, the "methodological" part of the Preface has been regarded as essentially a borrowing from Descartes; but Spinoza indicates no disagreement therewith.

The analytic and not the geometric-synthetic method "shows the true way [*vera via*] in which a thing has been methodically discovered," according to the Preface. Since Wolfson overlooked this assertion in his exposition, he was unable to see either the priority of the analytic or any significant difference between it and the geometric-synthetic method.[5] This assertion is not qualified or rejected by

---

[3] *Principles of the Philosophy of Rene Descartes, Demonstrated in the Geometrical Manner*, in B. Spinoza, *Earlier Philosophical Writings*, tr. Frank A. Hayes (Indianapolis: Bobbs-Merrill, 1963), 3–5, henceforth referred to as "Hayes".
[4] See Ep. XV to L. Meyer, *The Correspondence of Spinoza*, ed. A. Wolf (London: Frank Cass, 1966), 134–136; Gebhardt IV, 72–73.
[5] H. A. Wolfson, *The Philosophy of Spinoza* (Cleveland: World, 1958), Ch. II, "The Geometrical Method." Accordingly, the fact that "Descartes' philosophy ... was discovered by the analytic method" (I, 56), is without methodological significance; whether the order of proof is analytic or synthetic is a matter of indifference. It is therefore possible for Wolfson to say that it is "a literary pretension that (Spinoza's) entire philosophy was evolved from his conception of God"; but also that "the eternal existence of God ... is immediately known as an intuition"; and also that ". . 'God' is merely an appeasive term for the most comprehensive principle of the Universe" (II, 4; I, 375; I, 177).

the Preface: hence it is difficult to understand why Gueroult, who says the Preface was "revue, corrigée et approuvée par Spinoza," nonetheless says that "la méthode synthétique ... est entendue par Spinoza comme étant la véritable méthode d'invention."[6] Bidney made the decisive observation that "the geometric method did not provide any proof or demonstration of the truth of its major premises, namely, the definitions, postulates, and axioms which are accepted as given ."[7] The geometric-synthetic method cannot stand on its own feet, as an autonomous method of demonstration. Bidney never published, to our knowledge, the implications of this finding which he might have drawn for the *Ethics*. Only Strauss, among contemporaries, drew the conclusion that if synthetic demonstration cannot establish its premises, it must rely on a prior analytic procedure for their acquisition.[8] This prior analysis leading to the major premises of the geometric method of the *Ethics* must lie within the *Ethics* itself: we have no indications inside or outside the work that would point to another Spinozist publication that contains the analysis. This is less novel than it seems: some scholars have identified a discrepancy between Parts I and II of the *Ethics*, or have identified a second or new, discrepant beginning in *Ethics II*, especially with the introduction of the "Physical Treatise" after P 13.[9] Since the analytic is the *vera via* of discovery, it must necessarily begin by considering the phenomena as known pre-philosophically as required by the methodological statements of the *Treatise*.

II. *The Insufficiency of the Geometric-Synthetic Method*

Before turning to the analytic method, we must first establish that the geometric- synthetic method of the *Ethics* cannot be regarded as self-sufficient.

---

[6] M. Gueroult, *Spinoza* I (Paris: Aubier-Montaigne, 1968), 20, 35.

[7] D. Bidney, Introduction, in Hayes, xiv.

[8] L. Strauss, "How to Study Spinoza's Theologico-Political Treatise," *Persecution and the Art of Writing* (Glencoe: Free Press, 1952), 186–187, 189.

[9] H. Barker, "Notes on the Second Part of Spinoza's *Ethics*" in *Studies in Spinoza, Critical and Interpretive Essays* ed. S. Kashap (Berkeley: U. of California Press, 1972), 101–105; A. E. Taylor, "Some Incoherencies in Spinozism," Op. cit., 200; D. Lachterman, "The Physics of Spinoza's *Ethics*," in *Spinoza: New Perspectives*, ed. R. Shahan and J. Biro (Norman: U. of Oklahoma Press, 1978), 83.

(a) *Arbitrariness of the Primary Definitions*

If the geometric procedure is to be demonstrative, the Primary Definitions at the outset of the *Ethics* must be true. "A true idea must agree with that of which it is the idea": (E I, Ax. VI): the definition must be "real" and not merely nominal or stipulative. Since they are not accompanied by any justification, they must be self-evident or intuitively obvious. These requirements cannot be met by the Primary Definitions, nor does Spinoza's doctrine of definitions, as gathered from various writings, permit them to be met—as will appear in the sequel. Substance is defined (E I, Dt, III) as "that which is in itself and conceived through itself." In its double requirement this definition has no clear and explicit antecedent, as Wolfson's elaborate survey only confirms.[10] Even if, by some miracle, it were the universal conclusion of the prior tradition, it would not thereby acquire self-evidence. While the definition of substance has plainly a Greek and especially Aristotelian ancestry, the definition of God has its sources in Biblical theology. God is defined (Df. 6) as "a Being absolutely infinite, that is to say, a substance consisting of infinite attributes, each one of which expresses eternal and infinite essence." The self-intelligibility of substance is in clear tension with the problematic intelligibility of God as substance with a double infinity: the Greek ancestry is at variance with the Biblical. But in the *Ethics* only two of the divine attributes are adumbrated, extension and thought. Questions necessarily arise. Are only two of the divine attributes intelligible to the human mind? If so, what necessity underlies this conclusion? Is not the intelligibility of two attributes of the divine whole impaired by the unintelligibility of those to whom they must bear relations—the vastly greater remainder? Is not the whole fundamentally unintelligible? Can God be a substance, i.e., self-conceivable on these stipulations? On all these questions Spinoza preserves a resounding silence in the *Ethics*, a silence that inspires no confidence in the geometric method. It is not surprising that the arbitrariness of the Primary Definitions was ridiculed by Berkeley and rejected by Hegel. "The definitions from which Spinoza takes his start . . . *causa sui*, substance, attribute, mode,

---

[10] Wolfson, Op. cit., I, 64, 66.

etc. ... are solely and simply accepted and assumed, not deduced nor proved to be necessary."[11]

(b) *The Indeterminacy of the Primary Definitions*

If we consider Spinoza's treatment of definition in various places, it proves impossible to assign a determinate status to definitions within a geometric-synthetic method. Here our concern is with definitions only if connected with geometric method; and with method only if it involves definition. If a Spinozist statement asserts that definition is drawn from experience (e.g., *historia naturae*), or in general requires proof, we shall conclude, in the absence of statements to the contrary, that such definitions cannot be the starting points of geometric demonstration.

In the *Ethics*, as said above, there is no discussion of the status of definition. The only passage on definition (E I, P 8 S 2) argues only that a definition does not involve or express any certain number of individuals. His silence about definitions would be merely part of Spinoza's imitation of Euclid and unproblematic were the subject matter of the *Ethics* exclusively or primarily mathematical. Hence this imitation is necessarily partial: whereas Euclid is silent about method and knowledge, Spinoza discusses *"methodus"* in the scholia to E II, P 40 and there explains his classification of knowledge. In the first scholium, universals, and implicitly definitions, in so far as they involve genus and species, receive a certain critique. All the more striking then is it that in a work which begins *more geometrico* with Primary Definitions the sole thematic treatment of methodical knowing does not advocate or even once mention definition.

Instead of asking whether this omission is not itself deliberate and significant, it is customary to turn to the unpublished fragment, *On the Correction of the Understanding* (henceforth "*Correction*"), in order to find a methodology that will explain the geometric procedure of the *Ethics*. But neither the doctrine we find in that work, nor the status that it is permissible to assign that fragment, justify that function. The

---

[11] "I have heard, said I, Spinosa represented as a man of close, argument and demonstration." "He did, replied Crito, demonstrate; but it was after such a manner as any one may demonstrate anything. Allow a man the privilege to make his own definitions of common words, and it will be no hard matter for him to infer conclusions which in one sense shall be true and in another false, at once seeming paradoxes and manifest truisms," Bishop Berkeley, *Alciphron*, Seventh Dialogue, II, 334; G. W. F. Hegel, *Lectures on the History of Philosophy*, tr. E. Haldane, F. Simson (London: Routledge & Kegan Paul, 1896), III, 283.

Correction assuredly treats of *methodus*, of the true method or the *recta inveniendi via*,[12] and is the only extant treatise, as distinct from a private letter, which offers what approaches a doctrine of definition. Yet it never speaks of geometric method, or geometric order of demonstration, nor does it distinguish geometric-synthetic method from analytic. Definitions in the true method do not initiate a demonstration, but themselves presuppose a prior inquiry. The truth or evidentiality of definitions arises from a preparatory articulation of the whole of being, which distinguishes between *res creata* and *res increata*.[13] This distinction is absent from the *Ethics* and alien to its doctrine. Nevertheless the *res increata* might seem to bear an affinity to certain subjects of the Primary Definitions of E I, especially to substance and God. The second criterion of definitions of *res increata* is that they do not leave us in doubt about the existence of the things defined.[14] But if the definitions of substance and God in the *Ethics* were meant to conform to this doctrine of definition, the proofs of the existence of substance and God in E I, P 7 and P 11 would be redundant.

In the *Correction* Spinoza was groping for a methodology which combined the non-arbitrary evidentiality of beginnings, found in philosophical analysis, with the advantages of starting from known principles of the Whole, as in philosophical synthesis (see IV and V below). The young Spinoza was so confident that the completion of this methodology and of the *Correction* treatise was within his grasp that he wrote "I have composed a whole treatise on this subject [the First Cause] and also on the correction of the understanding."[15] It is reasonable to assume, following Wolf,[16] that the "treatise" referred to is the *Short Treatise on God, Man and his Well-Being*, which remained unpublished by Spinoza, and that the rest of this statement refers to the *Correction*, which remained a fragment. On the statement quoted, the *Short Treatise* should presumably exemplify the method of the *Correction*, but it is not demonstrated *more geometrico*. From these facts it appears that Spinoza did not regard the *Correction* as teaching a geometric method, or even an adequately articulated method. Accordingly, the *Correction* cannot supply the methodological foundations for the geometric method of the *Ethics*. The doctrine, methodological and definitional, of the unpublished *Correction* is in clear discrepancy

---

[12] Gutmann, 31; Gebhardt II, 34.
[13] Gutmann, 32-33; Gebhardt II, 35-36.
[14] Gutmann, 33; Gebhardt II, 35.
[15] Ep. VI, Wolf, Op. cit., 98; Gebhardt IV, 36.
[16] Wolf, ibid., 386.

with that of the major published writings, *Descartes*, *Treatise*, and *Ethics*. Therefore, when Spinoza says in the *Ethics* (E II, P 40 S1), after some exposition of his *"methodus"*, that he has destined these subjects for treatment in another work, the reference is most probably to a replacement for the *Correction*—or to a substantially revised version thereof. A similar conclusion applies to Spinoza's statement to Tschirnhaus in 1675 that, as regards "motion" and "method," "my views on these subjects have not been put into final shape."[17] We conclude that Spinoza expected his readers to be guided sufficiently by the methodological doctrine of the published writings.[18]

In the *Treatise*, the four principal "methodological" passages never mention geometric-synthetic method in demonstration, refer three times to *"methodus"* and once to definitions. In the first, we are required by *"nostra methodus"* to deduce and infer "the unknown from the known, insofar as it is known,"[19] but nothing permits the identification of the known with definitions. In the second, the definitions are acquired empirically. "The *methodus interpretandi naturae* consists chiefly in this, in composing a history of nature [*historia naturae*] and deducing therefrom definitions of natural things on certain fixed axioms."[20] In the third, the necessity of an empirical basis in *historia naturae* is essential in "philosophy"—we are not permitted to restrict it to some branch thereof which we would call "physics". "We have shown in Chap. VII that the meaning of Scripture should be gathered from its own history and not from the history of universal nature (*ex universali historia naturae*) which is the foundation of philosophy alone."[21] By the fourth, " ... we shall require a method (*methodus*) and order [*ordo*] similar to that which we use in interpreting nature from its history ... In the examination of natural things we try first of all to investigate what is universal and common to the whole of

---

[17] Ep. IX, Wolf, ibid., 301; Gebhardt, 271.

[18] In an early letter to Oldenbourg (Ep. IV, 1661) Spinoza maintains that the existence of the thing defined does follow in a definition of "a thing which is conceived through itself and in itself," the example being a definition of God. In the *Ethics*, however, the Primary Definitions of God and substance are followed by lengthy demonstrations of their existence. The early view of definition is not found in the account of definition given De Vries (Ep. VIII) and Tschirnhaus (Ep. LX). Spinoza's reply (Ep. XXXVII) to Bouwmeester's request for an assured "method" of treating "the most exalted subjects" does not mention definitions.

[19] Elwes, 113; Gebhardt III, 112.

[20] Elwes, 99; Gebhardt III, 98.

[21] Elwes, 195; Gebhardt III, 185.

nature—as motion and rest, and their laws and rules, which nature always observes, and through which it continually acts and from these we gradually proceed to the less universal . . ."[22] The presence of the prior *historia naturae* once more excludes identification of the method as geometric-synthetical. On the other hand, the mention of "motion and rest" suggests an identification with the procedure of *Ethics* II, and especially with that of the Physical Treatise, whose first axiom concerns motion and rest (see V below).

(c) *The Restricted Range of Geometric Method*

It is generally acknowledged that it is impossible in the *Ethics* to deduce geometrically any of the particular beings of the natural world, i.e., the "finite modes." Hence even if we were able to assign a determinate status to the Primary Definitions on the basis of Spinozist statements, the geometric method cannot be the method of Spinoza's philosophy. As Barker observed, "the First Part (of the *Ethics*) may be said to work out a set of formal determinations applicable to reality as a single whole, without much concern as to what, in actual fact, reality consists of," i.e., a multiplicity of finite modes. "Much of Part I becomes a mere formal exercise in the working out of the mutual relations of more or less arbitrary concepts."[23] But even the intelligible infinite attributes cannot be determined as extension and thought except on the basis of the finite modes which enter with experience. Hence even the determinancy of God's infinite attributes proves to lie outside the competence of geometric method.

Spinoza writes to De Vries: "We only need experience in the case of whatever cannot be deduced from the definition of a thing, as for instance, the existence of modes: for this cannot be deduced from the definition of a thing."[24] In accord with this assertion, Spinoza introduces near the outset of E II the axiom: "We neither sense nor perceive particular things except bodies and modes of thought." With this Ax 5 belongs Ax 2 ("Man thinks") and Ax 4 ("We sense [sentimus] that a certain body is affected in many ways"). Only on this experienced basis of particulars, at the inception of *Ethics* II, do we acquire knowledge that there are existent modes, and what their determinate properties are. But they are called "axioms": do they not fall within the geometric method? But in clear contradistinction to the axioms that follow the Primary Definitions of E I, these axioms assert

---

[22] Elwes, 104; Gebhardt III, 102.
[23] H. Barker in S. Kashap, Op. cit., 101, 102.
[24] Ep. X, Wolf, Op. cit., 109; Gebhardt IV, 47.

the existence of particular finite beings with determinate properties, and do so on the basis of internal and external sensation and feeling. The axioms of E I remain "geometrical" insofar as they are not based on experience, as these from E II are. These put a term to one methodological procedure in the *Ethics*, and, as will be shown, inaugurate another.

Already in E I we learn that what is finite cannot be deduced from the infinite. "That which is finite, and has a determinate existence cannot be produced by the absolute nature of any attribute of God" (E I, P 28). Nor can the finite be deduced from the infinite modes, as the context of E I, P 28 shows. A finite mode "must be determined by another, which is finite and has a determinate existence." Whereas God is only a "*causa immanens*" and not a transitive cause (E I, P 16), the finite modes, e.g., bodies, clearly have transitive causal relationships. The realm of finite modes is independent of the divine attributes and infinite modes, as regards the particular determinacy, or "production," of its members. Precisely because the geometric method begins with definitions of infinite being it reveals itself as not competent to account for the determinacy of finite being.

This conclusion appears indeed to be controverted by the assertion that "modes of the divine nature follow therefrom necessarily and not contingently" (E I, P 29 Dm). Moreover, "God is not only the efficient cause of the existence of things, but also of their essence" (E I, P 25). But the purport of these assertions does not bring them into contradiction with E I, P 28, on which we have primarily relied above. A body, i.e., a finite mode, determines another body, by transitive causality, because of the necessary condition that each is extended, but extension is an infinite attribute of God, hence the immanent cause of the finite determination. When extension, taken as infinite attribute, is "modified," it becomes the extension of a body that can determine another body. But from the infinite attribute of extension, no modifications can be deduced (E I, P 28). Spinoza does not tell us why there should be any modes. Hence that there are modes as distinct from substances, or from the one substance, is merely an empty, unsupported assertion, so long as we adhere to the deduction of the geometric method. Of course, if we understand Primary Definition V (of "mode") as a self-evidently true definition that entails the existence of its referent, then we shall indeed hold that there exist some modes of substance. But even if this be granted this procedure is empty, since we shall still not know what any particular mode is—i.e., what a modification of substance might mean in actuality, until we leave the geometric method behind us.

The barrenness of the geometric method is still more acute. It cannot even deduce what God is in the determinate sense: that his infinite attributes include extension and thought. Only on the basis of our experience of the existence and nature of finite modes does Spinoza, in E II, P 1 and P 2, infer that God is extension and thought. There he reasons that since "particular thoughts . . . are modes" and God must possess the attribute thus modified, thought is an attribute of God; and by a similar argument from finite to infinite, God is extended. But, as seen before, only the experiential axioms E II, A 2 and A4, introduce into the exposition the existence of particular thoughts and bodies. It is worth noting that the demonstations that God is a thinking and extended thing (E II, P 1, P 2) have a small but significant defect: they do not mention the experiential axioms (A2, A 4) on which they depend, but instead offer justification only from E I. This is not the only indication that Spinoza seeks to blur the "modal boundary" which delimits the synthetic method.

This "blurring" shows up in the fact that Spinoza already in Part I asserts as established the twin theses, God is extended and thinking, long before the propositions that assert them and the demonstrations that justify them are introduced in Part II. Spinoza first says, without justification (E I, P 14, C 2), and somewhat tentatively, that "extension and thought are either attributes of God or modes of the attributes of God." But in the following proposition (E I, P 15 S) he says that in P 14 he had already "concluded that extended substance is one of the attributes of God." This could be regarded as an egregious blunder, except that Spinoza calls our attention to his blunder, by compounding it with another: he says that substance is an attribute, in clear discord with the Primary Definitions of the synthetic system. Moreover, if Spinoza thought he had established in E I, P 14 that God is extended, he would not have offered the proof of that thesis in E II, P 2. Hence it is a reasonable inference that Spinoza's claim to have concluded that God is extended in E I, P 14, is a pretence of which he is fully aware. A similar argument could be made about the theses that God is a thinking being, and an intellect, which are asserted in Part I but again without justification. We can therefore agree that for these, and similar reasons, "as an apodictic system, *de Deo* [Part I] is patently ill-formed . . . "[25] This malformation is hardly the fruit of Spinoza's exaggerated confidence in "geometric" deduction; it has a well-deliberated structure. On the one hand, he blurs the modal boundary by his "geometric" deduction of conclusions of which it is incapable. On the other, by the inconsequence of certain conclusions,

---

[25] S. Umphrey, "*De Natura*," this volume, p. 275

whose visible basis is clearly experience, he calls our attention to that very same boundary.

III. *Analytic and Synthetic Method in the* Descartes

To understand why Spinoza chose the geometric order of demonstration in the *Ethics* we must understand why he chose it in his first publication, the *Descartes* (1663). It is reasonable to suppose that he expected readers to study the *Descartes* for this purpose: nowhere but here does he justify or even discuss the geometric method. In the *Descartes* Spinoza utilizes the geometric method to demonstrate what is in fundamental respects for him a false doctrine. The Preface identifies several false Cartesian doctrines, e.g., the "statements about will ... even though they seem to be satisfactorily proved with great care and completeness." "The foundations of knowledge laid by Descartes and the things erected upon them do not suffice ..."[26] We can then conclude that the geometric demonstration of Descartes' principles is a pseudo-demonstration, a fact to which Spinoza even invites the reader's attention. The geometric method then is neutral to the truth of the doctrine conveyed, or it is peculiarly suited for the communication of false doctrines, or both.

The Preface begins by identifying "the method of the mathematicians" with the geometric method of "demonstrating conclusions from definitions, postulates, and axioms ..." This is "the best and surest means of searching out and teaching the truth." All the more striking is it that when Descartes is introduced—"that splendid light of our age"—we learn that he did not employ the geometric method "used in the *Elements* of Euclid and in other Geometries." In his "philosophic writings" he preferred the analytic method "which shows the true way in which a thing has been methodically discovered, even, as it were, *a priori*." Both this statement, and the following description of synthetic method, are quoted in the Preface from Descartes' 2^d *Replies*, accompanying the *Meditations*. Synthetic method "uses a long series of definitions, assumptions, axioms, theories and problems, so that if anything in the consequences is denied, it is at once shown to be contained in the premises, and so extorts the assent of the most contrary and obstinate reader." The synthetic—plainly the "geometric"—method demonstrates only what is "contained in the premises," but not the premises themselves. If geometric demonstration is formally correct, the doctrine demonstrated may be true

---

[26] Hayes, Op. cit., 8, 9; Gebhardt I, 132, 132–133.

or false depending on the status of the premises. Only analysis as the *vera via* of discovery can establish the status of premises. Hence for Descartes "the true and best way of teaching" is the analytic.

For Descartes the geometric method "extorts the assent of the most contrary and obstinate reader," whereas only the analytic method contents "the eager learner" because it "shows the way in which the matter taught was discovered" (2^d *Replies*).[27] More precisely, the analytic method is addressed to the philosophic reader, the geometric-synthetic to the non-philosophic, as we learn from correlation with a distinction in the Preface to the *Meditations*. "In geometry, since each one is persuaded that nothing is advanced of which there is not a certain demonstration, those who are not entirely adept more frequently err in approving what is false, in order to give the impression that they understand it, than in refuting the true." But "in philosophy"everyone believes that all is problematical, and few give themselves to the search after truth."[28] The geometric method is not addressed to the philosophic reader because it is not suited to philosophy, as distinct from geometry. " . . . the presuppositions of geometric proofs harmonize with the use of our senses, and are readily granted by all . . . on the contrary, nothing in metaphysics causes more trouble than the making the perception of its primary notions clear and distinct" (2^d *Replies*).[29] Accordingly, the geometric demonstration of his metaphysics which Descartes appended to the 2^d *Replies*, even if a formally correct deduction, cannot have been intended by him as a genuine demonstration.

Why did Spinoza reject the analytic method used by Descartes in his philosophic writings in favor of the geometric-synthetic? The Preface, which scarcely addresses this question explicitly, suggests at first that the initiative lay with Ludwig Meyer. Meyer observes that most people are inexperienced in analytic and synthetic method, and many "have assumed the name Cartesian though unable to demonstrate anything." He hoped that "someone skilled in both analytic and synthetic order" would demonstrate Descartes' principles in geometric order; he learned that Spinoza had stated Part II of Descartes' *Prin-*

---

[27] R. Descartes, 2d Replies, *The Philosophical Works of Descartes*, tr. E. Haldane and G. Ross (New York: Dover, 1955), II, 48, 49; *Oeuvres de Descartes*, ed. Adam-Tannery, IX-1, 121–122.

[28] R. Descartes, Ep. Ded., *Meditations*, tr. Haldane and Ross, Op. cit., I, 135–136: Adam-Tannery, IX-1, 7.

[29] R. Descartes, 2d Replies, tr. Haldane and Ross, Op. cit., II, 49–50; Adam-Tannery, IX-1, 122.

ciples (the physics) geometrically; and he persuaded him to add a geometric version of Part I. This explanation gives no reason for the choice of the geometric: presumably the *vera via* of discovery, the analytic, would have been more appropriate. Moreover, Meyer's distress at the dogmatising of the Cartesians, even if it was shared by Spinoza, does not explain why the latter composed and published an essentially dogmatic, i.e. geometric version of Cartesianism, which suppressed the analytical proof of its premises. Nothing could be less faithful to the spirit of Descartes than to demonstrate the Cartesian metaphysics by a method Descartes declared inappropriate to metaphysics, and which he employed in the 2^d *Replies* only *ad hominem*—at the insistence of the authors of the 2^d *Objections*.

Light on the enigma begins to appear from the fact Meyer gives us that the initiative in applying the geometric method to Descartes originally lay with Spinoza. For one of his pupils he had demonstrated geometrically the Cartesian physics–Part II entire of the *Principles* and a portion of III. To Spinoza this is the least problematic part of Descartes' doctrine: the Preface indicates several Spinozist objections to his metaphysics, but none to his physics. But Spinoza had no intention of producing more competent Cartesians. To the same pupil he demonstrated geometrically "some important and rather difficult questions aired in metaphysics and not yet resolved by Descartes." At some point the promising pupil learned, as Spinoza's pupil Meyer learned, that one must know the analytic method of discovery as well as geometric-synthetic demonstration. But the analytic method cannot, for Spinoza, establish the premises of a Cartesian metaphysics which is erroneous; it must lead to the premises of Spinozist philosophy. The apprenticeship to the true philosophy is study of the geometric demonstration of Descartes' principles. The apprentice will remain a dogmatic Cartesian if he does not break the fetters of geometric demonstration and practice analysis. By identifying the false Cartesian doctrines "demonstrated" ("proved with great care and completeness") geometrically and by identifying analysis as the true way of discovery, Spinoza provokes the reflective reader to turn to analysis and philosophy. Just as unmistakably as Descartes, Spinoza presupposes two kinds of readers, a dogmatic non-philosopher and a competent "eager learner." Only on this assumption can we grasp why he "demonstrated" the erroneous philosophy of Descartes, while declaring, in the final paragraph of the Preface, that he publishes for no other purpose than "to urge men to the study of true and sincere philosophy."

IV. Philosophic Speech

The notions of philosophic communication implied in the foregoing are found partly in the precepts of the *Correction* and partly in the *Treatise*. Spinoza sets down three "rules of living" for philosophers in the *Correction*, which begin as follows. "To speak with a view to the capacity of the vulgar (*ad captum vulgi*) and to practice all those things which cannot hinder us from reaching our goal (i.e. the highest good). For we are able to obtain no small advantages from the vulgar provided we make as many concessions as possible to their capacity. Add to this that in this way they will lend friendly ears to the truth."[30] To accommodate philosophic speech to the capacity of the vulgar is, at least at certain times, an action not antithetical to, but requisite to the quest for wisdom. Spinoza's first rule is modelled on the first rule of Descartes' "morale par provision."[31] While pursuing the strictly private examination of his own opinions, the Cartesian philosopher practices intransigent conformism to the opinions and practices of those among whom he will live, even though these be "Persians or Chinese." In the *Treatise* Spinoza teaches that God and the prophets Jesus and Paul, in speaking *ad captum vulgi* or *ad captum alicuius*, i.e., to men who held vulgar opinions, accommodated themselves to the capacity of their addressees by professing or at any rate not questioning those opinions.[32]

Four kinds of possible readers are identified at the end of the Preface to the *Treatise*: 1) the "philosophic reader," identified as the primary addressee; 2) the philosophers, who do not require Spinoza's instruction; 3) the "vulgar," in whom "prejudices embraced under the name of religion" or of "superstition" are deeply rooted; and 4) those afflicted by the same passions as the vulgar. Category 4) refers to theologians: neither they nor the vulgar will benefit from a book whose purpose is to deny that "reason ought to be a handmaiden to theology." Nevertheless they can and may be expected to read the book: as shocking as the *Treatise* is to their opinions, it nonetheless accommodates itself to those opinions. More pertinent, even the philosophic reader is not, or not yet, a philosopher, but one who shares the vulgar opinions: he must be addressed on the grounds of those opinions. Thus, Spinoza's first sentence in Chapter I is an *ad*

---

[30] Gutmann, 7; Gebhardt II, 9–10.

[31] *Discours de la méthode III*, 2d paragraph.

[32] See L. Strauss, "How to Study Spinoza's *Theologico-Political Treatise*," Op. cit., 178.

captum utterance which is often later contradicted: "Prophecy or revelation is certain knowledge of some thing revealed by God to man."

As Spinoza indicates through his examples of *ad captum* speech in the Bible, the assertions of a speaker do not necessarily reflect the settled beliefs of the speaker: "Moses believed, or at least he wished to teach . . ."[33] Spinoza stresses that what God and certain prophets say to certain prophets or men contradicts what is said on other occasions to others, because it is acommodated "*ad captum vulgi*" or "*ad captum alicuius.*" At least some statements of the speakers must then be in deliberate or conscious contradiction with others, as well as with their own knowledge or settled beliefs. Since Spinoza forcibly draws attention to this type of contradiction in the Bible, the reader if a philosophic reader is forced to ask if the many and various contradictions in Spinoza's own statements are not themselves conscious or deliberate. Moreover, the ambiguity whether the Bible had one primary author, or two or more authors, is absent in Spinoza's work: could not all the difficulties of the *Treatise* be part of a single, controlling intention? Spinoza's interpretation of the Bible educates the reader to discern not merely the variety of forms of direct and indirect contradiction in that writing and his own, but also the disjunction in levels of discourse. Only rarely are these levels placed in immediate proximity, as at the end of Chap. 15. "As we cannot perceive by the natural light of reason that simple obedience is the path of salvation, and are taught by revelation only that it is so by the special grace of God, which our reason cannot attain, it follows that the Bible has brought a very great consolation to mortals." The passage continues: "All are able to obey, whereas there are but very few, compared with the aggregate of humanity, who can acquire the habit of virtue under the unaided guidance of reason." The philosophic few are compelled to suspect the ultimate seriousness of any Spinozist assertion or inquiry which is not guided by the natural light of reason.

In the *Ethics* the surface contradiction lies between the geometric form of exposition and the abandonment of that form, especially in Part II. It might be expected, on the basis of the *Descartes*, that Spinoza would clearly indicate in the *Ethics* that beginning of the analytic method which establishes the premises of the geometric. Instead he blurs in various ways, as said above, the limitation of the geometric and the introduction of a new method in II. In our consideration of the analytic we shall find (just as in the *Descartes*) that he has no intention of removing the arbitrariness of geometric demonstration: the

---

[33] Elwes, 102–103; Gebhardt III, 101.

methods will be disjunctive in procedure and doctrine. This conclusion has already been implied: the recommended philosophic method of the *Treatise* is in contradiction with the ostensible geometric method of the *Ethics*. The same philosophic reader, to whom we must assume both works are addressed, is a child of both the religious and philosophic traditions. The dogmatic beginning with biblical revelation in the *Treatise* must be complemented by the dogmatic beginning with substance metaphysics in the Primary Definitions of the *Ethics*.

V. Analytic Method and Kinds of Knowledge in Ethics II

Cartesian analysis is the immediate parent of Spinozist analysis, as the *Descartes* shows. Tonelli has given general definitions of descriptive statements of analysis and synthesis in the tradition before the 18th century.[34] To simplify somewhat, analysis is that procedure which begins from the sensible, seeks the causes or principles of the sensible understood as "effects," and culminates in elementary notions or first principles. Since synthesis proceeds in the opposite direction, or begins with those elementary notions and first principles, we can infer that it presupposes the analytic. Tonelli thus confirms analysis as the true way of discovery. Nevertheless, there is a grand dogma that Descartes is the founder of continental rationalism which excogitates its principles *a priori*, or exclusively by intuition and deduction, apart from experience. Tonelli's description of analysis seems not to fit Descartes, nor even the empiricists who sought first principles not of the beings, but of human knowledge or of the human mind. What must be preserved, however, from Tonelli is that the moderns shared with the ancient tradition the assumption that philosophy must begin with a non-arbitrary reflection on experience, i.e., with analysis. It is by analysis guided by experience of bodies that Descartes elicits extension as the intelligible in the piece of wax (*Medit.* II); and by which he elicits the simple, prior or absolute in the "questions" of *Regulae* V and VI which are saturated with experiential elements.

However, a prior and more fundamental reflection leads Descartes to the abandonment of the experienced articulation of the world into a heterogeneity of kinds or classes of things—men, animals, plants, inanimate beings, the man-made and non-man-made. In this sense he turns his back on experience just as surely as any other modern phy-

---

[34] G. Tonelli, "Analysis and Synthesis in XVIIIth Century Philosophy Prior to Kant," *Archiv für Begriffsgeschichte* (Bonn: 1976 [20]), 178–213.

sicist. He replaces the heterogeneity of kinds of things with the homogeneity of bodies, guided by, or justified by, the decision that science is exclusively "clear and distinct" cognition. Nonetheless, the clear and distinct is that which manifests itself immediately in the experience of bodies: what can be known only by an *inspectio mentis* in the piece of wax is the same extension that can be touched.[35] The Cartesian departure from the experience of heterogeneous kinds is compensated by the universal immediacy by which concepts are manifested in the experience of bodies; the abiding difficulty of this procedure is the return to the explanation of heterogeneous kinds. It is a question whether Descartes did not pay a heavy price for this immediacy: extension is not a true ultimate, or not that metaphysical essence of body which can account for the properties, even of homogeneous bodies. Descartes did not seek to determine the ultimate divisibility of extension, or those ultimate parts which could explain the resistance, impenetrability or *antitypia*, required of his laws of mechanics. He was content to postulate three grades of fineness of material parts. It is probable that this lack of metaphysical ultimacy did not distress Descartes: extension, figure and motion could be identified with the conceptual objects of his analytic geometry. In these respects Spinoza is his disciple.

Spinoza's analytic procedure similarly begins negatively, in the first scholium, following E II P 40, the only place in the work where he speaks of "this method of ours . . ." His thematic critique of imagination shows us that he is examining what is called (second scholium) "the first kind of knowledge," "*opinio vel imaginatio*," by which men inhabit the "common order of nature" (P 29). But the *Treatise* had investigated opinion and prejudice, and it is especially through speech that we remember and imagine things: the *Treatise* is the beginning of the analysis of the *Ethics*. In the first scholium, Spinoza instances transcendentals and then universals as reflecting the inadequacy of imagination, but the critique bears directly only on the universals. Spinoza seems to imply that if one begins with universals, or with things and attributes, one is led to abstractions such as Being (*ens*) which he at least once equates with *substantia*[36] with which the geometric demonstration of the *Ethics* begins. The tradition had formed universals

---

[35] R. Descartes, *Meditations*, tr. Haldane and Ross, Op. cit., I, 155; Adam-Tannery, IX-1, 24.

[36] "*Substantia (sive ens)*," Ep. IX, Wolf, Correspondence, op. cit., 107; Gebhardt IV, 44.

from the imagined, and apparently common, attributes of the kinds, and had abstracted ever "higher" or more general terms. In common with Descartes Spinoza begins with bodily wholes and parts instead of the heterogeneous kinds. But as against Descartes, he refuses the fundamental heterogeneity of *res cogitans* and *res extensa*: man is not in nature as a "kingdom within a kingdom": in this respect Descartes is the last ancient philosopher.

The Physical Treatise following P 13 begins with an axiom: "All bodies are either in a state of motion or rest." This beginning is the bond between experience and science. What would be acknowledged by any man in "the common order of nature" is simultaneously the first axiom of Spinoza's physics. It lacks any supporting geometric deduction; it has been prepared by the pseudo-geometric axiomatization of sense experience that premises the existence of bodies at the outset of E II. Axiom I presupposes the meaning of "a body"; the subsequent definition of "a body or individual" presupposes the meaning of motion: there is no unilateral deduction in either direction. More precisely, the definition of a body or individual presupposes the "law of inertia" and two other principles of motion given previously in three lemmata. Stated differently, the definition of a body or individual is the only definition in the Physical Treatise, but since motion is not defined even this definition is elliptical. The analytic procedure then scarcely relies on definitions, e.g., of essences, and to the extent that it uses them they are not *a priori* but experientially derived. While Spinoza's *"unum corpus sive individuum"* is a compound of "simplest bodies" (*corpora simplicissima*), it is not defined in terms of them. We are not told whether the simplest bodies are indivisible atoms or infinitesimally small particles or what they are. Scholarship has speculated that they may be corpuscles of aetherial fluid or oscillating pendula.[37] It suffices for Spinoza's science of nature that we assume that the parts of extension must possess the same hardness, impenetrability, etc., as that of experienced bodies. Ultimate definitions may or may not be possible, but they are not necessary. Even the ultimacy of extension found in Descartes is lacking; the very word *"extensio"* is literally absent from the Physical Treatise; it is alluded to, certainly, though not employed, in Lemma II, apparently to link up the analysis with the divine attribute in the geometric synthesis. But whereas the geometric exposition stresses

---

[37] D. Lachterman, "The Physics of Spinoza's *Ethics*" in Shahan and Biro, Op. cit., 84.

the extension of materiality of God as one of his two intelligible attributes, the analysis treats extension as posterior to motion and rest.

To be *"unum corpus sive individuum"* the definition requires, first, that the parts of a compound be pressed together by external bodies so that they lie one upon another, and, second, that the parts communicate their motion to one another by "a certain fixed ratio" (*certa quadam ratione*). The first condition by itself may suffice to designate what would customarily be called an inanimate body; and the following axiom appears to have the same reference, a body that has *"figura"* alone. However, both conditions apply to the compounds of Lemmata IV-VII, which preserve their *natura* or *forma* despite their ("metabolic") interchange of bodies with adjacent individuals, thanks to conservation of their *ratio*. The fact of having some *ratio* is deducible from prior axioms and laws of nature; only experience tells Spinoza that some bodies have an abiding identity, i.e., preserve the same *ratio*. Experience also both permits and justifies Spinoza's version of "metabolic" interchange, as well as constitutive features of the human body, the only distinctive kind of body that is explicitly acknowledged. But it is obvious that a "certain fixed ratio" in its fixity cannot accommodate the facts of growth and decline, and not even diurnal bodily change. Only much later in the *Ethics* does Spinoza speak of the change from childhood to maturity as a change of ratio, and hence as a change of identity: he does not hesitate to call this "death." Even the famous amnesia of the Spanish poet is called death.[38] Spinoza has no concern with articulating the degrees or kinds of ratio change that would permit him to describe the continuity of living bodies through change, whether of maturation or amnesia. He suggests that the wise man can alter or modify the relations of imagination and memory to reason so that a change results to the ratio underlying happiness or blessedness.[39] Because the parts of living bodies are not, e.g., organs, but rather the bodies known to the physicist, Spinoza's doctrine is an "ethics" and not a possible "philosophy of organism." The ratio which in physical terms would be an hypothesis, "in principle" calculable, but never practically calculable, is translated onto the practical plane of self-therapy in the experience of the wise man.

---

[38] Gutmann, 218–219; Gebhardt II, 240.
[39] Compare E IV, P 39 with V, P 10 and P 39, with regard to the "death" of the body in the change from infancy to maturity, and the "chief endeavor" of the wise man "to change the body of infancy" to a state in which memory and imagination are of little importance.

Similar considerations underlie the treatment of the mind-body relation. By P 13 "the object of the idea constituting the human mind is a body, or a certain mode of extension actually existing, and nothing else." In terms of geometric metaphysics, a modification of the attribute of thought is here conceived by means of a modification of the attribute extension. As has been noticed by others, this does not conform to the requirements of the substance doctrine. "Each attribute of a substance must be conceived through itself" (E I, P 10). In general, Spinoza appears to be governed by his explanation of Primary Definition II: "a body is not limited by a thought, nor a thought by a body." Nevertheless, P 13 asserts a relation of mind to body: what then is "limitation"? The relation of mind to body in P 13 could be regarded as merely one of awareness: limitation in the sense of causal determination may then be denied, and this denial is supported by many passages. To be sure, Spinoza appears to waver between a view which regards ideas or acts of mind to be sufficiently determined by antecedent acts of mind—finite modes by finite modes; and another view which regards bodily states, and even external impacting bodies, as causal sources of mind's ideas. [40] The latter view is strengthened by the recourse to experience when Spinoza considers action and passion in Part III. For example, "experience teaches" "that if the body be sluggish the mind at the same time is not fit for thinking." [41] The inverse causal sequence though rare is also found. When we groundlessly fear an evil, the fear vanishes when we have correct intelligence (E V, P 67). (Fear involves the body's *potentia agendi*.) In sum, Spinoza remains entirely faithful to Primary Definition II in one sense: no adequate knowledge of such mind-body causal sequences is claimed. Just as clearly "experience teaches"—or "nature teaches" as Descartes said in a similar context[42]—that such causal sequences occur. "There is no need to know the nature of the mind through its first cause" (Ep. XXXVII[43]).

Spinoza's celebrated doctrine of three kinds of knowledge (P 40, 2d scholium) does not refer to definitions or geometric method or order, as said before. As for the first kind of knowledge, "*opinio vel*

---

[40] " . . . Spinoza is really thinking of the body as determining the mind," H. Barker in S. Kashap, Op. cit., 149.

[41] *Ethics* III, P 2, S; Gutmann 131; Gebhardt II, 142.

[42] *Meditations*, tr. Haldane and Ross, Op. cit., I, 189–90; Adam-Tannery IX-1, 64–66. See the author's "The 'Teaching of Nature' in Descartes' Soul Doctrine," *Review of Metaphysics*, Vol. XXVI, No. 1, Sept. 1972.

[43] Wolf, *Correspondence*, Op. cit., 228.

imaginatio," it has now been more securely placed in the analytic procedure. "Reason and knowledge of the second kind" arises "from common notions and adequate ideas of the properties of things (P 38C, P 39C, P 49)." Spinoza's cited propositions refer us back exclusively to adequate knowledge of bodies, and what can be deduced therefrom, i.e., knowledge derived analytically. The corollaries of P 38 and P 39 both refer to what is common to all bodies, but the enunciations of P 38 and P 39 which speak of *"omnibus communia"* appear to have a wider reference than "all bodies."

To elicit the underlying problem, we note that by P 38 "that which is common to all things and which is equally in the part and the whole can only be adequately perceived." The whole in question cannot be limited to finite wholes. "If we advance *ad infinitum*, we may easily conceive the whole of nature to be one individual [*individuum*] whose parts, that is to say, all bodies, differ in infinite ways without any change of the whole individual" (Lemma VII, S). The common will be univocally present in the part and in the totality, the whole of nature. Thus the intelligible in Spinoza's analytic method does not alter, gain or lose, in being or intelligibility, by any "ascent" or "descent" from part to whole or whole to part, as in the pre-modern analytic and synthetic procedures. This is the "scientific" core of Spinoza's analytic *vera via*.

This whole-part univocity is sacrificed when Spinoza in P 45 and 46 purports to show that "adequate" knowledge is also exemplified by geometric deduction. If the whole-part univocals of P 38 were to be instantiated through the geometric metaphysics they would have to be "equally present" in God and finite modes or particular things. But this would impair the distinction of attribute and mode: they would have to be equally present in eternal and temporal being, in substance which is *in se* and in modes which are *in alio* (E I, Def. III, V), as modifications thereof. Accordingly, in P 45 and 46 Spinoza reduces the range of univocity to what is common to the part and whole of merely finite wholes: the common in that reduced sense may be deduced from "the eternal and infinite essence of God." This reduction makes intelligible his exclusion of geometric deduction from the range of, or examples of, adequate knowing in P 39–P 40, S2.

Spinoza's third kind of knowledge, *scientia intuitiva*, "advances from an adequate idea of the *essentia formalis* of certain attributes of God to the adequate knowledge of the essence of things." The notable example given should awaken caution: finding the fourth proportional to three given numbers does not disclose the essence of any particular thing. The geometric metaphysics is incapable of deducing any determinate quantities; it remains a qualitative or attributal metaphysics of traditional type; numerical ratios and proportions had entered only with the analytic account of the corporeal individual; and even there are not actually calculable. On the other hand, if we free "ratio" from a strict numerical meaning, the description given of *scientia intuitiva* remains in strong discord with E I, P 28: it is impossible to deduce the finite from the infinite. In the light of these considerations, it is not surprising that Spinoza gives a peculiarly lame proof that geometric method can attain *scientia intuitiva*, in the scholium, as distinct from the demonstration, of P 47. The proof begins with God's essence, appropriately enough, but does not even mention "the essence of things," the required concluding term of the deduction. In fact only in P 7 of Part III does Spinoza introduce *conatus* as "the actual essence of the thing itself." It is generally agreed that *scientia intuitiva* terminates in knowledge of particular things, ("*res singulares*," E II, P 36). Even were we to disagree with Bidney and others that the *conatus* of things is their inertial force or power[44]—and hence the product of analytic knowing—it would still remain that, on the geometric procedure, one could not deduce the *conatus* of this or that thing.

In Spinoza's *Ethics* the Whole which is expounded by the geometric method is at strong variance with the Whole discovered by the analytic procedure. The first Whole is a substance with attributes, the other a Whole which is a compound of parts. The one substance is indivisible and lacks parts (E I, P 12, P 13) and is constituted by its attributes; the other is a compound whole which is constituted by its component parts or individuals (E II, Lemma 7, S). In the Whole as substance, attribute is prior to mode in being; as a modification of an attribute, a mode has its being *in alio*. But in the Whole as a compound of parts, the part, or the constant ratio which constitutes it, is not derivative from, or a modification of, that Whole. And the individual part or thing, so far from being *in alio*, strives to persevere. "*in suo esse*" (III, P 7). As regards the Whole as substance, an attribute is not the sum or totality of its modes or modifications: the mode is not a part. But the Whole as compound individual is the totality of its parts, which are not derivative from the Whole: the part is not a mode. The geometric and analytic models of the Whole are disjunctive.

---

[44] ". . logically desire or the conatus is merely a principle of inertia," D. Bidney, *The Psychology and Ethics of Spinoza*, (New Haven: Yale University Press, 1940), 88.

VI.

The problem of Spinoza's Pantheism is located in the double name that designates the one identical Whole, *Deus sive natura*. The duality and the unity of this Whole receive their most authoritative articulation in the *Ethics* in the exposition of *natura naturans* and *natura naturata* (E I, P 29 S). Both together are "nature"; taken together they comprise and exhaust the Whole. But both together are also God: from God as *natura naturans*, or a substance whose attributes express his eternal and finite essence, there follows God as *natura naturata*, or all the modes of God's attributes in so far as they are considered as things which are in God. Thus the one Whole may be designated indifferently "*Deus sive natura*." At the same time, it may be observed that the distinction permits a certain harmonization between theism and pantheism: it may be construed as designed to distinguish between God and the beings that make up the world. It is not accidental that Spinoza uses a distinction employed for that purpose by Thomas Aquinas, and attributed it to him in the *Short Treatise*.[45] That Spinoza intends such a harmonization is confirmed by the theist attributes imputed to God in Part I, omnipotence, omniscience, perfection, and his occasional use of the language of creation. His consideration of the divine nature is especially revealing of his procedure. Since "neither intellect nor will appertain to God's nature," it is necessary that "we take these words in some significations quite different from those they usually bear" (E I, P 17 S). We need not enter into the details of Spinoza's identification of the divine will and intellect in order to see that his assertions that both will and intellect pertain to the essence of God, and that the modes or *natura naturata* "follow" from that essence, easily permit a theist construction.

The question now arises, however, whether this harmonization with theism leaves unimpaired the possibility of uniting God and the world, *natura naturans* and *natura naturata*, and hence *Deus* with *natura*, as pantheism requires. But precisely the derivation from the divine essence to the finite modes, as a cognitive procedure available to the human mind through geometric deduction, has been excluded, especially by E I, P 28, as shown previously. Moreover, it must be noted that the modes of *natura naturata* are "in God," in accordance with Biblical statement (*Acts* 17:28), but they are not said to be parts of God. God's modes are not parts—he is, as brought out before,

---

[45] *Short Treatise* I, 8; Gebhardt I, 47. See Wolfson, Op. cit., I, 254.

indivisible and without parts: whereas nature as the one compound whole has parts which are not modes, since not derivable from the divine essence. For the very reason that it is an accommodation to theism, the distinction of *natura naturans* and *natura naturata*, when carefully regarded, does not permit *Deus* and *natura* to designate the same whole, neither in their being nor in their being known.

To add one last clarification, according to Spinoza's "pantheist" statements, what follows from God's essence is complete or perfect. "The omnipotence of God has been actual from eternity" (E I, P 17 S). "Things have been brought into being by God in the highest perfection" (E I, P 38, S 2). Spinoza considers an objection to this conclusion, at the end of the Appendix to E I. Why did God not create all men in such a manner that they might be controlled by the dictates of reason alone? He first replies "because to him material was not wanting for the creation of everything, from the highest down to the very lowest grade of perfection." This answer leaves it uncertain whether or not God has in fact brought into being all the grades of perfection, even among human beings. Spinoza's second reply, immediately following, drops "creation" as well as the notion of a completed *scala naturae*. "To speak more properly, because the laws of his nature were so ample that they sufficed for the production of everything which can be conceived by an infinite intellect." But what is conceivable in principle to an infinite intellect is not now necessarily actual in fact. Despite the earlier assertion of the eternal actuality of omnipotence, we are left with the suggestion that the Whole is not yet complete or perfect, or is a process of progressive development.[46] However this may be, since "the laws of his nature," if taken to mean the infinite essence of God, cannot produce any finite things, nor any laws of nature determining the production of finite things, as seen above, it is entirely reasonable that Spinoza replace God's laws by "nature's laws" in the analogous passage in the Preface to *Ethics* III. "Nature's laws and rules whereby all things are and are changed from one form into others are everywhere and always the same." When speaking of God's laws in the Appendix just quoted above no "forms" were mentioned; forms are a function of the laws of nature introduced in the Physical Treatise. The forms do not abide; things, it is reasonable to surmise, take on all the forms which could be conceived by "an infinite intelligence." We are reminded of Descartes' view that "these laws [are] the cause that matter must take necessarily

---

[46] See L. Strauss, Preface to the English translation, *Spinoza's Critique of Religion* (New York: Schocken, 1965), 16.

all the forms of which it is capable" (Princ. III, 47). To maintain such a Cartesian view, according to Leibniz, who also relates it to Spinoza, "il faudroit supposer, que le même état de l'Univers revient toujours précisément après quelque période."[47] Nature is either unilinear development or eternal return of the same.

The Catholic University of America

---

[47] G. W. Leibniz, *Opera*, ed. Erdmann (Berlin: 1840), 142.

INDEX TO PROPOSITIONS OF THE *ETHICS*

Note: this index includes only individual propositions, etc., discussed, not all of those mentioned or referred to.

I D1:   (Schmitz) 233, (Franck) 261
I D2:   (Kennington) 313
I D3:   (Doney) 49–50, (Donagan) 91, (Kennington) 297–98
I D4:   (Donagan) 91, (Schmitz) 237
I D5:   (Kennington) 302
I D6:   (Schmitz) 233, (Kennington) 297–98
I A6:   (Hooker) 31
I A7:   (Doney) 40–41
I P2:   (Hooker) 27
I P3:   (Hooker) 27–29
I P4:   (Hooker) 24
I P5:   (Hooker) 21–27
I P6:   (Hooker) 21
I P7:   (Hooker) 19–20, (Franck) 250
I P8 S2:   (Franck) 250, (Kennington) 298
I P9:   (Donagan) 92
I P10:   (Donagan) 92
I P11:   (Weiss) 5–8, (Hooker) 17–19, 32–34, (Doney) 35–51, (Donagan) 93–94, (Franck) 263
I P12:   (Kennington) 315
I P13:   (Kennington) 315
I P14:   (Kennington) 303
I P25:   (Benardete) 59–61
I P28:   (Umphrey) 283, (Kennington) 302
I P29:   (Allison) 219
I P29 S: (Umphrey) 287–88, (Kennington) 316
I Appendix: (Umphrey) 282, (Kennington) 317–18

II D1:   (Benardete) 61–62
II A2:   (Kennington) 301, 303
II A4:   (Kennington) 301, 303
II A5:   (Kennington) 301
II P1:   (Kennington) 303
II P2:   (Kennington) 303
II P7:   (Jonas) 124 ff.
II P7 S: (Wilson) 106, (Franck) 265, (Umphrey) 286–87
II P8:   (Donagan) 102
II P11:   (Donagan) 98
II P12:   (Donagan) 98, (Wilson) 107

II P13:   (Donagan) 98, (Kennington) 313
II P13 S: (Wilson) 117
Axioms, Lemmas, etc., foll. II P13 S: (Donagan) 97, (Jonas) 124 ff.,
    (Umphrey) 289–90, (Kennington) 311–12, 315
II P15:   (Benardete) 62–63
II P19:   (Wilson) 114
II P21:   (Benardete) 64–65
II P23:   (Wilson) 115–16
II P29:   (Kennington) 310
II P29 S: (Donagan) 99
II P38:   (Benardete) 70–71, (Wilson) 118–19, (Franck) 259,
    (Kennington) 314
II P39:   (Wilson) 118–19
II P40 S1: (Benardete) 70, (Franck) 257–60, 268, (Kennington)
    298, 300, 310–311
II P40 S2: (Franck) 268–69, (Umphrey) 288, (Kennington) 298,
    300, 310–311, 313–15
II P45:   (Kennington) 314
II P46:   (Kennington) 314
II P49 S: (Franck) 265–66

III Preface: (Kennington) 317
III P2:   (Jonas) 124 ff., (Kennington) 313
III P6:   (Benardete) 66–67, 71
III P7:   (Kennington) 315
III P9:   (Wilson) 115, 118
III P31:   (Gildin) 169
III P57 S: (Benardete) 54

IV Preface: (Umphrey) 282
IV P39:   (Kennington) 312

V P10:   (Kennington) 312
V P23:   (Donagan) 102
V P28:   (Franck) 270
V P36:   (Umphrey) 281
V P36 S: (Umphrey) 288
V P39 S: (Wilson) 117–18, (Kennington) 312

INDEX OF NAMES

Acton, Lord, 139
Adickes, Erich, 209 n., 225
Alexander, 187
Alpakhar, Rabbi, 159, 192
Altmann, Alexander, 202 n.
Anselm, St., 18, 38
Apostles, 159
Appuhn, Charles, 158 n., 258
Aquinas, St. Thomas, 6, 47, 316
Arendt, Hannah, 139
Aristotle, 24, 53, 62, 64-65, 68, 70, 75, 90, 97, 121, 163, 206, 229, 252, 253-55, 259, 282, 283, 284, 286, 290, 291, 297
Armstrong, D. M., 96
Arnauld, A., 23
Aubrey, John, 155
Augustus, 187
Bacon, Francis, 178 n., 269
Bäck, Leo, 199 n.
Barker, H., 103 n., 296 n., 301, 313 n.
Barnes, Jonathan, 38 n.
Bayle, P., 207, 294
Beck, Robert N., 240 n.
Benardete, J., 281 n.
Bend, J. G. van der, 87, 240 n.
Berkeley, G., 200, 225, 297, 298 n.
Berlin, Isaiah, 150
Bidney, D., 296, 315 n.
Blondel, Maurice, 86
Blyenbergh, Willem van, 147-48, 176 n.
Bohr, Niels, 126-28
Boole, 4
Bouwmeester, 300 n.
Brahe, Tycho, 90
Caird, John, 86, 242 n.
Cassirer, Ernst, 255, 284 n.
Catiline, 144
Christ, Jesus, 159, 165-67, 183-84, 307
Cicero, 144
Cleon, 187
Cohen, Hermann, 175 n.
Cohen, Morris R., 153
Comte, Auguste, 149-50
Condorcet, 133
Copernicus, Nicholas, 90-91
Copleston, F. C., 86

Cromwell, 140
Curley, E. M., 73, 86, 114-16, 251, 262 n., 271 n., 288 n.
de Careil, Foucher, 136 n.
Descartes, René, 4, 6, 8, 10, 12, 13, 18, 22, 23-25, 27, 29, 30, 31-32, 37, 54, 59, 61, 64-65, 74, 75, 89-97, 100-102, 105, 108-110, 111-13, 120, 121-24, 176-77, 205, 215, 225, 240 n., 252, 260, 274 n., 276, 278 n., 282, 294 n., 295, 304-306, 307, 309-311, 313, 317-18
Deugd, Cornelius de, 251, 262 n., 271
Diderot, D., 134
Dilthey, W., 194 n.
Disraeli, 141
Donagan, A., 101 n., 120 n., 285 n.
Düsing, Klaus, 230 n.
Dummett, Michael, 89 n.
Duns Scotus, John, 286
Durkheim, Emile, 146
Edelmann, Johann Christian, 199 n.
Einstein, Alfred, 135, 146, 153
Eleatics, 75, 230, 241
Elwes, R. H. M., 71, 258-59, 266 n.
Engels, Friedrich, 138, 146
Epicurus, 215
Euclid, 3-4, 68, 95, 194, 248, 258-59, 274, 284, 295, 298, 304
Evans, Richard I., 152 n.
Ezekiel, 159
Fackenheim, Emil, 176 n., 193 n.
Fénelon, F., 294 n.
Feuerbach, L., 241
Fichte, J. G., 199-200
Findlay, J. N., 232 n.
Fleischmann, Eugène, 232 n.
Fløistad, Guttorm, 81
Frege, Gottlob, 89
Freud, Sigmund, 146, 151-52
Freudenthal, J., 194 n.
Friedman, Joel, 120 n.
Friedmann, Georges, 108 n.
Fromm, Erich, 152
Galileo, 90, 135, 282, 283
Gebhardt, Carl, 173, 175 n., 192 n.
Grossmann, Walter, 199 n.
Grunwald, Max, 199 n., 200 n.

Gueroult, Martial, 35, 91, 93, 99 n., 100–101, 294, 296
Hallett, H. F., 247–48
Hamann, J. G., 201, 202
Hampshire, Stuart, 17, 103 n.
Harris, Errol E., 86, 87, 103 n., 242 n., 282 n., 290 n.
Harris, H. S., 230 n.
Hartshorne, Charles, 38
Hegel, Georg Wilhelm Friedrich, 63, 74, 75–78, 79–80, 87, 200, 229–43, 297–98
Herder, J. G., 199, 209–210, 294
Herz, Marcus, 202
Himmelfarb, Gertrude, 139 n.
Hitler, Adolf, 140, 145–46, 148
Hobbes, Thomas, 155–57, 168–69, 170–71, 280 n.
Hooker, Michael, 41–45
Hubbeling, H. G., 251, 263
Hume, David, 19, 29, 30–31, 200, 212–13, 223 n., 291, 294
Jacobi, F. H., 199, 201–203, 207–208, 209–210, 213, 224, 230 n.
James, St., 183
Jefferson, Thomas, 140, 142 n.
Jeremiah, 159
Joachim, H. H., 54, 65, 82, 86, 242 n., 287 n.
Jonas, H., 123 n.
Jones, W. T., 247 n., 251
Kant, Immanuel, 29, 35, 56, 75, 141, 151, 199–227, 229, 273, 282
Kennington, Richard, 177 n., 269 n., 282 n.
Kierkegaard, S., 232
Kline, George, 93–94
Krakauer, Moses, 199 n.
Kuhn, Thomas S., 90 n.
Lachterman, D., 296 n., 311 n.
Lauer, Quentin, 229 n.
Leclerc, Ivor, 74
Le Clerc, J., 294 n.
Leibniz, Gottfried Wilhelm, 6, 23, 29, 64, 78, 83, 104–108, 113 n., 140, 200, 226–27, 274, 318
Lenin, 134
Lessing, G. E., 199, 201–202
Lichtenberg, 225
Livy, 187 n.
Locke, John, 33, 78, 140, 171
Machiavelli, Niccolo, 134, 135, 144, 149, 168, 187 n., 189 n.

McFarland, J. D., 213 n.
MacIntyre, Alasdair, 250
McMinn, J. B., 240 n.
McShea, Robert J., 168 n.
Madison, James, 142 n.
Maimonides, Moses, 6, 141, 149, 252, 259
Malebranche, N., 209, 223–24
Mandelstam, Nadezhda, 137
Mark, Thomas Carson, 109 n.
Martin, Gottfried, 223 n.
Martineau, James, 256
Marx, Karl, 133, 138–39, 144, 146, 149–52, 241
Matson, Wallace I., 103 n.
Mendelssohn, Moses, 199, 201–202, 208, 294
Meyer, Ludwig, 260–61, 295, 305–306
Mill, John Stuart, 136
Moses, 159, 164–65, 167, 180 n., 183–84, 187, 189, 276
Mure, G. R. G., 232 n.
Murray, J. Clark, 86
Nero, 146, 147
Newton, Isaac, 130, 273
Nicholson, Peggy, 116 n.
Odegard, Douglas, 103 n.
Oldenburg, Henry, 98, 174 n., 249, 300 n.
Ovid, 181 n.
Parkinson, G. H., 251, 271
Parmenides, 67
Paul, St., 165–67, 183, 307
Plato, 57, 63, 163, 208, 222, 223, 235, 252, 265, 287 n.
Pollock, Sir Frederick, 80, 83, 86, 133 n., 264
Powell, Elmer Ellsworth, 186 n.
Prophets, 165
Quine, W. V. O., 89
Radner, Daisie, 111–13
Randall, John H., Jr., 29
Reid, Thomas, 31
Rice, Lee E., 73
Rosen, S., 235 n., 240 n.
Rotenstreich, N., 231 n., 242 n.
Roth, Leon, 262
Rousseau, Jean-Jacques, 134, 171
Royce, Josiah, 74, 78–80, 82, 86
Ryle, Gilbert, 282
Sallust, 144
Schelling, F. W. J. von, 200, 230 n.

Scholz, H., 203 n., 205 n.
Schütz, Christian Gottfried, 203 n.
Schumpeter, Joseph, 144
Shmueli, E., 230 n., 240 n.
Socrates, 65–66, 273, 282
Solomon, 165
Solzhenitsyn, Alexander, 137, 140
Spencer, Herbert, 149–50
Stalin, Joseph, 148
Stoics, 238, 252
Strauss, Leo, 155 n., 156 n., 166 n., 168, 170, 175 n., 186 n., 191 n., 192 n., 193 n., 194 n., 195 n., 280 n., 296, 307 n., 317 n.
Strawson, P. F., 73, 97, 103
Switzer, Brian, 173 n.
Taylor, A. E., 86, 296 n.
Toland, John, 294 n.
Tonelli, G., 309
Tschirnhaus, 83, 86, 94, 255, 300
Umphrey, S., 303 n.
Urban, W. M., 80, 82, 84

Voltaire, 134
Vries, Simon de, 93, 262, 300 n., 301
Weber, Max, 146
Wernhan, A. G., 161 n.
White, W. H., 71, 258, 266 n.
Whittaker, Edmund, 134
Williams, Bernard, 250
Witt, Jan de, 136, 143, 145, 175 n.
Wittgenstein, Ludwig, 291
Wolf, A., 83, 86, 94 n., 95 n., 139, 299
Wolff, Christian, 205, 216
Wolfson, Abraham, 229 n.
Wolfson, Harry Austryn, 36, 84–85, 162 n., 251–52, 254, 258–59, 260 n., 268 n., 276 n., 288 n., 294, 295, 297, 316 n.
Woodbridge, Frederick J. E., 247, 252
Zimmerli, Walther Christoph 230 n.

www.ingramcontent.com/pod-product-compliance
Lightning Source LLC
Chambersburg PA
CBHW031406290426
44110CB00011B/287